Further praise for *In an Unspoken Voice*

"Peter Levine's first book, *Waking the Tiger*, changed the world of trauma treatment: somatic therapy, specifically Somatic Experiencing®, the name of the specific approach he developed, no longer alternative fringe practice, became a major player in the world of the mainstream psychotherapies. Like an anthropologist acquainting us with a different culture that he has made his own, Levine, in his new book, *In an Unspoken Voice*, systematically and engagingly initiates us into the ways of the body and the nervous system that animates it: how it works, what makes it tick, how to make friends with it, how to understand it, how to communicate with it and, last but not least, how to treat it and release it (and with it, us) from the hold of posttraumatic stress disorder (PTSD). No longer unspoken, all that is held in the body—in trauma and in health, in psychosomatic illness and in resilience—is described, articulated and made coherent. The result is a masterful, fluent book that seamlessly moves between evolution, science, Polyvagal theory, mind-body practice, impassioned defense of our animal natures, self-disclosure and specific step-by-step guide to treating trauma and restoring resilience. It is erudite, it is impassioned, it is learned and it is accessible."

> —Diana Fosha, PhD, director of The AEDP Institute, co-editor of *The Healing Power of Emotion: Affective Neuroscience, Development and Clinical Practice* and author of *The Transforming Power of Affect: A Model for Accelerated Change*

"To be traumatized is to be condemned to endless repetitions of unbearable experiences. In this beautifully written and engrossing book, Peter Levine explains how trauma affects our body and mind and demonstrates how to call upon the wisdom of our bodies to overcome and transform it. The accounts of his personal and therapeutic experiences, integrated with the essentials of the sciences of trauma and healing, are highly informative and inspiring. His distinctive voice should be widely heard by survivors, clinicians and scientists."

> —Onno van der Hart, PhD, Honorary Professor of the Psychopathology of Chronic Trauma, Utrecht University, Utrecht, The Netherlands, and co-author of *The Haunted Self: Structural Dissociation of the Personality*

"Like a wise old weaver Peter Levine painstakingly blends together strands of many dense colors into ever-fresh patterns emerging from his honed intelligence and fertile imagination. These strands comprise careful reflections on his own personal healing, his work with others, insights from studies with animals, different views from indigenous peoples here and elsewhere, various scientists exploring the biologies of the body, spiritual practices in many traditions and whatever else passes in front of his sparkling eyes. His first (and now iconic) book, *Waking the Tiger*, is now part of the canon for the education of therapists. This major new book is a welcome landmark in his long history of creating an intricate tapestry of Somatic theory and practice."

> —Don Hanlon Johnson, PhD, professor of Somatics at California Institute of Integral Studies, founder of the first accredited graduate studies program in the field and author of *Bone, Breath, and Gesture: Practices of Embodiment* and *Everyday Hopes, Utopian Dreams: Reflections on American Ideals*

"For more than forty years, Peter Levine has gently, humorously, and with stunning simplicity, shown us how trauma responses are part of a brilliant psychological self-protection system; a protection system that we, professionals and laypeople alike, unwittingly block with our many 'normal' responses. If you want to grasp the essence of how and why the trauma response can help people heal, read this book. If you want to help a traumatized person lessen the impact of the trauma while it's happening, read this book. If you want to understand your own journey through stress and trauma, read this book. If you want some trail markers for a path from the daze of dissociation to the reemergence of deep vibrant aliveness and spiritual feeling, read this book."

—Marianne Bentzen, international trainer in Neuroaffective Psychotherapy, Copenhagen, Denmark

"Peter Levine conveys his profound scientific understanding of posttraumatic stress disorder (PTSD) so vividly that the reader can sense, feel and identify with the many traumatized children and adults he has worked with. Levine helps us to understand the complexity of PTSD seen from the outside as well as felt from the inside. He invites us into a spiritual dimension that draws equally on science and experience. Through his poetic style the reader is conducted from the built-in reactions of the nervous system to deep mental scars, and to how the skilled PTSD therapist can guide far-reaching healing processes. Levine's understanding is vast in its scope, from an evolutionary understanding of the source of trauma to a spiritual dimension of how we as human beings can be strengthened by healing from trauma."

—Susan Hart, Danish psychologist, author of *Brain, Attachment, Personality: An Introduction to Neuroaffective Development* and *The Impact of Attachment: Developmental Neuroaffective Psychology*

"This book stands as a worthy sequel to Levine's groundbreaking *Waking the Tiger*. He expands his concepts of the neurophysiological basis for trauma with a thorough review of the science of trauma and his own creative theories, providing rich insights for application to the business of healing. Valuable case studies illustrate the 'whys' of the behavior of the trauma victim, and useful tools help the therapist enlist the body in the process."

—Robert Scaer, MD, author of *The Trauma Spectrum* and *The Body Bears the Burden*

"Peter Levine's approach to understanding and healing trauma is innovative, vital and thoroughly creative. The map for therapy that he introduces is very helpful to any healer of trauma. Once again Levine reminds us that our evolutionary ancestors are not so removed from us. That we and the other animals are all one family and that we should learn from them, as our survival and sanity depends on it. Levine's suggestion to change posttraumatic stress disorder (PTSD) to posttraumatic stress injury (PTSI) is much more realistic as we are healing the hurt and not the disorder."

—Mira Rothenberg, author of *Children with Emerald Eyes* and founder of Blueberry Treatment Centers

IN AN
Unspoken
Voice

*How the Body Releases Trauma
and Restores Goodness*

Peter A. Levine, PhD

Foreword by
Gabor Maté, MD

North Atlantic Books
Berkeley, California

Published by   and
North Atlantic Books   ERGOS Institute Press
P.O. Box 12327   P.O. Box 110
Berkeley, California 94712   Lyons, Colorado 80540

Cover and book design © Ayelet Maida, A/M Studios
Cover art © fotosearch.com

Author photograph © Gerry Greenberg
Printed in the United States of America

Figures 6.2a through 6.4d—From *Healing Trauma: A Pioneering Program for Restoring the Wisdom of Your Body* written by Peter Levine and published by Sounds True. Used with permission from Sounds True, www.soundstrue.com.

Diagrams A and B (color insert)—Netter illustrations from www.netterimages.com. © Elsevier Inc. All rights reserved. Used with permission.

Creative design of all other figures: Justin Snavely

In an Unspoken Voice: How the Body Releases Trauma and Restores Goodness is sponsored by the Society for the Study of Native Arts and Sciences, a nonprofit educational corporation whose goals are to develop an educational and cross-cultural perspective linking various scientific, social, and artistic fields; to nurture a holistic view of arts, sciences, humanities, and healing; and to publish and distribute literature on the relationship of mind, body, and nature.

North Atlantic Books' publications are available through most bookstores. For further information, visit our website at www.northatlanticbooks.com or call 800-733-3000.

Library of Congress Cataloging-in-Publication Data

Levine, Peter A.
    In an unspoken voice : how the body releases trauma and restores goodness / Peter A. Levine ; foreword by Gabor Maté.
        p. cm.
    Includes bibliographical references.
    Summary: "Based on findings from biology, neuroscience, and the emerging field of body-oriented psychotherapy, *In an Unspoken Voice* explains that trauma is not a disease or a disorder, but an injury caused by fright, helplessness, and loss and that this wound can be healed only if we attend to the wisdom of the living, knowing body"—Provided by publisher.
    ISBN 978-1-55643-943-8
    1. Psychic trauma. I. Title.
    RC552.T7L483 2010
    616.85'21—dc22

                                                              2010023653

4 5 6 7 8 9 10 11 UNITED 16 15 14 13 12 11

In all things in nature
there is something
of the marvelous.

—Aristotle (350 BC)

Acknowledgments

Everything responsible for our "human
existence" is due to an anonymous
multitude of others who lived before us,
whose achievements have been bestowed
upon us as gifts.
—H. Hass (1981)

FOR WHERE I STAND TODAY, I am indebted to the great scientific tradition and lineage of the ethologists, those scientists who study animals in their natural environments, who have contributed greatly to my naturalistic vision of the human animal. A most personal thanks to Nobel Laureate Nikolaas Tinbergen, whose suggestions and kind words of support encouraged me to pursue this naturalistic worldview. Though I have never met them, except through their written gifts to history, I would like to honor Konrad Lorenz, Heinz von Holst, Paul Leyhausen, Desmond Morris, Eric Salzen and Irenäus Eibl-Eibesfeldt. Other "virtual" teachers include Ernst Gellhorn, who informed my early neurophysiological thinking, and Akhter Ahsen, who helped consolidate my vision of the "undifferentiated and welded unity of the body and mind."

A giant, whose broad shoulders I stand on, is Wilhelm Reich, MD. His monumental contribution to the understanding of "life-energy" was taught to me by Philip Curcuruto, a man of few words and simple wisdom. My deep appreciation and personal debt go to Richard Olney and Richard Price, who taught me what little I know about self-acceptance. Having known (and been inspired by) Dr. Ida Rolf has been a catalyst in forming my identity as a scientist-healer. To Dr. Virginia Johnson, I thank you for your critical understanding of altered states of consciousness. And to Ed Jackson, thanks for trusting my nascent body/mind practice in the 1960s and for referring Nancy, my first trauma client.

I am grateful for the tremendous support and help from my friends. Over the years (beginning in 1978) I have had many stimulating discussions with Stephen Porges, already a leading figure in the field of psychophysiology. Over the following decades, our paths have continued to cross as we shared our parallel and interwoven developments and a special friendship. Thanks and admiration to Bessel van der Kolk for his voracious inquiring mind, his broad comprehensive vision of trauma, his professional life of research advancing the field of trauma to its modern status, and his courage to challenge existing structures. I fondly recollect our sharing Vermont summers on the banks of East Long Lake, swimming, laughing and talking trauma into the wee hours.

In putting this book together I am indebted to the creative challenge and tremendous editorial help from Laura Regalbuto, Maggie Kline and Phoebe Hoss; also thanks to Justin Snavely for his awesome technical help. And, once again, I appreciate the cooperative endeavor of a continuing partnership with North Atlantic Books; with Emily Boyd, project manager, and Paul McCurdy, the line editor.

To my parents, Morris and Helen, I give thanks for the gift of life, the vehicle for the expression of my work, and for their unequivocal support from the "other side" of the physical plane. To Pouncer, the Dingo dog who had been my guide into the animal world as well a constant companion, I have fond body-memories of play and goodness. At the age of seventeen (arguably, over a hundred human years), he continued to show me the vital joy of corporeal life.

Finally, I stand in awe of the many "coincidences," "chance" meetings, synchronicities and fateful detours that have impelled and guided me on my life's journey. To have been blessed by a life of creative exploration and the privilege to contribute to the alleviation of suffering has been a precious gift, a pearl beyond price.

Thanks for all my teachers, students, organizations and friends throughout the world who are carrying out the legacy of this work.

PETER A. LEVINE

Contents

Foreword

IN AN UNSPOKEN VOICE IS PETER LEVINE'S MAGNUM OPUS, the summation of his lifelong investigation into the nature of stress and trauma and of his pioneering therapeutic work. It is also the most intimate and poetic among his books, most revealing of his own experience both as a person and as a healer. It is also his most scientifically grounded and erudite.

An early heading in the beginning chapter reveals the essence of Peter's teaching: "the power of kindness." Injured in a motor vehicle accident, Peter finds his own healing potential unlocked by his willingness to attend fully to his physical/emotional experience, allowing it to unfold as it needs to. His process is facilitated by a compassionate human presence. The power of goodness—in this case, the organism's innate capacity to restore itself to health and balance—is encouraged by a bystander, an empathetic witness who helps to prevent trauma by embodying kindness and acceptance.

Not surprisingly, these are the very qualities Peter Levine considers essential in those called to do therapeutic work with traumatized human beings. As he says, the therapist must "help to create an environment of *relative* safety, an atmosphere that conveys refuge, hope and possibility." But pure empathy and a warm therapeutic relationship are not enough, for traumatized people are often unable to read or fully receive compassion. They are too suppressed, too stuck in primal defenses more appropriate to our amphibian or reptilian evolutionary predecessors.

So what is the therapist to *do* with human beings hurt and beaten down by past trauma? It is to help people listen to the unspoken voice of their own bodies and to enable them to feel their "survival emotions" of rage and terror without being overwhelmed by these powerful states. Trauma, as Peter brilliantly recognized decades ago, does not reside in the external event that induces physical or emotional pain—nor even in the pain itself—but in our becoming stuck in our primitive responses to painful events. Trauma is caused when we are unable to release blocked energies, to fully move through the physical/emotional reactions to hurtful experience. Trauma is not what happens to us, but what we hold inside in the absence of an empathetic witness.

The salvation, then, is to be found in the body. "Most people," Levine notes, "think of trauma as a 'mental' problem, even as a 'brain disorder.' However, trauma is something that also happens in the body." In fact, he shows, it happens first and foremost in the body. The mental states associated with trauma are important, but they are secondary. The body initiates, he says, and the mind follows. Hence, "talking cures" that engage the intellect or even the emotions do not reach deep enough.

The therapist/healer needs to be able to recognize the psychoemotional and physical signs of "frozen" trauma in the client. He or she must learn to hear the "unspoken voice" of the body so that clients can safely learn to hear and see themselves. This book is a master class in how to listen to the unspoken voice of the body. "In the particular methodology I describe," Levine writes, "the client is helped to develop an awareness and mastery of his or her physical sensations and feelings." The key to healing, he argues, is to be found in the "deciphering of this nonverbal realm." He finds the code in his synthesis of the seemingly—but only seemingly—disparate sciences that study evolution, animal instinct, mammalian physiology and the human brain, and in his hard-won experience as a therapist.

Potentially traumatic situations are ones that induce states of high physiological arousal but without the freedom for the affected person to express and get past these states: danger without the possibility of fight or flight and, afterward, without the opportunity to "shake it off," as a wild animal would following a frightful encounter with a predator. What ethologists call *tonic immobility*—the paralysis and physical/emotional shutdown that characterize the universal experience of helplessness in the face of mortal danger—comes to dominate the person's life and functioning. We are "scared stiff." In human beings, unlike in animals, the *state* of temporary freezing becomes a long-term *trait*. The survivor, Peter Levine points out, may remain "stuck in a kind of limbo, not fully reengaging in life." In circumstances where others sense no more than a mild threat or even a challenge to be faced, the trauma-tized person experiences threat, dread and mental/physical listlessness, a kind of paralysis of body and will. Shame, depression and self-loathing follow in the wake of such imposed helplessness.

The American Psychiatric Association's *Diagnostic and Statistical Manual of Mental Disorders* (DSM) "deals in categories, not in pain," in the incisive words of psychiatrist and researcher Daniel Siegel. Cen-tral to Peter Levine's teaching is that trauma cannot be reduced to the diagnostic traits compiled by the DSM under the rubric of PTSD, Post-traumatic Stress Disorder. Trauma is not a disease, he points out, but rather a human experience rooted in survival instincts. Inviting the full, if carefully graded, expression of our instinctive responses will allow the traumatic state to loosen its hold on the sufferer. Goodness, the restoration of vitality, follows. It springs from within. "Trauma is a fact of life," Levine writes. "It does not, however, have to be a life sentence." In our suffering lies also our salvation. As he shows, the same psycho-physiological systems that govern the traumatic state also mediate core feelings of goodness and belonging.

Peter's astonishing awareness of and attention to nuanced detail as he observes and describes his clients' "unfreezing" are at the heart of his teaching, as are his techniques to guide and facilitate his process. Reading this manuscript, I was impressed by how often I experienced "aha" moments as I recalled my own observations in my work with trau-matized and often addicted people. I could now understand and inter-pret these observations in a new way—and not only my clinical observations, but also my own personal experience. And that's impor-tant, for, as Peter recognizes, the therapist's attuning to his or her own experience serves as an essential guiding light leading the healing process along the right path.

Peter Levine and the reader complete their mutual journey with an exploration of spirituality and trauma. There is, he writes, "an intrin-sic and wedded relationship" between the two. For all our rootedness in a physical body, we humans are spiritual creatures. As the psychiatrist Thomas Hora astutely pointed out, "all problems are psychological, but all solutions are spiritual."

With this book Peter Levine secures his position in the forefront of trauma healing, as theorist, practitioner and teacher. All of us in the therapeutic community—physicians, psychologists, therapists, aspiring healers, interested laypeople—are ever so much richer for this summation of what he himself has learned.

GABOR MATÉ, MD

Author of *In the Realm of Hungry Ghosts:
Close Encounters with Addiction*

PART I

Roots:
A Foundation
to Dance On

We must go down to the very
foundations of life. For any merely
superficial ordering of life that leaves
its deepest needs unsatisfied is as
ineffectual as if no attempt at order
had ever been made ...

—*I Ching*, Hexagram #34
"The Well" (circa 2500 BC)

CHAPTER 1

The Power of an Unspoken Voice

When a man has learned within his heart
what fear and trembling mean,
he is safeguarded against any terror
produced by outside influences.
　　　　—*I Ching*, Hexagram #51 (circa 2500 BC)

NO MATTER HOW SELF-ASSURED WE ARE, in a fraction of a second, our lives can be utterly devastated. As in the biblical story of Jonah, the unknowable forces of trauma and loss can swallow us whole, thrusting us deep into their cold dark belly. Entrapped yet lost, we become hopelessly frozen by terror and helplessness.

Early in the year 2005, I walked out of my house into a balmy Southern California morning. The gentle warmth and soft sea breeze gave a lift to my step. Certainly, this was the kind of winter morning that makes everyone in the rest of the country (with the possible exception of Garrison Keillor of Lake Wobegon) want to abandon their snow shovels and move to the Southland's warm, sunny beaches. It was the beginning of a perfect kind of day, a day when you feel certain that nothing can go wrong, when nothing bad can possibly happen. But it did.

A Moment of Truth

I walked along, absorbed in happy anticipation of being with my dear friend Butch for the celebration of his sixtieth birthday.

I stepped out into a crosswalk...

... The next moment, paralyzed and numb, I'm lying on the road, unable to move or breathe. I can't figure out what has just happened. How did I get here? Out of a swirling fog of confusion and disbelief, a crowd of people rushes toward me. They stop, aghast. Abruptly, they hover over me in a tightening circle, their staring eyes fixed on my limp and twisted body. From my helpless perspective they appear like a flock of carnivorous ravens, swooping down on an injured prey—me. Slowly I orient myself and identify the real attacker. As in an old-fashioned flashbulb photo, I see a beige car looming over me with its teeth-like grill and shattered windshield. The door suddenly jerks open. A wide-eyed teenager bursts out. She stares at me in dazed horror. In a strange way, I both know and don't know what has just happened. As the fragments begin to converge, they convey a horrible reality: *I must have been hit by this car as I entered the crosswalk.* In confused disbelief, I sink back into a hazy twilight. I find that I am unable to think clearly or to will myself awake from this nightmare.

A man rushes to my side and drops to his knees. He announces himself as an off-duty paramedic. When I try to see where the voice is coming from, he sternly orders, "Don't move your head." The contradiction between his sharp command and what my body naturally wants—to turn toward his voice—frightens and stuns me into a sort of paralysis. My awareness strangely splits, and I experience an uncanny "dislocation." It's as if I'm floating above my body, looking down on the unfolding scene.

I am snapped back when he roughly grabs my wrist and takes my pulse. He then shifts his position, directly above me. Awkwardly, he grasps my head with both of his hands, trapping it and keeping it from moving. His abrupt actions and the stinging ring of his command panic me; they immobilize me further. Dread seeps into my dazed, foggy consciousness: *Maybe I have a broken neck,* I think. I have a compelling impulse to find someone *else* to focus on. Simply, I need to have someone's comforting gaze, a lifeline to hold onto. But I'm too terrified to move and feel helplessly frozen.

The Good Samaritan fires off questions in rapid succession: "What is your name? Where are you? Where were you going? What is today's date?" But I can't connect with my mouth and make words. I don't have the energy to answer his questions. His manner of asking them makes me feel more disoriented and utterly confused. Finally, I manage to shape my words and speak. My voice is strained and tight. I ask him, both with my hands and words, "Please back off." He complies. As though a neutral observer, speaking about the person sprawled out on the blacktop, I assure him that I understand I am not to move my head, and that I will answer his questions later.

The Power of Kindness

After a few minutes, a woman unobtrusively inserts herself and quietly sits by my side. "I'm a doctor, a pediatrician," she says. "Can I be of help?"

"Please just stay with me," I reply. Her simple, kind face seems supportive and calmly concerned. She takes my hand in hers, and I squeeze it. She gently returns the gesture. As my eyes reach for hers, I feel a tear form. The delicate and strangely familiar scent of her perfume tells me that I am not alone. I feel emotionally held by her encouraging presence. A trembling wave of release moves through me, and I take my first deep breath. Then a jagged shudder of terror passes though my body. Tears are now streaming from my eyes. In my mind, I hear the words, *I can't believe this has happened to me; it's not possible; this is not what I had planned for Butch's birthday tonight.* I am sucked down by a deep undertow of unfathomable regret. My body continues to shudder. Reality sets in.

In a little while, a softer trembling begins to replace the abrupt shudders. I feel alternating waves of fear and sorrow. It comes to me as a stark possibility that I may be seriously injured. Perhaps I will end up in a wheelchair, crippled and dependent. Again, deep waves of sorrow flood me. I'm afraid of being swallowed up by the sorrow and hold onto the woman's eyes. A slower breath brings me the scent of her perfume. Her continued presence sustains me. As I feel less overwhelmed, my fear softens and begins to subside. I feel a flicker of hope, then a rolling wave of fiery rage. My body continues to shake and tremble. It is alternately icy cold and feverishly hot. A burning red fury erupts from deep within my belly: *How could that stupid kid hit me in a crosswalk? Wasn't she paying attention? Damn her!*

A blast of shrill sirens and flashing red lights block out everything. My belly tightens, and my eyes again reach to find the woman's kind gaze. We squeeze hands, and the knot in my gut loosens.

I hear my shirt ripping. I am startled and again jump to the vantage of an observer hovering above my sprawling body. I watch uniformed strangers methodically attach electrodes to my chest. The Good Samaritan paramedic reports to someone that my pulse was 170. I hear my shirt ripping even more. I see the emergency team slip a collar onto my neck and then cautiously slide me onto a board. While they strap me down, I hear some garbled radio communication. The paramedics are requesting a full trauma team. Alarm jolts me. I ask to be taken to the nearest hospital only a mile away, but they tell me that my injuries may require the major trauma center in La Jolla, some thirty miles farther. My heart sinks. Surprisingly, though, the fear quickly subsides. As I am lifted into the ambulance, I close my eyes for the first time. A vague scent of the woman's perfume and the look of her quiet, kind eyes linger. Again, I have that comforting feeling of being held by her presence.

Opening my eyes in the ambulance, I feel a heightened alertness, as though I'm supercharged with adrenaline. Though intense, this feeling does not overwhelm me. Even though my eyes want to dart around, to survey the unfamiliar and foreboding environment, I consciously direct myself to go inward. I begin to take stock of my body sensations. This active focusing draws my attention to an intense, and uncomfortable, buzzing throughout my body.

Against this unpleasant sensation, I notice a peculiar tension in my left arm. I let this sensation come into the foreground of my consciousness and track the arm's tension as it builds and builds. Gradually, I recognize that *the arm wants* to flex and move up. As this inner impulse toward movement develops, the back of my hand also *wants* to rotate. Ever so slightly, I sense it moving toward the left side of my face—as though to protect it against a blow. Suddenly, there passes before my eyes a fleeting image of the window of the beige car, and once again—as in a flashbulb snapshot—vacant eyes stare from behind the spiderweb of the shattered window. I hear the momentary "ching-ing" thud of my left shoulder shattering the windshield. Then, unexpectedly, an enveloping sense of relief floods over me. I feel myself coming back into my body. The electric buzzing has retreated. The image of the blank eyes and shattered windshield recedes and seems to dissolve. In its place, I picture myself leaving my house, feeling the soft warm sun on my face, and being filled with gladness at the expectation of seeing Butch that evening. My eyes can relax as I focus outwardly. As I look around the ambulance, it somehow seems less alien and foreboding. I see more clearly and "softly." I have the deeply reassuring sense that I am no longer frozen, that time has started to move forward, that I am awakening from the nightmare. I gaze at the paramedic sitting by my side. Her calmness reassures me.

After a few bumpy miles, I feel another strong tension pattern developing from the spine in my upper back. I sense my right arm wanting to extend outward—I see a momentary flash; the black asphalt road rushes toward me. I hear my hand slapping the pavement and feel a raw burning sensation on the palm of my right hand. I associate this with the perception of my hand extending to protect my head from smashing onto the road. I feel tremendous relief, along with a deep sense of gratitude that my body did not betray me, knowing exactly what to do to guard my fragile brain from a potentially mortal injury. As I continue to gently tremble, I sense a warm tingling wave along with an inner strength building up from deep within my body.

As the shrill siren blasts away, the ambulance paramedic takes my blood pressure and records my EKG. When I ask her to tell me my vital signs, she informs me in a gentle professional manner that she cannot give me that information. I feel a subtle urge to extend our contact, to engage with her as a person. Calmly, I tell her that I'm a doctor (a half-truth). There is the light quality of a shared joke. She fiddles with the equipment and then indicates that it might be a false reading. A minute or two later she tells me that my heart rate is 74 and my blood pressure is 125/70.

"What were my readings when you first hooked me up?" I ask.

"Well, your heart rate was 150. The guy who took it before we came said it was about 170."

I breathe a deep sigh of relief. "Thank you," I say, then add: "Thank God, I won't be getting PTSD."

"What do you mean?" she asks with genuine curiosity.

"Well, I mean that I probably won't be getting posttraumatic stress disorder." When she still looks perplexed, I explain how my shaking and following my self-protective responses had helped me to "reset" my nervous system and brought me back into my body.

"This way," I go on, "I am no longer in fight-or-flight mode."

"Hmm," she comments, "is that why accident victims sometimes struggle with us—are they still in fight-or-flight?"

"Yes, that's right."

"You know," she adds, "I've noticed that they often purposely stop people from shaking when we get them to the hospital. Sometimes they strap them down tight or give them a shot of Valium. Maybe that's not so good?"

"No, it's not," the teacher in me confirms. "It may give them temporary relief, but it just keeps them frozen and stuck."

She tells me that she recently took a course in "trauma first-aid" called Critical Incident Debriefing. "They tried it with us at the hospital. We had to talk about how we felt after an accident. But talking made me and the other paramedics feel worse. I couldn't sleep after we did it—but you weren't talking about what happened. You were, it seemed to me, just shaking. Is that what brought your heart rate and blood pressure down?"

"Yes," I told her and added that it was also the small protective spontaneous movements my arms were making.

"I'll bet," she mused, "that if the shaking that often occurs after surgery were allowed rather than suppressed, recovery would be quicker and maybe even postoperative pain would be reduced."

"That's right," I say, smiling in agreement.

Horrible and shocking as this experience was, it allowed me to exercise the method for dealing with sudden trauma that I had developed, written about and taught for the past forty years. By listening to the "unspoken voice" of my body and allowing it to do what *it* needed to do; by not stopping the shaking, by "tracking" my inner sensations, while also allowing the *completion* of the defensive and orienting responses; and by feeling the "survival emotions" of rage and terror without becoming overwhelmed, I came through mercifully unscathed, both physically and emotionally. I was not only thankful; I was humbled and grateful to find that I could use my method for my own salvation.

While some people are able to recover from such trauma on their own, many individuals do not. Tens of thousands of soldiers are experiencing the extreme stress and horror of war. Then too, there are the devastating occurrences of rape, sexual abuse and assault. Many of us, however, have been overwhelmed by much more "ordinary" events such as surgeries or invasive medical procedures.[1] Orthopedic patients in a recent study, for example, showed a 52% occurrence of being diagnosed with full-on PTSD following surgery.

Other traumas include falls, serious illnesses, abandonment, receiving shocking or tragic news, witnessing violence and getting into an auto accident; all can lead to PTSD. These and many other fairly common experiences are all potentially traumatizing. The inability to rebound from such events, or to be helped adequately to recover by professionals, can subject us to PTSD—along with a myriad of physical and emotional symptoms. I dread to think how my accident might have turned out had I lacked my knowledge or not had the good fortune to be helped by that woman pediatrician and her scent of holding kindness.

Finding Method

Over the past forty years, I have developed an approach to help people move through the many types of trauma, including what I went through that February day when I was struck by a car. This method is equally applicable directly after the trauma or many years later—my first serendipitous client, described in Chapter 2, was able to recover from a trauma that occurred about twenty years prior to our sessions together. Somatic Experiencing®, as I call the method, helps to create physiological,

sensate and affective states that transform those of fear and helplessness. It does this by accessing various instinctual reactions through one's
awareness of physical body sensations.

Since time immemorial, people have attempted to cope with powerful and terrifying feelings by doing things that contradict perceptions
of fear and helplessness: religious rituals, theater, dance, music, meditation and ingesting psychoactive substances, to name a few. Of these
various methods for altering one's way of being, modern medicine has
accepted only the use of (limited, i.e., psychiatric) chemical substances.
The other "coping" methods continue to find expression in alternative
and so-called holistic approaches such as yoga, tai chi, exercise, drum-
ming, music, shamanism and body-oriented techniques. While many
people find help and solace from these valuable approaches, they are
relatively nonspecific and do not sufficiently address certain core physiological mechanisms and processes that allow human beings to transform terrifying and overwhelming experiences.

In the particular methodology I describe in these pages, the client is
helped to develop an awareness and mastery of his or her physical sensations and feelings. My observations, in visiting a few indigenous cultures,
suggest that this approach has a certain kinship with various traditional
shamanic healing rituals. I am proposing that a collective, cross-cultural
approach to healing trauma not only suggests new directions for treatment, but may ultimately inform a fundamentally deeper understanding of the dynamic two-way communication between mind and body.

Over my lifetime, as well as in writing this book, I have attempted
to bridge the vast chasm between the day-to-day work of the clinician
and the findings of various scientific disciplines, particularly ethology,
the study of animals in their natural environments. This vital field
reached a pinnacle of recognition in 1973 when three ethologists—
Nikolaas Tinbergen, Konrad Lorenz and Karl von Frisch—shared the
Nobel Prize in Physiology or Medicine.*

---

* Tinbergen's was for his study of animals in their natural environments, Lorenz's
  for his study of imprinting and Von Frisch's for his study of how the dance of honey
  bees communicates the location of pollen to the rest of the hive.

All three of these scientists utilized patient and precise observation to study how animals express and communicate through their bodies. Direct body communication is something that we reasoning, language-based human animals do as well. Despite our apparent reliance on elaborate speech, many of our most important exchanges occur simply through the "unspoken voice" of our body's expressions in the dance of life. The deciphering of this nonverbal realm is a foundation of the healing approach that I present in this book.

To convey the nature and transmutation of trauma in the body, brain and psyche, I have also drawn upon selected findings in the neurosciences. It is my conviction that clinical, naturalistic animal studies and comparative brain research can together greatly contribute to the evolution of methodologies that help restore resilience and promote self-healing. Toward this end, I will explain how our nervous system has evolved a hierarchical structure, how these hierarchies interact, and how the more advanced systems shut down in the face of overwhelming threat, leaving brain, body and psyche to their more archaic functions. I hope to demonstrate how successful therapy restores these systems to their balanced operation. An unexpected side effect of this approach is what might be called "Awakening the Living, Knowing Body." I will discuss how this awakening describes, in essence, what happens when animal instinct and reason are brought together, giving us the opportunity to become more whole human beings.

I aim to speak to the therapists who seek a better understanding of the roots of trauma in brain and body—such as psychological, psychiatric, physical, occupational and "bodywork" therapists. I also hope to reach the many medical doctors who are confounded by patients presenting inexplicable and mutable symptoms, the nurses who have long worked on the frontlines caring for terrified, injured patients and the policy makers concerned with our nation's problematic healthcare. Finally, I look for the larger audience of voracious readers of a wide variety of subjects—ranging from adventure, anthropology, biology, Darwin, neuroscience, quantum physics, string theory, relativity and zoology to the "Science" section of the *New York Times*.

Inspired by a childhood of reading Sherlock Holmes, I have attempted to engage the reader in the excitement of a lifelong journey of mystery and discovery. This voyage has carried me into a field that is at the core of what it means to be a human being, existing on an unpredictable and oftentimes violent planet. I have been privileged to study how people can rebound after extreme challenges and have borne witness to the resilience of the human spirit, to the lives of countless people who have returned to happiness and goodness, even after great devastation.

I will be telling some of this story in a way that is personal. The writing of this book has presented me with a very exciting challenge. I offer an account of my own experience as a clinician, scientist and inner explorer. My hope is that the occasional use of storytelling will help to create an accessible work that engages the clinical and scientific, but is sparse on jargon and is not unduly tedious and pedantic. I will utilize case vignettes to illustrate various principles, as well as invite the reader to participate in selected awareness exercises that embody these principles.

While directed to clinicians, physicians and scientists, as well as to interested laymen, ultimately this book is dedicated to those who have been tormented by the hungry ghosts of trauma. To these people, who live in a cage of anxiety, fear, pain and shame, I hope to convey a deeper appreciation that their lives are not dominated by a "disorder" but by an *injury that can be transformed and healed!* This capacity for transformation is a direct consequence of what I describe in the next section.

The Self-Regulating, Self-Knowing Body

In spite of my confusion and disorientation after the crosswalk accident, it was my thoroughly ingrained knowledge of trauma that led me first to request that the off-duty paramedic back off and allow me some space, and then to trust my body's involuntary shaking and other spontaneous physical and emotional reactions. However, even with my extensive knowledge and experience, I doubt whether I could have done this alone. The importance of the graceful pediatrician's quiet support was enormous.

Her noninvasive warmth, expressed in the calm tone of her voice, her gentle eyes, her touch and scent, gave me enough of a sense of safety and protection to allow my body to do what it needed to do and me to feel what I needed to feel. Together, my knowledge of trauma and the support of a calm present other allowed the powerful and profoundly restorative involuntary reactions to emerge and complete themselves.

In general, the capacity for *self-regulation* is what allows us to handle our own states of arousal and our difficult emotions, thus providing the basis for the balance between authentic autonomy and healthy social engagement. In addition, this capacity allows us the intrinsic ability to evoke a sense of being safely "at home" within ourselves, at home where goodness resides.

This capacity is especially important when we are frightened or injured. Most every mother in the world, knowing this instinctively, picks up her frightened child and soothes him or her by rocking and holding the child close to her body. Similarly, the kind eyes and pleasant scent of the woman who sat by my side bypassed the rational frontal cortex to reach directly into the recesses of my emotional brain. Thus, it soothed and helped to stabilize my organism just enough so that I could experience the difficult sensations and take steps toward restoring my balance and equanimity.

What Goes Up . . . Can Come Down

In 1998, Arieh Shalev carried out a simple and important study in Israel, a country where trauma is all too common.[2] Dr. Shalev noted the heart rates of patients seen in the emergency room (ER) of a Jerusalem hospital. These data were easy to collect, as charting the vital signs of anyone admitted to the ER is standard procedure. Of course, most patients are upset and have a high heart rate when they are first admitted to the ER, since they are most likely there as victims of some terrifying incident such as a bus bombing or motor vehicle accident. What Shalev discovered was that a patient whose heart rate had returned to near normal by the time of discharge from the ER was unlikely to develop posttraumatic stress disorder. On the other hand, one whose heart rate was still elevated upon leaving was highly likely to develop PTSD in the following weeks or months.* Thus, in my accident, I felt profound relief when the paramedic in the ambulance gave me the vital signs that indicated my heart rate had returned to normal.

Briefly, heart rate is a direct window into the autonomic (involuntary) branch of our nervous system. A racing heart is part of body and mind readying for the survival actions of fight-or-flight mediated by the sympathetic-adrenal nervous system (please see Diagram A after page 18 for a detailed depiction of the physiological pathways underlying the classic fight or flight response). Simply, when you perceive threat, your nervous system and body prepare you to kill or to take evasive countermeasures to escape, usually by running away. This preparation for *action* was absolutely essential on the ancient savannahs, and it is "discharged" or "used up" by all-out, meaningful action. In my case, however, lying injured on the road and then in the confines of the ambulance and the ER—where action was simply not an option—could have entrapped me. My global activation was "all dressed up with nowhere to go." If, rather than fulfilling its motoric mission in effective action, the preparation for action was interfered with or had lain dormant, it would have posed a great potential to trigger a later expression as the debilitating symptoms of posttraumatic stress disorder.

What saved me from developing these symptoms was the ability to bring down my fight-or-flight activation by discharging the immense survival energy through spontaneous trembling. This contained discharge, along with my *awareness* of the self-protective impulse to move my arms and shield my head, helped return my organism to equilibrium. I was able to surrender to these powerful sensations while remaining fully aware of my spontaneous bodily reactions, and with the

---

* Edward Blanchard and his colleagues questioned Shalev's data. However, in their study the vast majority of subjects were women and were only subjects who had sought treatment. Women tend to have more of a "freezing" stress response associated with the vagus nerve (which *lowers* heart rate)—in contrast to men, who tend to have a dominant sympathetic adrenal response. See Blanchard, E., et al. (2002). Emergency Room Vital Signs and PTSD in a Treatment Seeking Sample of Motor Vehicle Accident Survivors. *Journal of Traumatic Stress, 15* (3), 199–204.

pediatrician's steady presence and "holding of the space," I could restore my nervous system to equilibrium. By staying aware while "tracking" my spontaneous bodily reactions and feelings,* I was able to begin the process of moving through and out of the biological shock reaction. It is this *innate* capacity for self-regulation that let me regain my vital balance and restored me to sanity. This capacity for self-regulation holds the key for our modern survival—survival beyond the brutal grip of anxiety, panic, night terrors, depression, physical symptoms and helplessness that are the earmarks of prolonged stress and trauma. However, in order to experience this restorative faculty, we must develop the capacity to face certain uncomfortable and frightening physical sensations and feelings without becoming overwhelmed by them. This book is about how we develop that capacity.

Shake, Rattle and Roll ... Shiver, Quiver and Quake

The shaking and trembling I experienced while lying on the ground and in the ambulance are a core part of the innate process that reset my nervous system and helped restore my psyche to wholeness. Without it I would have surely suffered dearly. Had I not been aware of the vital purpose of my body's strange and strong sensations and gyrations, I might have been frightened by these powerful reactions and braced against them. Fortunately, I knew better.

I once described, to Andrew Bwanali, park biologist of the Mzuzu Environmental Center in Malawi, Central Africa, the spontaneous shaking, trembling and breathing that I and thousands of my therapy clients have exhibited in sessions as they recover from trauma. He nodded excitedly, then burst out, "Yes ... yes ... yes! This is true. Before we release captured animals back into the wild, we try to be sure that they have done just what you have described." He looked down at the ground and then added softly, "If they have not trembled and breathed that way [deep spontaneous breaths] before they are released, they will likely not

---

* These varied reactions included shaking, trembling and the restoration of biological defensive and orienting responses (including head and neck movements and the protective bracing of my arms and hands to protect my head).

survive in the wild ... they will die." His comment reinforces the importance of the ambulance paramedic's questioning the routine suppression of these reactions in medical settings.

We frequently shake when we are cold, anxious, angry or fearful.
We may also tremble when in love or at the climax of orgasm. Patients
sometimes shake uncontrollably, in cold shivers, as they awake from
anesthesia. Wild animals often tremble when they are stressed or confined. Shaking and trembling reactions are also reported during the
practices of traditional healing and spiritual pathways of the East. In
Qigong and Kundalini yoga, for example, adepts who employ subtle
movement, breathing and meditation techniques may experience ecstatic
and blissful states accompanied by shaking and trembling.

All of these "tremblings," experienced in diverse circumstances and
having a multiplicity of other functions, hold the potential for catalyz-
ing authentic transformation, deep healing and awe. Although the fearful trembling of anxiety does not in itself ensure a resetting and return
to equilibrium, it can hold its own solution when guided and experienced in the "right way." The distinguished Jungian analyst Marie-
Louise von Franz notes: "The divine psychic core of the soul, the self,
is activated in cases of extreme danger."[3] And, in the Bible, it is said that
"God is found where you have trembled."

What do all of these involuntary shakes and shivers have in common? Why do we quake when frightened or tremble in anger? Why
do we quiver at sexual climax? And what might be the physiological
function of trembling in spiritual awe? What is the commonality of all
these shivers and shakes, quivers and quakes? And what have they to
do with transforming trauma, regulating stress and living life to its
fullest?

These gyrations and undulations are ways that our nervous system
"shakes off" the last rousing experience and "grounds" us in readiness
for the next encounter with danger, lust and life. They are mechanisms
that help restore our equilibrium after we have been threatened or
highly aroused. They bring us back down to earth, so to speak. Indeed,
such physiological reactions are at the core of self-regulation and
resilience. The experience of emergent resilience gives us a treasure

beyond imagination. In the words of the ancient Chinese text, the *I Ching,*

> The fear and trembling engendered by shock comes to an individual at first in such a way that he sees himself placed at a disadvantage ... this is only transitory. When the ordeal is over, he experiences relief, and thus the very terror he had to endure at the outset brings good fortune in the long run.[4]

Learning to live through states of high arousal (no matter what their source) allows us to maintain equilibrium and sanity. It enables us to live life in its full range and richness—from agony to ecstasy. The intrinsic relationship of these spontaneous autonomic responses to the broad phenomenon of resilience, flow and transformation is a central theme of this book.

When, on the other hand, these "discharges" are inhibited or otherwise resisted and prevented from completion, our natural rebounding abilities get "stuck." Being stuck, after an actual or perceived threat, means that one is likely to be traumatized or, at least, to find that one's resilience and sense of OK-ness and belonging in the world have been diminished. Again, in the prescient words of the *I Ching:*

> This pictures a situation in which a shock endangers a man and he suffers great losses. Resistance would be contrary to the movement of the time and for this reason unsuccessful.[5]

On that sunny winter morning of my accident, I was able—with the help of the kind pediatrician—to allow those physiological processes to complete moment-by-moment, moving time forward and releasing the highly charged "survival energy" lurking in my body and seeking its intended expression. This immediate emotional and "physical" first-aid prevented me from getting "stuck," or locked in a vicious cycle of suffering and disability. How did I know what to do, as well as what to avoid, in this extremely stressful and disorienting situation? The short answer is that I have learned to embrace and welcome, rather than to fear and suppress, the primitive trembles, shakes and spontaneous body movements. The longer answer takes me back to the beginning of my last forty years of professional life as a scientist, a therapist and a healer.

Sympathetic–Adrenal Components of Fight or Flight

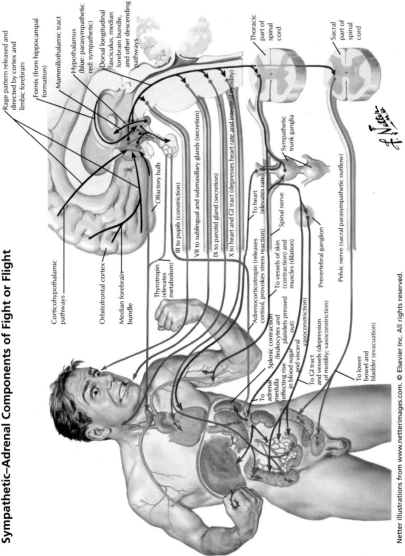

Rage pattern released and directed by cortex and limbic forebrain

Fornix (from hippocampal formation)

Mammillothalamic tract

Hypothalamus (blue: parasympathetic red: sympathetic)

Dorsal longitudinal fasciculus, median forebrain bundle, and other descending pathways

Corticohypothalamic pathways

Orbitofrontal cortex

Median forebrain bundle

Olfactory bulb

III to pupils (constriction)

VII to sublingual and submaxillary glands (secretion)

IX to parotid gland (secretion)

X to heart and GI tract (depresses heart rate and intestinal motility)

To heart (elevates rate)

Thoracic part of spinal cord

Sympathetic trunk ganglia

Spinal nerve

Sacral part of spinal cord

Thyrotropin (elevates metabolism)

Adrenocorticotropin (releases cortisol, provokes stress reaction)

To vessels of skin (contraction) and muscles (dilation)

Prevertebral ganglion

Pelvic nerve (sacral parasympathetic outflow)

To adrenal medulla (leukocytes and platelets pressed out)

Splenic contraction effecting rise in blood sugar

To GI tract and vessels (depression of motility; vasoconstriction)

To lower bowel and bladder (evacuation)

...and visceral vasoconstriction

Diagram A This is a detailed depiction of the physiological pathways underlying the classic fight-or-flight response. The illustrator was the late Dr. Frank Netter, one of the foremost medical illustrators.

The Vagus (10th Cranial) Nerve—"The Wanderer"

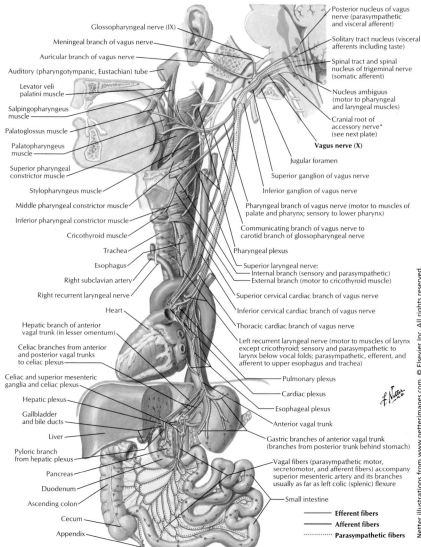

Glossopharyngeal nerve (IX)
Meningeal branch of vagus nerve
Auricular branch of vagus nerve
Auditory (pharyngotympanic, Eustachian) tube
Levator veli palatini muscle
Salpingopharyngeus muscle
Palatoglossus muscle
Palatopharyngeus muscle
Superior pharyngeal constrictor muscle
Stylopharyngeus muscle
Middle pharyngeal constrictor muscle
Inferior pharyngeal constrictor muscle
Cricothyroid muscle
Trachea
Esophagus
Right subclavian artery
Right recurrent laryngeal nerve
Heart
Hepatic branch of anterior vagal trunk (in lesser omentum)
Celiac branches from anterior and posterior vagal trunks to celiac plexus
Celiac and superior mesenteric ganglia and celiac plexus
Hepatic plexus
Gallbladder and bile ducts
Liver
Pyloric branch from hepatic plexus
Pancreas
Duodenum
Ascending colon
Cecum
Appendix

Posterior nucleus of vagus nerve (parasympathetic and visceral afferent)
Solitary tract nucleus (visceral afferents including taste)
Spinal tract and spinal nucleus of trigeminal nerve (somatic afferent)
Nucleus ambiguus (motor to pharyngeal and laryngeal muscles)
Cranial root of accessory nerve* (see next plate)
Vagus nerve (X)
Jugular foramen
Superior ganglion of vagus nerve
Inferior ganglion of vagus nerve
Pharyngeal branch of vagus nerve (motor to muscles of palate and pharynx; sensory to lower pharynx)
Communicating branch of vagus nerve to carotid branch of glossopharyngeal nerve
Pharyngeal plexus
Superior laryngeal nerve:
Internal branch (sensory and parasympathetic)
External branch (motor to cricothyroid muscle)
Superior cervical cardiac branch of vagus nerve
Inferior cervical cardiac branch of vagus nerve
Thoracic cardiac branch of vagus nerve
Left recurrent laryngeal nerve (motor to muscles of larynx except cricothyroid; sensory and parasympathetic to larynx below vocal folds; parasympathetic, efferent, and afferent to upper esophagus and trachea)
Pulmonary plexus
Cardiac plexus
Esophageal plexus
Anterior vagal trunk
Gastric branches of anterior vagal trunk (branches from posterior trunk behind stomach)
Vagal fibers (parasympathetic motor, secretomotor, and afferent fibers) accompany superior mesenteric artery and its branches usually as far as left colic (splenic) flexure
Small intestine

——— **Efferent fibers**
——— **Afferent fibers**
··········· **Parasympathetic fibers**

Diagram B This Netter illustration shows the intricate and robust relationship between the viscera and the brain. The dorsal vagus nerve (the tenth cranial nerve at the back/dorsal part of the brain stem) mediates the immobilization system. It acts upon most of the visceral organs. The (ventral/front) nucleus ambiguus mediates the social engagement system through its connections with the middle ear, face and throat.

CHAPTER 2

Touched by Discovery

The right way to wholeness is made up of
fateful detours and wrong turnings.
—C. G. Jung

To be touched by the revelation of love or scientific discovery is
among the greatest and most wondrous blessings of being alive.
While the year 1969 was a dud for romance, it was for me a time of
thrilling scientific illumination. While a momentous technical event
occurred in outer space that year, for me, an awakening in inner space
changed the course of my life.

At summer's beginning my friends and I sat glued to the TV screen,
our jaws dropped in awe. The Eagle lunar module had landed on the
Bay of Tranquility, and Neil Armstrong assuredly stepped onto the lunar
surface. Transfixed, we listened to the immortalized (though gram-
matically challenged) phrase: "One small step for man, one giant leap
for mankind." Men not only walked on the moon, they leaped in technological exuberance! Images of Earth were relayed from our nearest
celestial neighbor, offering a visual reminder that we were not at the
center of the universe.

In spite of that day's historical significance, I doubt that many people remember the month or even the year of the Apollo 11 moon land-
ing. However, that date, July 20, 1969, and the thrill of inner discovery
were indelibly etched in my mind. A "chance" event occurred around
the same time in my mind/body practice that was every bit as compelling. This singular event, a first step in a new professional life, gave birth

to a fresh perspective on the human condition, as well as confronting me with my own formidable hang-ups and inner trauma demons.

This incident was occasioned by the referral of a young woman from a psychiatrist who was aware of my keen interest in the fledgling fields of stress and mind-body healing. Nancy (not her real name) had been suffering from frequent migraines, hyperthyroidism, and fatigue, as well as chronic pain and debilitating premenstrual syndrome. Today, such symptoms would probably have been diagnosed as fibromyalgia and chronic fatigue syndrome. Her life was further diminished by severe panic-anxiety attacks and agoraphobia that kept her tied to home. I had been developing some body awareness–based relaxation and stress-reduction procedures that the psychiatrist thought might be beneficial to her.

Nancy entered my office, clinging nervously to her husband's arms. She was fidgeting with his hands; he was transparently burdened by her complete dependence. I noticed how tight her neck was, pulling in like an injured turtle, while her eyes were wide with the startled look of a deer in the headlights. Her posture was stooped, conveying a pervasive sense of fear and defeat. Nancy's resting heart rate was high—almost 100 beats per minute (which I was able to surmise from the pulsing of the carotid artery in her neck). Her breathing was so shallow as to seem barely able to sustain life.

At first I taught Nancy to become aware of, and then to release, her chronically tense neck and shoulder muscles. She appeared to be relaxing deeply. Her heart rate decreased to a more normal range as her breathing deepened. However, moments later she abruptly became intensely agitated. Her heart, pounding wildly, shot up to approximately 130 beats per minute. Her breath was rapid and shallow as she gasped erratically. Then, as I watched helplessly, she abruptly froze in terror. Her face turned deathly white. She appeared paralyzed and barely able to breathe. Her heart seemed to almost stop, dropping precipitately to about 50 beats per minute (an action of the heart I will discuss later in Chapter 6). Fighting my own impending panic, I was at a loss as to what to do.

"I'm dying. Don't let me die," she pleaded in a small taut voice. "Help me, help me! Please don't let me die." Her disturbing helplessness evoked, in my subconscious, an archetypal solution. Suddenly, in my mind's eye, a dreamlike image appeared: a tiger, crouched in readiness to strike, materialized out of the far wall of the room.

"Run, Nancy!" I commanded without thinking, "A tiger is chasing you. Climb those rocks and escape." Bewildered by my own outburst, I gazed in amazement as Nancy's legs began to tremble and then move up and down in what appeared to be spontaneous running movements. Her whole body started shaking—first convulsively, then more softly. As the shaking gradually subsided (over the better part of an hour), she experienced a feeling of peacefulness that, in her own words, "held her in warm tingling waves." (See Figure 2.1a and 2.1b.)

Fear/Immobility Cycle

Figure 2.1a This shows the vicious cycle by which fear and immobility feed off each other. It is what engulfs and traps us in the "black hole" of trauma.

Later, Nancy reported that during the session she had seen nightmarish images of herself as a four-year-old child, struggling to escape the grasp of the doctors who held her down in order to administer ether anesthesia for a "routine" tonsillectomy. Until now, she recounted, this event had been "long forgotten." To my utter amazement, these unusual gyrations turned Nancy's life around. Many of her symptoms improved significantly, and some disappeared altogether. The panic attack that occurred during the session was her last; and, over the next two years, until her graduation from graduate school, her chronic fatigue, migraines, and premenstrual symptoms improved dramatically. In addition, she reported the following "side effect"—she "felt more alive and happier than [she could] remember."

Restoration of Active Defense Responses

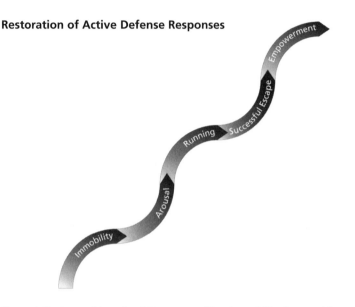

Figure 2.1b I was able to lead Nancy out of her immobility/fear and hyperarousal by allowing her to re-create the experience of running and successfully escaping from her would-be attackers. It is essential for the client to *feel* the sensation of running. Running without inner sensing has only limited value.

The Innate Capacity for Recovery

What allowed Nancy to emerge from her frozen symptomatic shell and reengage in life was the same mechanism that prevented me from becoming traumatized after I was hit by the automobile. The shaking and trembling, occurring in the warm and reassuring presence of a reliable other person, and allowed to continue to completion, helped both of us to restore equilibrium and wholeness, and to be freed from trauma's grip.

Through focused awareness and micro-movements to reenact and *complete* our unfinished, instinctually rooted protective actions, both Nancy and I were able to discharge the residual nervous system "energy" that had been activated for survival. Nancy experienced the long-delayed escape that her body wanted to make while she was being tied down and overpowered as a defenseless little girl. In short, we both experienced and *embodied* the innate and powerful wisdom of our instinctual responses as they mobilized to ward off mortal danger.

The mindful sensing of this protective primal force stood in stark contrast to the overwhelming helplessness that had engulfed each of us. The major difference between Nancy's experience and mine was that I had the luck of receiving self-administered first aid, and the fortunate presence of the pediatrician, to nip the potential PTSD symptoms in the bud. Nancy, like millions of others, unfortunately did not. She had suffered years of needless distress until we briefly revisited and "renegotiated" her childhood surgery in my office, some twenty years afterward.*

Had I not sensed the raw muscular power of my survival instincts, contrasting with my helpless condition, I surely would have developed the debilitating symptoms of PTSD that had so shadowed and crippled Nancy. I would have, like Nancy, been left too frightened to venture out confidently into the world again. Just as Nancy was able to escape her tormenters in retrospect, I was able to both escape my destruction and preventatively "reset" my nervous system in real time.

When acutely threatened, we mobilize vast energies to protect and defend ourselves. We duck, dodge, twist, stiffen and retract. Our muscles contract to fight or flee. However, if our actions are ineffective, we freeze or collapse. Nancy's four-year-old body had tried to escape from her masked predators. Her body wanted to run away and escape, but it could not. She was overpowered and held down against her will by all-powerful masked and gowned giants. In our hour together Nancy's body contradicted her panicky feelings of being overwhelmed and trapped. And as her body learned this, so did her mind.

When any organism perceives overwhelming mortal danger (with little or no chance for escape) the *biological* response is a global one of paralysis and shutdown. Ethologists call this innate response *tonic immobility* (TI). Humans experience this frozen state as helpless terror and

---

* I use the term *renegotiation* to refer to the reworking of a traumatic experience in contrast to the *reliving* of it.

panic. Such a state of shutdown and paralysis is meant to be temporary. A wild animal exhibiting this acute physiological shock reaction will either be eaten or, if spared, presumably resume life as before its brush with death; it will be none the worse for the encounter and perhaps wiser. It may be more vigilant (not to be confused with hypervigilant) about similar future sources of threat and thus of early intimations of danger. A deer might, for example, avoid certain rocky outcroppings where it had previously escaped the lunging attack of a mountain lion.

Humans, in contrast to animals, frequently remain stuck in a kind of limbo, not fully reengaging in life after experiencing threat as overwhelming terror or horror. In addition, they exhibit a propensity for freezing in situations where a non-traumatized individual might only sense danger or even feel some excitement. Rather than being a last-ditch reaction to inescapable threat, paralysis becomes a "default" response to a wide variety of situations in which one's feelings are highly aroused. For example, the arousal of sex may turn unexpectedly from excitement to frigidity, revulsion or avoidance.

Toward a Biology of Trauma

In an attempt to understand the episode with Nancy, I was pulled in several new directions. First, I realized that, if not for trusting my gut instincts and a little bit of blind luck, I might just as easily have inadvertently "retraumatized" Nancy, leading to a worsening of her already severe symptoms. In addition, like the gambler who hits the jackpot early in his career, I would soon find out that such dramatic—one-time—"cures" would not always be the case. I was drawn into a consuming journey to uncover just what had transpired that summer day in 1969. As I discovered, it was crucial to "titrate" (gradually access) these physiological reactions so that they were not overwhelming. Just exposing a client to his or her traumatic memories and having the person relive them was, at best, unnecessary (reducing integration and feelings of mastery and goodness) and at worst retraumatizing for the individual. I also learned that the shaking and trembling, which constitute the discharge reactions, were often so subtle as to be barely noticeable to an outside observer. Often the manifestation of the discharge was a gentle muscular fasciculation (minute muscular trembling and quivers) or temperature change—such as going from very cold to very hot. These changes are generally monitored by observing color changes in the hands and face.

Over the following decades, I explored the biological basis of trauma from a comparative study of animals and their nervous systems. This, I felt, would help me develop a systematic approach to healing trauma that could be reproduced reliably and systematically, as well as being sufficiently safe. This journey also fulfilled an early dream of mine: I became a (small) part of the space adventure. While still a Berkeley graduate student in medical biophysics, I was given a fellowship as a stress consultant at NASA for a year. My primary task—to help prepare our astronauts for the first space shuttle flight—gave me a unique opportunity to study people whose stress resilience was unusually robust. These observations inspired me to reflect back on my session with Nancy some years earlier: on her profound lack of resilience and her spontaneous transformation. It seemed possible that the astronauts' super-resilience was a skill that even the most highly traumatized individuals could learn to activate, a birthright that needed to be reclaimed.

A First Step: Serendipity Gained

In attempting to understand what had transpired that day with Nancy, I was struck by a "footnote" in an informal graduate seminar I was taking in comparative animal behavior. One of the professors, Peter Marler, had mentioned some peculiar behaviors exhibited by prey animals such as birds and rabbits when they were physically restrained. That night I awoke, shaking in excitement. Could Nancy's reaction (when held down by the doctors) be similar to those of the experimentally restrained animals? As for my "hallucination" of the crouching tiger, that was undoubtedly a creative "waking dream" stimulated by that inspiring graduate seminar.

In pursuing the arcane allusion from my seminar, I came across a 1967 article titled "Comparative Aspects of Hypnosis."[6] I brought this article, along with my ideas about it, to my graduate research advisor,

Donald M. Wilson.* His field was invertebrate neurophysiology, and he was familiar with these types of "freezing" behaviors. However, for one dedicated solely to the study of creatures like insects and lobsters, he was understandably skeptical about "animal hypnosis." Nonetheless, I remained fascinated by the broadly observed phenomenon of animal paralysis and spent endless hours in the musty, dusty stacks of the Life Sciences graduate library. At the same time, I continued to see more clients referred primarily by Ed Jackson, the psychiatrist who had referred Nancy to me. I was exploring with them how various imbalanced patterns of muscular tension and postural tone were related to their symptoms—and how releasing and normalizing these entrenched patterns often led to unexpected and dramatic cures. Then in 1973, in the acceptance speech for his share in the Nobel Prize in Physiology or Medicine,[†] the ethologist Nikolaas Tinbergen unexpectedly chose to talk not primarily about his study of animals in their natural environment, but about the observed human body as it goes through life and as it functions and malfunctions under stress. I was struck by his observations about the Alexander technique.[‡] This body-based reeducation treatment, which he and members of his family had undergone with notable health benefits (including a normalizing of his high blood pressure), paralleled my observations with my body-mind clients.

Clearly, I needed to talk to this elder. I managed to locate him at Oxford University; with unassuming generosity, this Nobel Laureate spoke to me, a lowly graduate student, via transatlantic cable on a number of occasions. I told him about my first session with Nancy and other clients, and about my speculation concerning the relationship of her reactions to "animal paralysis." He was excited about the possibility that animal immobility reactions might play an important role in humans

---

* Tragically, Donald Wilson was killed in a rafting accident in 1970.

† This transcript was published in the journal *Science* in 1974.

‡ The Alexander technique takes its name from F. Matthias Alexander, who first observed and formulated its principles between 1890 and 1900. It is an approach for reducing harmful postural habits that interfere with both the physical and the mental conditions of the individual as a whole.

under conditions of inescapable threat and extreme stress, and encouraged me to pursue this line of investigation.* I occasionally wonder if without his support, as well as that from Hans Selye (the first stress researcher) and Raymond Dart (the anthropologist who discovered *Australopithecus*), I might have thrown in the towel.

In a memorable phone conversation, Tinbergen chided me in his kind, grandfatherly voice, "Peter, we are, after all, just a bunch of animals!" According to recent polls, however, only half of the Western world (and even fewer in the United States) seem to believe in evolution and, thus, in our intimate relation to other mammals. Yet given obvious patterns in anatomy, physiology, behavior, and emotions, and since we share the same survival parts of the brain with other mammals, it only makes sense that we share their reactions to threat. Hence, there would be great benefit gained from learning how animals (particularly mammals and higher-level primates) respond to threat, and then observing how they rebound, settle and return to equilibrium after the threat has passed. Many of us humans, unfortunately, have become alienated from this innate capacity for resilience and self-healing. This, as we shall explore, has made us vulnerable to being overwhelmed and traumatized.

It was not until 1978, however, that I could plant my observations on firmer ground. While working at the NASA Ames labs in Mountain View, California, and continuing to develop my body-mind practice in Berkeley, I spent every spare moment frequenting the biology graduate library. One dark and rainy December day in 1978, I was making my usual library rounds. In that era, long before Google or anything remotely resembling a PC, my usual mode of library research was to pack a lunch and then leaf through the large volumes of possibly relevant journals. With this supposedly inefficient, meandering method, I came across many wonderful gems that I might not have discovered by a "high-tech" search engine. These formative research efforts set the theoretical groundwork for my life's work.

---

* At this time the chairman of my doctoral committee was quite dubious, even antagonistic, about my thesis.

One day I chanced upon a mind-blowing article by Gordon Gallup and Jack Maser that described how "animal paralysis" was evoked, with variables experimentally controlled.[7] This paper, which I discuss in Chapter 4, gave me the key that allowed me to weave observations of my body-mind clients (like Nancy) with an appreciation for how certain fear-based survival instincts both shape trauma and inform its healing. I was fortunate to have the freedom to speculate in this manner since trauma had not yet been formally defined as posttraumatic stress disorder (PTSD), and would not be for over a decade. For this reason, I am happy to say, I never pigeonholed trauma as a reified and incurable disease, as it became known in the early PTSD literature.

A synchronous and full-cycle return occurred several years ago. I was presenting my work at a conference titled "Frontiers in Psychotherapy," put on by the Psychiatry Department at the University of California, San Diego, School of Medicine. At the end of my talk, a lively, impish man jumped up to introduce himself: "Hi, I'm Jack Maser!" I shook my head, dubious at first; not quite believing my ears, I burst into spontaneous laughter. After exchanging a few words, we arranged to lunch together. At this time he shared with me his delight in discovering that his animal work had found a clinical application in real-life therapy. I was sort of a clinical godchild to his experimental godfather.

In 2008, Jack Maser forwarded to me an article that he and a colleague, Stephen Bracha, had just published. In this article they proposed a fundamental change to the "Bible" of psychiatric diagnosis. They wanted to include the concept of tonic immobility in explaining trauma.[8] My jaw dropped so far that a bird might have flown in and nested there. The *Diagnostic and Statistical Manual of Mental Disorders*, or *DSM*, is the encyclopedic book that psychologists and psychiatrists use to diagnose "mental disorders," including Posttraumatic Stress Disorder. (The *DSM* is now in its "IV-R" edition, the "R" denoting a partial revision of the fourth edition.) The next edition—the *DSM-V*—will (ideally) be a significant step forward.

The previous versions of the PTSD diagnosis have been careful not to suggest a mechanism (or even a theory) to explain what happens in the brain and body when people become traumatized. This absence is important for more than academic reasons: a theory suggests rationales for treatment and prevention. This avoidance, and sole reliance on taxonomy, is an understandable overreaction to the Freudian theory's previous stranglehold on psychology. I believe that it is only with intimate collaboration that science and praxis will co-evolve into a lively, vibrant partnership capable of generating truly innovative therapies. An open multidisciplinary effort could begin to help us discern what is or is not effective and to improve at our primary aim of helping suffering people heal!

The article by Jack Maser and Steven Bracha offers a spirited challenge to those entrusted to write the *DSM-V.* In their audacious commentary, these two researchers put forth the bold premise that there exists a theoretical basis for the mechanisms underlying PTSD: an evolutionary *(instinctual)* basis for trauma, similar to what I had observed with Nancy in 1969. With this article, I had come full circle. Gallup and Maser's 1977 experimental studies on fear and "animal paralysis" had inspired my explanation for her behavior. Now Maser and Bracha concluded their 2008 article with these tickling couple of sentences:

> Along swith the many changes that are being suggested for *DSM-V,* we urge the planners to seek out empirical studies and/or theories that place psychopathology in an evolutionary context. The field will then have a connection to broader issues in biology, the data on psychopathology can be placed within a widely accepted concept, and clinicians will have the possibility of developing more effective behavioral treatments (e.g., Levine, 1997).[9]

Oh, what divine delight! I could not help but wonder if my lecture at the San Diego Medical Conference had contributed in part to stimulating Maser and Bracha to make this proposal. The mere possibility that I might somehow, through fateful detours and twisted turns, have influenced the course of the psychiatric diagnosis of trauma (or at least contributed to the dialogue) was mind-blowing. Let us take a brief look at that diagnostic history.

CHAPTER 3

The Changing Face of Trauma

M OST PEOPLE THINK OF TRAUMA AS A "MENTAL" PROBLEM, even as a "brain disorder." However, trauma is something that also happens in the body. We become scared stiff or, alternately, we collapse, overwhelmed and defeated with helpless dread. Either way, trauma defeats life.

The state of being scared stiff has been portrayed in the various great cultural mythologies. There is, of course, the Gorgon Medusa who turns her victims to stone by exposing them to her own wide-eyed terrified gaze. In the Old Testament, Lot's wife is turned into a pillar of salt as a punishment for witnessing the terrifying destruction of Sodom and Gomorrah. If these myths seem too remote, we need only look at children throughout the world playing "statue." How many countless generations of kids have used this game to help them master the primordial terror (often lurking in their dreams) of being scared stiff? To these stories we can add our contemporary myth of the "disease" that psychiatry has named posttraumatic stress disorder or PTSD. Indeed, when compared with historical mythologies, modern science has certain advantages and disadvantages in accurately comprehending the universal human experience of terror, horror, injury and loss.

The indigenous peoples throughout South America and Mesoamerica have long understood both the nature of fear and the essence of trauma. What's more, they seemed to know how to transform it through their shamanic healing rituals. After colonization by the Spanish and Portuguese, the indigenous peoples borrowed their word *susto* to describe what happens in trauma. Susto translates graphically as "fright paralysis" and as "soul loss."[10] Anyone who has suffered a trauma knows, first, paralyzing fright, followed by the bereft feeling of losing your way in the world, of being severed from your very soul.

When we hear the term *fright paralysis*, we may think of a startled deer, stunned motionless by oncoming headlights. Humans react similarly to trauma: thus Nancy, her startled face wide-eyed and frozen in fear. The ancient Greeks also identified trauma as being paralyzing and corporeal. Zeus and Pan were invoked to instill terror and paralysis in the enemy during times of war. Both had the capacity to "freeze" the body and induce "*pan*-ic." And in the great Homeric epics, the Iliad and the Odyssey, trauma was portrayed as ruthlessly destructive to self and families.

By the time of the American Civil War—when young men were suddenly exposed to their comrades being blown into pieces by cannon fire; to the noise and terror of chaos; and to stinking, rotting corpses far beyond anything they were prepared for—the term used to describe traumatic post-combat breakdown was *soldier's heart.** This name conveyed both the anxious, arrhythmic heart, pounding in sleepless terror, as well as the heartbreak of war, the killing of brothers by brothers. Another term from the Civil War era was *nostalgia*, perhaps a reference to the unending weeping and inability to remain oriented to the present and go on with life.

Shortly before World War I, Emil Kraepelin, in an early diagnostic system published around 1909, called such stress breakdown "fright neurosis."[11] After Freud, he recognized trauma as a condition arising from an overwhelming stress. Freud had defined trauma as "a breach in the protective barrier against stimulation [(over)stimulation—my addition], leading to feelings of overwhelming helplessness." Kraepelin's definition was largely lost in the nomenclature of trauma, yet it recognized the central aspect of fright—although the word "neurosis" has pejorative associations.

---

* This descriptive term was probably borrowed from the Swiss in the mid-1600s, where it was also called nostalgia *(Heimweh)*—and yes, the armies of the "neutral" Swiss cantons were at each other's throats for centuries!

In the wake of World War I, combat trauma was reincarnated as *shell shock*, simple, honest and direct. This bluntly descriptive phrase almost resounds like the maddening explosions of shells, shattering the stunned and trapped men into shaking, urinating and defecating uncontrollably in the cold, wet trenches. Like susto, this raw descriptive term had nothing distancing, dispassionate or disinfected about it.

However, by World War II, any real reference to soldiers' suffering was stripped of dignity and neutered to *battle fatigue* or *war neurosis*. The first term suggested that if a soldier heeded Grandma's advice and took a good long rest, all would be just fine. This dismissive minimizing was especially insulting, and even ironic, given a suffering soldier's profoundly disturbed capacity for restorative sleep. Even more demeaning was the pejorative use of the word *neurosis*, implying that a soldier's "shell shock" was somehow due to a "character defect" or a nagging personal weakness—perhaps an "Oedipal complex"—rather than to one's entirely appropriate terror of exploding shells or stark grief for fallen comrades and the horror of men killing men. These newer monikers separated civilians, families and doctors from the jagged reality of the soldiers' profound suffering.

In the aftermath of the Korean War, all remaining poignancy was excised from the next generation of war trauma terminology. The term used here for combat trauma, *operational exhaustion* (which was resurrected as *combat operational exhaustion* for the Iraq war), certainly had nothing gritty or real in respect to the horrors of war. It was an objectified term, more applicable to a laptop computer of today when left on too long and needing a reboot.

Finally, the current terminology, derived largely from the experiences of the Vietnam War, is *posttraumatic stress disorder*. As PTSD, the universal phenomenon of terror and paralysis—in which the nervous system has been strained to the breaking point, leaving body, psyche and soul shattered—is now fully sanitized as a medical "disorder." With its own convenient acronym, and serving the dispassionate nature of science, the archetypal response to carnage has now been artificially severed from its ravaging origins. Where it was once aptly conveyed by the terms *fright paralysis* and *shell shock*, it is now simply a disorder, an objectified collection of concrete and measurable symptoms; a diagnosis amenable to vested research protocols, detached insurance companies and behavioral treatment strategies. While this nomenclature provides objective scientific legitimacy to the soldiers' very real suffering, it also safely separates doctor from patient. The "healthy" ("protected") doctor treats the "ill" patient. This approach disempowers and marginalizes the sufferer, adding to his or her sense of alienation and despair. Less noticed is the likely burnout in the unprotected healer, who has been artificially hoisted onto a precarious pedestal as false prophet.

Recently, a young Iraq veteran took issue with calling his combat anguish PTSD and, instead, poignantly referred to his pain and suffering as PTSI—the "I" designating "injury." What he wisely discerned is that trauma is an injury, not a disorder like diabetes, which can be managed but not healed. In contrast, posttraumatic stress injury is an emotional wound, amenable to healing attention and transformation.

Nonetheless, the medical model persists. It (arguably) functions fairly effectively with diseases like diabetes and cancer, where the doctor holds all of the knowledge and dictates the necessary interventions for a sick patient. This is not, however, a useful paradigm for trauma healing. Rather than being a disease in the classical sense, trauma is instead a profound *experience* of "dis-ease" or "dis-order." What is called for here is a cooperative and restorative process with the doctor as an assisting guide and midwife. A doctor who insists on retaining his or her protected role as "healthy healer" remains separate, defending him- or herself against the ultimate helplessness that lurks, phantom-like, in all of our lives. Cut off from his or her own feelings, such a doctor will not be able to join with the sufferer. Missing will be the crucial collaboration in containing, processing and integrating the patient's horrible sensations, images and emotions. The sufferer will remain starkly alone, holding the very horrors that have overwhelmed him and broken down his capacity to self-regulate and grow.

In a common therapy resulting from this isolating orientation, the therapist instructs the PTSD victim to assert control over his feelings, to manage his aberrant behaviors and to alter his dysfunctional thoughts.

Contrast this alignment to that of shamanic traditions, where the healer and the sufferer join together to reexperience the terror while calling on cosmic forces to release the grip of the demons. The shaman is always first initiated, via a profound encounter with his own helplessness and feeling of being shattered, prior to assuming the mantle of healer. Such preparation might suggest a model whereby contemporary therapists must first recognize and engage with their own traumas and emotional wounds.*

The Power of Myth

Mythology is a function of biology.
—Joseph Campbell
in *Myth and the Body*

Healing has been hindered by a nomenclature and a paradigm that, in separating the healer from the wounded, denies the universality of our responses to terror and horror. The aspiration to reinvigorate a contemporary approach to healing trauma requires each of us to connect to our biological commonality as instinctual beings; thus, we are linked not only by our common vulnerability to fright but by our innate capacity to transform such experiences. In pursuing this link, we can learn much from mythology and from our animal brethren. It is the weaving together of heroic myth and biology ("mytho-biology") that will help us comprehend the roots and mysterium tremendum of trauma.

Medusa

Mythology teaches us about courageously meeting challenges. Myths are archetypal stories that simply and directly touch the core of our being. They remind us about our deepest longings, and reveal to us our

---

* In the opposite direction we see that a declining number of office-based psychiatrists in the United States are providing psychotherapy. According the results from a national ten-year survey from the National Ambulatory Medical Care Survey (NAMCS), the percentage of office visits to psychiatrists that involved psychotherapy dropped from 44% in 1996–1997 to 29% in 2004–2005.

hidden strengths and resources. They are also maps of our essential nature, pathways that connect us to each other, to nature and to the cosmos. The Greek myth of Medusa captures the very essence of trauma and describes its pathway to transformation.

In the Greek myth, those who looked directly into Medusa's eyes were promptly turned into stone ... frozen in time. Before setting out to vanquish this snake-haired demon, Perseus sought counsel from Athena, the goddess of knowledge and strategy. Her advice to him was simple: under no circumstances should he look directly at the Gorgon. Taking Athena's advice to heart, Perseus used the protective shield fastened on his arm to reflect the image of Medusa. This way he was able to cut off her head without looking directly at her, and thus avoided being turned into stone.

If trauma is to be transformed, we must learn not to confront it directly. If we make the mistake of confronting trauma head on, then Medusa will, true to her nature, turn us to stone. Like the Chinese finger traps we all played with as kids, the more we struggle with trauma, the greater will be its grip upon us. When it comes to trauma, I believe that the "equivalent" of Perseus's reflecting shield is how our body responds to trauma and how the "living body" personifies resilience and feelings of goodness.

There is more to this myth:

Out of Medusa's wound, two mythical entities emerged: Pegasus the winged horse and the one-eyed giant Chrysaor, the warrior with the golden sword. The golden sword represents penetrating truth and clarity. The horse is a symbol of the body and instinctual knowledge; the wings symbolize transcendence. Together, they suggest transformation through the "living body."* Together, these aspects form the archetypal qualities and resources that a human being must mobilize in order to heal the Medusa (fright paralysis) called trauma. The ability to perceive and respond to the *reflection* of Medusa is mirrored in our instinctual natures.

---

*In the analytic psychology of Jung, the image of the one-eyed giant holding a golden sword conveys the archetype of the "deep" (non-egoic) self.

In another version of this same myth, Perseus collects a drop of blood from Medusa's wound in two vials. The drop from one vial has the power to kill; the drop in the other vial has the power to raise the dead and restore life. What is revealed here is the dual nature of trauma: first, its destructive ability to rob victims of their capacity to live and enjoy life. The paradox of trauma is that it has both the power to destroy and the power to transform and resurrect. Whether trauma will be a cruel and punishing Gorgon, or a vehicle for soaring to the heights of transformation and mastery, depends upon how we approach it.

Trauma is a fact of life. It does not, however, have to be a life sentence. It is possible to learn from mythology, from clinical observations, from neuroscience, from embracing the "living" experiential body, and from the behavior of animals; and then, rather than brace against our instincts, embrace them. With guidance and support, we are capable of emulating animals in learning (like Nancy and I did) to shake and tremble our way back to life. In being able to harness these primordial and intelligent instinctual energies, we can move through trauma and transform it. In Chapter 4 we begin with a study of our instinctual roots as revealed in the animal experience.

CHAPTER 4

Immobilized by Fear

Lessons Learned from Animals

It is life's only true opponent,
only fear can defeat life.
> —Yann Martel, *Life of Pi*

The only thing we have to fear
is fear itself.
> —Franklin Delano Roosevelt,
> First Inaugural Address, 1933

All higher animals exhibit fear reactions. By understanding the biological nature of fear, we are able to grasp the very taproot of trauma. This knowledge also illuminates our innate capacity to rebound from the contracted states of fear and terror. In many primate groups, predator and cohort attacks are unpredictable, frequent and unremitting.* These primates see members of their tribe torn to pieces by hyenas, panthers and other large cats. Terror is likely their frequent companion; but, ultimately, survival requires that such strong emotional reactions be essentially transitory.

We share with our proximal ancestors, the monkeys and apes, a heritability of predation anxiety. This destiny prompted one author to call primate existence, "one continual nightmare of anxiety."[12] Prehistoric peoples must have spent long hours each day huddled together in dark, cold caves with the certain knowledge that they could be picked off at

---

* Bonobos are a notable exception to cohort attacks, largely through the strategy of free sex for all, as well as their matriarchal organization.

any moment and torn to shreds. Though most of us no longer dwell in caves, we retain an intense expectation of lurking danger, be it from others of our own species or from predators.

In calming a frightened nation against panic, Franklin D. Roosevelt described fear's destructive nature as "nameless, unreasoning, unjustified terror which paralyzes needed efforts to convert retreat into advance." It is such paralyzing fearfulness that has outlasted its survival utility in humans. Such intractable fear prevents a person from returning to balance and normal life. The ability to transition readily between intense emotional states is popularly referred to as "flow," as "being present" or "in the moment" as opposed to being stuck in one's past history. How mammals rebound from extreme fear and other intense emotional states such as rage and loss is instructive for our own recovery from trauma. It is also a key to our very sanity and capacity to live fully and spontaneously.

The Posture of Danger

As surely as we hear the blood in our ears,
the echoes of a million midnight shrieks
   of monkeys,
whose last sight of the world was the eyes
   of a panther,
have their traces in our nervous systems.
—Paul Shepherd (in *The Others*)

On the Serengeti

We are troop animals and have a close kinship with other pack mammals. We live in family groups and tribes, join clubs, rely on neighbors and friends, form political parties and identify with our national (and even international) community. Recognizing our mammalian status provides us with important information on the nature of trauma and recovery, as well as on how we interact with our clients, and with other humans.

A herd of gazelle grazes peacefully in a lush wadi. The snap of a twig, the rustling of some bushes, a fleeting shadow or a few molecules of a particular scent alert one member of the herd. It *arrests* its movement and stiffens in readiness. This abrupt cessation of movement makes the animal less likely to be detected by the predator. It also lets the gazelle "pause," giving it the opportunity to organize an optimal escape route. In addition, the other animals of the herd instantly attune to its postural shift by arresting their activity as well. They all scan *together* (many more ears, noses and eyes), better to localize and identify the source of threat. There is a similar response to potential threat from an army squad on patrol in enemy territory.

Imagine strolling leisurely in an open meadow. A shadow suddenly moves into the periphery of your vision. How do you respond? Instinctively, your previous motions stop. You may crouch slightly in a flexed posture, and your heart rate will change as your autonomic nervous system is engaged. After this momentary "arrest" response, your eyes open wide. Without willing it, your head turns in the direction of the shadow (or sound) in an attempt to locate and identify it. Your neck, back, legs and feet muscles are working together to turn your body, which extends and lengthens. Your eyes narrow as your pelvis and head shift horizontally to give an optimal, panoramic view of your surroundings. What is your internal state? What other intangible aspects of yourself do you feel or sense in response to seeing the moving shadow? Most people will feel alert and engaged, even curious. Perhaps you feel a hint of excitement and anticipation or, possibly, of danger.

Animals and humans also need to know if one of their own has aggressive intentions. Ignoring such signals may well put you in harm's way. In sessions with hundreds of rape victims, I have discovered that many could recall the early presence of danger signals that they had ignored or overridden. They could remember the man staring at them as they left a restaurant or the fleeting shadow as they passed a street corner.

I have also worked with several rapists who graphically described precisely how they knew (from a woman's posture and gait) who was fearful (or propped up with false bravado) and would thus be easy prey. The precision and accuracy of these perpetrators' assessments were truly unsettling. Although their capacity to empathize and read subtle emotions was greatly impaired, their predatory ability to read fear and helplessness was expertly honed. They made deliberate use of the innate skills that we tend to dismiss at our own peril.

One's posture and facial muscles signal emotional states, not only to others, but to oneself as well.[13] We shall see in the following sections that, as social creatures, it is through empathy that we make our deepest communications. To do this we must be able to "resonate" with the sensations and emotions of others; we must, in other words, be able to feel the same things as those around us feel. The way we indicate this is primarily nonverbal; it is through our postures and expressive emotions.

Biological, or postural, tuning is also the foundation for the "therapeutic resonance" that is vitally important in helping people heal from trauma. A therapist who is not aware of how his or her own body reacts to (i.e., resonates with) the fear, rage, helplessness and shame in another person will not be able to guide clients by *tracking* their sensations and navigating them safely through the sometimes treacherous (albeit therapeutic) waters of traumatic sensations. At the same time, by learning how to track their own sensations, therapists can avoid *absorbing* the fear, rage and helplessness of their clients. It is important to understand that when therapists perceive that they must protect themselves from their clients' sensations and emotions, they unconsciously block those clients from therapeutically experiencing them. By distancing ourselves from their anguish, we distance ourselves from them and from the fears they are struggling with. To take a self-protective stance is to abandon our clients precipitately. At the same time, we also greatly increase the likelihood of their exposure to secondary or vicarious traumatization and burnout. Therapists must learn, from their own successful encounters with their own traumas, to stay present with their clients. This is the reason healing trauma must necessarily engage the awareness of the living, sensing, "knowing" body in *both* client and therapist. "Perhaps the most striking evidence of successful empathy," says the analyst

Leston Havens, "is the occurrence in our bodies of sensations that the patient has described in his or hers."[14]

Through the Eyes of a Neuroscientist

The ability to detect danger in the posture of others has been studied by the neuroscientist Beatrice Gelder.[15] Her research has demonstrated that the brain of an observer reacts more powerfully to the body language of a person in a posture denoting fear than it does even to a fearful facial expression. Like the Gorgon Medusa, looks of fear can paralyze or, at least, evoke our own potent fear-based reactions. Yet, as powerful as facial expressions are in conveying danger, a person's uptight posture and furtive movements make us even more uncomfortable.* Wouldn't you, too, startle to the sudden recoiling of the hiker in front of you a split second *before* you heard the hissing and rattle of a coiled snake? This type of imitative behavior occurs throughout the animal world. If, for example, one bird in a flock on the ground suddenly takes off, all the other birds will follow immediately after; they do not need to know why. The hypothetical contrarian bird that stays behind may not live to pass its genes to the next generation.

In combination, a fearful face, hypervigilance and a tight constricted posture are powerfully compelling. They trigger us to prepare our bodies for action, to locate the source of threat and then to respond immediately. Perhaps a perceived threat comes from an "uptight" person readying to strike out in aggravated fear. In our day-to-day life, most of us deal with chronically fearful or angry people by simply avoiding them whenever we can. On the other hand, when you meet people whose posture expresses grace and acceptance, you are calmed by their ease. Thus, we are particularly affected by the serenity, compassion and

---

* These experiments were carried out with still photos taken from video clips of actors imagining opening a door and seeing a mugger. Doubtless these effects would be of a much greater magnitude with a real threat or even just acting but showing subjects moving pictures.

profound quiet of people like Nelson Mandela, Thich Nhat Hanh, the Dalai Lama or a loving mother peacefully nursing her infant.

Gelder's research shows the power of fearful postures in activating specific areas of an observer's brain—areas that happy and neutral postures leave inactive.* In addition, these brain regions, stimulated by the recognition of frightened body stances, are further differentiated from regions involved in the reading of fearful faces. Postural recognition centers include multiple brain regions, some that process emotions and others that primarily *prepare us for action.* According to Gelder, "You could almost say that when you see a fearful body you react with your whole body." This observation supports the basic Darwinian tenet that the human ability to rapidly read bodies and to respond both unequivocally and instantaneously is highly advantageous. Reading others' bodies predisposes us to actions that increase our chances of survival. In order to be effective and immediate, such *postural resonance* bypasses the conscious mind. Rational deliberation could compromise survival by confusing and slowing us down. Survival reactions under threatening circumstances generally need to be swift and sure, not pondered. According to researchers Rizzolatti and Sinigaglia, "our perceptions of *the motor acts and emotive reactions* [italics mine] of others appear to be united by a mirror mechanism that permits our brain to immediately understand what we are seeing, feeling, or imagining others to be doing, as it triggers the same neural structures ... that are responsible for our own actions and emotions."[16]

Had our neocortical (thinking) brain preempted our instinctual lower (action-based) circuitry, you might have an inner dialogue something like this: "That guy's jaw and shoulders look tight and angry as he comes near. His eyes are shifty ... but his shirt—well, it's certainly a pleasant color and looks like the one I almost bought at Macy's." While your

---

*When neutral postures are shown (such as pouring a glass of water), only the parts of the brain associated with vision (area 17 in the neocortex) are activated. So far as I know, the researchers have not enlisted extraordinarily peaceful beings, such as the Dalai Lama, for the positive postures.

survival "bottom-up" processing center is alerting your body (*Avoid this guy, period—no discussion!*), your "top-down" processing is meandering through a much slower language-based analysis.

Just like the gazelles, humans are acutely attuned to danger and prepared to act decisively to meet it. The posture, gestures and facial expressions of people tell the untold tale of what did and did not happen when threatened and overwhelmed. Habitual postures tell us what paths need to be retraced and resolved. In order to facilitate bottom-up processing, therapists need to have a precise feel for the instinctual imperative that was thwarted in their client at a moment of overwhelming fright. The traumatized body-mind was, in other words, poised in readiness but failed to fully orchestrate its meaningful course of action. As in my accident (Chapter 1) we have to help clients discover just where in her body she readied for action, and which action had been blocked in its execution.

Other research confirms the pertinence of instantaneous body reading. A recent study carried out by the U.S. Army suggests that the speed with which the brain reads emotions in the body language of others and interprets sensations in one's own body is central to avoiding imminent threats like hidden booby traps, who might be carrying a hidden bomb or who had recently buried one.[17] In this same article, the neurologist Antonio Damasio adds that "emotions are practical action programs that work to solve a problem, often before we're conscious of it. These processes are at work continually, in pilots, leaders of expeditions, parents, in all of us."

Therapeutic approaches that neglect the body, focusing mainly on thoughts (top-down processing), will consequently be limited. I propose instead that, in the initial stages of restorative work, bottom-up processing needs to be standard operating procedure. In other words, addressing a client's "bodyspeak" first and then, *gradually*, enlisting his or her emotion, perception and cognition is not merely valuable, it's essential. The "talking cure" for trauma survivors should give way to the unspoken voice of the silent, but strikingly powerful, bodily expressions as they surface to "sound off" on behalf of the wisdom of the deeper self.

Challenges of Therapy

Therapists working with traumatized individuals frequently "pick up" and mirror the postures of their clients and hence their emotions of fear, terror, anger, rage and helplessness. The way we respond to these signifiers will be pivotal in helping traumatized individuals deal with those difficult sensations and emotions. If we recoil because we cannot contain and accept them, then we abandon our clients ... if we are overwhelmed, then we are both lost. If we embody some small portion of a Dalai Lama–like equanimity and "composure," we are able to share and help contain our client's terrors in a "blanket of compassion."

We should not underestimate how compelling instinctual fear reactions are and how readily they can become maladaptive. In the event of a fire, for example, people will tend to adopt the uptight, frightened body posture of the person next to them. They are then readied to spring into action and flee the movie theater. However, such behavior can also set the ground for contagious panic. As each person mirrors the fear posture of those nearby, he or she simultaneously senses fear and transmits that fear-posture to others in the group. Transmittance of fear through postural resonance creates an escalating situation, a positive feedback loop (with negative consequences). Panic contagion can spread to the whole group almost instantly. FDR presciently warned us about avoiding this kind of contagion. If a moment presents itself, we may beneficially ask ourselves, is there really something threatening? In the example of the theater fire you could, before running, assess the situation independently. If you smell smoke then there should be no hesitation; on the other hand, if you see a group of teenagers laughing, then your rational brain might tell you to check things out some more before running full steam toward the exit. Rational assessment can be an efficient tempering of the extreme instinctual command when the person next to us (whom we are mirroring) is mistaken or overreacting. However, often in therapy the attempt to place reason over instinct is a serious failure, a likely disaster.

In the therapy situation, the therapist must strike a balance between mirroring a client's distress enough for them to learn about the client's sensations, but not so much as to increase the client's level of fear as in contagion panic. This can only happen if the therapist has learned the ins and outs of his or her own sensations and emotions and is relatively comfortable with them. Only then can we really help clients contain their troubling sensations and emotions so that they can learn that, no matter how horrible they feel, it will not go on forever.

Fear Paralysis

On the Serengeti, one herd member's startled reaction cues the other gazelles to anticipate the worst and vigilantly scan the environment in an attempt to locate the potential source of threat. If, however, they fail to detect the stalking predator, they readily let down their guard and innocently return to grazing.* Moments later, another gazelle arrests to the sound of a twig snapping and, once again, the herd is alerted, the animals' "collective nervous system" activated, tuning and readying them for all-out action. They stiffen in unison as their muscles tense in preparation for maximal exertion in flight.

Seizing the moment, a stalking cheetah leaps from its cover of dense shrubbery. The herd springs together as one organism, darting away from the advancing predator. One young gazelle falters for a split second, then recovers its footing. In a blur, the cheetah lunges toward its intended victim. The chase is on at a blazing sixty-five miles an hour! At the moment of contact (or just before, as it senses that the end is near), the young gazelle collapses to the ground. The stone-still animal has entered an altered state of consciousness shared by all mammals when death appears imminent. It is not "pretending" to be dead and may, in fact, be uninjured.[18] It is in a state of *fear paralysis.*

---

* This transition is orchestrated by the autonomic nervous system between states of sympathetic arousal and parasympathetic rebound and relaxation. This fluid shifting maintains an overall quality of "relaxed alertness."

Paralysis, an Ancestral Root

We die so that we can live.

—A father opossum to his
children in the animated
film *Over the Hedge*

One's first line of defense against a predator, an attacker or other source of danger is generally an *active defense*. You duck, dodge and retract; you twist and raise your arms to protect against a mortal blow. And most well known, you flee from potential predators or fight them when you perceive that you are stronger than your adversary, or if you have become trapped by them. In addition to the well-known fight and flight reactions, there is a third, lesser-known reaction to threat: immobilization. Ethologists call this "default" state of paralysis *tonic immobility* (TI). It's one of the three primary instinctual responses available to reptiles and mammals when faced with threat from predation. It occurs when active responses are not likely to be effective in escaping or removing the source of threat (as by fighting). The familiarity of the other two, fight or flight, is due largely to the overarching and extended influence of Walter B. Cannon's eminent work carried out in the 1920s on the sympathetic–adrenal nervous system.[19] Far less appreciated, though, are the profound implications of the human immobility response in the formation and treatment of trauma.[20] Taking into account the more than seventy-five years of ethological and physiological research since Cannon's discovery, fight-or-flight could be updated with the acronym "the A, and four Fs": *Arrest (increased vigilance, scanning), Flight (try first to escape), Fight (if the animal or person is prevented from escaping), Freeze (fright—scared stiff) and Fold (collapse into helplessness). In two sentences: Trauma occurs when we are intensely frightened and are either physically restrained or perceive that we are trapped. We freeze in paralysis and/or collapse in overwhelming helplessness.* Note: Although some recent authors tend to call the initial arrest response "freezing," I will avoid possible confusion by using the term "freezing" only to describe behaviors involving tonic immobility.*

---

* This earlier usage is, for example, consistent with that of such ethologists as A. Eric Salzen and Desmond Morris. See Desmond Morris, *Primate Ethology*,

In freezing, your muscles stiffen against a mortal blow, and you feel "scared stiff." On the other hand, when you experience death as being unequivocally imminent (as when bared fangs are ready to annihilate you), your muscles collapse as though they have lost all their energy. In this "default" reaction (when it has become chronic, as it does in trauma), you feel that you are in a state of helpless resignation and lack the energy to fuel your life and move forward. This collapse, defeat and loss of the will to live are at the very core of deep trauma.

Being "scared stiff" or "frozen in fear"—or, alternatively, collapsing and going numb—accurately describes the *physical, visceral, bodily* experience of intense fear and trauma. Since the body enacts all of these survival options, it is the body's narration that therapists must address in order to understand these reactions and to mobilize them in transforming trauma.

It may help therapists (and their clients) to know that immobility appears to serve at least four important survival functions in mammals. First, it is a last-ditch survival strategy, colloquially known as "playing opossum." Rather than pretense, though, it is a deadly serious innate biological tactic. With a slow, small animal like the opossum, flight or fight is unlikely to be successful. By passively resisting, in the grand tradition of Gandhi, the animal's inertness tends to inhibit the predator's aggression and reduce its urge to kill and to eat. In addition, a motionless animal is frequently abandoned (especially when it also emits a putrid odor like rotting meat) and not eaten by such predators as the coyote—unless, of course, this animal is very hungry.* With such "death feigning," the opossum may live to escape, plodding along into another day. Similarly, the cheetah may drag its motionless prey to a safe place, removed from potential competitors, and return to her lair to fetch her cubs (so as to share the kill with them). While she is gone, the gazelle may awaken from its paralysis and, in an unguarded moment, make a

---

(London: Weidenfield and Nicholson, 1969); A. Eric Salzen (1991), "On the Nature of Emotion," *Journal of Comparative Psychology*, 5, 47–110; and Salzen (1967), "Social Attachment and a Sense of Security," *Social Sciences Information 12*, 555–627.

* Abandoning the prey may serve to protect the predator from being poisoned by eating infected carrion.

hasty escape. Second, immobility affords a certain degree of invisibility: an inert body is much less likely to be seen by a predator. Third, immobility may promote group survival: when hunted by a predator pack, the collapse of one individual may distract the pack long enough for the rest of the herd to escape.

Last, but by no means least, a fourth biological function of immobility is that it triggers a profoundly altered state of numbing. In this state, extreme pain and terror are dulled: so if the animal does survive an attack it will be, even though injured, less encumbered by debilitating pain and thus possibly able to escape if the opportunity arises. This "humane" analgesic effect is mediated by the flooding of endorphins, the body's own profound morphine pain-relief system.[21] For the gazelle, this means that it will not have to suffer the full agony of being torn apart by the cheetah's sharp teeth and claws. The same is most likely true for a rape or accident victim.[22] In this state of analgesia, the victim may witness the event as though from outside his or her body, as if it were happening to someone else (as I observed in my accident). Such distancing, called *dissociation*, helps to make the unbearable bearable.

The African explorer David Livingstone graphically recorded such an experience in his encounter with a lion on the plains of Africa:

> I heard a shout. Startled, in looking half round, I saw the lion just in the act of springing upon me. I was upon a little height; he caught my shoulder as he sprang, and we both came to the ground below together. Growling horribly close to my ear, he shook me as a terrier does a rat. The shock produced a stupor similar to that which seems to be felt by a mouse after the first shake of the cat. *It caused a sort of dreaminess in which there was no sense of pain nor feeling of terror, though quite conscious of all that was happening. It was like what patients partially under the influence of chloroform describe, who see all the operation, but feel not the knife. This singular condition was not the result of any mental process. The shake annihilated fear, and allowed no sense of horror in looking round at the beast.* This

peculiar state is probably produced in all animals killed by the carnivore; and if so, is a merciful provision by our benevolent creator for lessening the pain of death. [italics mine][23]

While Livingstone attributes this gift to his "benevolent creator," one need not invoke "intelligent design" to appreciate the biologically adaptive function of diminishing the sharp edges of serious pain, terror and panic. If one is able to stay broadly focused and perceive things in slow motion, one is more likely to be able to take advantage of a potential escape opportunity or think of an ingenious strategy to evade the predator. For example, a friend of mine told me about a time when he was withdrawing money from an ATM for an international trip. As he turned from the machine, a group of thugs grabbed him, holding a knife to his throat. As in a dream, he serenely told them that it was their lucky day, and that he had just withdrawn a lot of money for a trip he was taking the next day. The astonished muggers calmly took the money and slipped away into the darkness. I am sure that some degree of dissociation helped him to survive his ordeal without being so terrified as to be unable to strategically deal with this dreadful situation.

Indeed, the adaptive and benevolent value of dissociation is illustrated by another riveting tale, this time by the adventurer Redside, from the jungles of the Indian subcontinent:

[He had] stumbled when crossing a swift stream, dropping his cartridge belt into the water ... now out of ammunition, he noticed a large tigress stalking him. Turning pale and sweating with fright, he began retreating ... But it was already too late. The tigress charged, seized him by the shoulder and dragged him a quarter of a mile to where her three cubs were playing. As he recalled it afterward, Redside was amazed that his fear vanished as soon as the tigress caught him and he hardly noticed any pain while being dragged and intermittently mauled while the tigress played "cat and mouse" with him for perhaps an hour. He

vividly remembered the sunshine and the trees and the
look in the tigress's eyes as well as the intense "mental
effort" and suspense whenever he managed to crawl away,
only to be caught and dragged back each time while the
cubs looked on and playfully tried to copy mama. He said
that, even though he fully realized his extreme danger, his
mind somehow remained "comparatively calm" and "without dread." He even told his rescuers, who shot the tigress
just in time, that he regarded his ordeal as less fearful than
"half an hour in a dentist's chair."[24]

Although Livingstone and Redside appeared to be surprisingly
unscathed by their unpleasant encounters with predatory cats, Livingstone nonetheless developed an inflammatory reaction in that shoulder that broke out for the rest of his life on the anniversary date of the
attack. Unfortunately, for many traumatized individuals, such dissociative reactions or "body memories" are not minor and transitory, but
lead to a wide variety of enduring, so-called psychosomatic (physical)
symptoms (which might aptly be called "somatic dissociation"[25]) as well
as to an inability to focus, orient and function in present time—in the
here and now. While traumatized humans don't actually remain physically paralyzed, they do get lost in a kind of anxious fog, a chronic partial shutdown, dissociation, lingering depression, and numbness. Many
are able to earn a living and/or raise a family in a kind of "functional
freeze" that severely limits their enjoyment of life. They carry their
burden with diminished energy in an uphill struggle to survive, despite
their symptoms. In addition, we human beings, who cleave to symbols
and images, may continue to see (in the mind's eye) ourselves at death's
door long after the real danger has passed. A vision of the mugger or
rapist holding a knife at your throat can endlessly recycle itself, as though
it is still happening.

How Biology Becomes Pathology

Although the states of immobilization and dissociation (like those just
described by Livingstone and Redside) are dramatic, they do not

necessarily lead to trauma. Even though he didn't develop any limiting fears, Livingston did exhibit a localized anniversary reaction on his affected shoulder. In the case of my accident, I notice that I am now a bit more cautious when crossing streets—especially in Brazil, where I often teach, and where moving vehicles can be a considerable challenge to pedestrians. Otherwise, I don't exhibit any type of fear or anxiety reaction in respect to traffic. Perhaps my friend who was robbed is also a little more careful about going to an ATM at night. But neither my friend nor Livingstone nor Redside nor I was traumatized; though we undoubtedly experienced arrest, terror, immobilization and dissociation. Speaking for myself, I feel (and friends have confirmed) that I was actually made stronger and more resilient by successfully navigating my accident and its sequel. My friends noticed that I seemed more grounded, focused and playful.

This brings me to the central question: what determines whether acute exposure to a (potentially) traumatizing event will have a long-term debilitating effect as in posttraumatic stress disorder? And how does understanding the dynamics of the immobility response postulate clinical solutions to this crucial question?

Let me reiterate. Generally, an animal *in the wild*, if not killed, recovers from its immobility and lives to see another day. It is wiser but none the worse for wear. For example, a deer learns to avoid a certain rock outcropping where it was ambushed by a mountain lion. While my observational hypothesis is based on field observations and is not empirically proven, my interviews with wildlife managers throughout the world have supported it. In addition, it is difficult to imagine how individual wild animals (or their entire species, for that matter) would have ever survived if they routinely developed the sorts of debilitating symptoms that many humans do.* This natural "immunity" is clearly not the case for us modern humans ... but why and what can we do about it?

---

* The same is clearly *not* true of animals placed in laboratory conditions. As Pavlov first observed, stressed experimental animals are readily traumatized.

Long-Lasting Immobility

As I was completing my doctoral dissertation at Berkeley in 1977, I continued with my daily visits to the musty stacks of the graduate library, where I stumbled upon the critical key in my understanding of trauma. This article by Gordon Gallup and Jack D. Maser informed the central question of how the normally time-limited immobility response becomes long-lasting and eventually unending.[26] For their work, I would like to make a personal nomination for them to retroactively receive the 1973 Nobel Prize in Physiology or Medicine—along with the three ethologists previously mentioned.

In a carefully thought-out and well-controlled experiment, the authors demonstrated that if an animal is both frightened and restrained, the period during which it remains immobilized (after the restraint is removed) is dramatically increased. There is a nearly perfect linear correlation between the level of fear an animal experiences when it is restrained, and the duration of immobility.[27] When an animal is not subjected to fear before being restrained, immobility generally lasts from *seconds* to about a minute. This spontaneous capacity is called "self-paced termination."[28] In dramatic contrast, when both repeatedly frightened and repeatedly restrained, the experimental animal may remain immobilized for as long as seventeen hours!

It is my clinical experience and understanding that such a robust *potentiation* has profound clinical implications for the understanding and treatment of human trauma. I shall discuss how the "potentiation," or enhancement, of immobility by fear can lead to a self-perpetuating feedback loop causing an essentially permanent quasi-paralysis in the traumatized individual. This condition, I believe, underpins several of trauma's most debilitating symptoms, especially numbing, shutdown, dissociation, feelings of entrapment and helplessness.

A few years ago, in Brazil, I had the opportunity to observe the interaction between fear and immobility within a laboratory setting and thereby gained direct verification of the seminal work of Gallup and Maser on tonic immobility. Although there are very few researchers in this important field, I found one actively involved in experimental animal research on tonic immobility at the laboratory of Leda Menescal de Oliveira at the Federal University, School of Medicine in Ribeirao Preto, Brazil. Her work has focused on the brain pathways activated in tonic immobility.[29]

Leda and her group were exceedingly generous in sharing their time and expertise. During my visit I was able to directly observe and participate in the experimental methodology of earlier researchers whose written work had inspired me in the 1970s. These experiments carried out in a dimly lit room involved gently picking up a guinea pig, holding it securely, turning it upside down, and then placing it on its back in a V-shaped wooden trough. When this is done *without a struggle*, the experimental animal lies motionless for seconds to a minute or two, then flips over and calmly walks off in self-paced termination from immobility. The laboratory guinea pigs may have some inherent fear of humans (a possible confounding variable). Yet these animals still appear to come out of their immobility relatively quickly, and aftereffects were not apparent, thus presumably nonexistent or very mild.

A vivid illustration of self-paced termination comes from the arts. In the play *Picasso at the Lapin Agile,** the young Pablo takes the jacket from the pretty young woman he has brought up to his Paris loft. Coolly executing a seductive ruse, he reaches outside the window to where a white dove is perched on the ledge. Slowly, but without hesitation, he firmly takes the bird in his hands. As he turns it over, the bird ceases all movement. He then drops it to the street, three stories below. The young woman gasps, reflexively bringing her hand to her mouth. At the last moment, the dove rights itself and flies off, unharmed, into the Montmartre night. Picasso then turns to his voluptuous human prey, drawing her immobile body into a lecherous embrace.

This is an instructive glimpse of how animals negotiate immobility and how the consensual sexual act and orgasmic release involve some immobility in the absence of fear. Immobility, in the absence of fear, is

---

* Embellished from Steve Martin's play *Picasso at the Lapin Agile* (New Village Arts Theater, Carlsbad, California, January 2010).

benign and even pleasurable, as in the example of a mother cat carrying its limp kitten securely in its mouth.

Returning to the laboratory: Self-paced termination clearly *does not occur when an animal is purposefully frightened before being captured* (or when it comes out of immobility) and/or is repeatedly placed on its back. In the latter case, the guinea pig (or other animal) remains paralyzed for far longer than a few minutes. When this fear-induced process is repeated numerous times, the animal remains immobile for a significantly longer period—so much so that we went out for lunch and returned to find it still inert on its back.

Applications to Trauma Therapy

Only a handful of behavioral scientists have been seriously interested in tonic immobility as the biological foundation of trauma. Some of these recent authors have suggested that immobility is *intrinsically* traumatic.[30] It is my experience that this view is misleading. It limits our understanding of trauma and restricts the possibility of effective therapeutic intervention. My clinical work with thousands of clients has confirmed that immobility can be encountered *with or without fear.* Indeed, I believe that it is only when the immobility becomes inextricably and simultaneously coupled with intense fear and other strong negative emotions that we get the entrenched trauma feedback loop in the form of persistent posttraumatic stress disorder. My experience, beginning with Nancy (in Chapter 2) and then working with so many more traumatized clients, has taught me that the very key to resolving trauma is being able to *uncouple and separate the fear from the immobility.* However, before returning to animals, I shall consider the studies of two observant individuals: the neurologist K. L. Kahlbaum and the fictional detective Sherlock Holmes.

As one of the earliest pioneers to scientifically study tonic immobility in humans (which he called *catatonia*), Kahlbaum had it right when, in 1874, he wrote, "In most cases catatonia is *preceded* by grief and anxiety, and in general by depressive moods and affects aimed against the patient by himself."[31] He is saying, I believe, that *both immobility and a significant exposure to fear or grief need to occur* for (transient states of) tonic immobility to be converted to a paralysis/self-induced depressive feedback loop—that is, to a state of chronic catatonia, or (arguably) posttraumatic stress disorder.

Sherlock Holmes, the very epitome of a careful and precise observer, seems to confirm Kahlbaum's perception in the story of Mr. Hall Pycroft: Holmes says to Watson, "I had never looked upon a face that had such marks of grief . . . and of something beyond grief . . . of a horror, such as comes to few men in a lifetime. His brow glistened with perspiration. His cheeks were of the dull dead white of a fish's belly and his eyes were wild and staring . . . He looked at his clerk as though he failed to recognize him."[32] Such a combination of wild agitation, deathly white complexion and frantic dissociation (staring wide-eyed as though without recognition) accurately describes acute human fright paralysis. While traumatized individuals may not exhibit all of these characteristics all of the time, they do form the undercurrent of traumatic shock as PTSD.

The few psychologists who write about tonic immobility (TI) as a model for trauma seem to agree that both fear and restraint (or, at least, the perception that one cannot escape) are required to induce TI. Here I am in full agreement. However, in a recent excellent review article, Marx and colleagues[33] add, "Everything we know about the animal and human literature to date suggests that the TI response may itself be traumatic."* It is here that I respectfully differ: my clinical experience forces me to part ways from that speculation.

After more than four decades of observing my traumatized clients à la Holmesian discernment, and guiding them out of frozen states of terror and horror, I have found that the dynamic elements of fear, tonic immobility and trauma paint a far more complex and nuanced portrait. I am convinced that the state of immobility is not in and of itself traumatic. When, for example, immobility is induced in non-traumatized subjects through "hypnotic catalepsy," they frequently experience that

---

* Although domestic animals appear to not reliably enter TI, indicating that at least some degree of fear—or at least unfamiliarity—may be necessary to induce TI. However, if traumatized or highly anxious subjects are induced into hypnotic catalepsy (to the dismay of the unsuspecting clinician), they may have abrupt panic attacks or even prolonged catatonia-like states.

immobility as neutral, interesting or even pleasurable. Mammal mothers routinely pick up their young to move them about, and those babies, when in the clutches of a loving mother's jaws, stop squirming and go limp. Also, during sexual congress, and particularly at orgasm, the female of many mammal species becomes immobile at this pinnacle of pleasure leading (arguably) to an increased likelihood of fertilization. Contrast this to trauma, where intense fear (and other strong negative affects), when coupled with the immobility response, becomes entrapping and therefore traumatic. *This difference suggests a clear rationale for a trauma therapy model that separates fear and other strong negative affects from the (normally time-limited) biological immobility response. Separating the two components breaks the feedback loop that rekindles the trauma response.* This, I am convinced, is the philosopher's stone of informed trauma therapy.

Marx and colleagues do seem to amend their position in a direction more compatible with mine when they suggest that "for clinical purposes, it may matter less if TI among humans is an 'all or none' phenomenon, as the *intensity* of the TI response among humans may be an important factor in the onset and maintenance of posttraumatic psychopathology."[34] Questions like this exemplify important areas for interdisciplinary discussion. Indeed, one of the impediments to the progress of truly effective trauma therapy has been that clinicians, experimentalists and theoreticians have not worked in ongoing partnerships to address such pivotal questions.

To summarize: It is my observation that a precondition for the development of posttraumatic stress disorder is that a person is both frightened and perceives that he or she is trapped. *The interaction of intense fear and immobility is fundamental in the formation of trauma, in its maintenance and in its deconstruction, resolution and transformation.* I shall elaborate on the therapeutic implications of this relationship in Chapters 5 through 9.

The Shame, Blame, Immobility Spiral

It should be no surprise, given the nature of fear-induced immobility, that a majority of rape victims predictably describe feeling paralyzed (sometimes also suffocated) and unable to move. Being held down and terrorized by someone much larger, stronger and heavier is virtually guaranteed to induce long-lasting immobility and, thus, trauma. Rape not only forces one to keep still, it induces an inner immobility because of the terror (fear-potentiated immobility). In one study, 88% of the victims of childhood sexual assault and 75% of the victims of adult sexual assault reported moderate to high levels of paralysis during the assault.[35] In addition, because of the high levels of dissociation, it is likely that many victims do not remember feeling paralyzed or deny the paralysis because they feel so guilty for not having "fought back."

Similarly, soldiers under fire can rarely flee or even physically fight. They must frequently stay pinned close to the ground (resisting both active fight and flight urges), while "calmly" trying to steady, aim and fire their guns. I interviewed a soldier who was threatened with a court martial for "cowardice under fire." He was an embedded translator with a special-forces assault team in Iraq—although the only foreign languages he knew were Hungarian and Serbo-Croatian; he did not know Farsi or any Arabic language! He had not been trained for combat duty, and when his crack Marine unit was ambushed, he did not fire back. While interviewing this broken, devastated, humiliated and terrified soldier, I came to see that his "refusal" to fire back was, in fact, involuntary paralysis—a normal reaction to the highly abnormal situation of seeing the blood, death and dismemberment of his comrades. Unlike the Marines, he had had no training to override his fear.* His instinctual response to overwhelming threat precluded action.[36]

This story speaks to modern cultures that tend to judge immobilization and dissociation in the face of overwhelming threat as a weakness tantamount to cowardice. Beneath this castigating judgment lies a pervasive fear of feeling trapped and helpless. This fear of fear and helplessness, and of feeling trapped, can come to dominate a person's

---

* Although, in threatening situations, special-service warriors experience about the same rush of the stress hormone cortisol as any other soldier does, the formers' levels typically drop off much faster than do those of less well-trained troops.

life in the form of persistent and debilitating shame. Together, shame and trauma form a particularly virulent and interlocked combination.

Self-blame and self-hatred are common among molestation and rape survivors, who judge themselves harshly for not "putting up a fight," even where fight was not a viable survival option. However, both the experience of paralysis and the critical self-judgment about "weakness" and helplessness are common components of trauma. In addition, the younger, the more developmentally immature or insecurely attached the victim is, the more likely it is that he or she will respond to stress, threat and danger with paralysis rather than active struggle. People who lack solid early attachment bonding to a primary caregiver, and therefore lack a foundation of safety, are much more vulnerable to being victimized and traumatized and are more likely to develop the entrenched symptoms of shame, dissociation and depression.[37] In addition, since the psychophysiological patterns of trauma and shame are similar, there is an *intrinsic* association of shame and trauma. This includes the collapse of shoulders, slowing of heart rate, aversion of eyes, nausea, etc.[38]

Shame also feeds into the common misperception of traumatized individuals that they are, somehow, the cause of (or, at least, deserving of) their own misfortune. Another (powerfully corrosive) factor comes into play in the formation of shame: while it appears to be an almost structural component of trauma, all too frequently trauma is inflicted by the people who are supposed to protect and love the child. Children who are molested by family and friends, of course, bear this additional confused and chaotic burden. Shame becomes deeply embedded as a pervasive sense of "badness" permeating every part of their lives. Similar erosion of a core sense of dignity is also found in adults who have been tortured, on whom pain, disorientation, terror and other violations have been deliberately inflicted.[39] While the principles of uncoupling fear from immobility discussed in this chapter apply to these cases, the therapeutic process is generally much more complex. It requires a broader skill for negotiating the therapeutic relationship so that the therapist does not get tangled up in taking on the (projected) role of the perpetrator(s) or rescuer.

As They Go In, So They Come Out: The Rage Connection

When a pigeon that is blithely pecking at some grain is quietly approached from behind, gently picked up, and then turned upside down, it becomes immobilized. The pigeon will, like the guinea pigs I saw in Brazil, or Picasso's dove in the play, remain in that position, with its feet stuck straight up in the air. In a minute or two, it will come out of this trancelike state, right itself, and hop or fly away. The episode is resolved.

However, if the pecking pigeon is first frightened by the approaching person, it will try to fly away. When it is caught after a frantic pursuit, and then forcibly held upside down, it will again succumb to immobility. This time, however, the terrified animal will not only remain frozen much longer, but when it comes out of its trance, it will likely be in a state of "frantic agitation." It may thrash about wildly, pecking, biting or clawing randomly, or it may scurry away in a frenzy of undirected movement.[40] When all else fails, this last-ditch (and disorganized) form of defense may yet save its life.

Similarly, when a well-fed household cat catches a mouse, the latter, restrained by the cat's paws, stops moving and becomes limp. Without resistance from the mouse, the cat becomes bored and will sometimes gently bat the inert animal, seemingly trying to revive it and restart the game anew (not unlike Jimmy Stewart slapping his swooning heroine to bring her out of her faint). With each reawakening, chasing and reactivated terror, the mouse goes deeper and longer into immobility. When it does eventually revive, it frequently darts away so quickly (and unpredictably) that it may even startle the cat. This sudden, non-directed burst of energy could just as easily cause it to run at the cat, as well as away from it. I have even seen a mouse ferociously attack the nose of an astounded cat. Such is the nature of exit from immobility, where induction has been repetitive and accompanied by fear and rage. Humans, in addition, *reterrorize themselves out of their (misplaced) fear of their own intense sensations and emotions*. This is similar to what may happen when catatonic psychiatric patients come out of their immobility. They are often extremely agitated and may attack the staff. I once had the opportunity to work with a patient who had been in a catatonic state for two or three years. After carefully sitting by his side (getting closer, over the period of several days), I spoke to him softly about the shaking and trembling that I observed with people and animals when they come out of shock. I had also talked with the chief psychiatrist, and he agreed that they would not give him an injection of thorazine (or straitjacket him) if he came to in an agitated state, unless he was clearly dangerous to himself or others. Two weeks later I got a call from the psychiatrist. The man had begun to shake and tremble, started to cry and was released to a transitional living situation six months later.

To review, fear both greatly enhances and extends immobility and *also makes the process of exiting immobility fearful and potentially violent.* An individual who is highly terrified upon entering the immobility state is likely to move out of it in a similar manner. "As they go in, so they come out" was an expression that Army M.A.S.H. medics used when describing the reactions of their war-wounded patients. If a soldier goes into surgery terrified, and needing to be held down, he or she will likely come out of anesthesia in a state of frantic and possibly violent disorientation.

The same consequences are sadly true when children are frightened and abruptly separated from their parents before surgery.[41] If they go into the surgery in an agitated state, are held down and then surrounded by gowned and "masked monsters," they come out of the anesthesia frightened and drastically disoriented. David Levy, in 1945, studied hospitalized children, many of them being treated for injuries requiring immobilization, such as splints, casts and braces. He found that these unfortunate children developed shell-shock symptoms similar to those of the soldiers returning from the war fronts in Europe and North Africa.[42] Some sixty-five years later, a troubled father recounts "an all-too ordinary" story about his son Robbie's "minor" knee surgery, a virtual guarantee for trauma.

> The doctor tells me that everything is okay. The knee is
> fine, but everything is not okay for the boy waking up in

a drug-induced nightmare, thrashing around on his hospital bed—a sweet boy who never hurt anybody, staring
out from his anesthetic haze with the eyes of a wild animal, striking the nurse, screaming "Am I alive?" and forcing me to grab his arms ... staring right into my eyes and
not knowing who I am.[42]

The immobilization effects Levy observed in children also occur in
adult patients. In a recent medical study, more than 52% of orthopedic patients being treated for broken bones were shown to develop full-
blown posttraumatic stress disorder, with a majority not recovering and
worsening over time.[44]

This result should come as no real surprise when one recognizes
that many orthopedic procedures follow frightening accidents, stressful ambulance rides endured while one is strapped down and terrifying
and depersonalizing emergency room visits. Further, many of these
patients have also undergone immediate surgeries, and often in an agitated state. This chain of events often precedes immobilization and is
followed by painful rehabilitation regimens. In a recent study of children undergoing even "minor" orthopedic procedures, to quote the
authors, "High levels of posttraumatic stress disorder symptoms (in
over 33% of all children studied) are common in the recovery period
after pediatric orthopedic trauma, even among patients with relatively
minor injury. Children admitted to the hospital after injury are at high
risk for such symptoms."[45]

Although hospitals have become more humane (particularly for children—though from the above study not nearly enough), there is still
inadequate attention to preventing undue fear in people who must
undergo painful procedures or general anesthesia. Indeed, some of those
ill-fated individuals partially "awaken" during anesthesia and many
develop some of the most horrific and complex PTSD symptoms.[46] In
the words of one survivor (a surgical nurse herself), "I feel a cosmic hol-
lowness, as if my soul has left my body and can't return ... horrifying
nightmares are my companion ... often shocking me wide awake. When
my eyes pop open, there is still no respite because the walls and ceiling

turn blood red."[47] This riveting description illustrates the horror of enduring the combination of terror, extreme pain, and being unable to move or to communicate one's situation.

Biologically, the orthopedic patients, soldiers, rape victims and hospitalized children are reacting like wild animals fighting for their life after being frightened and captured. Their impulse to attack in an "aggravated rage" or to flee in frantic desperation is not only biologically appropriate; in fact, it is a frequent biological outcome. As a captured and terrified animal comes out of immobility, its survival may depend on its violent aggression toward the still-present predator. In humans, such violence, however, has produced tragic consequences to the individual and society. I had the opportunity to speak with the mother of Ted Kaczynski (the "Unabomber," whose vendetta was waged against the impersonality of technology) and with the father of Jeffrey Dahmer (a serial killer who dismembered his victims). They both told me horrific stories of how their young children were "broken" by terrifying hospital experiences. Both parents described how, after terrifying hospitalizations, each of these children retreated into his own world. While such experiences of rage leading to perverted violence are (fortunately) rare, the terror and anger evoked by medical procedures is (unfortunately) not.

Rage Turned Against the Self

With humans, the impulse toward violent aggression may become terrifying in itself and is then turned against the self, as Kahlbaum so presciently observed in his seminal work on catatonia.[48] This turning inward (or "retroflection") results in further paralysis, suppression, passivity and resignation. The flipping between shutdown and outbursts of "impotent" and misdirected rage becomes the individual's stereotypic reaction to later challenges that require much more nuanced and subtly differentiated feeling-based responses.

In my accident (see Chapter 1), as I came out of shock, I experienced "a rolling wave of fiery rage" as my body continued its shaking and trembling; then I felt a "burning red fury" erupting "from deep within my belly." I really wanted to kill the girl who'd hit me, and I thought, *How could that stupid kid hit me in a crosswalk? Wasn't she paying any attention? Damn her!* I wanted to kill her, and it felt like I could have. Because rage is about wanting to kill, it is not hard to understand how frightening this urge can be; and how the rage could turn to fear as a way of preventing such murderous impulses.

By allowing my body to do what *it* needed to do—by not stopping the shaking while tracking my inner body sensations—I was able to allow and contain the extreme survival emotions of rage and terror *without becoming overwhelmed.* Containment, it must be understood, is NOT suppression; it is rather building a larger, more resilient vessel to hold these difficult affects. And mercifully, this way, I came through the accident's aftermath unscathed by trauma and more resilient to future challenge.

As people revisit, move through and then move out of immobility in therapy, they frequently experience some rage. These primal sensations of fury (when contained) represent movements back into life. However, rage and other intense body sensations can be frightening if they occur abruptly. In effective therapy, the therapist supports and carefully guides the client through this powerful process. Guidance should be done slowly, by using a graduated approach so that the client is not overwhelmed.

Ultimately, rage is (biologically) about the urge to kill.[49] When some women who have been raped begin to come out of shock (frequently months or even years later) they may have the impulse to kill their assailants. Occasionally, they have had the opportunity to carry out this impulse in action. Some of these women have been tried and sentenced for murder because the time elapsed was viewed as evidence of premeditation. Injustices have most certainly occurred due to general ignorance of the biological drama those women were playing out. A number of these women may have been acting upon the profound (and delayed) self-protective responses of rage and counterattack that they experienced as they came out of agitated immobility; and thus their reprisal (though much delayed) may have been biologically motivated, and not necessarily premeditated revenge, despite the outward appearance. These killings might have been prevented if effective treatment for the traumatized women had been available at the time.

In contrast, non-traumatized individuals who feel angry are well aware that (as much as they may "feel like murdering" even a spouse or their children) they obviously wouldn't actually try to kill the object of their anger. As traumatized individuals begin to come out of immobility, they frequently experience eruptions of intense anger or rage. But fearing that they may actually hurt others (or themselves), they exert a tremendous effort to deflect and suppress that rage, almost before they feel it.

When one is flooded by rage, the frontal parts of the brain "shut down."[50] Because of this extreme imbalance, the capacity to stand back and observe one's sensations and emotions is lost; rather, one *becomes* those emotions and sensations.* Hence, the rage can become utterly overwhelming, causing panic and the stifling of such primitive impulses, turning them inward and preventing a natural exit from the immobility reaction. Maintaining this suppression requires a tremendous expenditure of energy. One is, essentially, doing to oneself what experimenters have done to animals to reinforce and protract their immobilization. Traumatized individuals repeatedly frighten themselves as they begin to come out of immobility. The "fear-potentiated immobility" is *maintained from within*. The vicious cycle of intense sensation/rage/fear locks a person in the biological trauma response. A traumatized individual is literally imprisoned, repeatedly frightened and restrained—by his or her own persistent physiological reactions and by fear of those reactions and emotions. This vicious cycle of fear and immobility (a.k.a. fear-potentiated immobility) prevents the response from ever *fully* completing and resolving as it does in wild animals.

---

* This is a central dilemma in working with so-called Borderline Personality Disorder.

The Living Dead

Rage/counterattack is one consequence of repetitive fear-induced immobilization; the other is death. Death might occur, for example, when the cat persists in recapturing the mouse, repeating the cycle many times. The cat bats his prey until the mouse finally goes so deeply into immobility that it dies, even though uninjured. While only a few humans actually die from fright, chronically traumatized individuals go through the motions of living without really feeling vital or engaged in life. Such individuals are empty to the core of their being. "I walk around," said a gang-rape survivor, "but it's not me anymore ... I am empty and cold ... I might as well be dead," she told me on our first session.

Chronic immobility gives rise to the core emotional symptoms of trauma: numbness, shutdown, entrapment, helplessness, depression, fear, terror, rage and hopelessness. The person remains fearful, unable to imagine safety from a never-ending (internal) enemy and unable to reengage in life. Survivors of severe and protracted (chronic) trauma describe their lives as those of "the living dead." Murray has poignantly written about this state: "here it is as if the person's primal springs of vitality had dried up, as if he were empty to the core of his being."[51] In the poignant 1965 film *The Pawnbroker*, Rod Steiger plays Sol Nazerman, an emotionally deadened Jewish Holocaust survivor who, despite his prejudice, develops a fatherly affection for a young black teenager who works for him. When, in the final scene, the boy is killed, Sol impales his own hand on the spike of a memo spindle so that he can feel something, anything.

Trauma and Immobility: A Way Out

In review: *Trauma arises when one's human immobility responses do not resolve; that is, when one cannot make the transition back to normal life, and the immobility reaction becomes chronically coupled with fear and other intense negative emotions such as dread, revulsion and helplessness.* After this coupling has been established, *the physical sensations of immobility by themselves evoke fear.* A traumatized individual has become conditioned to be fearful of his or her internal (physical) sensations that now generate the fear that extends and deepens (potentiates) the paralysis. Fear begets paralysis, and fear of the sensations of paralysis begets more fear, promoting yet a deeper paralysis. In this way, a normally time-limited adaptive reaction becomes chronic and maladaptive. The feedback loop closes in on itself. In this downward spiral, the vortex of trauma is born.

Successful trauma therapy helps people resolve trauma symptoms. The feedback loop is broken by *uncoupling fear from immobility* (see Figures 4.1a and 4.1b). Effective therapy breaks, or depotentiates, this trauma-fear feedback loop by helping a person safely learn to "contain" his or her powerful sensations, emotions and impulses without becoming overwhelmed. Thus, the immobility response is enabled to resolve as it is evolved to do.

Uncoupling fear and allowing the normally time-limited immobility reaction to complete is, in principle, a straightforward matter. The therapist helps reduce the duration of immobility by gently diminishing the level of fear. In other words, the therapist's job is to aid a client to gradually uncouple the fear from the paralysis, so as to gradually restore self-paced termination. In this way the (fear-immobility) feedback loop is broken; colloquially, it runs out of gas. As a client learns to experience the physical sensations of the immobility in the *absence* of fear, trauma's grip is loosened, and equilibrium is restored. In the next four chapters, I discuss how therapists can help clients learn how to uncouple the fear from the immobility and restore active defensive responses. When clients achieve this, they often describe the physical sensation of immobility (in the absence of fear) with a mixture of curiosity and profound relief or, often, "as though waking from a nightmare."

There is an important caveat to this simple "prescription." Where trauma has been lengthy and deeply entrenched, other factors come into play: primarily, one's very faculty for change and reengagement in life becomes impaired. This aspect has been poignantly portrayed in Louise Erdrich's compelling novel *The Master Butchers Singing Club.* In the first chapter, the male protagonist, Fidelis, leaves the trenches

Charting Duration of Immobility Amongst Different Scenarios

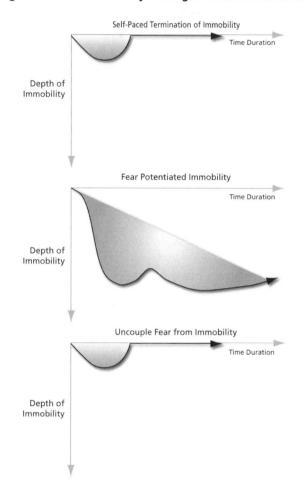

Figure 4.1a This figure illustrates the duration and severity of "freezing" in three situations. The first scenario is similar to an opossum being attacked and playing dead. The opossum freezes, and the predator, losing interest in this inert carrion, walks off in search of livelier prey. Left alone, the opossum "shakes off" this encounter and goes on its way, none the worse. This is called *self-paced termination*. The second scenario illustrates what happens when an animal emerging from immobility is restrained and frightened. It is thrust back into terror, and the immobility is far deeper, lasting for a much longer time. This paralyzing terror is the effect of *fear-potentiated immobility* and leads to PTSD. This is why the phrase "time heals all wounds" simply does not apply to trauma. The third scenario shows what happens in a successful therapy session. The therapist gradually guides the client to briefly touch into the immobility sensations, and then guides her to uncouple the immobility from the fear. In this way she can discharge the underlying hyperarousal and return to equilibrium.

Fear/Immobility Cycle

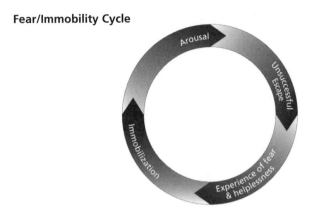

Figure 4.1b This is how we become trapped in the fear/immobility cycle.

of World War I and returns to his mother's cooking and kindness. He sleeps for the first time in his own familiar, comfortable bed, an experience that he has not known for years.

> Now that he was home, he understood, he must still be vigilant. Memories would creep up on him, emotions sabotaging his thinking brain. To come alive after dying to himself was dangerous. There was far too much to feel, so he must seek, he thought, only shallow sensations.

We also learn that, "as a child, Fidelis had breathed lightly and gone motionless … whenever as a child sorrow had come down upon him." As a young soldier, "he'd known from the first that in his talent for stillness lay the key to his survival." The human need to *gradually* return from the land of the walking dead to the land of the living needs to be understood, respected and honored. Too much, too soon, threatens to overwhelm the fragile ego structure and adaptive personality. This is why the rate at which people resolve trauma must be gradual and "titrated."

Instinct and Reason

In the final analysis, I believe that it is the dynamic balance between the most primitive and the most evolved/refined parts of the brain that allows trauma to be resolved and difficult emotions to be integrated and transformed. Effective treatment is a matter of helping individuals keep the "observing" prefrontal cortex online as it *simultaneously* experiences the raw primitive sensations generated in the archaic portions of the brain (the limbic system, hypothalamus and brain stem; see Figure 4.2). The key to this delicate undertaking is being able to safely sense both intense and subtle body sensations and feelings. It turns out that there is a paired brain structure that appears to do exactly that: wedged in between the limbic system and the prefrontal cortex are the insula (nearer to the limbic system) and cingulate (nearer to the cortex). Briefly, the insula receives input from the internal structures of the body, including muscles, joints and viscera. Together, insula and cingulate help us make sense of these primitive sensations by weaving them into nuanced feelings, perceptions and cognitions.[52] Accessing that function is a key to the approach of transforming trauma and difficult emotions described in the following chapters.

Balancing Instinct and Reason

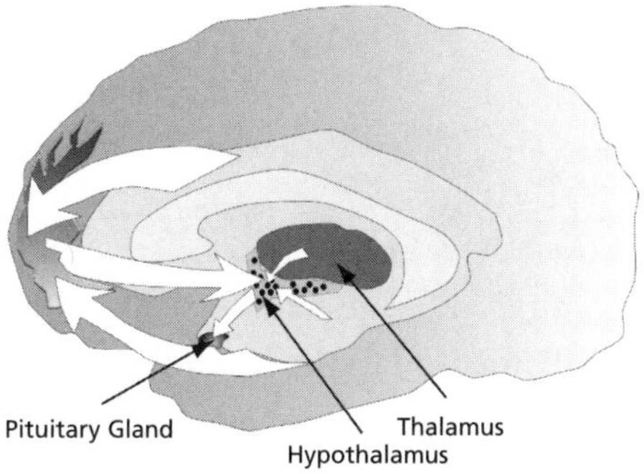

Pituitary Gland   Thalamus
Hypothalamus

Figure 4.2 This illustrates the importance of keeping the prefrontal cortex online during activation of survival-based arousal in the brain stem and limbic system. Note how nerve impulses flow between the instinctual brain structures of the thalamus and hypothalamus (which controls the secretion of the pituitary gland that is vital for maintaining organ and cellular homeostasis) and the frontal lobe (or rational brain).

Restoring the balance and rhythm between instinct and reason also plays a central part in healing the mind/body split. Integration of brain and body, of right and left cerebral hemispheres, and of primitive and evolved brain regions promotes wholeness and makes us fully human. Until then, we are, as Margaret Mead noted, "the missing link between apes and humans."

CHAPTER 5

From Paralysis to Transformation

Basic Building Blocks

Fear is the mind killer. Fear is the little
death that brings total obliteration.
I will face my fear. I will permit it to pass
over me and through me.
And when it has gone past me, I will turn
to see fear's path.
Where the fear has gone there will be
nothing. Only I will remain.
—*Dune* by Frank Herbert

If you do not understand the nature of
fear, you will never find fearlessness.
—Shambhala Buddhism

In the previous chapter we explored just how experimental animals and humans become trapped in fear-dominated paralysis; and, thus, how they become traumatized. In this chapter, I introduce the "antidote" for trauma: the core biological mechanisms that therapists must be aware of and able to elicit in their clients in order to assist in resolving their traumatic reactions. The engaging of these biological processes is equally essential whether treating the acute phase immediately following threatening and overwhelming incidents, such as rape, accidents and disasters, or in transforming chronic PTSD.

Until the core physical experience of trauma—feeling scared stiff, frozen in fear or collapsing and going numb—unwinds and transforms,

one remains stuck, a captive of one's own entwined fear and helplessness. The sensations of paralysis or collapse *seem* intolerable, utterly
unacceptable; they terrify and threaten to entrap and defeat us. This
perception of seemingly unbearable experiences leads us to avoid and
deny them, to tighten up against them and then split off from them.
Resorting to these "defenses" is, however, like drinking salt water to
quench extreme thirst: while they may give temporary relief, they only
make the problem drastically worse and are, over the long haul, counterproductive. In order to unravel this tangle of fear and paralysis, we
must be able to voluntarily contact and experience those frightening
physical sensations; we must be able to confront them long enough for
them to shift and change. To resist the immediate defensive ploy of
avoidance, the most potent strategy is to move toward the fear, to contact the immobility itself and to consciously explore the various sensations, textures, images and thoughts associated with any discomfort that
may arise.

When working with traumatic reactions, such as states of intense
fear, Somatic Experiencing®* provides therapists with nine building
blocks. These basic tools for "renegotiating" and transforming trauma
are not linear, rigid or unidirectional. Instead, in therapy sessions, these
steps are intertwined and dependent upon one another and may be
accessed repeatedly and in any order. However, if this psychobiologi-
cal process is to be built on firm ground, Steps 1, 2 and 3 *must occur
first and must follow sequentially*. Thus, the therapist needs to:

1. Establish an environment of *relative* safety.
2. Support initial exploration and acceptance of sensation.
3. Establish "pendulation" and containment: the innate power of
   rhythm.

---

* This is a method I have developed over the past forty years.

4. Use titration to create increasing stability, resilience and organization. Titration is about carefully touching into the smallest "drop" of survival-based arousal, and other difficult sensations, to prevent retraumatization.
5. Provide a corrective experience by supplanting the passive responses of collapse and helplessness with active, *empowered*, defensive responses.
6. Separate or "uncouple" the conditioned association of fear and helplessness from the (normally time-limited but now maladaptive) biological immobility response.
7. Resolve hyperarousal states by gently guiding the "discharge" and redistribution of the vast survival energy mobilized for life-preserving action while freeing that energy to support higher-level brain functioning.
8. Engage self-regulation to restore "dynamic equilibrium" and relaxed alertness.
9. Orient to the here and now, contact the environment and reestablish the capacity for social engagement.

Step 1. Establish an environment of relative safety

After my accident, the first inkling my body had of being other than profoundly helpless and disoriented was when the pediatrician came and sat by my side. As simple as this seems, her calm, centered presence gave me a slight glimmer of hope that things might turn out OK. Such soothing support in the midst of chaos is a *critical* element that trauma therapists must provide for their unsettled and troubled clients. This truly is the starting point for one's return to equilibrium. The therapist must, in other words, help to create an environment of *relative* safety, an atmosphere that conveys refuge, hope and possibility. For traumatized individuals, this can be a very delicate task. Fortunately, given propitious conditions, the human nervous system is designed and attuned both to receive and to offer a regulating influence to another person.[53] Thankfully, biology is on our side. This transference of succor, our mammalian birthright, is fostered by the therapeutic tone and working alliance you create by tuning in to your client's sensibilities.

With the therapist's calm secure center, relaxed alertness, compassionate containment and evident patience, the client's distress begins to lessen. However minimally, his or her willingness to explore is prompted, encouraged and owned. While resistance will inevitably appear, it will soften and recede with the holding environment created by the skilled therapist. One possible roadblock, however, happens between sessions; when they are without their therapist's calm, regulating presence, clients may feel raw and thrown back into the lion's den of chaotic sensations when exposed to the same triggers that overwhelmed them in the first place. The therapist who provides only a sense of safety (no matter how effectively) will only make the client increasingly dependent—and thus will increase the imbalance of power between therapist and client. To avoid such sabotage, the next steps are aimed at helping the client move toward establishing his or her own agency and capacity for mastering self-soothing and feelings of empowerment and self-regulation.

Step 2. Support initial exploration and acceptance of sensation

Traumatized individuals have lost both their way in the world and the vital guidance of their inner promptings. Cut off from the primal sensations, instincts and feelings arising from the interior of their bodies, they are unable to orient to the "here and now." Therapists must be able to help clients navigate the labyrinth of trauma by helping them find their way home to their bodily sensations and capacity to self-soothe.

To become self-regulating and authentically autonomous, traumatized individuals must ultimately learn to access, tolerate and utilize their inner sensations. It would, however, be unwise to have one attempt a sustained focus on one's body without adequate preparation. Initially, in contacting inner sensations, one may feel the threat of a consuming fear of the unknown. Or, premature focus on the sensations can be overwhelming, potentially causing retraumatization. For many wounded individuals, their body has become the enemy: the experience of almost any sensation is interpreted as an unbidden harbinger of renewed terror and helplessness.

To solve this perplexing situation, a therapist who (while engaging in initial conversation) notices a momentary positive shift in a client's affect—in facial expression, say, or a shift in posture—indicating relief and brightness, can seize the opportunity and try to direct the client toward attending to her sensations. "Touching in" to positive experiences gradually gives a client the confidence to explore her internal bodily landscape and develop a tolerance for *all* of her sensations, comfortable and uncomfortable, pleasant and unpleasant.

The client can now begin to allow the underlying disowned sensations—especially those of paralysis, helplessness and rage—to emerge into consciousness. She develops her experience of agency by choosing between the two opposing states: resistance/fear and acceptance/exploration. With a gentle rocking back and forth, oscillating between resistance and acceptance, fear and exploration, the client gradually sheds some of her protective armoring. The therapist guides her into a comforting rhythm—a supported shifting between paralyzing fear and the *pure* sensations associated with the immobility. In Gestalt

Figure and Ground Perception

Figure 5.1 This figure demonstrates the alternation of figure and ground perception. Do you see the vase or the face? Keep looking. Now what do you see now? You will probably notice that the vase and face alternate but cannot be perceived at the same time. This is a useful concept in understanding how fear is uncoupled from immobility. When one experiences pure immobility, one cannot (like vase and face) also feel fear at the same time. This facilitates expansion and the gradual discharge of activation shown in Figure 5.2.

psychology, these back-and-forth movements between two different
states are described as figure/ground alternations (see Figure 5.1). This
shifting, in turn, reduces fear's grip and allows more access to the quin-
tessential and unencumbered (by emotion) immobility sensations. This
back-and-forth switching of attention (between the fear/resistance and
the unadulterated physical sensations of immobility) deepens relaxation
and enhances aliveness. It is the beginning of hope and the acquiring
of tools that will empower her as she begins to navigate the interoceptive (or the direct felt experiencing of viscera, joints and muscles) landscape of trauma and healing. These skills lead to a core innate
transformative process: pendulation.

Step 3. Pendulation and containment: the innate power of rhythm

> Expecting the worst, you look, and instead,
> here's the joyful face you've been wanting
>   to see.
> Your hand opens and closes and opens and
>   closes.
> If it were always a fist or always stretched
>   open,
> you would be paralyzed.
> Your deepest presence is in every small
>   contracting and expanding.
> The two as beautifully balanced and
>   coordinated as birdwings.
>   —Rumi (1207–1273)

> All God's children got rhythm, who could
> ask for anything more?
>   —*Porgy and Bess*

While trauma is about being frozen or stuck, pendulation is about the
innate organismic rhythm of contraction and expansion. It is, in other
words, about getting unstuck by knowing (sensing from the inside),

perhaps for the first time, that no matter how horrible one is feeling, those feelings *can and will* change. Without this (experienced) knowledge, a person in a state of "stuckness" does not want to inhabit his or her body. In order to counter the seemingly intractable human tendency to avoid horrible and unpleasant sensations, effective therapy (and the promotion of resilience in general) must offer a way to face the dragons of fear, rage, helplessness and paralysis. The therapist must inspire trust that their clients will not be trapped and devoured by first giving them a little "taste treat" of a pleasant internal experience. This is how our clients move toward self-empowerment. Confidence builds with the skill of pendulation.

One surprisingly effective strategy in dealing with difficult sensations involves helping a person find an "opposite" sensation: one located in a particular area of the body, in a particular posture, or in a small movement; or one that is associated with the person's feeling less frozen, less helpless, more powerful and/or more fluid. If the person's discomfort shifts even momentarily, the therapist can encourage him to focus on that fleeting physical sensation and so bring about a new perception; one where he's discovered and settling on an "island of safety" that feels, at the very least, OK. Discovering this island contradicts the overarching feelings of badness, informing the person that somehow the body may not be the enemy after all. It might actually be grasped as an ally in the recovery process. When enough of these little islands are found and felt, they can be linked into a growing landmass, capable of withstanding the raging storms of trauma. Choice and even pleasure become a possibility with this growing stability as new synaptic connections are formed and strengthened. One gradually learns to shift one's awareness between regions of relative ease and those of discomfort and distress.

This shifting evokes one of the most important reconnections to the body's innate wisdom: the experience of pendulation, the body's *natural restorative* rhythm of contraction and expansion that tells us that whatever is felt is time-limited ... that suffering will not last forever. Pendulation carries all living creatures through difficult sensations and emotions. What's more, it requires no effort; it is wholly innate. Pendulation is the primal rhythm expressed as movement from constriction to expansion—and back to contraction, but gradually opening to more and more expansion (see Figure 5.2). It is an involuntary, internal rocking back and forth between these two polarities. It softens the edge of difficult sensations such as fear and pain. The importance of the human ability to move through "bad" and difficult sensations, opening to those of expansion and "goodness," cannot be overstated: it is pivotal for the healing of trauma and more generally, the alleviation of suffering. It is vital for a client to know and *experience* this rhythm. Its steady ebb and flow tell you that, no matter how bad you feel (in the contraction phase), expansion *will inevitably* follow, bringing with it a sense of opening, relief and flow. At the same time, too rapid or large a magnitude of expansion can be frightening, causing a client to contract precipitously against the expansion. Hence, the therapist needs to moderate the scale and pace of this rhythm. As clients perceive that movement and flow are a possibility, they begin to move ahead in time

Cycles of Expansion and Contraction

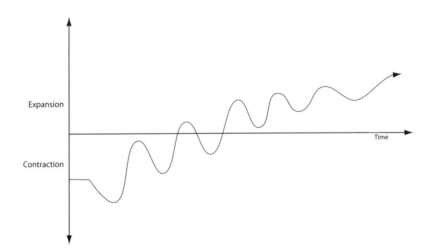

Figure 5.2 This figure describes the cycle of expansion and contraction through the process of pendulation. This vital awareness lets people learn that whatever they are feeling will change. The perception of pendulation guides the gradual contained release (discharge) of "trauma energies" leading to expansive body sensations and successful trauma resolution.

by accepting and integrating *current* sensations that had previously overwhelmed them.

Let's look at three universal situations that register this innate capacity of pendulation to restore feelings of relief and life flow: (1) We have all watched the inconsolable anguish of a child who, after a nasty fall, runs screaming to its mother and collapses in her arms. After a short time, the child begins to orient back out to the world, then seeks a moment's return to its safe haven (perhaps through a glance back at mother or a connection through touch); and then, finally, returns to play as if nothing ever happened. (2) Consider the adult who is struck down by the gut-wrenching reaction to the sudden loss of a loved one. One may collapse, feeling that this experience will go on forever, resulting in one's own death. Grieving can stretch out for quite a long time, but there is a clear ebb and flow in the tide of anguish. Gradually the rhythm of acceptance and pain yields a calming release and a return to life. (3) Finally, recall the last time you were driving and experienced a shockingly close call with disaster. Your nerves were raw with fear (hair standing on end) and rage, and your heart was pounding wildly, ready to explode in your chest. Then a wave of relief reminded you that you haven't been catapulted into the horror of an accident. This moment of relief is usually followed by a second "flashback" of the near miss, which provokes another round of lessened startle, followed by yet another wave of restorative relief. This reparative rhythm occurs involuntarily, usually in the shadow of awareness, thankfully allowing one to focus on the task at hand. Thus, pendulation allows you to recover your balance and return to life's moment-to-moment engagement.

When this natural resilience process has been shut down, it must be gently and gradually awakened. The mechanisms that regulate a person's mood, vitality and health are dependent upon pendulation. When this rhythm is experienced, there is, at least, a tolerable balance between the pleasant and the unpleasant. People learn that whatever they are feeling (no matter how horrible it seems), it will last only seconds to minutes. And no matter how bad a particular sensation or feeling may be, knowing that it will change releases us from a sense of doom. The brain registers this new experience by tuning down its alarm/defeat bias.

Where before, there was overwhelming immobility and collapse, the nervous system now finds its way back toward equilibrium. We cease to perceive everything as dangerous, and gradually, step by step, the doors of perception open to new possibilities. We become ready for the next steps.

Step 4. Titration

Steps 3 and 4—pendulation and titration—together form a tightly-knit dyad that allows individuals to safely access and integrate critical survival-based, highly energetic states. Together, they allow trauma to be processed without overwhelm, and hence the individual is not retraumatized.

In Steps 5, 6 and 7, the gradual restoration of active defensive and protective responses—along with the carefully calibrated termination of the immobility reaction is accomplished. This, along with the discharge of bound energy, reduces the hyperarousal. Together these steps lie at the heart of transforming trauma. In particular, the egress from immobility is associated with intense arousal-based sensations, along with the powerful emotions of rage and frantic, fearful flight. This is the reason the process of trauma release must be worked in tiny increments.

I use the term *titration* to denote the gradual, stepwise process of trauma renegotiation. This process operates like certain chemical reactions. Consider two glass beakers, one filled with hydrochloric acid (HCl) and the other with lye (NaOH). These extremely corrosive substances (the acid and the base, respectively) would cause severe burning if you were to place your finger in either beaker; indeed, if you were to leave that finger there for a few moments, it would simply dissolve since both of these chemicals are so caustic. Naturally, you would want to make them safe by neutralizing them; and, if you knew a little chemistry, you might mix them together to get a harmless mixture of water and common table salt, two of the basic building blocks of life. This reaction is written $HCl + NaOH = NaCl + H_2O$. If you simply poured them together, you would get a massive explosion, surely blinding yourself and any other individuals in the lab. On the other hand, if you skillfully use a glass valve (a stopcock), you could add one of the chemicals to the other *one single drop at a time*. And with each drop there would be a small "Alka-Seltzer fizzle," but soon all would be calm. With each drop the same minimal reaction would repeat (see Figure 5.3). Finally, after a certain number of drops, both water and crystals of salt would begin to form. With several titrations, you would inevitably get the same neutralizing chemical reaction, but without the explosion. This is the effect that we want to achieve in resolving trauma: when dealing with potentially corrosive forces, therapists must somehow neutralize those sensations of intense "energy" and the primal emotional states of rage and non-directed flight without unleashing an explosive abreaction.

Titration

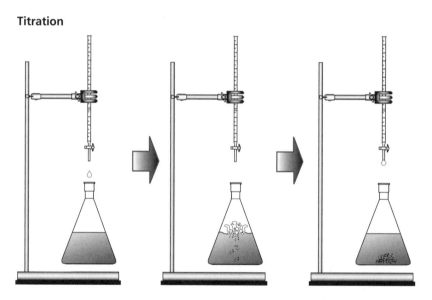

Figure 5.3 Titration in the chemistry lab is a way of combining two corrosive and potentially explosive substances in a controlled mixing that transforms the reactants gradually.

Step 5. Restoring active responses

During my accident, as I was propelled into the windshield of the car, my arm stiffened to ward off the impact to my head. The amount of energy that goes into such a protective response is vast; muscles stiffen to maximal exertion to fend off a lethal blow. Also, at the moment my shoulder smashed into the glass and I was propelled into the air and onto the road, my body went limp.

When your muscles "give up" like that and collapse, you feel helpless and defeated. However, underneath that collapse, those flaccid (hypotonic) muscles still carry the signals to protect you even though they have "lost" their power, liveliness and ability to do so.

Our human sensorimotor memory is poised and ready to carry out its marching orders to champion our protection and safety. In my case, with interoceptive awareness, the active bracing pattern was gradually restored, and energy began to return to my arms. I allowed my muscles to do what they had "wanted" to do and were prepared to do in the moment prior to impact before they collapsed into helplessness. Bringing that into consciousness allowed me to experience a deepening sense of empowerment. Similarly, twenty-four-year-old Nancy (my very first trauma client from Chapter 2) and I discovered, unwittingly, that (rather than continuing to feel overpowered and overwhelmed by the surgeons as she had at age four), she could now escape from being held down and terrorized. These new experiences contradicted and repaired both of our experiences of helpless terror.

Briefly, the way these active self-protective responses are reestablished is as follows: Specific tension patterns (as experienced through interoceptive awareness) "suggest" particular movements, which then can express themselves in minute or micro-movements. The positions that my arms and hands spontaneously and powerfully assumed during the accident had protected my head from smashing into the windshield and then from being cracked open on the pavement. Later, when I was in the ambulance, I revisited these instinctual reflexive movements and expanded them through sensation awareness—a process that allowed me to consciously experience the activation of muscle fibers as my body prepared for movement. These actions had previously been incomplete and remained nonconscious. By slamming forcefully, first into the windshield and then onto the pavement, these muscular reflexes had been truncated, leaving me with collapsed and constricted muscles and a vast reservoir of latent energy. Instead of feeling helpless and victimized by this dreadful event, I created a powerful sense of agency and mastery. In addition, the restoration of defensive responses has the effect of automatically titrating the energies of rage. In other words, the explosive energy that would be expressed as rage and non-directed flight was now channeled into effective, directed healthy aggression.

Empowerment derives directly from expelling the physical attitude of defeat and helplessness and restoring the biologically meaningful active defense system—that is, the embodied triumph of successful protection and the visceral actuality of competency. Such renegotiation (as we shall see in Step 6) also helps to dissolve the entrenched guilt and self-judgment that may be byproducts of helplessness and repressed/dissociated rage. By accessing an active and powerful experience, passivity of paralysis and collapse is countered.

Because of the central importance of restoring these lost (rather, misplaced) instinctive active responses in healing trauma, I will—at the risk of repetition—address this subject from a slightly different angle. It can be said that the *experience of fear* derives from the primitive responses to threat where escape is *thwarted* (i.e., in some way—actual or perceived—prevented or conflicted).[54] Contrary to what you might expect, when one's primary responses of fight-or-flight (or other protective actions) are executed freely, one does *not necessarily* experience fear, but rather the pure and powerful, *primary* sensations of fighting or fleeing. Recall, *the response to threat involves an initial mobilization to fight or flee.* It is only when that response fails that it "defaults" to one's freezing or being "scared stiff" or to collapsing helplessly.

In my case, in the ambulance, it was in my limbs—in the micromovements of my arms rising upward to protect my head from mortal injury—that I first felt an opposite experience that contradicted my sensation of helplessness. For Nancy, it was her legs running to escape the doctor's surgical knife. In both cases, consciously feeling our way through these active self-protective reflexes with precision brought us the physical sense of agency and power. Together, these experiences countered our feelings of overwhelming helplessness. Step by step, our bodies learned that we were not helpless victims, that we had survived our ordeals, and that we were intact and alive to the core of our beings.

Along with instilling active defensive responses (which reduces fear), individuals learn that when they experience the physical sensations of paralysis, it is with less and less fear—each time trauma loosens its grip. With such a body-based epiphany, the mind's interpretation of what happened and the meaning of it to one's life and who one is shifts profoundly.

Step 6. Uncoupling fear from immobility

My clinical observations, drawn from more than four decades of work with thousands of clients, have led me to the solid understanding that the "physio-*logical*" ability to go into, and then come out of, the innate (hard-wired) immobility response is *the key* both to avoiding the prolonged debilitating effects of trauma and to healing even entrenched symptoms.[55] Basically, this is done by separating fear and helplessness from the (normally time-limited) biological immobility response as described in Chapter 4. For a traumatized individual, to be able to touch into his or her immobility sensations, even for a brief moment, restores self-paced termination and allows the "unwinding" of fear and freeze to begin.

Of equal importance in resolving trauma is therapeutic restraint in not allowing the unwinding to occur precipitously. As with the nontitrated chemical reaction, abrupt decoupling can be explosive, frightening and potentially retraumatizing to the client. Through titration, the client is *gradually led into and out of the immobility sensations many times*, each time returning to a calming equilibrium (the "Alka-Seltzer fizzle"). In exiting from immobility, there is an "initiation by fire"; the intense energy-packed sensations that are biologically coupled with undirected flight and rage-counterattack are released. Understandably, people commonly fear both entering and exiting immobility, especially when they are not aware of the benefit of doing so. Let us look more deeply into these fears.

The fear of entering immobility: We avoid experiencing the sensations of immobility because of how powerful they are and how helpless and vulnerable they make us feel. Some of these even mimic the death state. When you consider how the thought of something as routine as being compelled to sit rigidly still in the dentist's chair can cause you to wince, you begin to understand the challenge of voluntarily entering immobility mode. You may anticipate the pain of being trapped with no way to escape. For anxious or traumatized individuals, having to lie immobile during an MRI or CT scan can be downright terrifying. For children, these procedures may be vastly more difficult. Sitting quietly at one's desk, unable to move for hours at a stretch, is a challenge for any youngster. For an anxious or "sensitive" child, it can be unbearable, perhaps even contributing to attention-deficit hyperactivity disorder. This may be especially true for children who have had to undergo immobilizing procedures, such as when casts or metal braces are required for orthopedic correction of hips, legs, ankles or feet during the developmental stage when a child would normally be learning how to walk, run and explore the world.

Even adults who meditate often struggle with sitting still. Those few fortunate ones who can crawl into a warm bed, lie absolutely still, and drift quickly off into a restorative sleep are bestowed a most precious blessing. However, for many (perhaps even a majority), bedtime is often fraught with anxiety. It can become a nightmare in itself. In frustration, you may try to lie still while "counting sheep." Mind spinning, you are unable to let go and surrender into Morpheus's waiting arms. And then when some people awaken during (or shortly after) REM sleep, their bodies are still literally paralyzed by the neurological mechanisms designed to inhibit running or fighting (or even actively moving) in a dream for self-protection and prevention against hurting someone else. Waking up from this normal "sleep paralysis" can be terrifying, particularly when people experience themselves detaching from their bodies, a frequent component of immobility. For others, the sleep-induced REM paralysis is a curious, enjoyable, even "mystical," out-of-body experience. For those who perceive this detaching from their bodies as terrifying, panic reactions are typical. In traumatized people, fear-potentiated immobility is their wrenching companion, day and night.

Although avoidance of immobility is understandable, it has a price. Whatever experiences you turn away from, your brain-body registers as dangerous; or colloquially, "that which we resist persists." Thus, the time-honored expression, "time heals all wounds," simply does not apply to trauma. In the short run, the suppression of immobility sensations *appears* (to our denial-biased mind) to keep the paralysis and helplessness at bay. However, in time, it becomes apparent that evasive maneuvers are an abject failure. This "sweeping under the rug" not only prolongs the inevitable, it often makes the eventual encounter with immobility even more frightening. It is as if the mind recognizes the extent of our resistance and in response interprets it as further evidence of peril. If, on the other hand, one is able to utilize the vital assistance of titration and pendulation, one can touch gently and briefly into that deathlike void without coming undone. Hence, the immobility response can *move ahead in time* toward its natural conclusion, self-paced termination.

The fear of exiting immobility: In the wild, when a prey animal has succumbed to the immobility response, it remains motionless for a time. Then, just as easily as it stopped moving, it twitches, reorients and scampers off. But if the predator has remained and sees its prey returning to life, the story has a very different ending. As the prey comes back to life and sees the predator standing ready for a second (and this time lethal) attack, it either defaults to all-out rage and counterattacks, or it attempts to run away in frantic non-directed flight. Thus reaction is wild and "mindless." As I mentioned in Chapter 4, I once saw a mouse counterattack a cat that had been batting it about with its paws (bringing the mouse out of its stupor), and then scurry away, leaving the cat dazed, like Tom-cat in a Tom and Jerry cartoon. Just as the immobilized animal (in the presence of the predator) comes out ready for violent counterattack, so too does a traumatized person abruptly swing from paralysis and shutdown to hyper-agitation and rage. Fear of this rage and the associated hyper-intense sensations prevents a tolerable exit from immobility unless there is education, preparation, titration and guidance.

The fear of rage is also the fear of violence—both toward others and against oneself. The exiting of immobility is inhibited by the following double bind: to come back to life, one must feel the sensations of rage and intense energy. However, at the same time, these sensations evoke the possibility of mortal harm. This possibility inhibits sustained contact with the very sensations that bring relief from the experience of immobility, thereby leading to resolution. Recall the prescience of Kahlbaum (in Chapter 4) when he wrote in 1874: "In most cases catatonia is *preceded* by grief and anxiety and in general by depressive moods *and affects aimed against the patient by himself.*"[56] Because the rage associated with the termination of immobility is both intense and potentially violent, frequently traumatized people inadvertently turn this rage against themselves in the form of depression, self-hatred and self-harm.

The inability to exit from the immobility response generates unbearable frustration, shame and corrosive self-hatred. The therapist must approach this Gordian knot carefully and untangle it through deliberate and careful titration, along with reliance on the experience of pendulation and a resolve to befriend intense aggressive sensations. In this way, the individual is able to move out of this "kill or be killed" counterattack bind. As one begins to open gradually to accepting one's intense sensations, one enhances the capacity for healthy aggression, pleasure and goodness.

It is no surprise, then, that traumatized individuals constrict and brace against their rage as socialized animals. But let us look at the cumulative consequence of suppressing rage. Tremendous amounts of energy need to be exerted (on an already strained system) to keep rage and other primitive emotions at bay. This "turning in" of anger against the self, and the need to defend against its eruption, leads to debilitating shame, as well as to eventual exhaustion. This involution adds another layer to the complexity and seeming intransigence of the festering traumatic state. For these reasons, titration becomes even more crucial as a measure to interrupt this self-perpetuating "shame cycle."

In the case of molestation and other forms of previous abuse, a substratum of self-reproach has already been laid beneath a later trauma during adulthood. Indeed, because immobility is experienced as a passive response, many molestation and rape victims feel tremendous shame for not having successfully fought their attackers. This perception and the overwhelming sense of defeat can occur regardless of the reality of the situation: the relative size of the attacker doesn't matter; nor does the fact that the immobility might have even protected the victim from further harm or possibly death.* And I haven't even included here the additional blanket of confusion and shame that occurs within the complex dynamics of secrecy and betrayal in the incestuous family.

As traumatized individuals begin to reown their sense of agency and power, they gradually come to a place of self-forgiveness and self-acceptance. They achieve the compassionate realization that both their immobility and their rage are a biologically driven, instinctual imperative and *not* something to be ashamed of as if it were a character defect. They own their rage as undifferentiated power and agency, a vital life-preserving force to be harnessed and used to benefit oneself. Because of its profound importance in the resolution of trauma, I'll repeat myself: the fear that fuels immobility can be categorized, broadly, as two separate fears: the fear of entering immobility, which is the fear of paralysis, entrapment, helplessness and death; and the fear of exiting immobility, of the intense energy of the "rage-based" sensations of counterattack. Caught in this two-sided clamp (of entering and exiting), immobility repels its antidote implacably so that it seems impossible to break through it. However, when the skillful therapist assists clients in uncoupling the fear from the immobility by restoring "self-paced termination of immobility," the rich reward is the client's capability to move forward in time. This "forward experiencing" dispels fear, entrapment and helplessness by breaking this endless feedback loop of terror and paralysis.

As fear uncouples from the immobilization sensations, you may scratch your head and ask, where does the fear go? The short and confounding answer is that when titrated, "fear" simply does not really exist as an independent entity. The actual acute fear that occurred at the time of the traumatic event, of course, no longer exists. What happens, however, is that one provokes and perpetuates a new fear state (one

---

* It is not clear when fighting or succumbing is the best survival strategy for rape. A dependent child experiencing molestation, however, really has little choice but to succumb.

literally frightens oneself) and becomes one's own self-imposed predator by bracing against the residual sensations of immobility and rage. While paralysis itself need not actually be terrifying, what is frightening is our *resistance* to feeling paralyzed or enraged. Because we don't know it is a temporary state, and because our bodies do not register that we are now safe, we remain stuck in the past, rather than being in present time. Pendulation helps to dissolve this resistance. We might best heed the words of the 1960s jug band Dan Hicks and his Hot Licks: "It's me I'm afraid of ... I won't scare myself."

During therapy, a graduated (titrated) progression or "forward moving of experiencing" keeps building on itself until the fear (now receding into the background) is eclipsed by a fully experienced immobility response. Frequently, one notices this physical sensation and acknowledges it with simple comments such as "I feel paralyzed, like I can't move," or "it feels like I am dead," or even "it's funny—I am dead and it doesn't frighten me." In addition, individuals may even experience blissful states similar to those reported in studies about near-death experiences. In exiting immobility, people may report that they feel "tingling vibrations all over my body" or "I feel deeply alive and real."

As the innate response of paralysis naturally resolves, sensations of "pure energy" are accepted; the individual opens into a mother lode of existential relief, transformative gratitude and vital aliveness. The mystic poet William Blake celebrated the intrinsic relationship between energy and the body: "The Body is a portion of the Soul discerned by the Senses, the chief inlet of the Soul in this age. Energy is the only life and is from the Body ... and energy is pure delight."

Step 7. Resolve arousal states by promoting discharge of the vast survival energy mobilized for life-preserving action

As one's passive responses are replaced by active ones in the exit from immobility, a particular physiological process occurs: one experiences waves of involuntary shaking and trembling, followed by spontaneous changes in breathing—from tight and shallow to deep and relaxed. These involuntary reactions function, essentially, to discharge the vast energy that, though mobilized to prepare the organism to fight, flee or otherwise self-protect, was not fully executed. (See Chapter 1 for my own experience of such reactions after my accident, and Chapter 2 for Nancy's as she discharged the arousal energy that had been bound up in ever-increasing symptoms since her early-childhood tonsillectomy.) Perhaps the easiest way to visualize the release of energy is through an analogy from physics. Imagine a spring fastened firmly to the ceiling above you. A weight is attached to the free end of the spring (see Figure 5.4). You reach up and pull the weight down toward you, stretching the spring and creating in it potential energy. Then as you release the spring, the weight oscillates up and down until all of the spring's energy is discharged. In this way, the potential energy held in the spring is transformed into the kinetic energy of movement. The spring finally comes to rest when all the stored potential energy that has been converted to this kinetic energy is fully discharged.

Discharge of Traumatic Activation and Restoration of Equilibrium

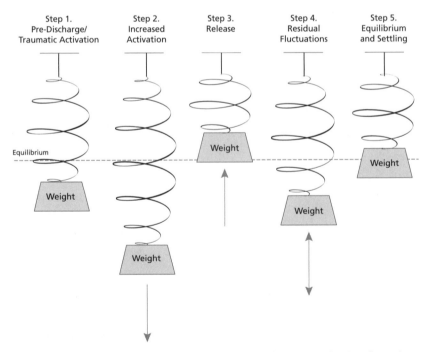

Figure 5.4 Stretching the spring increases its potential energy. Releasing the spring transforms this potential into kinetic energy, where it is discharged and equilibrium restored.

Similarly, your muscles are energized ("stretched") in preparation for action. However, when such mobilization is not carried out (whether fight-or-flight or some other protective response such as stiffening, twisting, retracting or ducking), then that potential energy becomes "stored" or "filed" as an unfinished procedure within the implicit memory of the sensorimotor system. When a conscious or unconscious association is activated through a general or specific stimulus, all of the original hormonal and chemical warriors reenergize the muscles as if the original threat were still operating. Later this energy can be released as trembling and vibration. Risking oversimplification, I can say that an amount of energy (arousal) similar to what was mobilized for fight-or-flight must be discharged, through effective action and/or through shaking and trembling. These can be dramatic as with Nancy (Chapter 2), while others are subtle. They may be expressed as gentle fasciculations and/or changes in skin temperature. Along with these autonomic nervous system releases, the self-protective and defensive responses that were incomplete at the time of the incident (and lie dormant as potential energy) are frequently liberated through micro-movements. These are almost imperceptible and are sometimes referred to as "premovements"). In this way, Steps 4 through 7 link together.

Step 8. Restore self-regulation and dynamic equilibrium

A direct consequence of discharge of the survival energy mobilized for fight-or-flight is the restoration of equilibrium and balance (as in the previous example of the spring). The nineteenth-century French physiologist Claude Bernard, considered the father of experimental physiology, coined the term *homeostasis* to describe "the constancy of the internal environment *[milieu intérieur]* as the condition for a free and independent life."[57] More than a hundred and fifty years later, this remains the underlying and defining principle for the sustenance of life. However, since equilibrium is not a static process, I will use the term *dynamic equilibrium* instead of homeostasis to describe what happens when the nervous system becomes hyperaroused in response to threat and is then "reset," only to be aroused and reset once again. This continual resetting both restores the prethreat level of arousal and promotes

the shifting state (process) of relaxed alertness. Over time this con-
tributes to the building of a robust resilience. Finally, the interoceptive
experience of equilibrium, felt in viscera and in your internal milieu, is
the salubrious one of goodness: that is, the background sense that—
whatever you are feeling at a given moment, however dreadful the upset
or unpleasant the arousal—you have a secure home base within your
organism.

Step 9. Reorient to the environment in the here and now

Trauma could appropriately be called a disorder in one's capacity to be
grounded in present time and to engage, appropriately, with other
human beings. Along with the restoration of dynamic equilibrium, the
capacity for presence, for being in "the here and now," becomes a reality. This occurs along with the desire and capacity for embodied social
engagement.

The capacity for social engagement has powerful consequences for
health and happiness. As young children we are wired to participate in
the social nervous systems of our parents and to find excitement and
joy in such engagement. In addition, fascination with the face of another
person generalizes to the environment and to the wonder of "new-
ness." Colors become vibrant, while one perceives shapes and textures
as though seeing them for the first time—the very miracle of life
unfolding.

In addition, the social engagement system is intrinsically self-calming
and is, therefore, built-in protection against one's organism being
"hijacked" by the sympathetic arousal system and/or frozen into submission by the more primitive emergency shutdown system. The social
engagement branch of the nervous system is probably both cardio-
protective and immuno-protective. This may be why individuals with
strong personal affiliations live longer, healthier lives. They also maintain
sharper cognitive skills into old age. Indeed, one study examining the
effects of playing bridge in reducing dementia symptoms concluded
that the main independent variable was socialization (rather than com-

putational skills per se).* And, finally, to be engaged in the social world is not only to be engaged in the here and now, but also to feel a sense of both belonging and safety. So, ultimately freeing clients from the repercussive isolation that fear and immobility create has the potential of bringing not only freedom from debilitating symptoms, but also the potential to generate energy into the establishment of satisfying con- nections and relationships.

---

* The so-called 90+ study at the University of Southern California began in 1981. It has included more than 14,000 people aged 65 and older and more than 1,000 aged 90 or older. Dr. Kawas, a senior investigator, concluded, "Interacting with people regularly, even strangers, uses easily as much brain power as doing puzzles, and it wouldn't surprise me if this is what it's all about."

CHAPTER 6

A Map for Therapy

The map may not be the territory,
but it sure helps you to get around.
—Me (PAL)

Ancient Unspoken Voices

Just as maps are useful in finding a particular part of the city, maps of the human organism* are important in navigating the landscape of trauma and informing its healing. The groundbreaking work of Stephen Porges, director of the Brain Body Center at the University of Illinois, Department of Psychiatry, has provided an eloquent, well-reasoned and broadly supported "treasure map" of the psychophysiological systems that govern the traumatic state. These same systems also mediate core feelings of goodness and belonging. Porges's *polyvagal theory of emotion*[58] illuminates the pathways for recovery and integration described in Chapter 5. In addition, his model clarifies why certain common approaches to trauma psychotherapy frequently fail.

Briefly, Porges's theory states that, in humans, three basic neural energy subsystems underpin the overall state of the nervous system and correlative behaviors and emotions. The most primitive of these three (spanning about 500 million years) stems from its origin in early fish

---

* Merriam-Webster's definition of *organism* is "a complex structure of interdependent and subordinate elements whose relations and properties are largely determined by their function in the whole." Organism describes a wholeness, which derives not from the sum of its individual parts (i.e., bones, chemicals, muscles, nerves, organs, etc.); rather, it emerges from their dynamic, complex interrelation. Body and mind, primitive instincts, emotions, intellect, and spirituality all need to be considered together in studying the organism.

species.* The function of this primitive system is immobilization, metabolic conservation, and shutdown. Its target of action is the internal organs. Next in evolutionary development is the sympathetic nervous system. This global arousal system has evolved from the reptilian period about 300 million years ago. *Its function is mobilization and enhanced action (as in fight or flight); its target in the body is the limbs.* Finally, the third, and phylogenetically most recent, system (deriving from about 80 million years ago) exists *only* in mammals. This neural subsystem shows its greatest refinement in the primates, where it mediates complex social and attachment behaviors. It is the branch of the parasympathetic nervous system that regulates the so-called mammalian or "smart" vagus nerve, which is neuroanatomically linked to the cranial nerves that mediate facial expression and vocalization. This most recently acquired system animates the unconsciously mediated muscles in throat, face, middle ear, heart and lungs, which together communicate our emotions, both to others and to ourselves.[59] This most refined system *orchestrates relationship, attachment and bonding* and also mediates emotional intelligence. Figure 6.1 summarizes the basic mammalian nervous subsystems. For more detail, see Diagram B after page 18, which shows the complex wandering of the vagus nerve affecting and being affected by most of the internal organs. The basic functions of these phylogenetic systems are summarized in Figures 6.2a through 6.2d.

Nervous systems are tuned to assess potential risk in the environment—an unconscious evaluative process that Porges calls "neuroception."† If one perceives the environment to be safe, one's social engagement system inhibits the more primitive limbic and brain stem structures that control fight or flight. After being moderately startled, you might, for example be calmed by another person—as when a mother says to her child, "It's ok; that was only the wind blowing."

Generally, when threatened or upset, one first looks to others, wishing to engage their faces and voices and to communicate one's feelings

---

* Namely, in the cartilaginous and even jawless fish, in which it regulates metabolic energy conservation.

† Any situation that can increase one's sense of safety has the potential of enlisting the evolutionarily more advanced neural circuits that support the behaviors of the social engagement system.

Simplified Block Diagram of the Polyvagal Components

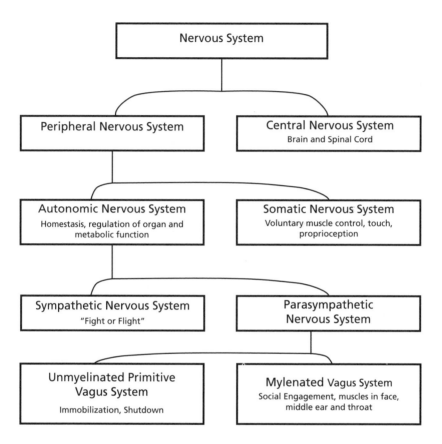

Figure 6.1

to secure collective safety. These are called attachment behavior. Attachment is virtually the only defense young children have, as they cannot usually protect themselves by fighting or fleeing. Attachment for security is a general mammalian and primate survival strategy against predation. By dealing with threat in quantity, the individual is less likely to be "picked off." In addition, if someone in your own group is threatening you, you may first try to "make nice" before resorting to fighting or fleeing.

However, when "pro-social" behaviors do not resolve the threatening situation, a less evolved system is engaged. We mobilize our fight-or-

Phylogenetic Hierarchy of Response Strategies

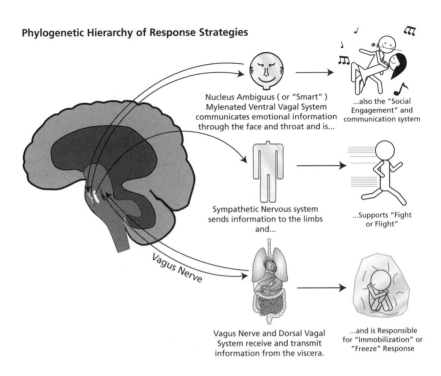

Nucleus Ambiguus (or "Smart")
Mylenated Ventral Vagal System
communicates emotional information
through the face and throat and is...

...also the "Social
Engagement" and
communication system

Sympathetic Nervous system
sends information to the limbs
and...

...Supports "Fight
or Flight"

Vagus Nerve

Vagus Nerve and Dorsal Vagal
System receive and transmit
information from the viscera.

...and is Responsible
for "Immobilization" or
"Freeze" Response

Figure 6.2a This figure shows which part of the body is affected by each of the evolutionary subsystems.

flight response. Finally, in this "hierarchy of default"—when neither of
the more recently acquired systems (social engagement or fight/flight)
resolves the situation, or when death appears imminent—the last-ditch
system is engaged. This most primitive system, which governs *immobility, shutdown and dissociation*, takes over and hijacks all survival efforts.*

---

* For a thorough discussion of the structure and complexities of dissociation, the
reader is referred to the following comprehensive article: van der Hart, O., Nijenhuis, E., Steele, K., & Brown, D. (2004). Trauma-Related Dissociation: Conceptual Clarity Lost and Found. *Australian and New Zealand Journal of Psychiatry*,
38, 906–914. These authors define dissociation, contextually, thus: "Dissociation
in trauma entails a division of an individual's personality, that is, of the dynamic,
biopsychosocial system as a whole that determines his or her characteristic mental and behavioral actions. This division of personality constitutes a core feature
of trauma. It evolves when the individual lacks the capacity to integrate adverse
experiences in part or in full, can support adaptation in this context, but commonly
also implies adaptive limitations. The division involves two or more insufficiently
integrated dynamic but excessively stable subsystems."

The concept of *default hierarchies*—first described by the preeminent neurologist of the later nineteenth century, Hughlings Jackson[60]—remains a fundamental principle of neurology* and is a primary assumption in Porges's theory. Basically, Jackson observed that when the brain is injured or stressed, it reverts to a less refined, evolutionarily more primitive level of functioning. If there is subsequent recovery, this regression will reverse, returning the individual to the more refined functions. This is an example of "bottom-up processing," so important in trauma therapy.

Evolutionary Roots

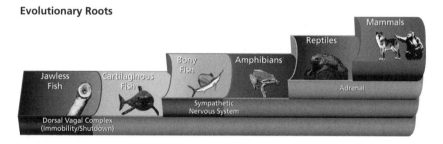

Figure 6.2b This shows the neural control of the three phylogenetic systems: primitive vagus, sympathetic/adrenal and "smart" (mammalian) vagus.

The more primitive the operative system, the more power it has to take over the overall function of the organism. It does this by inhibiting the more recent and more refined neurological subsystems, effectively preventing them from functioning. In particular, the immobilization system all but completely suppresses the social engagement/attachment system. When you are "scared to death," you have few resources left to orchestrate the complex behaviors that mediate attachment and calming; social engagement is essentially hijacked. The sympathetic nervous system also blocks the social engagement system, but not as completely as does the immobilization system (the most primitive of the three defenses).

---

* Jacksonian dissolution is, essentially, the precursor of Paul McLean's triune brain theory. See McLean's *The Triune Brain in Evolution: Role in Paleocerebral Functions* (New York: Springer, 1990).

Polyvagal Theory: Phylogenetic Stages of Nervous Control

Stages	Autonomic Nervous System Component	Behavioral Functions	Lower Motor Neurons
III	Myelinated Vagus	• social communication • self-soothing • calming • inhibit sympathetic adrenal influences	Nucleus Ambiguus
II	Sympathetic Adrenal System	Mobilization (active avoidance)	Spinal Cord
I	Unmyelinated Vagus	Immobilization (death feigning, passive avoidance)	Dorsal Motor Nucleus of the Vagus

From Stephen Porges, PhD

Figure 6.2c This summarizes the phylogenetic stages of the sympathetic and poly-vagal systems.

Immobility and hyperarousal are, as I have explained, organismic responses to threat and prolonged stress. When they are *operative*, danger (in the case of fight or flight) and doom (with immobility) are what an individual perceives—regardless of the reality of the external situation. The human nervous system does not readily discriminate between a potential source of danger in the environment, such as an abruptly moving shadow, or distress about a situation long past.* Where the distress is generated internally (by muscles and viscera), one experiences an obsessive pressure to locate the source of threat or (when that's not possible) to manufacture one as a way of explaining to oneself that there is an identifiable source of threat.

Highly traumatized and chronically neglected or abused individuals are dominated by the immobilization/shutdown system. On the other hand, acutely traumatized people (often by a single recent event and without a history of repeated trauma, neglect or abuse) are generally dominated by the sympathetic fight/flight system. They tend to suffer from flashbacks and racing hearts, while the chronically traumatized

---

* It is most probable that sensory afferents, both from the external senses (e.g., sight and sound) and from the interior of the body (from muscles, viscera and joints), converge in the thalamus at the uppermost portion of the brain stem and, from there, proceed to the insula and cingulate cortex.

Polyvagal Theory: Emergent "Emotion" Subsystems

	Ventral Vagal System	Sympathetic Nervous System	Dorsal Vagal System
Heart Rate	+ / −	+	−
Bronchi	+ / −	+	−
Gastrointestinal		−	+
Vasodilation		+	
Sweat		+	
Adrenal		+	
Tears	+ / −		

From Stephen Porges, PhD

Figure 6.2d This shows the effect the phylogenetic systems have in either increasing (+ sign) or decreasing (- sign) the activity of the various organ systems.

individuals generally show no change or even a decrease in heart rate. These sufferers tend to be plagued with dissociative symptoms, including frequent spacyness, unreality, depersonalization, and various somatic and health complaints. Somatic symptoms include gastrointestinal problems, migraines, some forms of asthma, persistent pain, chronic fatigue, and general disengagement from life.

In some exciting research, the brain activity of people suffering from posttraumatic stress disorder (PTSD) was recorded by functional magnetic resonance imaging (fMRI) while they were read a "traumatic script," which was a graphic and detailed description of someone's serious trauma (such as an accident or rape).[61] The fMRI, scanning the location and the intensity of brain activity, portrayed them as a rainbow of colors.* So, for example, blue (cold) colors indicated a relative reduction in brain activity, while red (hot) colors might indicate an increase. The distress of the volunteers was intensified by the fact that their heads were immobilized, confined in a noisy clanging metal basket. In these studies, at least 30% of the subjects exhibited a decrease in activity of the insula and the cingulate cortex. The PTSD of these volunteers was characterized by dissociation and (vagal) immobility. On the other hand, about 70% of the subjects studied suffered primarily

---

* While brain maps are useful, these are somewhat artificial situations, as fMRIs are more like static snapshots of dynamic brain circuitries.

from the simpler symptoms of sympathetic hyperarousal and showed a dramatic increase in the activity of these same areas.[62] The insula and the cingulate are the parts of the brain that receive sensory information from receptors inside the body (interoception) and form the basis of what we feel and know as our very identity.[63] Underactivity portrays dissociation, while overactivity is associated with sympathetic arousal.

In my long clinical experience, I found that many (perhaps even a majority of) persons exhibit some symptoms of both systems. The expression of symptoms appears to depend on a variety of factors, including the type and severity of a person's trauma, the age at which it occurred, and which traumatic patterns and content were activated during treatment. There are also most likely constitutional and gender factors at play as well. In addition, these symptom constellations tend to change over time and even within a single session.* Most important, treatment must be approached differently according to which of these three systems is activated during sessions and which lie dormant.

To effectively guide the processes of healing and transformation in their clients, therapists must be able to perceive and track the physiological footprints and expressions of these organismic systems. Since each of the hierarchical polyvagal systems has its own unique pattern of autonomic and muscular expressions, therapists need to perceive these indicators—skin color, breathing, postural signs and facial expressions—in order to determine the stage (immobilization, hyperarousal or social engagement) their clients are in and when they are transitioning to another.

As we saw with Nancy in Chapter 2, a patient can undergo a wild roller-coaster ride between the three evolutionary subsystems, which demand parallel changes in strategy.† When, for example, the individual

---

* Remember that because fMRIs are fixed images, they would not be able to pick up such dynamic changes.

† To make matters more complex, one often observes indications of concurrent combinations of sympathetic arousal and parasympathetic (vagal immobility) activation. This occurs particularly at high-stress and transition points. Concomitant indicators include low heart rate (vagal/parasympathetic) along with cold hands (sympathetic).

is in sympathetic hyperarousal, the therapist can observe a tightening of the muscles in the front of the neck (particularly the anterior scalenes, the sternocleidomastoids and the upper shoulder muscles), a stiffened posture, a general jumpiness, darting eyes, an increase in heart rate (which can be seen in the carotid artery in the front of the neck), dilation (widening) of the pupils, choppy rapid breathing and coldness in the hands, which may appear bluish particularly at the finger tips, as well as pale skin and cold sweat in the hands and forehead. On the other hand, a person going into shutdown often collapses (as though slumping in the diaphragm) and has fixed or spaced-out eyes, markedly reduced breathing, an abrupt slowing and feebleness of heart rate, and a constriction of the pupils. In addition, the skin often turns a pasty, sickly white or even gray. And, finally, the person who is socially engaged has a resting heart rate in the low to mid-seventies, relaxed full breathing, pleasantly warm hands and a mild to moderate pupil aperture. Therapists are rarely trained to make such observations (though they can get a little coaching from watching episodes of the TV series *Lie to Me*).

Of the three primary instinctual defense systems, the immobility state is controlled by the most primitive of the physiological subsystems. This neural system (mediated by the unmyelinated portion of the vagus nerve) controls energy conservation and is triggered only when a person perceives that death is imminent[64]—whether from outside, in the form of a mortal threat, or when the threat originates internally, as from illness or serious injury.* Both of these challenges require that one hold still and conserve one's vital energy. When this most archaic system dominates, one does not move; one barely breathes; one's voice is choked off; and one is too scared to cry. One remains motionless in preparation for either death or cellular restitution.

This last-ditch immobilization system is meant to function *acutely and only for brief periods*. When chronically activated, humans become trapped in the gray limbo of nonexistence, where one is neither *really* living nor *actually* dying. A therapist's first job in reaching such

---

* It can also be evoked by intense and unremitting stress.

shut-down clients is to help them mobilize their energy: to help them, first, to become aware of their physiological paralysis and shutdown in a way that normalizes it, and to shift toward (sympathetic) mobilization. The next step is to gently guide a client through the sudden defensive/self-protective activation that underlies the sympathetic state and back to equilibrium, to the here-and-now and a reengagement in life.

Generally, as a client begins to exit the freeze state, the second most primitive system (sympathetic arousal) engages in preparation for fight or flight. Recall how Nancy went from sympathetic arousal (her heart rate shooting up wildly) to helpless terror and then abruptly to shutdown (her heart rate dropping precipitately), and then finally to mobilization and discharge when she activated her running muscles and escaped from the image of the tiger. The important therapeutic task in the sympathetic/mobilization phase is to ensure that a client *contains* these intense arousal sensations without becoming overwhelmed (I described this process in Chapter 5). In this way, they are experienced as intense but manageable waves of energy, as well as sensations associated with aggression and self-protection. These sensory experiences include vibration, tingling, and waves of heat and cold (I described both of these phenomena in Chapter 1 and in my report on Nancy in Chapter 2).

When one is able to ride the sometimes bucking bronco of one's arousal sensations through, and begin to befriend them in a slow and steady way, one is gradually able to discharge the energy that had been channeled into hyperarousal symptoms. This initial stage and foundational piece of the self-regulation pie, and the basic ingredient for restoring equilibrium, is what brought both Nancy and me out of limbo and back to life. Only after this point of intervention does the social engagement system, the third evolutionary subsystem, begin to come back online. An individual who has been able to move out of immobility, and then through sympathetic arousal, begins to experience a restorative and deepening calm. Along with these sensations of OK-ness and goodness, an urge, even a hunger, for face-to-face contact emerges.* Because

---

* The social engagement system controls the voice, ear and facial muscles, which are all used together in nuanced communication.

that yearning may have been painfully unmet during critical periods of infancy, childhood and adolescence (or may have been associated with shame, invasion and abuse), many traumatized individuals also need particular guidance to negotiate this intimacy barrier. This therapeutic guidance can occur only when it becomes physiologically possible to access the social engagement system—that is, when the nervous system is no longer hijacked by the immobilization and the hyperarousal systems.

The intentional use of a mental or physical health practitioner's own intact heartfelt human expression can be profoundly therapeutic. In spite of the raw dominance of the vagal immobilization and sympathetic arousal systems in suppressing social engagement, the power of human contact to help change another's internal physiological state (through face-to-face engagement and appropriate touch) should not be underestimated. Thus, as I discussed in Chapter 1, the pediatrician with the kindly face who sat by my side after my auto accident gave me the glimmer of hope I needed at that exact moment in order to go on.

The gentle power of the human face to soothe the "savage beast" is portrayed in a film with the revealing title *Cast Away*. Tom Hanks plays the lead character, Chuck Noland, who is marooned on a remote, uninhabited island as the sole survivor of an airplane crash. Also washed ashore is some of the plane's cargo, which includes a white volleyball printed with the Wilson brand name. He aptly names the ball "Wilson" and offhandedly adopts it as his mascot.* To his surprise, it begins to take on a life of its own, becoming the confidant for Noland's innermost thoughts. One day, in a fit of impotent rage, Noland throws the ball into the sea, but then—realizing how deeply he has become attached to Wilson—he dives in to retrieve it. Back on the beach, he affectionately draws childlike facial features[65] (eyes, mouth and nose) on the round volleyball.† Wilson now becomes his most intimate companion, sharing

---

* Screenwriter William Broyles Jr. actually spent a full week marooned on a desert island, and many aspects of the 2000 film were informed by his firsthand experiences.

† The power of simple contours representative of the human face may trace back to an innate pattern recognition that is already functioning just after birth. A number of clever experiments have been devised, all showing that the newborn is drawn preferentially to simple (curving) contours and not attracted, for example, to angular shapes.

his troubled thoughts, deepest yearnings and anguished feelings of loneliness and despair, as well as his joyful triumphs. Noland's bonding with Wilson is eerily reminiscent of the ethologist Konrad Lorenz's orphan ducklings and their powerful attachment (imprinting) to a white ball after their mother was removed from their life shortly after their hatching.[66] Once they were permanently bonded to the ball as their surrogate mother, they preferred it even to a live, soft, feathery mother duck.

Finally, Hanks's character realizes that the island is apparently outside of any shipping lanes and that he will never be rescued if he remains on it. In his ill-fated attempt to leave on a raft he has made, Wilson is swept away during a fierce storm, and Hanks is inconsolable in his grief.

Face-to-face, soul-to-soul contact is a buffer against the raging seas of inner turmoil. It is what helps you calm any emotional turbulence. So, in spite of the vast primal power of the immobilizing and hyper-arousal systems, therapists should recognize the power of facial recognition and social engagement in calming their clients, and in meeting people's deepest emotional needs and motivating many behaviors, both conscious and unconscious. Lest I leave you in the lurch, Noland, at death's door, is finally rescued. Upon returning home he takes all of the surviving packages and, traveling across the country, delivers them to their rightful owners. Yes, that's right: face-to-face.

Deprived of face contact (and even a person who is blind from birth uses his or her hands to "see" other faces), we are (like Hanks's character) cast away, adrift from our deepest needs and sense of purpose in life. Most of us would go insane without some kind of face-to-face contact. Along with facial recognition, the sound, intonation and rhythm of the human voice (prosody) have an equally calming effect. Even with clients who cannot tolerate face-to-face contact, the sound of the therapist's voice—like the mother's cooing to her infant—can be deeply soothing and enveloping.

In a revealing commentary, Dr. Horvitz, a leading computer scientist, recently demonstrated his voice-based system, which asks patients about their symptoms and responds with empathy.[67] When a mother said that her child was having diarrhea, the animated *face* on the screen said, in a supportive tone, "Oh, no; sorry to hear that." This simple acknowledgment put the woman at ease and helped her to interact with the program in a secure and empowered manner. One physician told Horvitz that "it was wonderful that the system responded to human emotion ... I have no time for that." Perhaps this computer system is the equivalent of Chuck Noland's volleyball. Its programmed "empathy" was certainly helpful but a meager substitute for the real thing. It is a depressing commentary on the growing alienation of our postmodern, twenty-four-hour texting culture. While so many of our young keep in touch with dozens of people every hour in cyber-relationships, authentic face-to-face engagement is clearly on an apocalyptic wane. How sad and disturbing that the physician believed he didn't have the minuscule time for such basic and salutary human communication— contact that would help humanize them both. If practiced regularly, it might even help both patient and physician stave off Alzheimer's or other forms of dementia.[68]

Why Therapy Fails

Many traumatized individuals, and especially those who have been chronically traumatized, live in a world with little or no emotional support, making them even more vulnerable. After a devastating event— be it violence, rape, surgery, war or an automobile accident—or in the aftermath of a childhood of protracted neglect and abuse, traumatized individuals, even those who share a residence with a friend, family member or intimate partner, tend to isolate themselves. Alternatively, they cling desperately to other people in the hope that they will somehow help and protect them. Either way, they are bereft of the real intimacy— the salubrious climate of belonging—that we all crave and need in order to thrive. Traumatized individuals are, at the same time, terrified of intimacy and shun it. So either way, avoidant or clinging, they are unable to maintain the balanced, stable and nurturing affiliations we all need, the egalitarian bond characterized by the Jewish theologian Martin Buber as the "I-thou" relationship.[69]

When their loneliness becomes too stark, traumatically disconnected individuals may seek increasingly more unrealistic (and sometimes dangerous) "hook-ups." They see each new relationship possibility (or impossibility) as providing the caring protection that will calm their inner anxieties and buoy up their fragile sense of self. Having had a neglectful or abusive childhood predisposes them to chaotic relationships. These individuals continue to look for love "in all the wrong places"—a folly the song reminds us of. Even when one's idealized (fantasy) rescuers become abusive, one seems oblivious to the early signs of that abuse and becomes increasingly ensnared in a damaging liaison precisely because it is so familiar or "like family."

Correcting such maladaptive patterns is the bane of many trauma therapists, who look on helplessly as their clients are repeatedly triggered and seduced into self-destructive affairs, reenacting their original trauma. Many therapists hold to the hope that *they* can somehow provide their clients with the positive, affirmative (I-thou) relationship that will assuage a client's fractured psyche and restore his or her wounded soul to wholeness. However, what often happens is that a client's dependency upon the therapist escalates and gets entirely out of hand–as shown so conspicuously in the gem of a film *What About Bob?* (1991). In it, Bob, the "abandoned" client, is so dependent, and his feelings about being left alone are so intolerable, that he tracks down his psychiatrist like a sleuth and follows him on a family vacation on Cape Cod.

On the other hand, if a client experiences the therapist, who is supposed to be a healer, as a "proxy" abuser, the therapy often culminates in the client's profound disappointment and/or seething rage. Traumatized individuals are not made whole through the therapeutic relationship alone. Even with the best of intentions, and highly developed empathic skills, a therapist often misses the mark here. The polyvagal theory and the Jacksonian principle of dissolution help us to understand why and how this happens.[70] When the traumatized person is locked in either the immobilization response or the sympathetic arousal system, the social engagement function is physiologically compromised; the former, in particular, both inhibits sympathetic arousal and can almost completely suppress the social engagement system.

A person whose social engagement system is suppressed has trouble reading positive emotions from other people's faces and postures and also has little capacity to feel his or her own nuanced positive affects. Thus, one finds it difficult to know if that other person can be trusted (whether he or she is threatening or safe, friend or foe). According to the polyvagal theory, being in shutdown (immobility/freezing/or collapse) or in sympathetic/hyperactivation (fight or flight) greatly diminishes a person's capacity to receive and incorporate empathy and support. The facility for safety and goodness is nowhere to be found. To the degree that traumatized people are dominated by shutdown (the immobility system), they are physiologically unavailable for face-to-face contact and the calming sharing of feelings and attachment. And while immobilization is rarely complete (as it is, for example, in catatonic schizophrenia), its ability to suppress life and one's capacity for social engagement is extreme. A young man describes his dark plight as follows: "I feel all alone in the universe, dissociated from the human race … I am not sure that I even exist … Everyone is part of the flower; I am still part of the root."* It is not surprising that, try as they may, many traumatized clients are little able to receive support and caring from their well-intentioned therapists—not because they don't want to, but because they are stuck in the primitive root of immobility with its greatly reduced capability for reading faces, bodies and emotions; they become cut off from the human race.

For this reason such a client may not be readily calmed by the positive feelings and attitude of empathy the therapist provides, and may even perceive the therapist as a potential threat. Unable to recognize caring feelings in the face and posture of others, such a client finds it extremely difficult to feel that anyone is safe or can really be trusted. And when high hopes are placed on the therapist, one small misstep or inadvertent fumble on the latter's part can bring the entire relationship crashing down.

As highly dissociated and shut-down clients involuntarily retreat, they experience additional *self-recrimination and shame*. Tormented by

---

* Indeed, the brain stem's immobilization system is the "root" of the default hierarchy.

this loss of control, they are unable to accept and respond to the warmth and security offered by their therapist and may engage in unproductive transference and "acting out." The inherent disconnect that then occurs often leaves both client and therapist bewildered and frustrated, feeling that they are failing in their respective roles. The client may perceive this breakdown as a devastating confirmation of his or her inadequacy, adding to a lifetime of (many perceived) failures. Therapists may also feel confused, helpless, inadequate and self-reproaching. Such situations, where the two partners are locked against one another, can readily become intractable Gordian knots. These therapeutic cul-de-sacs may eventually result in termination of treatment.

A Way Out

Shut-down and dissociated people are not "in their bodies," being, as we have seen, nearly unable to make real here-and-now contact no matter how hard they try. It is only when they can *first* engage their arousal systems (enough to begin to pull them up, out of immobility and dissociation), and *then discharge that activation*, that it becomes physiologically possible to make contact and receive support. Fortunately, there is a way to escape the immobilization system's domination of the two less primitive systems—a way that healing practitioners must learn to exercise.

This therapeutic solution is supported by Lanius and Hopper's fMRI work mentioned earlier.[71] This compelling research, recording activity in the part of the brain associated with the awareness of bodily states and emotions, makes a clear differentiation between sympathetic arousal and dissociation in traumatized subjects. The brain area associated with awareness of bodily states and emotions is called the right anterior insula and is located in the frontal part of the limbic (emotional) brain, squeezed in directly under the prefrontal cortex—the locus of our most refined consciousness. The research showed that the insula* is strongly

---

* These same brain regions (in the medial temporal lobe) that process memory and emotion, when malfunctioning, contribute to delusions of identity. To people with injury here, their mother looks and sounds exactly as she should, but they have lost the sensation of her presence; she seems somehow unreal.

inhibited during shutdown and dissociation, and it confirmed that these traumatized individuals are unable to feel their bodies, to differentiate their emotions, or even to know who they (or another person) really are.[72] On the other hand, when subjects are in a state of sympathetic hyperarousal, this same area is highly activated. This dramatic *increase* in the activity of the right anterior insula strongly suggests a clear differentiation of little or no body awareness (in immobility/shutdown and dissociation) to a kind of "hyper-sensation" in sympathetic arousal. In addition, the sympathetic state, at least, provides the possibility of coherent awareness, processing and resolution. These data support the crucial steps to trauma resolution outlined in Chapter 5 (Step 5) and further clarify the strategy of helping clients move from shutdown to mobilization while learning to manage their physical (bodily) sensations as they shift into sympathetic arousal.

A related, and seminal, research study was carried out by Bessel van der Kolk.[73] He and his colleagues read a traumatic story to a group of clients and compared two brain regions in each (measured with fMRI). The researchers found that the amygdala, the so-called fear or "smoke detector," lit up with electrical activity; at the same time, a region in the left cerebral cortex, called Broca's area, went dim. The latter is the primary language center—the part of the brain that takes what we are feeling and expresses it with words. That trauma is about wordless terror is also demonstrated in these brain scans. Frequently when traumatized people try to put their feelings into words—as when, for example, one is asked by the therapist to tell about his or her rape—they speak about it as though it had happened to someone else (see the story of Sharon in Chapter 8). Or clients try to speak of their horror, then become frustrated and flooded, incurring more shutdown in Broca's area, and thus enter into a retraumatizing feedback loop of frustration, shutdown and dissociation.

This language barrier in traumatized individuals makes it especially important to work with sensations—the only language that the reptilian brain speaks. Doing so both helps people to move out of shutdown and dissociation and diminishes a client's frustration and flooding when working with traumatic material.

The body must be doing something to keep the insula, the cingulate cortex, and Broca's area online. Even though the capacity for engagement is inhibited by the sympathetic nervous system, it is not thoroughly squelched in the debilitating way it was by the more primitive immobility system. In sympathetic arousal, clients are better able to respond to their therapist's promptings and suggestions, as well as to be more receptive to his or her calming presence. In turn, it is this very receptivity that helps to attenuate the sympathetic arousal. When a client begins to make the breakthrough out of immobility and into sympathetic arousal, the astute therapist seizes this momentary opportunity, first by detecting the client's shift and then by facilitating the awareness of his or her transition. The therapist endeavors to enlarge the client's awareness of what is going on in him- or herself while simultaneously helping the client avoid being overwhelmed by the intense sympathetic arousal. Such guidance helps clients move out of immobility and through complete cycles of activation, discharge/deactivation and equilibrium (steps 7 and 8 in Chapter 5). In this way, the individual learns that what goes up (gets activated) can, and will, come down. *Clients learn to trust that moderate activation unwinds on its own when one doesn't avoid and recoil from it: that is, when one doesn't interfere with the natural course of one's sensations of arousal.* Thus a therapist can seize the day—by giving clients the gift of this bodily experience.

The Brain/Body Connection

Whatever increases, decreases, limits or extends the body's power of action, increases, decreases, limits or extends the mind's power of action. And whatever increases, decreases, limits or extends the mind's power of action, also increases, decreases, limits or extends the body's power of action.

—Spinoza (1632–1677), *Ethics*

Many therapists, realizing how difficult it is to reach highly dissociated and shut-down clients, have developed valuable cognitive and emotional methods to help connect with them.[74] Somatic approaches can also be enormously useful, or even critical, in this healing effort. They help clients move out of immobility, into sympathetic arousal, through mobilization, into discharge of activation and then finally onward to equilibrium, embodiment and social engagement. The following somatically based awareness exercises begin this process by helping individuals move out of shutdown and dissociation.

The first is a simple exercise that clients can do by themselves to help enliven their body-sense and minimize shutdown, dissociation and collapse. By being able to practice in the privacy of their own homes, clients can spare themselves potential embarrassment or shame in their awakening process. This exercise, and those that follow, are meant to be done regularly, over time, for maximum benefit—and therapists should practice the exercises themselves.

For ten minutes or so (a few times a week), take a gentle, pulsating shower in the following way: at a comfortable temperature, expose your body to the pulsing water. Direct your awareness into the region of your body where the rhythmical stimulation is focused. Let your consciousness move to each part of your body. For example, hold the backs of your hands to the shower head, then the palms and wrists, then your head, shoulders, underarms, both sides of your neck, etc. Try to include each part of your body, and pay attention to the sensation in each area, even if it feels blank, numb, or uncomfortable. While you are doing this, say, "This is *my* arm, head, neck," etc. "I welcome you back." You can also do this exercise by gently tapping those same parts of your body with your fingertips. When done regularly over time, this and the following exercises will help reestablish awareness of your body boundary through awakening skin sensations.

A sequel to this shower exercise involves bringing boundary awareness into the muscles. You start by using a hand to grasp and gently squeeze the opposite forearm; then you squeeze the upper arm, the shoulders, neck, thighs, calves, feet, etc. The important element is to be mindful of *how your muscles feel from the inside* as they are being squeezed. You can begin to recognize the rigidity or flaccidity of the tissue as well as its general quality of aliveness. Generally, tight, constricted muscles are associated with the alarm and hypervigilence of the sympathetic arousal system. Flaccid muscles, on the other hand, belie how the body collapses when dominated by the immobilization system. In the case of flaccid muscles, you need to linger and gently hold them, almost as though you were holding a baby. With the practice of gentle, focused touch and resistance exercises, you can learn to bring life back into those muscles as the fragile fibers learn to fire coherently and thus vitalize the organism.

These two exercises are best done regularly, several times per week. As body consciousness grows, so, too, will a more palpable sense of boundary awareness, as well as greater aliveness. For some clients, classes in gentle yoga or martial arts, such as tai chi, aikido or chi gong, can be beneficial in restoring connection to their bodies and defining body boundaries. For these classes to be helpful, it is important that the teacher have some experience in working with traumatized individuals.

Changing the Paradigm

Most psychotherapists work with clients when both are sitting in chairs. Since sitting requires little proprioceptive and kinesthetic information to maintain an erect posture, the body easily becomes absent, disappearing from its owner. Recall the fMRI study of Lanius and Hopper, where dissociated patients showed a great reduction of activity in the parts of the brain (insula and cingulate) that register body sensations. In contrast, a standing position requires one to engage in at least a modicum of interoceptive activity and awareness to maintain one's balance via proprioceptive and kinesthetic integration. Often, this simple change in stance can make the difference between whether or not a client is able to stay present in the body while processing difficult sensations and feelings. Another supportive variant is to invite the client to sit on a suitable-sized gymnastic ball. Since balancing on a ball requires making multiple adjustments to maintain equilibrium, not only does it help one to be in touch with internal sensations due to the feedback from this pliable surface, but in addition, explorations in muscle awareness, grounding, centering, protective reflexes and core strength bring a whole new dimension to developing a body consciousness. Naturally, the therapist has to be sure that the client is present and integrated enough not to fall off the ball and possibly sustain an injury.

The following is another technique to help clients remain conscious of their bodily sensations while at the same time learning how to manage assertion and aggression. First, have your client stand up and face you. It is important to check whether she is comfortable with the distance between the two of you. Next, ask the client to notice what she is aware of as her feet contact the ground. Then encourage her to broaden her perception, moving up through her ankles, calves and thighs. To encourage a sense of groundedness, continue this exercise by proposing a slow and gentle weight shift from one foot to the other. Also, you could suggest that your client think of her feet as suction cups (like the feet of a frog) flexibly rooted in the earth. Next, have the client bring her attention to her hips, spine, neck, and then head. Now have her notice how her shoulders hang from her neck like a tent. Awareness of breathing is evoked as the client is asked to sense her shoulders as they gently rise and fall with each breath. Now bring her attention to her chest and belly; and, using breath, help the client locate the center of gravity in her abdomen. Again have her slowly shift her weight from side to side between her two feet, and then have her add a slight sway from front to back. This type of movement requires a fairly sophisticated proprioceptive ability (joint position) and sense of muscle tension (kinesthesia).* As your client practices this, have her imagine a plumb line from her center down to the floor between her feet. Finally, have her notice how this line moves with her gentle swaying. A client who has developed this centered awareness is ready to move to the position shown in Figure 6.3a.†

---

* Along with the vestibular system, this is how we know where we are in gravity space.

† These figures are taken from *Healing Trauma: A Pioneering Program for Restoring the Wisdom of Your Body* written by Peter Levine and published by Sounds True. Used with permission from Sounds True, www.soundstrue.com.

Figure 6.3a   **Figure 6.3b**
Physical awareness exercise to cultivate the experience of healthy aggression. Hand positioning for evoking healthy aggression (in Figure 6.3a).

The idea, now, is to have the client feel her feet on the ground, feel her center and then push firmly, but gently, into the therapist's hand (see Figure 6.3b). As the therapist, you will offer just enough resistance to allow the client to sense herself pushing out from her center. You will be asking her to feel how the movement seems to originate from her belly and is expressed through her shoulders and into her arms and hands. Continue to check with the client to ascertain whether the resistance feels right—not too much or too little—and whether the distance feels safe enough. Should the client feel unsafe, first ask whether she can indicate where she would like you to stand. Now suggest that she try to notice *where in her body* it feels unsafe or unstable, and then to notice what happens if she brings her attention back to her feet and legs. Ask her to attempt to recapture a sense of the grounding established at the beginning of the exercise. When your client is able to feel a sense of safety, ask her to notice *where in her body* she feels safe now and to describe how she experiences her (often brand-new) sense of self. Repeat this resistance activity several times, having your client push with both hands, until there is a loosening up and developing sense of confidence. The next progression of this exercise involves more of a give and take between the therapist and the client, each of you alternately pushing and receiving the movement. When one's body is able to experience a relaxed sense of strength, one's mind is able to experience a relaxed sense of focused alertness.

The next somatic tool is designed to help posttraumatic stress disorder survivors learn that even when they feel paralyzed, there is a latent active response of running and escaping inside of them. A new experience of this dormant defense contradicts the traumatic encounter with being frozen and trapped (see Figure 6.4). It is essential for the therapist to have a pillow placed on the floor that is firm and thick enough to safely absorb the impact of vigorous running movements if they should occur. Begin by asking the client to run in place from a seated position. Encourage him to gently alternate his legs, lifting and stepping down, as he attends to the way his hips, legs, ankles and feet organize themselves from the inside out. The key element is to have the client stay fully aware of his legs as he makes this movement. In other words, the client needs to remain present to his bodily experience, rather than just mechanically performing or dramatizing the act of running. This is not role-playing, but rather an intentional heightening of kinesthetic and proprioceptive perception, telling a client how his body and brain together are designed to protect him by engaging innate escape movement patterns. Later, when the client brings up traumatic material that involves feeling paralyzed and unable to escape, have him put his story aside and, again, feel his legs. Have him begin to run in place as before in order to incorporate his new empowered awareness. In this way, the direct experiencing of "body wisdom" develops as the muscles discharge their latent energy.

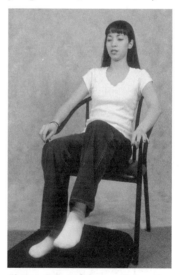

Figure 6.4 Safely practicing the running escape response to counter feeling trapped and helpless. It is important to cultivate the *awareness* of running.

Tummy Talk

It has long been known that the brain can influence our internal organs. When this process goes awry, one becomes the unfortunate bearer of what has been referred to as psychosomatic illness. The principal idea of the *one-way* effect of mind over body evolved as the "psychosomatic paradigm" of the 1930s through 1950s. Today, it remains conventional wisdom, and few doctors deny that an overwrought mind and unsettled emotions affect the human body in the form of "functional" disorders, which include high blood pressure, gastrointestinal symptoms, chronic pain, fibromyalgia and migraines, as well as a multitude of other, so-called idiopathic diseases. In 1872, however, long before the rise of psychosomatic medicine, the amazing Charles Darwin realized that there was a vital *two-way* connectivity between brain and body:

> When the heart is affected it reacts on the brain; and the state of the brain reacts through the pneumo-gastric on the heart; so *under any excitement, there will be much mutual action and reaction between these, the two most important organs in the body.*[75] [italics mine]

The "pneumo-gastric" nerve Darwin speaks of is none other than the vagus nerve described in Porges's polyvagal theory. The primitive (unmyelinated) vagus nerve of the immobilization system connects the brain with most of our internal organs. This enormous nerve is the second largest nerve in our body, comparable in size to the spinal cord. In particular, this nerve largely serves the gastrointestinal system, influencing ingestion, digestion, assimilation and elimination. It also significantly affects the heart and lungs, as Darwin clearly recognized.

Furthermore, embedded within the lining of the gastrointestinal wall itself there is a massive plexus of nerves. This complex network of sensory, motor and interneurons (those nerve cells that connect *between* the sensory and motor neurons) integrates the digestive and eliminative organs so that they function coherently.* This intricate system has about

---

* This diffuse brain lines the entire alimental canal (almost 30 feet from the esophagus to the anus).

the same number of neurons and white matter as does a cat's brain. Because of this complexity, it has sometimes been called the *second* or *enteric brain;* the other three are the reptilian (instinctual), the paleo-mammalian (limbic/emotional) and the primate (enlarged, rational) neo-cortex. The enteric nervous system is our oldest brain, evolving hundreds of millions of years ago. It produces many beneficial hormones, includ-ing *95% of the serotonin in the body,** and thus is a primary natural med-icine factory and warehouse for feel-good hormones.[76]

Amazingly, as much as *90% of the vagus nerve that connects our guts and brains is sensory!* In other words, for every one motor nerve fiber[†] that relays commands from the brain to the gut, nine sensory nerves send information about the state of the viscera to the brain. The sen-sory fibers in the vagus nerve pick up the complex telecommunications going on in the gut and relay them, first up to the (mid) brain stem and then to the thalamus. From there, these signals virtually influence the entire brain, and subliminal "decisions" are made that profoundly influ-ence our actions. Many of our likes and dislikes, our attractions and repulsions, as well as our irrational fears, are the result of these implicit computations in our internal states.

It can be said that humans have *two* brains: one in the gut (the enteric brain) and the "upstairs brain," sitting within the vaulted dome of the cranium. These two brains are in direct communication with each other through the hefty vagus nerve. And if we go with the numbers—nine sensory/afferent nerves to every one motor/efferent nerve—our guts apparently have more to say to our brains (by a ratio of 9:1) than our brains have to say to our guts![‡]

Let's look more deeply at the functions of this massive nerve, which not only connects organs and brain, but functions primarily in the direc-tion of *gut to brain.* Why is it even important for the body to talk to

---

* It should be noted that excess levels of serotonin in the gut also lead to problematic states.

† Motor neurons that act on the viscera are called viscero-motor neurons.

‡ In addition, there are multiple and bidirectional "neuropeptide" systems studied by Candice Pert and others. See Pert et al.'s *Molecules of Emotion: The Science behind Mind-Body Medicine* (New York: Simon and Schuster, 1999).

the brain in the first place? From the perspective of evolution (and the general parsimony of nature), it is unlikely that such a myriad of nerve fibers would be allotted to making bidirectional communication possible if that linkage weren't vitally important.

Most of us have experienced butterflies in our stomach when asked to make a public speech. On the other hand, some people are known for "having gall," while others are quite "bitter" or "bilious." And then too, at times we may have "knots in our guts" and are "twisted up inside."* Or we may be "heavyhearted" or nursing a "heartache." And blessed are the times when we have surrendered to the pure mirth of a spontaneous "belly laugh." Or, again, we may be "openhearted and filled with warmth in our bellies," feeling an inner peace and love for the whole world. On the occasions when we have accomplished notable achievements, our chests may "swell with pride." Such is the variety of poignant messages emanating from our viscera.

When aroused to fight or flight (sympathetic arousal), our guts tighten, and the motility of the gastrointestinal system is inhibited. After all, there is no sense in spending a lot of metabolic energy on digestion when it is best used to speed up the heart's rhythm and to strengthen its contraction, as well as to tense our muscles in readiness for impending action. When we are mortally threatened, or when the threat is internal (say, from the flu or from eating a bacterially infected food), our survival response is to vomit or to expel the contents of our intestines with diarrhea, and then to lie still so as to conserve energy. It seems possible that prey animals also resort to this reaction when a predator suddenly springs on it from within striking distance. In this case, the violent expulsion of the animal's intestinal contents may actually lighten its weight and give it a better chance of escaping. This fraction-of-a-second advantage could mean the difference between life or death. I have seen this happen on several occasions when a mountain lion has

---

* It is interesting that many autistic children have GI abnormalities. See Hadhazy, A. (2010). Think Twice: How the Gut's "Second Brain" Influences Mood and Well-Being. *Scientific American*, February 12.

lunged at a group of deer drinking from the North St. Vrain River, which runs behind my Colorado home.

The powerful effects of both the sympathetic and the vagus nerves on the viscera serve critical survival functions. The activation of these two systems is meant to be brief in response to acute emergency. When they become stuck (in either sympathetic overdrive or vagal overactivity), the survival function is drastically subverted: one may end up suffering from a painfully knotted gut, as in the case of persistent sympathetic hyperarousal, or be tormented by spasms of twisting cramps and disruptive diarrhea in chronic vagal hyperactivity.* When equilibrium is not restored, these states become chronic, and illness ensues.

Together, these complex systems (the vagus and the enteric plexus), not unlike a great marriage, put gut and brain in either blissful harmony or in dreadful unending battle. When there is a coherent balance between the two, the hedonic (concerned with pleasure or pleasurable sensations) fulcrum is tipped toward heaven; when the regulatory relationship is disordered, the gates of hell are opened wide like the great maw of misery.

The Medium Is the Message

Our nervous system assesses threat in two basic ways. First of all, we use our external sense organs to discern and evaluate threat from salient features in the environment. So, for example, a sudden shadow alerts one to a potential risk, while the large looming contours of a bear or the sleek, crouching silhouette of a mountain lion let one know that one is in grave danger. *We also assess threat directly from the state of our viscera and our muscles—our internal sense organs.* If our muscles are tense, we unconsciously interpret these tensions as foretelling the existence of danger, even when none actually exists. Tight muscles in the neck and shoulders may, for example, signal to the brain that you are

---

* As previously mentioned, many people experience a combination of sympathetic and vagal hyperactivity—a fact that makes the symptom profile more complex. For example, in the case of patients diagnosed with irritable bowel syndrome (IBS) or "spastic colon," there is often a vacillation between constipation and diarrhea.

likely to be hit. Tense legs, along with furtive eyes, may tell you that you need to run and escape, and taut arms may signal that you're ready to strike out. We suffer even greater distress when our guts are persistently overstimulated by the vagus nerve. If we are nauseated, twisted in our guts, feel our muscles collapsing, and lack in energy, we feel helpless and hopeless—even though there is no actual decimating threat. In other words, *the churning itself signals grave threat and dread to the brain*, even when nothing is currently wrong—at least not externally.

Our muscular and visceral states color both our perceptions and our evaluation of the intentions of others. While we may believe that certain individuals will do us no harm, we still feel endangered.* Even something as neutral as a room, a street corner or a sunlit meadow may seem ominous. Conversely, experiencing relaxed (and well-toned) muscles and belly can signal safety even when a person's daily affairs are in turmoil. As an illustration of this point, I overheard a person saying after receiving a full-body massage, "The world's not such a bad place after all. I feel terrific." While a wonderful massage is a great way to give a person a new way of feeling good, it will take a major shift in the ongoing dialogue on the brain-gut highway to free up more than ephemerally the congestion caused by chronic stress and trauma.

The intense visceral reactions associated with threat are meant to be acute and temporary. Once the danger has passed, these reactions (be it inhibition of gastric motility by the sympathetic nervous system or violent overstimulation of motility by the primitive vagus nerve) need to cease in order to return the organism to equilibrium, fresh and flowing in the here and now. When balance is not restored, one is left in acute and, eventually, chronic distress.

In order to prevent trauma as well as to reverse it when it has already occurred, individuals must become aware of their visceral sensations.†

---

* Therapists may be taken aback when certain clients perceive them as a threat or as either a hero or a villain.

† Many medical texts still teach that no sensations or feelings arise from the guts. The only thing we feel in our guts, they say, is pain—and then only when the pain is referred to areas like the lower back.

In addition, our gut sensations are vital in orchestrating positive feelings of aliveness and in directing our lives. They are also the source of much of our intuition. As we can learn from traditional, shamanic and spiritual practices, embraced for thousands of years throughout the world, feelings of goodness are embodied directly as visceral sensations. When we ignore our "gut instincts," it is at our own great expense, if not peril.

In states of immobilization and shutdown, the sensations in our guts are so dreadful that we routinely block them from consciousness. But this strategy of "absence" only maintains the status quo at best, keeping both brain and body hopelessly stuck in an information traffic jam. It is a recipe for trauma and a diminished life, a cardboard existence. The following is another simple exit strategy for undoing the brain/gut knot.

An Effective Sound: "Voo"

The first seat of our primal consciousness
is the solar plexus, the great nerve-centre
situated behind the stomach. From this
centre we are first dynamically conscious.

—D. H. Lawrence, *Psychoanalysis and the Unconscious*

Along with multitudes of other people, I have experienced various chanting and ancient "sounding" practices that facilitate healing and help open the "doors of perception." Singing and chanting are used in religious and spiritual ceremonies among every culture for "lightening the load" of earthly existence. When you open up to chant or sing in deep, resonant lower belly tones, you also open up your chest (heart and lungs), mouth and throat, pleasurably stimulating the many serpentine branches of the vagus nerve.*

Certain Tibetan chants have been used successfully for thousands of years. In my practice, I use a sound borrowed (with certain modifications)

---

* I recommend the wonderful Swedish film *As It Is in Heaven* (2004).

from some of these chants. This sound opens, expands and vibrates the viscera in a way that provides new signals to a shut-down or overstimulated nervous system. The practice is quite simple: make an extended "voooo ..." (soft *o*, like *ou* in *you*) sound, focusing on the vibrations stimulated in the belly as you complete a full expiration of breath.

In introducing the "voo" sound to my clients, I often ask them to imagine a foghorn in a foggy bay sounding through the murk to alert ship captains that they are nearing land, and to guide them *safely home*. This image works on different levels. First of all, the image of the fog represents the fog of numbness and dissociation. The foghorn represents the beacon that guides the lost boat (soul) back to safe harbor, to home in breath and belly. This image also inspires the client to take on the hero role of protecting sailors and passengers from imminent danger, as well as giving him or her permission to be silly and thereby play. Most important are the image's physiological effects. The sound vibrations of "voo" enliven sensations from the viscera, while the full expiration of the breath produces the optimal balance of oxygen and carbon dioxide.[77]

Begin the exercise by finding a comfortable place to sit. Then slowly inhale, pause momentarily, and then, on the out breath, gently utter "voo," sustaining the sound throughout the entire exhalation. Vibrate the sound as though it were coming from your belly. At the end of the breath, pause briefly and *allow* the next breath to slowly fill your belly and chest. When the in breath feels complete, pause, and again make the "voo" sound on the exhalation until *it* feels complete. It is important to let sound and breath *expire fully*, and then to pause and *wait* for the next breath to enter (be taken) *on its own*, when *it* is ready. Repeat this exercise several times and then rest. Next, focus your attention on your body, primarily on your abdomen, the internal cavity that holds your organs.

This "sounding," with its emphasis on both waiting and allowing, has multiple functions. First of all, directing the sound into the belly evokes a particular type of sensation while keeping the observing ego "online." People often report various qualities of vibration and tingling, as well as changes in temperature–generally from cold (or hot) to cool and warm. These sensations are generally pleasant (with a little practice, at least). Most important, they *contradict* the twisted, agonizing, nauseating, deadening, numbing sensations associated with the immobility state. It seems likely that the change in the *afferent* messages (from organs to brain) allows the 90% of the sensory (ascending) vagus nerve to powerfully influence the 10% going from brain to organs so as to restore balance.* Porges concurs on this key regulatory system: "The afferent feedback from the viscera provides a major mediator of the accessibility of prosocial circuits associated with social engagement behaviors."[78]

The salubrious sensations evoked by the combination of breathing and the sound's reverberations allow the individual to contact an inner security and trust along with some sense of orientation in the here and now. They also facilitate a degree of face-to-face, eye-to-eye, voice-to-ear, I-thou contact and thus make it possible for the client to negotiate a small opening into the "social engagement system," which is then able to help him or her to develop a robust resilience through increasing cycles of sympathetic arousal (charge) and discharge and thereby to deepen regulation and relaxation. Charles Darwin, I can happily imagine, would have knowingly winked his approval at the "voo" clinical application of his astute, anatomical and physiological 1872 observation.

Another exercise can provide clients with a way to manage and regulate distressing arousal symptoms. This "self-help" technique is taken from a system of "energy flows" called Jin Shin Jyutsu.† Figures 6.5A–D demonstrate a simple Jin Shin sequence to help clients learn to regulate their arousal and deepen their relaxation.[79] Again, I suggest that therapists experiment first on themselves before teaching these exercises to their clients. Encourage your clients to practice at home, first

---

* See the next section for a more detailed explanation of how feedback influences core regulation.

† Jin Shin Jyutsu®, an ancient healing system for "harmonizing the life energy in the body," has been passed down from generation to generation by apprenticeship. The art fell into obscurity until the early 1900s when it was dramatically revived by Master Jiro Murai in Japan and then brought to the United States by Mary Burmeister. In 1979, I had the privilege of meeting this vital octogenarian in Scottsdale, Arizona, where she continued to practice and teach well into her eighties.

Jin Shin Jyutsu Energy Flows

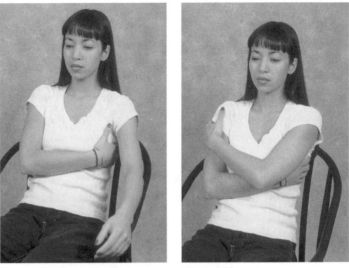

Figure 6.5a   **Figure 6.5b**

These figures show the arm/hand positioning for containing arousal and promoting self-compassion.

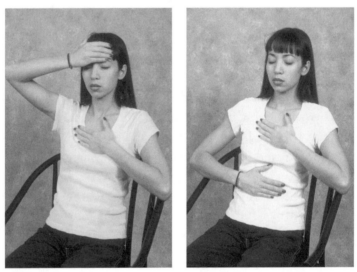

Figure 6.5c   **Figure 6.5d**

These figures show the the arm/hand positioning that help to establish energy flows between upper and lower body segments. These exercises promote relaxation.

at times when they are not upset and then when they are. Each position can be maintained for two to ten minutes. What the client looks for is a sensation of either energy flow or relaxation.

A Note on Feedback and Core Regulation

In 1932 Sir Charles Sherrington received the Nobel Prize in Physiology or Medicine for showing that the nervous system is made up of a combination of excitatory and inhibitory nerve cells. It is the balance of these two neural systems that allows us to move our limbs in a smooth, coordinated, accurate way. Without inhibition, our movements would be wildly spastic and uncoordinated. While Sherrington's work was primarily on the sensory/motor system (at the level of the spinal cord), the balancing of excitatory systems by inhibitory ones occurs throughout the nervous system and is considered a fundamental principle of it. This organization is the basic architecture of *self-regulation*. Let us look at an analogy from ordinary life:

In its simplest form (mechano-electric) regulation is what allows our house temperature to be kept in a comfortable range, regardless of the outside temperature. So let us say that on a winter's day we would like to keep the indoor temperature at a comfortable 70 degrees. To do this, we would set the thermostat at the desired temperature. This turns on the furnace. However, the furnace is not turned on all the time. If it were, the temperature would continue to rise, and we would have to open windows to bring the temperature down. But then, as the temperature dropped, we would have to close the window. The reason that we don't have to do all of this is that the temperature is controlled by a *negative feedback loop*. Like Sherrington's inhibitory system, the temperature rises, say to 72 degrees, and the furnace shuts off until the temperature drops to 68 degrees, at which time the furnace turns on again. This brings the temperature back to 72 degrees, giving us an average temperature of 70 degrees. With the aid of a light cotton sweater, a relatively comfortable environment is reached. If, on the other hand, the furnace were to turn *up* as the temperature rose, we would have rather quite an uncomfortable situation. Not only would we have to take our pullover off, but we would soon be going around the house stark naked. In the first example we have a smoothly regulated temperature mediated by a negative feedback system (with positive consequences). In the second situation, we have a *positive feedback loop* with negative consequences; our house becomes a sauna and sweat lodge.

In distress and trauma, I believe that a *positive feedback loop*, with *extremely negative consequences*, is set up. Indeed, most of us recognize that primal negative emotions readily turn into self-reinforcing, runaway positive feedback loops. Fear and anger can readily explode into terror and rage. Here trauma is the ouroboros, the serpent swallowing its own tail, eternally re-creating itself.

In the reciprocal enervation discovered by Sherrington, the nervous system operates primarily as a negative feedback system much like—but infinitely more complicated than—a house thermostat. Self-regulation of the complex nervous system exhibits what are called *emergent properties*, which are often somewhat unpredictable and rich in nuance. They frequently lead to finding new and creative solutions and are cherished when they happen in life and in psychotherapy. So while the nervous system operates under the principle of self-regulation, the psyche operates under the emergent properties of *creative self-regulation*. We might say that as the nervous system self-regulates, the psyche engages with these emergent properties: that is, to creative self-regulation. The relationship between the viscera and the brain is a complex self-regulating system. The richness of creative emergent properties allows these "sounding" and breathing techniques (like the "voo" sound) to initiate change throughout the nervous system. In a situation of inescapable and mortal threat, the brain stem, or reptilian brain, sends intense signals to the viscera, causing some of them to go into hyperdrive (as with the gastrointestinal system) and others to constrict and close down, as with the bronchioles of the lungs or the beating of the heart. In the first instance (hyperdrive), we get symptoms like butterflies, knots in the gut or rumbling, uncontrollable diarrhea. With the lungs, we have feelings of tightness and suffocation, which, when chronic, can lead to the symptoms of asthma. Likewise, the effect of the primitive vagus on the heart is to decrease the beat to a level so low that it can actually lead to (voodoo) death.[80] Because these sensations feel so dreadful, they themselves become the source of threat. So rather than coming from outside, the threat now emanates from deep within one's bowels, lungs, heart and other organs and can cause the exact same effect upon the viscera that the original threat evoked. This situation is the unfortunate setup for a positive feedback loop with disastrous negative consequences. In addition, because traumatized individuals are experiencing (intense) threat signals, they *project* this inner turmoil outward and thus perceive the world as being responsible for their inner distress—and so remove themselves from both the real source of the problem and its potential solution. This dynamic also wreaks havoc not only on the body but also on relationships.

The "voo" sound—by, first of all, focusing awareness upon the inner locus of the real problem—allows one to begin to change one's experience from dreadful to pleasant and thus moves the situation from being a positive feedback loop (with negative consequences) to being a negative feedback loop, which helps restore homeostatic balance, equilibrium and, hence, feelings of goodness. This shift, even if only brief, opens an opportunity for the client to experience the warmth of the supportive therapeutic relationship, which, in turn, also provides a buffer against the rush of (sympathetic) hyperarousal soon to follow. Then the self-regulatory system (negative feedback loop) brings down arousal, allowing for much deeper, more stable and enduring sensations of goodness, as well as a more resilient nervous system and psyche.

CHAPTER 7

Mapping the Body, Mending the Mind
SIBAM

The Body is the Map of the Mind.
—J. D. Landis, *Solitude*

The Body as Instrument of the Self

Physical sensations are the very foundation of human consciousness. As the biological creatures that we are, our bodies are designed to respond in an ever-changing, challenging and often dangerous world. A new baby must gradually learn to discern the meaning of the sensations that his or her body is experiencing. Babies learn about their body/mind self through action and interaction with their parents and with the environment that surrounds them. Infants live within a sea of sensations. Fortunately most parents catch on fairly quickly to their newborn's code. They know when she is signaling the various and unmistakable sensations of hunger, pain, anger and tiredness because babies instinctively communicate those internal states, inducing their caregivers to provide relief. It is a matter of survival. Later, however, this evolutionary brilliance serves more than a life-or-death function. Sensations actually form the bedrock for a child's gradual maturation toward authentic autonomy and independence.

As you grow, you are defined by how your body interacts with your environment. What you do physically—whether experiencing pleasure or pain, success or failure—is registered by your body and recorded in your mind. Your knowing about the world, as you interact with it, comes from the totality of your sensations, both external and internal. Sir Charles Sherrington, winner of the 1932 Nobel Prize in Physiology or Medicine, said that "the motor act is the cradle of the mind." Fifty years later another such laureate, Roger Sperry, elaborated on Sherrington's iconic premise:

> In so far as an organism perceives a given object, it is prepared to respond with reference to it ... The presence or absence of adaptive reaction potentialities, ready to discharge into motor patterns, makes the difference between perceiving and not perceiving.[81]

In a series of astonishing experiments stimulated by the "Sperry Principle," Richard Held and Alan Hein had adult subjects wear special prism goggles that made everything appear to be upside down.[82] After some time (usually a week or two), the brains of the subjects who were free to move about actively, touching and manipulating their environment, adapted so that they actually saw the environment as right side up again. The subjects who were not allowed to move around and explore, however, did not experience visual normalization. Held also carried out experiments that illustrate the developmental significance of motor responses.[83] Newborn kittens were put on a movable apparatus and placed within a circular enclosure. One group of kittens walked and pulled the apparatus around the enclosure with them, while the other kittens were pulled along passively. Both groups had exactly the same visual experiences moving around the enclosure. The kittens that were moved around passively, not actively exploring their environment, were unable later to use sight to guide their movements. They could not place their paws properly or move away from a place where they could fall. This deficit was swiftly reversed when they could actively move around, exploring their environments.

Finally, in this parade of Nobel Prize recipients, Gerald Edelman, the American biologist who won the prize in 1972 for his work on immunology, has proposed a theory of what he calls Neural Darwinism.[84] This complex theory recognizes the intrinsic relation of motor activity, from our past and present explorations of the environment, as the underpinning of experience and memory. Collectively, these Nobel recipients see "mindedness" (including our complex structure of meaning making) as deriving from the fine tuning and categorization of our actions, sensations, feelings and perceptions. Turning earlier theories on their heads, we are now aware that, rather than being the hierarchical, top-dog commander in chief, our thoughts are a complex elaboration of *what we do and how we feel.*

Thought can indeed be said to function as an "explanation" to ourselves: a reminder of what we are doing and feeling. Thinking and symbolizing help us to make categories of events, people or locations, such as "safe" and "dangerous." The evolution of thoughts, symbols and verbal communication, *derived from sensations*, gave our earliest ancestors a crucial edge, allowing them to share successes and failures and to pass them on to others. As hunters and gatherers, survival meant being *fully in* our bodies just like the babies. Excessive mental rumination would have surely meant sudden death or slow starvation. However, over the millennia, the innate intelligence of the body was abandoned for the exclusivity of rationality, symbolization and language. Our bodies came to exist solely (as a character in a Jules Feiffer cartoon quipped) "to transport our heads from place to place ... Otherwise we would have no need for them." On the contrary, consciousness actually unfolds through the development of body awareness, of learning to understand the nuances and the meaning of our internal physical sensations, and of our emotional feelings as well.

Trauma and the Body/Mind

Under ordinary circumstances, physical sensations are signals for action: to fight or flee when threatened, to chase down a wild turkey or open the fridge and make a sandwich when hungry, to go the bathroom when the urge presses, to make love when aroused by passion, to sleep when tired, to break into song when the mood strikes or to plant your feet and raise your voice in anger and assertiveness when your boundaries are violated. In all these instances, *the body initiates and the mind follows.*

Having an intimate relationship with, and understanding of, your physical sensations is critical because they, in signaling action, guide you through the experiences and nuances of your life. If one has been traumatized, however, one's sensations can become signals not for effective action but, rather, for fearful paralysis, helplessness or misdirected rage. When some of one's bodily signals become harbingers of fear, helplessness, impotent rage and defeat, he or she is typically avoided like the plague at a dear cost mentally, emotionally and physically. While attempting to shut down distressing sensations, one pays the price of losing the capacity to appreciate the subtle physical shifts that denote comfort, satisfaction or warning of clear and present danger. Sadly, as a result, the capacity for feeling pleasure, garnering relevant meaning and accessing self-protective reflexes also shuts down. You can't have it both ways; when feelings of dread are held at bay, so are the feelings of joy.

The good news is that human beings are generally flexible and resilient: we are ordinarily able to learn from and integrate a variety of life experiences. These experiences, whether uplifting or downbeat, flow easily through our body/mind stream of consciousness as long as we are not chronically over- or underaroused. The body/mind keeps flowing through new encounters with vitality, bouncing back into the stream of things unless there is a significant disruption. In this case, the person is knocked off that normal course—whether it is from a single episode, such as a disaster, an accident, surgery or rape, or from a chronic stressor, such as abuse or ongoing marital stress. When such disruptions fail to be fully integrated, the components of that experience become fragmented into isolated sensations, images and emotions. This kind of splitting apart occurs when the enormity, intensity, suddenness or duration of what happened cannot be defended against, coped with or digested. Personal vulnerability, such as age, genetics and gender also account for this psychic implosion. The result of this inability for the body/mind to integrate is trauma, or at the very minimum, disorientation, a loss of agency and/or a lack of direction.

Trapped between feeling too much (overwhelmed or flooded) or feeling too little (shut down and numb) and unable to trust their sensations, traumatized people can lose their way. They don't "feel like themselves" anymore; loss of sensation equals a loss of a sense of self. As a substitute for genuine feelings, trauma sufferers may seek experiences that keep them out of touch—such as sexual titillation or succumbing to compulsions, addictions and miscellaneous distractions that prevent one from facing a now dark and threatening inner life. In this situation, one cannot discover the *transitory* nature of despair, terror, rage and helplessness and that the body is designed to cycle in and out of these extremes.*

Helping clients cultivate and regulate the capacity for tolerating extreme sensations, through reflective self-awareness, while supporting self-acceptance, allows them to modulate their uncomfortable sensations and feelings. They can now touch into intense sensations and emotions for longer periods of time as they learn how to control their arousal. Once a client has the experience of "going within and coming back out" without falling apart, his or her window of tolerance builds upon itself. This happens through achieving a subtle interplay between sensations, feelings, perceptions and thoughts. I believe that the *people who are most resilient, and find the greatest peace in their lives, have learned to tolerate extreme sensations while gaining the capacity for reflective self-awareness.* Although this capacity develops normally when we are very young, one can learn it at any time in life, thankfully.

Children gradually learn to interpret the messages their bodies give them. Indeed, it is by learning to coordinate movements (behaviors) and sensations into a coherent whole that a child learns who he or she is. By remembering actions that have proven to be effective, and discarding those that are not, children learn how to anticipate what the most appropriate response is and how to time its execution for maximum effect. In this way, they experience agency, satisfaction and pleasure. When a child is overwhelmed by trauma or thwarted by neglect, this developmental sequence is aborted or, if already developed, breaks down; and negative emotions come to dominate his or her existence.

---

* Recall Step 3 (pendulation and containment) from Chapter 5.

After being traumatized, a child's relationship with his or her body often becomes formless, chaotic and overwhelming; the child loses a sense of his internal structure and nuance. As the body freezes, the "shocked" mind and brain become stifled, disorganized and fragmented; they cannot take in the totality of experience and learn from it. These children, who have become "stuck" at some point along a once meaningful and purposeful course of action, engage in habitually ineffective and often compulsive patterns of behavior. These often play out in symptoms like those of attention deficit hyperactivity disorder or obsessive-compulsive disorder. The child's uncoordinated fragmented efforts are not registered as normal, explicit, narrative memories but rather are encoded in the body as implicit, procedural memories including discomfort, constriction, distress, awkwardness, rigidity, flaccidity and lack of energy. Such memories are encoded not primarily in the neocortex but, instead, in the limbic system and brain stem. For this reason behaviors and memories cannot be changed by simply changing one's thoughts. One must also work with sensation and feeling—really with the totality of experience.

The SIBAM Model

Human beings, in general, and therapists, in particular, make contact through a kind of "body resonance." As described in Chapter 4, we humans are programmed to experience sensations similar to those of people with whom we are in close proximity.[85] Imagine the scenario of being in a room filled with anxious conspiracy theorists as compared to one with blissful, meditating monks.

Resonance forms the basis for the empathic attunement needed to form intimate relationships.[86] In treating traumatized individuals, a therapist first needs to cultivate a deep and enduring relationship with his or her own body. Only when a therapist's embodiment skills are intact and engaged can he or she mentor and self-empower a client. Similarly, by refining their own capacity *to observe the subtle behaviors of others*, therapists can provide their clients feedback that helps them become aware of their sensations and feelings. Together, these two tools—*somatic resonance* and *subtle observation*—are of incalculable power and benefit. In the words of the analyst Leston Havens, "Perhaps the most striking evidence of successful empathy is the occurrence in our bodies of sensations that the patient has described in his or hers."[87]

During the 1970s, I developed a model that allowed me to "track" the processes whereby my clients processed experiences. This model, which I call SIBAM, is based on the intimate relationship between our bodies and our minds. The model examines the following five channels, with the first letters of each element making up the acronym.

> **S**ensation
> **I**mage
> **B**ehavior
> **A**ffect
> **M**eaning

The SIBAM model stands in sharp contrast to the established hierarchical framework, codified as *cogito ergo sum* or "I think; therefore I am," which has been the foundational premise of the standard, cognitive-behavioral therapies. In contrast, my five-element model is the essence of "bottom-up," sensorimotor processing aimed at guiding the client through different "language" and brain systems, from the most primitive to the most complex; from physical sensations to feelings, perceptions and, finally, to thoughts. Sensation, Image, Affect and Meaning are tracked by the client, while Behavior is directly observed by the therapist. This approach allows for an intimate tracking of the multiple layers and textures of the totality of experience.

The Sensation Channel

In this channel, I refer to *physical sensations that arise from within the body*, from receptors lying in the interior of our organisms. These sensations are also known in the literature as *interoceptive*. They ascend via nerve impulses from the interior of the body to the thalamus in the upper brain stem, where they are transferred to many, if not most, regions of the brain. Four subsystems, or categories, make up the sensation channel in order of increasing depth: the kinesthetic, the proprioceptive, the vestibular and the visceral receptors.

The Kinesthetic Receptors

The first subsystem within the sensation channel is kinesthesia. The kinesthetic sense signals the state of tension of our muscles* and relays this information to the brain. When you feel "uptight," it is because you are receiving excess nerve impulses coming from muscles in your shoulders and other areas—such as neck, jaw or pelvis—as well as from an overactive mind.

The Proprioceptive Receptors

The second subsystem, called *proprioception*, gives us *positional* information about our joints. Together, kinesthesia and proprioception tell us *where* we are in space, as well as the velocity of any body part. One could, for example, conduct a symphony with one's eyes closed and then at the end place a finger precisely on the tip of one's nose without looking—an extraordinary but possible feat of sensation and coordination.

The Vestibular Receptors

The vestibular subsystem derives from microscopic hairs embedded within the semicircular canals of the inner ear. There are two of these canals positioned at right angles to each other. When we move (accelerate and decelerate in any direction), fluid in these canals "sloshes" over the hairs, bending them. Each hair is connected to a receptor, and these receptors then send afferent impulses to the brain stem. Information from this sense lets us know our position with respect both to gravity and to any change in velocity (i.e., acceleration and deceleration).

---

* It does this specifically from what are called "stretch receptors"—specialized fibers in the muscle called intrafusal fibers.

The Visceral Receptors

The fourth subsystem, which provides the deepest level of interoception, derives from our viscera and blood vessels. In Chapter 6 I described the vagus nerve, which connects the brain stem to most of our internal organs. This massive nerve is second only to the spinal cord in total number of neurons. Over *90% of these nerve fibers are afferent:* that is, the vagus nerve's main function is to relay information from our *guts upward to our brains.* Thus, the colloquialisms "gut instinct," "gut feelings" and even "gut wisdom" have a robust anatomical and physiological basis. Visceral sensations also originate from receptors in the blood vessels—as sufferers from migraines know all too well, the abrupt dilation of blood vessels (after strong constriction) causing their excruciating pain. However, we are also receiving all sorts of other ambient information from our blood vessels. We feel relaxed and open when our blood vessels and viscera gently pulse like jellyfish, causing sensations of warmth and goodness to surge through our bodies. When the vessels and viscera are constricted, we feel cold and anxious.

The Image Channel

While *image* commonly refers to visual representation, I use it more generally to refer to *all* types of *external* sense impressions, which originally come from *stimuli that arise from outside the body* and that we have also incorporated into the brain as sense memory. These external ("special") senses include sight, taste, smell, hearing and the tactile sense.* Counter to common parlance, I use the same word—Image— to categorize all of these external senses. Indeed, the I in the SIBAM model could refer, equally, to any of the externally generated *I*mpressions (i.e., visual, auditory, tactile, olfactory, etc.). For example, if a person is physically touched by another person, he or she will experience

---

*The senses of sound and touch are actually similar. In the inner ear there is a membrane called the basilar. Sound waves make this membrane vibrate, stimulating hair receptors to send impulses to the brain. The hairs on our skin function in a similar way. Indeed, deaf individuals have some sense of hearing through the skin.

both the *external* impression of being touched as well as the *internal* (interoceptive) sensation of his or her response to that touch. So if we have been touched inappropriately, it will be necessary to separate the actual tactile impression from our internal response to this stimulus in each new situation in order to free ourselves from reflexively reacting from past experience.

The visual impression, or Image, is the primary way modern humans access and store external sense information, unless they are visually impaired. The largest portion of our sensory brain is dedicated to vision. There are, however, other therapeutically oriented reasons for my including all of the external senses in the Image channel. At the moment a trauma takes place, all of a person's senses automatically focus on the most salient aspect of the threat. This is usually a visual image, though it could also be sound, touch, taste or smell. Many times it is a combination of several or, even, all of the above sense impressions simultaneously. For example, a woman molested by an alcoholic uncle may panic on seeing a man who looks vaguely like him or whose breath smells of alcohol and who walks with a loud, lumbering gait. These fragmentary snapshots come to represent the trauma. They become, in other words, the intrusive image or *Imprint*. For me, the image of the shattered glass and the eyes of the teenage driver kept intruding on my consciousness and flooding me with fear and dread.

When reworking such embedded sensory images, a process of diffusing the adrenalin charge of the compressed "trauma snapshot" is necessary in order to uncouple associations that are symptomatic. An important therapeutic technique "expands and neutralizes" this fixation and helps the person recover the multisensory experience he or she may have had prior to the threat that caused the fragmentation. The following vignette illustrates this principle of expanding the "visual aperture."

Imagine that early one summer morning, you are walking along a beautiful hillside. There is a babbling brook meandering beside the pathway. A gentle breeze makes the multicolored flowers look as if they are dancing on the meadow. You are touched by the sight of drops of morning dew sitting on a blade of grass. The sunshine warms your skin, and the scent of the flowers is nothing less than intoxicating. You are taking this all in. Then, unexpectedly, a large snake appears on the trail. You stop and hold your breath. All that you had perceived a moment ago is gone ... or is it? Not really. What happens is that your perception has constricted to focus narrowly on the source of the threat. Most everything else retreats into the background, into the hidden crevices of your mind, so as not to distract you from what you must identify and do: to keep your attention solely focused on the snake and to slowly back away. After feeling safe again, you may return to the full sensory experience of the morning. When a traumatized individual is able to expand his or her sensorial impressions, associated hyperarousal begins to ease, allowing that widened perceptual field to return to its prethreat status, and thus enhances the capacity of self-regulation.

Before my accident, as detailed in Chapter 1, I was taking in the scene: the colors, sounds, scents and warmth of that perfect day. In the instant that l was struck, these pleasant images paled. Now my attention was riveted only on the image of the "predator": the spiderweb cracks of the windshield, the beige grille of the car and the terrified face of the wide-eyed teenager. Luckily, in my self-administered first aid, I was able to return to the start of that perfect day, with the sensuous sights, sounds and smells of the precious moments before the impact.

The Behavior Channel

Behavior is the only channel that the therapist is able to observe directly; all others are reported *by* the client. Although the therapist is able to surmise much about a client's inner life from a resonance with her own sensations and feelings, such inferences cannot take the place of the client also accessing and communicating his own sensations, feelings and images to the therapist.* The therapist can *infer* a client's inner states from reading his body's language, the unspoken language of his actions/inactions or tension patterns. For example, the therapist, in

---

* It takes a good deal of experience for therapists to be able to distinguish between their "own" sensations and those that they are "picking up" from their clients. Analysts sometimes call this *projective identification.*

noting a particular body behavior, may direct the client to focus on what he may be experiencing in his body (Sensation). If, say, the therapist observes a slight rising of the client's left shoulder (Behavior), she can bring the latter's attention to this postural adjustment and allow the client to contact the sensations of the asymmetrical tension pattern. Similarly, the client may be encouraged to access the other channels of experiencing (Image, Affect or Meaning) during the execution of this postural behavior. This will be clarified by the case examples in the next chapter.

Behavior occurs on different levels of awareness, ranging from the most conscious voluntary movements to the most unconscious involuntary patterns. These levels are similar to the gradations of consciousness I have examined in the sensation category. We will now briefly examine behaviors that occur in the following subsystems: gestures, emotion and posture, as well as autonomic, visceral and archetypal behaviors.

Gestures

The most conscious behaviors are the voluntary ones: that is, the overt gestures that people generally make with their hands and arms when they are trying to communicate. These movements are the *most superficial* level of behavior. People frequently use voluntary gestures to convey "pseudo-feeling" states to others. We have all seen politicians deliberately exaggerate their gestures for emphasis and effect. If you know the real thing, you can readily discern the fundamental disconnect or incongruity between one's *attempt* to convey what one is trained to express (e.g., opening one's arms to the audience or holding a hand to one's heart) and what one is really feeling. At the same time, even volitional gestures can convey feelings, both to others and to oneself.

For example, one can interpret the nonverbal communication of the clenched fist as either a threat enhancing aggression or as the setting of clear boundaries and quelling fear. Here are some common gestures to experiment with: Rub your forehead with your hand and notice how that feels. Now stroke the back of your neck. What do these two gestures convey to you? Do they make you feel more or less secure? How about when you are wringing your hands versus when they are steepled, fingertip to fingertip? What differences do you notice?

Emotion

Facial expressions are at the next level of behavior and are generally considered to be largely involuntary. These micro-expressions are what the renowned Paul Ekman[88] studied in his pioneering research spanning over four decades. With practice and patience, one can develop the skills necessary to observe these very brief changes of muscle tension (often in a fraction of a second) throughout parts of the face.* The *specific patterns* of these muscle contractions communicate the full range of emotional nuances to oneself and to others.† Giving clients feedback about their facial expressions can help them contact emotions of which they may be partially or fully unaware.

Posture

The third level of less conscious awareness in the behavior category is *posture*. Here I'm not referring to gross voluntary postural adjustments like those demanded by parents or teachers, such as "sit-up straight," "don't slump" or "shoulders back," which refer to voluntary movements. These belong instead to the category of voluntary gestures. Sir Charles Sherrington, the grandfather of modern neurophysiology, alleges that "much of the reflex reaction expressed by the skeletal musculature is not motile, but postural, and has as its result not a movement but the steady maintenance of an attitude."[89] I would add that *postures are the platforms from which intrinsic movement is initiated.* In the words of A. E. Gisell, a student of Sherrington's, "the requisite motor equipment for behavior is established well in advance of the behavior itself." In underscoring how important posture is in the generation of new behaviors, sensations, feelings and meanings, Gisell added, "The embryogenesis of mind must be sought in the beginnings of postural behavior."[90]

---

* Another way to learn is by watching the TV series *Lie to Me*.

† This is the basis for the method of acting taught by Konstantin Stanislavsky.

Although relatively few therapists have cultivated the precise reading of postures, they are still being impacted by them. We all subconsciously mirror the postures of others and register them *as sensations in our own bodies.* This occurs presumably through the operation of mirror neurons and postural resonance. Since spontaneous postural changes are generally subtle, it takes a lot of practice to observe them. Resonance is particularly compelling with survival-based postures such as the nuanced varieties associated with the premovements and movements of flight, fight, freeze/fright and collapse.

If a posture is rigid from bracing or is collapsed, we can assume that it was a *preparation* for some particular action, an action that was thwarted and that the muscles are still programmed to complete. If this dormant sensorimotor trajectory had not been impeded, it would most likely have had a more triumphant outcome—as it still can retroactively. In recounting my accident, I described what I was aware of in my body as I lay helpless in the ambulance. It was, first, from a subtle twisting sensation in my spine that I felt my arm initiate an upward move to protect my head from being smashed on the windshield and, consequently, on the road.

Observing spontaneous (intrinsic) postures gives the therapist a vital window into the state of a client's nervous system and psyche. The body benevolently shows us when we are preparing to act and precisely what incipient premovement action is being prepared for. Most often, we as keen observers see before our very eyes a bodily orchestration unfolding that neither the therapist nor the client could ever have rationally predicted. The therapist begins by noticing postures that show rigidity, retraction, poised preparation for flight, twisting and collapse, as well as those of openness and expansion. I think of the unforgettable postural ease in someone like Nelson Mandela who, despite both the magnitude of his trauma and his advanced age, maintains a natural, graceful posture. And numerous people have described how they felt deeply relaxed and open in the presence of the Dalai Lama. The adroit therapist both sees and senses the opposite of such grace in a client whose spine becomes more rigid, braced against a perceived assault, or collapses (sometimes nearly imperceptibly) while experiencing difficult sensations and emotions. In the same manner therapists (and mothers, fathers and friends) are also able to observe and reflect momentary states of grace and goodness in others.

Autonomic Signals (Cardiovascular and Respiratory)

Visible autonomic behaviors include respiratory and cardiovascular sign-posts. Breathing that is rapid, shallow and/or high in the chest indicates sympathetic arousal. Breathing that is very shallow (almost imperceptible) frequently indicates immobility, shutdown and dissociation. Breathing that is full and free with a complete expiration, and a delicate pause before the next inhalation, indicates relaxation and settling into equilibrium. This type of spontaneous and restorative breath can be easily distinguished from a person who is "trying" to take a deep breath. Often, this kind of voluntary forced deep breath can actually increase imbalance in the nervous system and, at the very least, gives only temporary relief.[91]

Next are signs from the cardiovascular system, which include heart rate and the tone of the smooth muscles lining certain blood vessels. Heart rate can, as I have said, be monitored by observing the carotid pulse, which is visible as a pulsation in the neck. A therapist can, with a little practice, discern increases and decreases in rate, as well as estimate their magnitude. It is also possible to estimate changes in blood pressure from the strength or weakness of the pulse.

The therapist can identify the tonus of the blood vessels by noting alterations in skin color, although doing so requires a refined level of perception. In the case of a very high tone (vasoconstriction), a client's cold fingers will have, for example, a whitish/bluish tint, reflecting—along with increased heart rate—sympathetic hyperarousal. On the other hand, when the blood vessels are relaxed and dilated, or open, the fingers are a lively pinkish hue. Yet another variation arises when the capillary vessels dilate abruptly, causing a red flush, noticeable particularly in the face and neck. In addition, the observer can some-times actually feel a wave of heat emanating from the client's body.*

The next observation point is pupil size. A very wide pupil is asso-ciated with high sympathetic arousal, while a very small pupil can be indicative of immobility and dissociation. "Pinhole"-sized pupils can also be an indicator of drug use—generally of opiates. Interestingly, these opiates are also released by the body's own internal pain relief system[92] and are an integral part of the immobility system and dissoci-ation.[93]

Visceral Behavior

Visceral behavior refers to the motility of the gastrointestinal tract, whose movements can actually be "observed" by the sounds that it makes. The wonderful onomatopoetic word for these intestinal rum-blings and gurglings is *borborygmus* (plural: *borborygmi*). An entire sys-tem of body-therapy is based upon listening to a spectrum of these gut sounds with an electronic (fetal) stethoscope while different parts of the body are touched and gently manipulated.[94]

A therapist who is able to track all of the various behavior indica-tors discussed above has access to critical information that will help her to time various interventions efficaciously. She knows, for example, that cold hands generally indicate fear and stress; while warm ones signify relaxation. Flushed skin can reflect emotions like rage, shame and embar-rassment. What is not widely known is that flushed skin can also be the sign of a strong release of energy and a movement toward greater alive-ness. As with all such observations, sequence must be understood together with *context*: no single indicator stands alone. And, of course, the content that the client is currently processing must be considered in the mix. In this way, the therapist can artfully map an accurate topog-raphy relating what he is observing (Behavior) to what the client is expe-riencing (Sensation). In general, there is a correspondence between the level of Sensation and Behavior: that is, when the therapist gives the

---

* I am not sure how much is due to the actual radiation of heat and how much is the result of somatic resonance.

client feedback about a change in the latter's autonomic nervous system, such as heart rate or skin color (Behavior), he or she will generally be drawn to exploring autonomic Sensations, such as the level of cardiopulmonary/sympathetic arousal.

Archetypal Behaviors

Last, but not least, is the subsystem of archetypal behaviors coming from the deep "collective unconscious." In tracking people's postural shifts, I began to notice subtle hand and arm gestures that were clearly different from voluntary ones. These gestures often appeared at moments of significant therapeutic movement and frequently indicated pleasingly unforeseen resources and shifts toward flow and wholeness. Moreover, I became fascinated by the similarity of these involuntary gestures to those of the sacred dances that I had seen at various cultural performances presented at University of California–Berkeley's Zellerbach Hall. These hand/finger/arm movements, called *mudras*, are all-embracing and inclusive, across the spectrum of the human experience and throughout the world. Particularly in Asia, the way one's hands and fingers are poised communicates very deep and universal meanings, ones that are related more than just personally to dancer or audience member.* When the therapist observes such spontaneous mudras, then pauses, taking the time to bring them to the client's attention, the client can then use that information to explore how his "outside" posture feels on the "inside." It is not surprising, at this juncture, for the client to contact a treasure chest of powerful resources of connection, empowerment, flow, goodness and wholeness. I believe that these archetypal movements arise at unique moments when the instinctual is seamlessly wedded with one's conscious awareness—when the primitive brain stem and the highest neocortical functions integrate.

In summary, Behavior is the only category that the therapist is *directly* aware of. As clients become aware—at first only marginally—of their

---

* The legendary actor of the Peking Opera, Mei Lanfang, used hundreds of specific hand gestures to communicate several unspoken or subtextual emotional aspects of whichever character he was performing.

own behaviors, they may incorporate these perceptions into an observer role where they are reminding themselves to note sensations associated with those behaviors. When linked with thoughts, this is a powerful tool to dissolve compulsions and addictions.

The Affect Channel

The two subtypes in the fourth channel are the categorical emotions and the felt sense, or contours of sensation-based feeling.

Emotions

Emotions include the categorical ones described by Darwin and refined in extensive laboratory studies by Paul Ekman. These distinct emotions include fear, anger, sadness, joy and disgust. Again, these are feelings that the client is experiencing internally and that the therapist can deduce from the client's face and posture even when the client is unaware of them.

Contours of Feeling

Another level of affect—the registration of contours of feeling—is, perhaps, even more important to the quality and conduct of our lives than are the categorical emotions. Eugene Gendlin extensively studied and described these softer affects and coined the term *felt sense*.[95] When you see dew on a blade of grass in the morning light or visit a museum and delight in a beautiful painting, you're usually not experiencing a categorical emotion. Or when meeting a good friend you haven't seen for months, you're probably not feeling fear, sorrow, disgust or even joy. Contours are the sensation-based feelings of attraction and avoidance, of "goodness" and "badness." You experience these nuances countless times throughout the day. While it's easy to imagine a day without perceiving any of the categorical emotions, try for a moment to conjure up a day without any felt sense affects. On such a day you would be as lost as a ship at sea with no rudder or bearings. These contours guide us throughout the day, giving us orientation and direction in life.

The Meaning Channel

Meanings are the labels we attach to the totality of experience—that is, to the combined elements of sensation, image, behavior and affect. Meanings are like descriptive markers that we use to get a quick handle on the whole spectrum of inner experience so that we can communicate these to others and to ourselves. We all have fixed beliefs, or meanings, that we take to be the unequivocal truth. When a person is traumatized, his or her beliefs become excessively narrow and restrictive. Examples of these crystallized mantras are: "You can't trust people"; "The world is a dangerous place"; "I won't ever make enough money to support myself"; or "I'm unlovable." These beliefs are often connected to primal fears and are, by and large, negative and limiting.

As incredible as this might sound, we are likely to be programmed to have negative beliefs for survival purposes. For example, if you are walking in an area where you are confronted by a bear, you have likely gained the meaning that "this is a dangerous place" and "don't go that way next time." Unfortunately, when one has been traumatized or deeply conditioned through fear while young and impressionable, such meanings become pervasive and rigidly fixed. Later in life, rather than a client freely accessing the full spectrum of developing sensations and feelings, conclusions are drawn based on meanings born out of past trauma or early conditioning. I have called this kind of limiting prejudgment *premature cognition.*

Using the SIBAM model, the therapist can help the client work through the first four channels of awareness in order to reach *new* meanings. When cognition is suspended long enough, it is possible to move through and experience flow via these different channels (and subsystems) of Sensation, Image, Behavior and Affect. Then it is probable for *fresh new* Meanings to emerge out of this unfolding tapestry of body/mind consciousness. As an example, a client may start with specific fixed beliefs such as "my spouse is not behaving properly" or "I am unlovable." The therapist, rather than trying to talk them out of the belief, may instead encourage the client to examine the physical loci of these thoughts, to notice which areas are tense, which are open and spacious, and to locate any feelings of collapse. More importantly, perhaps, clients are also asked to note a vacancy of feeling. A common example (especially in clients who have had sexual trauma) is the sense that one cannot feel one's pelvis at all, or that it is disconnected from one's torso or legs. A client asked to scan his body from head to toe might convey an uncanny absence of pelvic sensations. Of course, such an absence gives the therapist an idea of what the client is avoiding.

Working with the Five Elements of SIBAM

The SIBAM model includes the neurophysiologic, behavioral and somatic aspects of an individual's experience, whether traumatic or triumphant. When there is a successful outcome, or a corrective experience occurs during therapy, the elements of SIBAM form a fluid, continuous and coherent response that is appropriate to the immediate situation. When individuals suffer from unresolved trauma, these various aspects of traumatic association and disassociation continue in fixed, now-maladaptive patterns that are distortions of current reality.

An example of this fixity follows: A woman loves nature, parks, meadows and grassy knolls; however, every time she smells new-mown grass she feels nauseated, anxious and dizzy. Her belief (M) is that grass is something to be avoided. The olfactory and visual image (I) is associated with, or coupled to, the sensations of nausea and dizziness (S) coming from her visceral and vestibular systems. This positive feedback loop, with negative consequences, is an enigma. Part of the event is disassociated from her awareness: she has no idea why this happens; she just knows that she has a strong dislike (M) of grass. As this woman explores her sensations and images, seeing and smelling cut grass in her mind's eye, she takes time to explore her bodily sensations in detail. As she does, she has a new sensation of being spun in the air and held at the wrists and legs. Next she gets a tactile image of her bullying brother giving her an airplane spin on the front lawn of her childhood house when she was four or five years old.

She feels scared (old A), but as she trembles and breathes, she realizes that she is no longer in danger. She now orients (B) by looking around at the peaceful office and then turning her head toward the open face of her therapist. Feeling intact with this newfound safety, she settles a bit. She experiences a spontaneous breath (new B), feeling secure in her belly (new S) now. Then she notices some tightness around her wrists (old S) and the impulse to pry her wrists loose (new S). Now, she feels a wave of anger (new A) building up inside as she yells "Stop!" using the motor muscles of her vocal cords (new B). She settles again and feels (new I) the tactile pleasure of lying on the soft new-mown grass in the warmth of the springtime sunshine. Fresh grass is no longer associated with unpleasant sensations (old M); green, freshly groomed grass is good, parks are wonderful places and "all is well" (new M). She no longer feels nauseated or anxious again in that situation.

The simple example above shows us how the elements of this biological model fit together to create a web of either fixity or flow. In nature, when one feels an internal sensation, frequently an image appears simultaneously or shortly afterward. If a client is bothered by an image, a sensation may accompany it that he is not aware of. When, with the therapist's guidance, the client becomes conscious of both elements, a behavior, affect or new meaning generally follows.

Once we understand the process and do not interfere with it, biology works to move it along. The sensation-based brain stem has the job of bringing homeostasis and, thus, goodness back to the body. Therefore, it *naturally* follows that when the client's body's behavior becomes conscious in the safety of the present moment, the thwarted movements come to an intrinsic resolution or a corrective experience—as happened with me, Nancy and the woman in the example above. This resolution leads to a discharge of energy, resulting in a fresh, new affect (A) that brings with it brand-new options or meanings. If the client is unaware of behavior or sensation, the fixed image generally leads to fixed affects and/or thoughts that were troubling the client to begin with. When a fixed behavior does not complete in a new way, the result is a habitual, or (over) coupled, affect. Because behavior reflects preparatory, protective and defensive orienting responses, assisting clients to follow their sensorimotor impulses to completion, as they come out of freeze, is a key to unlocking the constrictive and limiting prison of posttraumatic stress disorder.

The therapist's task as healer is to notice which SIBAM elements a client presents with are old, conditioned, ineffectual patterns and which are missing completely because they are unconsciously hidden. When we can read this map, we can provide the somatic tools to free the client from being tangled up in these habituated physiological associations from the past. In this way people are, thankfully, restored to a healthy, flexible and dynamic way of relating to all of the new experiences life brings.

PART II

The Body as Storyteller: Below Your Mind

We use our minds not to discover facts but to hide them. One of the things the screen hides most effectively is the body, our own body, by which I mean, the ins and outs of it, its interiors. Like a veil thrown over the skin to secure its modesty, the screen partially removes from the mind the inner states of the body, those that constitute the flow of life as it wanders in the journey of each day.

—Antonio Damasio, *The Feeling of What Happens*

CHAPTER 8

In the Consulting Room

Case Examples

To acquire knowledge, one must study;
but to acquire wisdom, one must observe.
—Marilyn vos Savant

You can observe a lot just by looking.
—Yogi Berra, catcher, New York Yankees
(circa 1950s)

The therapist who is familiar with bodily feelings has a privileged window onto the primal life of the psyche and soul. No amount of talk alone can match this vantage point. Long before the advent of psychiatry, the French philosopher Pascal noted that "the body has its reasons that reason can not reason." The Austrian Wittgenstein, in this same tradition, wrote that "the body is the best picture of the mind." And the Australian F. M. Alexander, around the turn of the nineteenth century, made an extensive study of peoples' postures and concluded, "When psychologists speak of the unconscious, it is the body that they are talking about."

The current lack of the appreciation of the body in psychotherapy caused the analyst Musad Kahn[96] to lament, "I have not come across any paper that discusses the contribution made to our knowledge and experience of a patient from our looking at him or her in their person as a body as against looking at merely the verbal material and affective responses in the analytic situation."

Somatically oriented therapists provide their clients with carefully paced feedback in the form of invitations to explore their emerging bodily sensations. This feedback is based largely on the therapist's ability to observe and track the postural, gestural, facial (emotional) and physiological shifts throughout a session in order to bring them into a client's conscious awareness. This allows both client and therapist to uncover unconscious conflicts and traumas that are well beyond the reach of reason. Freud seems to have grasped this concept in his early work when he says, "The mind has forgotten, but the body has not—thankfully." Yes, thankfully! Though Freud seems to have abandoned this premise, his student Wilhelm Reich spent his entire career studying how conflicts are lodged in the body. "When it comes to the consulting room," he remarked, "there are really just two animals and two bodies."[97]

In this chapter, I will use examples from my own cases to illustrate the principles outlined in Chapters 5 through 7. In the very beginning of session work, a client may not understand the therapist's feedback about her unconscious attitudes. But as the client becomes more conscious of her sensations, she is able to use them to access innate resources and to deepen her capacity to "know" herself through the subtle promptings of her body. In the first case (Miriam), I introduce expressive, but hidden, body language. This case is relatively straightforward and demonstrates some basic body-oriented observational skills that therapists can utilize with their clients to facilitate their awakening and to enhance integration of their sensations, feelings, perceptions and meanings.

Miriam: In the Unspoken Language of the Body

Miriam enters the room, tentatively sits down, and folds her arms tight across her chest. This posture gives the impression of rigid self-protection. Of course, one may have many reasons for folding one's arms: she could be comforting herself or even keeping herself warm. It is the overall context that tells the story. Miriam is agitated, pumping her crossed legs repeatedly. Her face is visibly constricted; her lips are thin and pulled tight. Miriam offers that she feels discontented and resentful about her marriage and work situation. She finds herself "in bad moods a lot" and frequently has trouble staying asleep at night. When she wakes up, it is often because of cramps in her belly and restlessness in her legs. She describes this intrusive experience by grumbling, "It's like they kick at night and wake me up." Her family doctor thinks that she may have "restless leg syndrome" or depression, and suggested an antidepressant medication. However, she first wants to try and "talk things out."

Miriam's body language reflects both her distress and her "resistance." This resistance is there for a reason: it is the physical expression of how she is protecting herself. In part, Miriam is defending herself as though from an outside "attack." However, she is protecting herself primarily from her disowned sensations and feelings. Resistance needs to be worked with gently and indirectly. Frontal confrontation is generally ill advised: to "attack" resistance directly is likely to intensify it or to break it down precipitously. Such a sudden demolition of a defense is likely to bring with it overwhelm, chaos and possible retraumatization.

Observing resistance *at the bodily level* allows the therapist to monitor the person's developing capacity to befriend her sensations and feelings as the session progresses; and, thus, to assess the efficacy and intensity of various therapeutic interventions, both verbal and nonverbal. As the client begins to feel safe enough (through appropriate reflection, pacing and mirroring), she begins to feel she is seen and respected; and then, naturally, her guarding postures will gradually diminish. If the client, on the other hand, tries too hard to open up (for example, by divulging more about herself than she is physically and emotionally ready to), her body will reflect that by intensifying resistance or in non-congruent changes in her nonverbal and verbal behaviors. However, when a therapist can track the client's burgeoning awareness and provide support in tracking her self-protective somatic mechanisms (without pushing into—or backing away from—them), the deeper levels of the body's unconscious communication system begin to speak, both to the therapist and to the client.

While, initially, Miriam is not conscious of her protective posture of habitually holding her arms crossed, it is still a relatively voluntary gesture. As she feels safer and more confident, these unspoken narrations emerge as more spontaneous, rather than habitual, expressions. As she gains deeper access to fledgling feelings, core issues begin to surface, ready to be explored.

Miriam continues to talk about her difficulties at work and with her husband, Henry. Although these are the same problems she was struggling with a few minutes ago, this time there is more animation in her voice. She gestures with her arms, extending them slightly outward in front of herself. Her hands are nearly at right angles to her wrists, almost as though she were pushing something away. I make a similar movement with my arms so as to "mirror" her movements and help her to feel and trust her own (disowned) movements.*

---

* Recall the discussion in Chapter 4 of Beatrice Gelder's work demonstrating how attuned we humans are to the survival-based postures of others. These findings also relate to research on mirror neurons. A mirror neuron is a neuron that fires both when an animal acts and when it observes the same action performed by another animal. Thus, the neuron mirrors the behavior of the other, as though the observer herself were performing the very same act. Such neurons have been directly observed in primates and are found in the premotor cortex and in the insula and cingulate, suggesting their importance in communicating internal bodily states and emotions. The neuroscientist Stephanie Preston, the Dutch primatologist Frans de Waal and other neuroscientists have independently posited that the mirror neuron system is centrally involved in empathy and that since it is the body that is being mirrored, intimate moments are nonverbal in nature. In humans, brain activity consistent with that of mirror neurons has been found in the premotor cortex and the inferior parietal cortex. See Chapter 4 for specific references to this research.

I bring Miriam's attention to her extending her arms and bending her wrists and suggest that she repeat the movements slowly. I ask her to try to focus on *how* her arms feel when she makes the movement, so that she gets a sense of how the movement feels physically from the inside. At first, she seems puzzled. After a few times, she pauses, smiles and says, "It feels like I'm pushing something away . . . no, more like holding something away . . . I need more space, that's what it's really like." She sweeps her arms from in front of herself and then off to both sides, creating a 180-degree range of free motion. She lets out a deep and spontaneous breath: "I don't feel as suffocated, and my belly isn't hurting like it was when we started." She extends her arms, flexing her wrists again. This time she holds them out for several seconds, almost at arm's length. "It's the same problem . . . at work and with my husband, too." She now places her hands gently on her thighs. "It's so hard for me, I don't know why but . . . I don't feel like I have a right to do this . . . like I don't have a right to my own space."

I ask her if it's more of a feeling or a thought. She pauses, giggles and replies, "Hah, I guess it's really a thought." Now there's a deeper laughter.

By contacting her nonverbal bodily expression, Miriam is able to go beneath the veneer of her ruminative thoughts about Henry and her work, to explore freely the story her body is beginning to tell. With this emergent kinesthetic and proprioceptive awareness, she has begun to sense into the *neuromuscular attitude* that underlies her internal conflicts.

After settling into her bodily experience, Miriam starts to get wound up again. I observe her carotid pulse and notice an increase in her heart rate, along with pressured, rapid, shallow breathing. I ask her to put her questionings aside for a moment and place her focus back on her body. Relieved by this suggestion, she closes her eyes.

"I feel more solid now . . . like there's more of me."

When I ask her to try and identify *where* in her body she feels the solidity, she says, "I don't know; I just feel that way."

"Just take your time," I suggest. "Don't try too hard. Just settle inside your body and see what you begin to notice."

Miriam closes her eyes. She seems a little confused and doesn't speak for a minute or two. "Its mostly in my arms and legs ... They feel like they have more substance ... They feel more solid ... *I* feel that way."

At this point, Miriam initiates further, this time self-directed, exploration by closing her eyes without my suggestion. After a minute or two, her jaw begins to tremble almost imperceptibly. I wait to see if she will notice this on her own.

"I feel strange," Miriam says, "kind of shaky inside ... I don't like this ... It makes me feel kinda weird inside ... like I'm getting out of control, like I'm not myself, like it's not me."

I reassure her by explaining that new sensations often feel uncomfortable and alien at first, and encourage her to "just let it happen ... try to suspend labeling or judging sensations for a bit." Miriam tells me that she's feeling worse, even more uncomfortable. I acknowledge this but gently and firmly encourage her "to hang in a little bit longer," to shift her attention to her arms and legs for a while—to the places in her body where she had been feeling rooted a short time ago.

"Huh, they don't feel shaky ... actually they feel strong ... I feel my jaw shaking ... That's where I feel shaky ... My legs feel solid."

The juxtaposition of the empowering sensations of her arms and legs supports her ability to experience the "shaky" sensations associated with the weakness without being swallowed up by them. Her breathing is now deep, continuous and spontaneous. Her skin has a warm rosy glow, indicating that the social engagement system is starting to function, to come online.

I suggest that she slowly begin to open her eyes and look around.

"That's funny," she says. "Things seem a little clearer; the colors are brighter and ... I think warmer, too. Actually, I feel a little warmer, and the trembling is less ... or not so scary ... It feels like I could go back inside now ... Do you want me to do that?"

"That's up to you," I say, knowing how important the element of choice is. "What I can tell you, though, is that you are starting to be able to go inside yourself, and you seem less scared and helpless."

She looks at me momentarily, but then averts her gaze downward to the floor. Slowly she looks upward, contacting my eyes. A single tear rolls down her cheek. "Yes that's right, I don't feel so scared ... In some ways I feel a little excited ... Yes I want to go on ... It's scary, but I think I can do it ... I just need some help ... your help." More tears stream from her eyes. Her words stumble as she chokes: "It's hard for me to ask ... It feels emotional ... I don't think I have so much experience in asking for help."

This acknowledgment lets me know that the social engagement system is operative, and that deeper exploration is possible. "Yes, I'm glad to give you support," I respond. When I ask her if she has any ideas of what kind of support might be helpful, she responds that just to do what I've been doing is what she wants. I ask her to be more specific.

"I'm not sure," she says. "Actually, I think it has to do with feeling that you're here, here for me. When you give me feedback, that helps keep me in touch with what I feel ... in a way with who *I* am."

"When you say that,"—I see her face relax—"you seem to let go more deeply." Miriam smiles, and I continue, "It's different than a few minutes ago, when you spoke of not having had the experience of asking for help."

"Yes," she adds, "it's really different to ask you for support in helping me to learn how to be there for myself ... That way I don't feel less than you, I feel more equal ... I like that ... I feel like if I didn't want to do something that you suggested to do, I could tell you that now." Without prompting, Miriam holds out her arms and hands again and sweeps them around in a horizontal semicircle. "Yes, these are my boundaries. I can set my limits—that feels good ... and I *can* tell you what I need."

We both smile. Miriam closes her eyes and sits quietly for several minutes. While it may seem simplistic, having the actual, kinesthetic, proprioceptive experience of being able to form and hold boundaries gives Miriam a significant physical experience that contradicts the pervasive sense of powerlessness that has driven her perception of the world.

Rather than being folded defensively across her chest, her arms now lie resting on her legs—exemplifying a more open stance and a willingness to look inward.

Miriam continues, "First I started to feel the shaking again ... It became more intense, but then it started to settle down on its own." She is now beginning to self-regulate by moving through activation/deactivation cycles. "I felt some warmth starting in my belly and then spreading out in waves ... That felt really good ... I could even feel the warmth flowing into my hands and legs ... but then my gut started to knot up. I started feeling a little sick, nauseous and queasy. I realized that I was thinking about Evan, my first husband. Actually, I saw a picture of him walking toward me. He was killed a month after we were married ... I think that I never got over it ... I couldn't believe it happened ... In a way I still don't ... I dream about Evan a lot. It's always the same dream. He comes to me; I'm despondent. I ask him why he left me. He doesn't answer me, but turns his back and walks away. I wake up wanting to cry, my throat is all tight, but I don't want Henry to know. I feel so terrible; like there's something wrong with me ... I don't want to cause him any pain."

"Miriam, I'm going to ask you to say something and notice what happens inside when you say the words. But remember these are my words. They might not mean anything to you. I'm only asking you to try them out and then just to notice how your body responds. Try not to think too much about it; just do it. Does that feel OK to you?" I say this not because it is true (or false) but so that the person can observe the effect the sentence has on their body sensations and feelings.

She nods. "Yes, that's OK. I'd like to do something about these feelings, these dreams, if I can."

"Ok, here's the sentence: 'I don't believe it happened; I don't believe you're really dead.'" The purpose of this is to bring into consciousness the direct body experience of denial so that it can be dealt with.

Miriam holds her breath and turns pale; her heart rate drops sharply, from about 80 to 60, indicating that the vagal immobility/shutdown system may have kicked in. "Are you OK, Miriam?" I ask.

"Yes ... but my guts are queasy and tight ... like a cold hard fist ... I feel sick again ... It's worse this time ... but I think that I can handle it. I'll tell you if it's too much."

Wanting to reinforce her developing capacity to assess her capability to handle difficult sensations, I ask her, "What gives you that sense, Miriam, that you can handle it?"

"Well, mostly I feel it in my arms and legs again. They still feel strong now, even if they're shaky." With her eyes still closed, Miriam starts to tremble visibly.

"That's OK," I encourage. "Just try and be with it. Know that if you need to, you can open your eyes. OK if I place my foot next to yours?"*

"Yes, I would like that ... Yes, that feels better." The trembling increases in intensity; it settles, increases and settles several times. Miriam takes a deep spontaneous breath and then becomes still. She seems peaceful; the color of her hands and face indicates a significant rise in temperature. Sweat begins to break out on her forehead.

"How are you doing now, Miriam?"

"I feel really hot ... like waves of heat burning me ... It's so intense, like nothing I've ever felt before; maybe once when I ... was with ... oh my god!"

"OK," I offer, "just sit quietly; just let it settle."

Tears start streaming as Miriam begins to cry softly. "It feels so deep. I couldn't feel this before. It was just too much when he died. It's different ... I can feel the pain in my body and I won't be destroyed ... Actually the pain in my belly is completely gone ... and it feels warm there ... a soft kind of warm." This is an example of linking islands of safety (see Step 2 in Chapter 5). The linking of resources starts with the sensations of strength and solidity in Miriam's arms and legs as she is able to form boundaries. Then experiencing the visceral sensations of warmth and expansion gives her a developing sense of empowerment and of intact goodness. This "chaining" of resources allows her to

---

* I do this to help her keep connected with me as she goes inside, as well as to feel more grounded.

gradually experience the sensations and feelings of paralysis and help-lessness, which form the core of her traumatic experience. As she does this without being overwhelmed, time has in a sense moved ahead from the frozen past of denial into the present. In the following phase of the session, Miriam accesses the "unfinished business" of anger, loss and guilt. In moving from fixity to flow, she awakens her sensual aliveness.

At this point, I suggest to Miriam that she just sit quietly with her body, that she sort of meditate and wait for any sensations, feelings, pictures or words. She becomes rather still, but not frozen like she appeared earlier in the session. However, after a while she tightens up again:

"I don't really have a picture ... Well, I sort of do, but it's more like I'm thinking about him, about my first husband. And I feel tense all over."

"Look," I suggest, "maybe sit with the tension a little longer and see what develops with the feeling that's in your body."

She seems to drop in again. "My belly feels so tight, it could explode."

"And if it explodes?" I ask.

She is quiet; then, a torrent of tears. "I don't really have a picture of him, but I do have that tightening in my gut again ... What should I do?"

I suggest that she focus on the tightness and make the "voo" sound (see Chapter 6) to help her "open" her guts.

"You're always inside of me. I can never get away from you ... Why are you there? I don't understand ... Hmm," she intones, becoming curious as she goes along. After a few minutes, her legs begin to trem-ble again. The shaking intensifies and spreads—this time, with little jerks into her shoulders. A deep spontaneous breath emerges, and tears stream from her eyes.

Miriam reaches out tentatively with her arms and quickly pulls them back. After another breath she speaks as if to her first husband: "Evan, I'm holding on to you. You're in my guts. I won't open to Henry ... I just keep holding on to you." She starts to cry, but then continues, "I think I'm mad at you. I can't believe I'm saying it, but I'm mad at you for leaving. You left me alone. I hate that you died." She clenches her hands and yells: "I hate you! I hate you! ... Don't leave me, damn it! ... I hate you!" She begins to cry again, this time sobbing deeply.

When she starts to talk, I suggest that she should "maybe just let things settle."

"Yeah, I think you're right ... There's something I'm trying to get away from." Some time passes, and Miriam cries gently, her legs trembling softly. "I haven't opened to Henry. I've been pushing him away. No wonder we're always in conflict. And when he tries to get physical, I just want to push him away ... I felt guilty about that."

Her hands make a pushing movement again. Gradually, her movements become softer: her hands open out into a supine position, and she gently brings them toward her chest in a gesture of reaching and taking into the heart a tentative embrace.

I don't say anything, and Miriam continues, "I needed to protect myself ... I felt so hurt and guilty."

"And how do you feel inside now?" I ask to keep her in the moment.

"Well, actually I feel really good."

"And how do you know that?"

"Well, it's mostly that I feel a lot of space inside myself."

"Where do you feel that?"

"I feel that in my belly and chest ... My head feels like it's got more room too, but mostly my belly and chest, they feel really open ... It feels like a cool breeze is in my body. My legs feel really powerful, and I have a lot of ... I feel shy to say it ... I feel warm and tingling in my, in my ... vagina ... It feels like I really want Henry." She pauses.

"I did what I had to do then," she went on, "but it's time to let go. I was so afraid of my hurt ... but even more afraid of my anger. It's like, if I felt what I felt, I might hurt Henry somehow ... It doesn't make sense logically, but that's what was all twisted up inside of me." She adds, "But I don't need to do that anymore."

Miriam takes a full easy breath and says with a broad joyful grin, "That breath took me and tickled me and laughed me." She laughs freely, looks around the room, then slowly at my face.

She puts her hands to her face—first, to cover it in embarrassment, but then gently holds and strokes it shyly. Tears roll down her cheeks.

"I feel finished ... for now, I mean," she says. "I know there's other stuff, but I just want to sit in your yard by the river for a few minutes, then take a walk ... Thanks ... See you next week."

Bonnie: A Forgotten Moment

The mind has forgotten but the body has
not—thankfully.
—Sigmund Freud

Bonnie is not an aggressive person, but she is by no means a pushover, either. Most of her peers and friends see her as well adjusted, even-handed and assertive. It was therefore surprising to her colleagues, and to herself, when for no apparent reason she became increasingly submissive and unpredictably explosive. At the point when her behavior threatened her relations with her colleagues, she became concerned.

During my Berkeley training class in 1974, Bonnie raised her hand when I requested a volunteer for a demonstration session. This was to be a demonstration that would start solely with symptoms or behavior issues rather than with any recall of a compelling event. I will frequently work without a historical link in order to prevent the client from bypassing bottom-up processing and prematurely jumping to an abstract, interpretational level. Neither I nor Bonnie's classmates knew her "story" when she elected to work with me on her symptoms in front of the group. Bonnie herself did not make the connection between her behavioral changes and an event that had transpired a year and a half earlier and that, as far as she was concerned, was irrelevant.

I asked Bonnie to recall a recent encounter with a colleague that illustrated her sudden shift in behavior, and then we both noted her bodily reactions. Bonnie described feeling a sinking sensation in her belly. I noticed that her shoulders were hunched over and brought that to her attention. When asked to describe how she felt in that position, she replied, "It makes me hate myself." Bonnie was taken aback by this sudden outburst of self-loathing. Rather than analyzing *why* she felt that way, I guided Bonnie back to the sensations in her body.* After a

---

* This is an important difference between "talk therapy" and body-oriented therapy. Rather than trying to help patients make new meanings or *understand* their problems, body therapy creates a space for the "body story" to unfold and complete. When this occurs, new meanings and insights emerge spontaneously, generated by the patients themselves, as an integral part of this process.

pause she reported that her "heart and mind were racing a million miles an hour."

She then became disturbed by what she described as a "sweaty, smelly, hot sensation" on her back, which left her feeling nauseated. Bonnie now seemed more agitated—her face turned pale, and she felt an urge to get up and leave the room. After reassurance, Bonnie chose to remain and continued tracking her discomfort. It intensified and then gradually diminished. Following this ebb and flow, Bonnie became aware of another sensation—a tension in the back of her right arm and shoulder. When she focused her attention on this, she started to feel an urge to thrust her elbow backward. I offered a hand as a support and as a resistance so that Bonnie could safely feel the power in her arm as she pushed it slowly backward. After pushing for several seconds, her body began to shake and tremble as she broke out into a profuse sweat. Her legs also began moving up and down as if they were on sewing machine treadles.

As Bonnie's arm continued its slow press backward, the body shaking decreased, and Bonnie felt as though her legs were getting stronger. She said that they felt "like they wanted to, and could, move." She reported noticing a strong urge propelling her forward. Suddenly, a picture flashed before her—a streetlight and the image of the couple that had "helped her." "I got away ... I got away ...," she cried softly. It was then she remembered molding into the man's torso as he held a knife to her throat. She went on, "I did that to make him think I was his ... Then my body knew what to do, and it did it ... That's what let me escape."

Then the story that her body had been telling emerged in words: eighteen months earlier, Bonnie had been the victim of an attempted rape. While walking home after visiting a friend in another neighborhood, a stranger had pulled her into an alley and threatened to kill her if she didn't cooperate. Somehow, she was able to break free and run to a lighted street corner where two passersby yelled for the police. Bonnie was politely interviewed by the police and then taken home by a friend. Surprisingly, she could not remember how she had escaped, but she was tearfully grateful to have been left unharmed. Afterward, her life appeared to return to normal, but when she felt stressed or in conflict, *her body* was still responding as it had when the knife was held to her throat.

Bonnie found herself helpless and passive or easily enraged under everyday stress, not realizing that this was a replay of the brief pretense at submissiveness that probably saved her life. Her "submission" successfully fooled the assailant, allowing a momentary opportunity for the instinctual energy of a wild animal to take over, propelling her arms and legs in a successful escape. However, it had all happened so fast that she had not had the chance to integrate the experience. At a primitive level, she still didn't "know" that she had escaped, and remained identified with the "submissiveness" rather than with her complete two-phase strategy that had in fact saved her life. Motorically and emotionally, it was like part of her was still in the assailant's clutches.

After processing and completing the rape-related actions, Bonnie now reported having an overall sense of capability and empowerment. She was "back to even more of her [old] self" in place of the previous submissive self-hatred. This new self came from being able to *physically feel* the motor response of elbowing her assailant, and then to *sense* the immense power in her legs that had, in fact, carried her to safety.

This is a case where symptoms did not emerge full-blown for twelve to eighteen months after the traumatic experience. Hence, it was not readily apparent that they were sequelae to a precipitating event. For reasons largely unknown, it is not uncommon for symptoms to be delayed by six months or even one and a half to two years. In addition, symptoms may only manifest after yet another traumatic encounter occurs—sometimes years later.

How many of our own habitual behaviors and feelings are outside of our conscious awareness or are long *accepted* as part of ourselves, of who we are, when in fact they are not? Rather, these behaviors are reactions to events long forgotten (or rationalized) by our minds but remembered accurately by our bodies. We can thank Freud for correctly surmising that both the imprints of horrible experiences, as well as the antidote, and latent catalyst for transformation, exist within our bodies.

Sharon: September 11, 2001

The body has its reasons
that reason cannot reason.

—Pascal

Through the Body's "I"

Just as she did every morning at work, Sharon was reading over her emails. It was a crisp, clear, New York autumn day—the kind of a day that makes one feel excited to be alive. Startled by a thunderous, deafening crash, she turned to witness the walls in her office moving twenty feet in her direction. Though Sharon was immediately mobilized, springing to her feet and readying to flee for her life, she was slowly and methodically led down eighty floors via stairwells filled with the suffocating, acrid smell of burning jet fuel and debris. After finally reaching the mezzanine in the north tower of the World Trade Center one hour and twenty minutes later, the south tower suddenly collapsed. The shock waves lifted Sharon into the air, violently throwing her on top of a crushed, bloody body. An off-duty police detective discovered her, dazed and disoriented, atop the dead man. He helped her find her way out of the wreckage and away from the site, through absolutely thick, pitch-blackness. She met a few other survivors sitting in front of a church, and together they gave thanks to be alive.

In the weeks following her miraculous survival, a dense yellow fog enveloped her in a deadening numbness. Sharon felt indifferent by day, merely going through the motions of living with little passion, direction or pleasure. Just a week before she had loved classical music; now it no longer interested her: she "couldn't stand listening to it." Numb most of the time, she was periodically assaulted by panic attacks. Sleep became her enemy; at night she was awakened by her own screaming and sobbing. For the first time in her life, this once highly motivated executive could not imagine a future for herself; terror had become the organizing principle of her life.*

Sharon's terror was not focused on anything in particular; it appeared everywhere, projected "out there"—onto a world that felt threatening, even when everything was objectively safe and predictable. It kept her from flying, riding the subway or being in public places. She was constantly on guard, whether awake or asleep. Sharon saw me on a television interview, tracked me down through my institute and then traveled four days and nights, by train, to see me in Los Angeles, where I was teaching. On December 1, 2001, we did the session summarized below.

When she enters the room, dressed smartly in an orange business suit, Sharon walks straight to a chair and sits down without seeming even to notice me. It makes me eerily uncomfortable when, almost before I had introduced myself, she begins talking about the horrors of the event, blandly, as though it had happened to someone else.† Had I not comprehended her words, I might have thought she was talking about a boring office party rather than a personal confrontation with death and dismemberment. Listening to her emotionally disconnected narrative left me squirming, wanting to get up and leave the room. I am unsettled at what lies hidden underneath her blandness.

My introspection is interrupted, drawn to the intimation of a slight, expansive gesture made by Sharon's arms and hands as she speaks; it's as though she were reaching toward something to hold on to. Is Sharon's body telling another story, *a story* that is hidden from her mind? I ask her to put her verbal narrative aside for the moment and to place her

---

* The sense of a foreshortened life, of wordless despair, is a central characteristic of severe trauma. The person is in a fundamental way stuck in the horrific imprint of the past and thus cannot imagine a future different from the past.

† This is an effect of dissociation. It is as though Sharon is describing what happened to another person; it is as though she is outside of her body, observing, but not really being present. She lives back at the moment of shock where dissociation is what allowed her to survive the unimaginable horror and terror. In the Hollywood, Hitchcock version of trauma, the sufferer is barraged by flashbacks. In real life, though, the numbing or shutting-down phase is often more significant and is generally characteristic of severe and/or chronic trauma. These are the people who become the "walking dead."

attention, instead, on the nascent message her hands are communicating to both of us. I encourage her to pursue this avenue by *slowly* repeating the movement and keeping her focus on its physical sensation.* Moving slowly and focusing attention on a movement allows it to be felt in a special way. When clients do this, most often they will experience their arms (or other part of the body) moving as if on its own ("like my arm is moving me!"). People will often smile or laugh because the sensation of the arm moving itself seems so unusual.†

Perplexed at first, Sharon describes the gesture as though she is "holding something." A noticeable shift occurs in her body; her face is visibly less strained and her shoulders less rigid. Unexpectedly, a fleeting image of the Hudson River appears in her mind's eye, the daily view from the living room in her apartment across the river from Manhattan.

Jumping back to the narrative story, Sharon becomes agitated as she tells me how she is haunted, revisited, by the smoldering smoke plumes, which she now sees every day from this same window. They evoke the horribly acrid smells from that day; she feels a burning in her nostrils. Rather than letting her go on "reliving" the traumatic intrusion, I firmly contain and coax her to continue focusing on the sensations of her arm movements. A spontaneous image *emerges*, one of boats moving on the river. They convey to her a comforting sense of timelessness, movement and flow. "You can destroy the buildings, but you can't drain the Hudson," she pronounces softly. Then, rather than going on with the horrifying details of the event, she surprises herself by describing *(and feeling)* how beautiful it had been when she had set out for work on that "perfect autumn morning."

---

*Frequently, people will make exaggerated gestures as a way of avoiding feeling the underlying sensations.

†I believe that this is because these very slow ("intrinsic") movements, when done mindfully, operate through the gamma efferent system. This system is intimately connected to the brain stem–autonomic nervous system and involves the extra pyramidal motor system. Voluntary movement, on the other hand, is controlled by the alpha motor system and is independent of the autonomic nervous system. Gamma-mediated movements tend to "re-set" the nervous system away from extremes of activation.

This process is an example of expanding the "aperture" of an image to its pretraumatic state (as described in Chapter 7). Up to the moment before the impact of the jet, it had been a perfect day, infused with vibrant colors and gentle scents. These sense impressions still exist somewhere in the catacombs of consciousness, but they have been over-ridden by the traumatic fixation. Gradually restoring the full spectrum of the disparate parts of an image is an integral component of resolving trauma.*

Sharon's body and images are beginning to tell a story that contrasts markedly with the one her words are relaying, almost as though narrated by two entirely different persons. As she holds the images of the Hudson River, along with the associated body sensations, she becomes aware of a tentative sense of relief. She now innocently recalls how she had been excited to come to work that day. Her gesture is stronger and more definite. Continued attention to the physical feeling of the gesture deepens her sense of relaxation, stimulating an almost playful curiosity. As she looks quizzically at her hands, first one then the other, I breathe a sigh of relief. Such a seemingly insignificant shift has profound implications—playful curiosity being one of the prima facie "antidotes" for trauma. Curious exploration, pleasure and trauma cannot coexist in the nervous system; neurologically, they contradict one another.†

This capacity to experience the positive bodily feelings (of interest and curiosity), while remaining in contact with her feelings of terror and helplessness, allows Sharon to do something she would not have been able to do a few minutes before. She can now begin to stand back and "simply" observe these difficult, uncomfortable, *physical* sensations and images without becoming overwhelmed by them.‡ They are, in

---

*Returning to these positive, expansive sights is not an avoidance, but rather an integral part of trauma resolution.

† This is similar to the widely accepted principle of reciprocal inhibition discovered by the Nobel Prize–winning physiologist Sir Charles Sherrington.

‡ This is the inherent capacity to pendulate (to rhythmically shift between states of distress/contraction and pleasure/expansion; see Step 3 in Chapter 5). Pendulation is an essential ingredient in the alchemy of transformation—it is what brings people into present time.

other words, kept at bay. This dual consciousness induces a shift that allows sensations to be felt as they are: intrinsically energetic, vital and in present time, rather than as fragments, triggers and harbingers of fear and helplessness from the past. This felt distinction makes it possible for Sharon to review and assimilate many details of the horrific event without reliving it. This new "dexterity" for revisiting, without reliving, a traumatic experience is essential in the process of recovery and reengagement that I call *renegotiation.*

People need to disengage the emotional and mental *associations* from the raw physical sensations they have come to experience as precursors of disaster but that are, ultimately, sensations of vitality. Reestablishing these enlivening affects is a central core of effective trauma treatment. Interestingly, it is also found in ancient healing practices, such as meditation, shamanism and yoga.

Taking the Plunge

When the first plane hit the building, only ten stories above her office, the explosion sent a shock wave of terror through her body. People's immediate reaction to such terrifying events is to arrest, orient and then escape. This usually entails an intense urge to run. However, trapped eighty stories above ground with thousands of other people, Sharon needed to inhibit this primal reaction. Against the intense impulses to flee, she compelled herself to stay "calm" and walk in an orderly line down the stairs along with dozens of other terrified individuals; this was the case even though her body was "adrenaline-charged" to run at full throttle. Surely Sharon also felt the potential for any one of the other trapped office workers to suddenly panic and start a stampede that would further imperil them all. They, like her, also had to restrain their powerful primal urge to run. As Sharon slowly recounts the details of the escape, while *feeling her bodily response, step-by-step,* she recalls encountering yet another moment of stark terror when she found the door at the seventieth floor locked and impassable.

Because of the physical comfort she found in contacting the spontaneous, expansive gestures and the images of the Hudson River, I now trust that Sharon can more safely face some of this highly charged material without becoming overwhelmed and consequently retraumatized.* In following her "body story," islands of safety (Steps 1 through 3 in Chapter 5) are beginning to form in Sharon's stormy trauma sea. The safety experienced from these internal islands allows her to deal with increasing levels of arousal and to move through them without undue distress.

From this assessment, I guide her back to the moment of the explosion and then have her locate where and *how* that violent imprint feels *in her body*. As she attends to this "felt sense," she becomes aware of an overall feeling of agitation in her legs and arms and tight "lumps" in her gut and throat. She says that she feels stuck. Here I introduce her to using the "voo" sound as a way to help her dissolve and transform the stuck sensations (see Chapter 6). As she focuses on those uncomfortable physical sensations (with the help of the vibratory sounds), the inclination to try to understand or explain them is reduced. With keenly focused attention, I guide her away from interpreting what she is feeling because I do not want the meaning to come from a mental place. The body needs to tell what's on its "mind" *first* in order for new perceptions to arise in present time. (This warning about "premature cognition" was displayed on a bumper sticker I recently saw: "Reality: It's not what you think!")

Sharon quietly takes some moments to reflect. In suspending the compulsion for understanding, she experiences a sudden "burst of energy coming from deep inside my belly." Does it have a color, I ask? "Yes, it's red, bright red, like a fire." Though visibly startled by its intensity, she does not recoil from its potency. Her experience shifts into (what she recognized as) a strong urge to run, concentrated in her legs and arms. However, with the very *thought* of running she again "freezes." I sense that she is caught between the real and necessary desire to escape and her "unconscious" mind, which associates fleeing with being trapped. As on the stairwell, she had to *restrain* her powerful escape impulse and

---

* To the nervous system, being overwhelmed by an event is really little different than being overwhelmed by similar sensations and emotions that are internally generated.

walk slowly—even though she was in mortal danger. This dilemma was compounded with the shock of finding the door locked on the seventieth floor. Then, when she eventually reached the mezzanine, the south tower collapsed and she was thrown violently into the air. Finally, there was the stark horror of finding herself lying semiconscious on a dead body.

Two Brains

Sharon was caught in a conflict between two very different centers in her brain: the raw, primitive self-preservation messages from the brain stem and limbic system were demanding that she run for her life, while her frontal cortex was sending messages of inhibition and restraint. It was telling her to be "reasonable" and walk calmly in an orderly line. In our session, it was crucial to *separate* the terrifying *expectations* of being trapped from her somatic *biological impulses to act on and "metabolize" that survival energy*. In order to *uncouple* the two, I ask if she can focus on the intense "electricity" she describes experiencing in her body and imagine taking it somewhere where she had previously enjoyed running. She stiffens in response to that invitation. She says, "It would make me feel too anxious." I then surprise her by asking her *where* she feels the anxiety and *what* it feels like (see the Epilogue to this case). Disarmed, Sharon blurts out, "I don't know. Oh, it's my neck and shoulders and my chest feels like I can't breathe ... My legs are so tight that ... I don't know, they feel like they could ..."

"Like what?" I ask.

"Like they want to run," she responds. Then, with a little reassurance, she begins to feel the sensations of running along a path in her favorite park. After a few minutes, I observe a gentle trembling in her legs. I ask her what she is feeling, to which she responds, "I could really feel the running; it was full-out ... and I don't feel the anxiety anymore."

"OK, Sharon," I interject, "but *what* do you feel?"

"Well, actually I feel good, relieved ... I feel tingly and relieved; and my breath feels really deep and easy; and my legs are warm and relaxed." A tear gently streaks down her cheek. Her face and hands have an even pink color.

This was the beginning of Sharon's *separating* the powerful *biological* urge to escape from her mental and emotional expectation that she would again be trapped and overwhelmed. By imagining—with full engagement in her bodily experience—the sense that she was running, unfettered, in a safe place, she was able to *complete* the frozen action locked in her body.* Just having Sharon imagine running would not have had much of an effect. However, first approaching the place where she was trapped, revisiting *(touching into)* that moment of terror and then experiencing the (new) possibility of completing that motor act was the therapeutic denouement.[98]

Having felt her highly charged physically sensations, *just as they were*, not as she feared or imagined they were, was the linchpin to uncoupling the catastrophic thoughts, as well as the emotions of terror and panic, from her actual physical experience. During this process, which lasted almost two hours, and which was punctuated with cycles of soft trembling and gentle sweating, she gradually developed the capacity to tolerate her sensations until they came to their natural completion. I believe evidence exists supporting the idea that this fulfilled and successful action "switched" certain critical brain circuits, allowing her to experience the possibility of meaningful, effective action rather than helpless anxiety.[99] In this way her immobilizing anxiety transformed into a "flowing wave of warm energy." The vast "life or death" energy of survival had metamorphosed, through cycles of trembling discharge, into feelings of aliveness and goodness.

After directly experiencing this relief as a sensation in her body (a sensation that directly contradicted her paralyzing terror) Sharon regained a sense of aliveness and the *felt* reality that she had, indeed, survived and that her life had a future with expanding possibilities. She no longer felt trapped in the horror of the event; it began to recede to the past where it belonged. And it was now possible to travel on the

---

* Until this was done, Sharon still experienced herself as being stuck in the stairwell. All of her thoughts had revolved around this deeply imprinted belief. By having the (new) *physical* sensation of running at a heightened level of arousal, Sharon contradicts her previous, bodily, experience of helpless freezing.

subway to hear her favorite music at Lincoln Center. A new and different meaning for her life arose out of a new and different experience at the instinctual bodily level.

This was the story Sharon's body told. It is reminiscent of Antonio Damasio's prose:

> We use our minds not to discover facts but to hide them. One of the things the screen hides most effectively is the body, our own body, by which I mean, the ins and outs of it, its interiors. Like a veil thrown over the skin to secure its modesty, the screen partially removes from the mind the inner states of the body, those that constitute the flow of life as it wanders in the journey of each day.[100]

Epilogue
Our feelings and our bodies are like water
flowing into water. We learn to swim
within the energies of the [body] senses.
—Tarthang Tulku

To review, human beings have been designed over millennia, through natural selection and social evolution, to live with and to move through extreme events and loss, and to process feelings of helplessness and terror *without* becoming stuck or traumatized. When we experience difficult and particularly horrible sensations and feelings, our tendency, however, is to recoil and avoid them. Mentally, we split off or "dissociate" from these feelings. Physically, our bodies tighten and brace against them. Our minds go into overdrive trying to explain and make sense of these alien and "bad" sensations. So, we are driven to vigilantly attempt to locate their ominous source in the outside world. We believe that if we feel the sensations, they will overwhelm us forever. The fear of being consumed by these "terrible" feelings leads us to convince ourselves that avoiding them will make us feel better and, ultimately, safer. There are many examples of this in our lives: we may avoid a café or certain songs that remind us of a former loved one or avoid the intersection where we were rear-ended a year ago.

Unfortunately, the opposite is true. When we fight against and/or hide from unpleasant or painful sensations and feelings, we generally make things worse. The more we avoid them, the greater is the power they exert upon our behavior and sense of well-being. What is not felt remains the same or is intensified, generating a cascade of virulent and corrosive emotions. This forces us to fortify our methods of defense, avoidance and control. This is the vicious cycle created by trauma. Abandoned feelings, in the form of *blocked physical sensations*, create and propel the growing shadow of our existence. As we saw with Sharon, when we focus in a particular way *on physical sensations*, in a short period of time they shift and change; and so do we.

Premature Cognition

Sharon's misdirected beliefs (though largely subconscious) are efforts to understand, to make sense of her experience and to help her justify *why* she feels so bad. These "explanations" will do nothing to help her move through her fright response and complete the inhibited actions that form the basis of her continued trauma response (the *how*). Mentation, at this stage, only interferes with resolution. For this reason I coach her to resist the seduction to understand and, instead, to fully engage with what she is *now* physically feeling in her body. The consequence of "premature cognition" is to take the person out of his or her sensate experience before it completes and has the opportunity to generate new perceptions and new meanings.

The Experience of Anxiety Is Not Universal

If you ask several anxious people what they are feeling, they may all *say* that they are feeling "anxiety." However, you are likely to get several different responses if they are then queried with the epistemological question, "How do you *know* that you are feeling anxiety?" One may state, "I know because something bad will happen to me." Another will say that he is feeling strangulated in his throat; another that her heart is leaping out of her chest; and yet another that he has butterflies or a

knot in his gut. Still other people might report that their neck, shoulders, arms or legs are tight; yet others might feel ready for action; while
still others might sense that their legs feel weak or that their chests are
collapsed. All but the first reply are specific and varied *physical* sensations. And if the person who feared that "something bad will happen
to me" was directed to do a scan of her body, she would have discovered some *somatic/physical* sensation driving and directing that thought.
With a little practice we can actually start to separate out emotions,
thoughts and beliefs from the underlying sensations. We are then
astounded by our capacity to tolerate and pass through difficult emotional states, such as terror, rage and helplessness, without being swept
away and drowned. If we go *underneath* the overwhelming emotions
and touch into *physical sensations*, something quite profound occurs in
our organism—there is a sense of flow, of "coming home." This is a
truth central to several ancient spiritual traditions, particularly certain
traditions in Tibetan Buddhism.[101]

The Transformative Power of Sensation

To understand the transforming power of direct sensate experience, it
is necessary to "dissect" certain emotions such as terror, rage and helplessness (see Chapter 13). When we perceive (consciously or unconsciously) that we are in danger, specific *defensive postures* necessary to
protect ourselves are mobilized in our bodies. Instinctively we duck,
we dodge, we retract and stiffen, we prepare to fight or flee; and when
escape seems impossible, we freeze or fold into helpless collapse. All of
these are *specific innate bodily responses*, powerfully energized to meet
extreme situations. They allow a woman weighing one hundred and
twenty pounds to lift a car off her trapped child. It is the same primal
force that propels a gazelle to sprint at seventy miles per hour in order
to escape the pursuing cheetah.

These survival energies are organized in the brain and specifically
expressed as patterned states of muscular tension in *readiness for action*.
However, when we are activated to this level and, like Sharon, are
prevented from *completing* that course of action—as in fighting or

fleeing—then the system moves into freeze or collapse, and the energized tension actually remains stuck in the muscles. In turn, these unused, or partially used, muscular tensions set up a stream of nerve impulses ascending the spinal cord to the thalamus (a central relay station for sensations) and then to other parts of the brain (particularly the amygdala), signaling the continued presence of danger and threat. Said simply, *if our muscles and guts are set to respond to danger, then our mind will tell us that we have something to fear.* And if we cannot localize the cause of our distress, then we will continue to search for one; a good example of this was Sharon's struggle to understand her experience. We see this in Vietnam vets who are terrified by the sounds of the 4th of July fireworks, even though they "know" rationally that they are not in any danger. Other examples are people who fear driving a car after they have been involved in an accident or people who fear even leaving the house because they do not know where these danger signals are originating from. In fact, if we cannot find an explanation for what we are feeling, we will surely manufacture one, or many. We'll often blame our spouses, children, bosses, neighbors (be they next door or another nation) or just plain bad luck. Our minds will stay on overdrive, obsessively searching for causes in the past and dreading the future. We will stay tense and on guard, feeling fear, terror and helplessness *because* our bodies continue to signal danger to our brains. Our minds may or may not "agree," but these red flags (coming from nonconscious parts of the brain) will not disappear until *the body* completes its course of action. This is how we are made—it is our biological nature, hardwired into brain and body.

These bodily reactions are not metaphors; they are literal postures that inform our emotional experience. For example, tightness in the neck, shoulders and chest and knots in the gut or throat are central to states of fear. Helplessness is signaled by a literal collapsing of the chest and shoulders, along with a folding at the diaphragm and weakness in the knees and legs. All of these "postural attitudes" represent action potentials. If they are allowed to complete their meaningful course of action, then all is well; if not, they live on in the theatre of the body.

If frightening sensations, such as the ones Sharon was experiencing, are not given the time and attention needed to move through the body and resolve/dissolve (as in trembling and shaking), the individual will continue to be gripped by fear and other negative emotions. The stage is set for a trajectory of mercurial symptoms. Tension in the neck, shoulders and back will likely evolve over time to the syndrome of fibromyalgia. Migraines are also common somatic expressions of unresolved stress. The knots in the gut may mutate to common conditions like irritable bowel syndrome, severe PMS or other gastrointestinal problems such as spastic colon. These conditions deplete the energy resources of the sufferer and may take the form of chronic fatigue syndrome. These sufferers are most often the patients with cascading symptoms who visit doctor after doctor in search of relief, and generally find little help for what ails them. Trauma is the great masquerader and participant in many maladies and "dis-eases" that afflict sufferers. It can perhaps be conjectured that unresolved trauma is responsible for a majority of the illnesses of modern mankind.

Renegotiation

The concept of renegotiation is completely different from cathartic "traumatic reliving," or flooding, a common form of trauma therapy still used after "critical events" like rapes, natural disasters and horror, like the World Trade Center attack that Sharon experienced on 9-11. Recent studies suggest that these therapies often do little to help and can actually be retraumatizing.[102]

One of the pitfalls of various trauma therapies has been their focus on the reliving of traumatic memories along with the intense abreaction of emotions. In these exposure-based treatments, patients are prodded into the dredging up of painful traumatic memories and abreacting emotions associated with these memories, specifically those of fear, terror, anger and grief. These cathartic approaches fall short as they often reinforce sensations of collapse and feelings of helplessness.

Adam: Holocaust Survivor

Adam was a financially successful businessman in his mid-sixties when I worked with him. He had a wife and family and was the owner of a multinational electronics company. As a quiet, kindly person, he was well liked by his employees and his acquaintances; yet Adam had no truly intimate friendships. Recently, his first grandchild was born. By all outward appearances, life has been good. It was the suicide of his son at the age of twenty-seven years that has broken this man of fierce, though subdued, determination. It has reduced him to obsessive self-blame and self-hatred.

"There was always something different about Paulo," Adam stated matter-of-factly. "He was a sensitive child who was easily frightened. When he was around the age of four years old, for reasons unknown, he would awaken in the middle of the night screaming and crying."

By late adolescence Paulo talked frequently of suicide. "Life is too hard," he had repeated numerous times. Adam made sure that his son was never left alone during his darkest times. He had been fatigued by this decade-long ordeal, but he persisted in his committed vigil. Despite Adam's exhaustive efforts to save his son, Paulo—no longer able to bear his pain—hanged himself in the bathroom. It was there that Adam found his limp, lifeless body. After the shock of Paulo's suicide, Adam found that for the first time in his life he could not push ahead. Rather than feeling shattered by grief, Adam felt nothing . . . a state familiar to him even before losing his son. But this time, the numbness rendered him so fully shut down that he could not function. Life for him just stopped.

After several months of paralyzing inertia, Adam made an appointment to see a psychiatrist. He was prompted to do this by a family friend who advised him to get some medication for his despondent condition. After taking a personal history, the psychiatrist suggested that Adam's past was preventing him from grieving his son's death and gave him the diagnosis of "complicated bereavement." Although the idea that his early life was "traumatic" or even implicated in his current malaise perplexed Adam, he agreed to talk to me.

Adam was born a motherless child. A massive heart attack during labor necessitated an emergency cesarean to save her only child. She died just as he was being born two months prematurely. Since his father had been conscripted into the Russian army, Adam was given to his father's brother to be raised by his uncle and his wife. The aunt, who was supposed to care for him, was instead a cruel, likely psychotic, woman who repeatedly beat him.

Beyond the torment of this treacherous beginning, rife with abandonment and abuse, Adam's life moved through a series of further trials and sorrows. At the age of four years, his uncle and two older stepsisters were deported and exterminated by the Nazis. He was then passed on to a series of Christian families who tried to hide his Jewish origins. During this time he would, according to these families, scream in the middle of the night—just as Paulo had done when he was the same age.

At the age of nine, Adam was given to a group of fugitives living in the forest. He "loved being there" because the people liked him and for the first time ever, he felt wanted. "That year was the best of my life," he told me. Even though he loved and felt protected by his "forest family," his night fits continued and grew in intensity. His crying and screaming would never subside, despite all attempts to soothe him. Since he could not even be awakened, the noise of his fits put his forest family in grave danger. So tragically, before his tenth birthday, Adam was sent back to the village, where he wandered aimlessly as an orphan.

One night, Adam was taken to the police station and interrogated. As he had been instructed, he gave the Nazis his Christian name. The police told him he would be punished if he lied. Next, they forced him to remove his pants in full view of everyone. To hide his shame, nine-year-old Adam stared at the wall, only to see a crucifix. This terrified him, causing him to believe that he would end up on a cross if he were caught lying. He was then taken to a concentration camp. "Being delivered alive to the concentration camp," he said, "was a relief; at least I was with other Jews."

Upon entering the camp, one of the prisoners from the village asked Adam his name. Now among his own people, Adam gave the name he had grown up with, and the names of those whom he believed to be his parents. The man then exclaimed, "No, no, that's not your real family name." And he told him the names of his biological parents and how they had both died. Adam remembered being unspeakably relieved to know that the cruel mother he had experienced was not his real mother.

While in the concentration camp, Adam witnessed people being brutally beaten, tortured and shot. Many others succumbed to suicide, often by hanging themselves. During his internment, Adam was without any real comfort or support to help him deal with such terror and horror. For most of us, Adam's experience is unimaginable. If we were to honestly ponder the effect it would have had on us, we would be deeply disturbed by such terrible knowledge. Yet, to observe Adam in his life, he appeared, at least on the surface, little different from you or me, only more successful by modern-day standards.

As an orphan from birth and a survivor of the most unimaginable atrocities and human suffering, Adam had risen above this torment. He immigrated to South America at the age of nineteen, hoping "to escape his past." There he settled and built his business, becoming a powerful, financially successful, international entrepreneur. Yet, when this extraordinary human being was referred to me, he had been reduced to a broken man. He was stooped over and shuffled as he entered the room. His posture and movements reminded me of patients I have seen in the back wards of psychiatric hospitals. His eyes looked blankly at the floor, and he seemed not to notice that I was even present. I had no idea where to begin. On the one hand, he was so shut down that it seemed like nothing I could say or do would reach him; but on the other hand, I feared that if I were able to bring up feelings, they might overwhelm him so completely that he would collapse into a bottomless catatonic despair. How could I reach this man without destroying him? I felt lost and intimidated by the scope and delicate challenge of my task.

By rote, Adam went on and on with the litany he had told the psychiatrist. There was not a trace of feeling in his narrative: "That all happened so long ago," he added with a small tired sigh. I listened, finding myself quite uncomfortable at hearing such horror described without affect. In a strange way, though, I was relieved that he had no feeling; that way I wouldn't have to feel either. Intellectually, I distanced myself from feeling and from Adam. I was able to do this by falling back on a clinical analysis, wondering what mechanism he had used to wall himself off from his horrific experiences and how he had kept himself from winding up wandering in the streets, like he had done as an orphan, or in the back ward of some mental institution.

As a way to try to initiate a little contact, I questioned Adam about his work, his family and friends—any topic where I thought there might be an entry point to even a tiny trace of positive feeling. Nothing came of this. I found myself, strangely, asking him to describe the last few hours of his day. Puzzled, he told me of missing his flight and frantically renting a car to drive the two hundred miles from Curitiba to São Paulo to meet with me. At the rental lot near the airport he recalled seeing children flying kites that they had made from things found at the garbage dump.* I caught the first flicker on his otherwise expressionless face. But then, just as quickly, his face became flat again, and his body slumped forward in resignation. Not wanting him to collapse, I asked him to stand up with his knees slightly bent. Standing requires the activation and coordination of the proprioceptive and kinesthetic systems. This had the effect of keeping Adam's awareness online by engaging the arousal branch of his nervous system. This intervention is the opposite of allowing a client to collapse, activating the shutdown response and thus perpetuating the mortifying feelings of shame and defeat. While he was standing erect with relaxed knees, I then directed Adam to "look inside" and find some place within his body where he could "find the picture of the children playing with their improvised kite."† At first, he reported feeling more anxious (due to sympathetic hyperarousal), but with encouragement, Adam was able to locate a small

---

* The exuberance of ghetto kids joyfully flying such improvised kites is portrayed in the classic film *Black Orpheus (Orfeu Negro)*, a reworking of the Greek myth set in Rio de Janeiro.

† At this point I did not want to ask Adam to try to feel something (this would only lead to frustration and failure), but rather to interest him in initiating exploration (in "finding the picture inside").

circle of warmth in his belly. I asked him to "just get to know that sensation for a little while."

He abruptly opened his eyes, surprising himself with his own words: "This could be dangerous."

"Yes," I agreed, "it could be; that's why it's important to learn about feeling, just a little bit at a time. Your body has been frozen for a long time; it will take some time to thaw," I add. It was important that I validate his legitimate fear and offer him an image (thawing from freeze) that would help mitigate his fear, inviting him to explore his internal experience.

Adam then sat down and looked around the room. I asked him to describe what he saw.* This provided the opportunity to connect the warmth in his belly with how he perceived the external world in the here and now. He looked perplexed. "Oh, I didn't notice those flowers before—or the table they're on." Almost like the inquisitive expression of someone coming out of a coma, his face showed another minute flickering of awakening. He looked around noticing an oriental carpet and a painting. "They have colors, rich colors," he said innocently.

"So as you look at those colors, I want you to find the place inside of your body that can feel—even, just the tiniest bit, those colors."[†]

He looked back at me with a puzzled expression, perhaps awaiting further instructions. But then he closed his eyes and went inside. "It feels warmer in my belly, and the circle, it's growing bigger in size."

After a few moments I asked him to stand again: "Adam, I'm going to ask you to do something that might seem strange ... I'm going to ask you to visualize the picture of the children with their kites ... Feel your feet on the ground and how your legs support you. Now feel *your* arms as *you* hold the kite string ... and imagine that you are there in the field with the children."

---

* This is done to amplify figure ground perception and presence.

† It is important to take a little piece of new internal experience like this and connect it to external perceiving. This is the "figure ground" that gives rise to the "experience of now."

Adam responded almost gleefully, "I can feel that in my arms and in my belly ... It's even warmer and bigger ... I can see the colors; they are bright and warm ... I see the kites dancing in the clouds."

After a few quiet moments Adam sat down and looked around the room. "Take all the time you need, Adam ... Just feel the rhythm of that ... of the inside and the outside."*

His eyes went back and forth between the table with the flowers and the painting. He focused on the table and started to describe the color and grain of the wood as warm ... he paused ... "like the warm feeling inside." He closed his eyes again, without my instruction this time, rested for a bit and then opened them slowly and turned toward me, unabashedly looking into my eyes. This was the first time that Adam's social engagement system (see Chapter 6) had awakened and come online.

Adam's body showed some tentative aliveness; his drooping face assumed a colorful, almost vibrant, tone, and his stooped posture extended and straightened. Adam was like a tightly curled, newborn banana leaf turning and reaching toward the sun, confiding in its warmth as it slowly unfurls itself. He was in wonder of the room—as though seeing it for the first time. He looked at his hands and then gently held the fingers of one hand in the other. He then moved his hands to his upper arms and held his shoulders, arms crossed over his chest. It was as though he were holding and nurturing himself. He surprised us both by saying, "I'm alive."

By learning that he could begin to feel, Adam became, in that moment, like the child, proud with the wondrous creation of his kite. That was the beginning of a gradual, rhythmical learning for Adam. Now, he could begin to feel his body-self without opening too widely the dark door of violence and horror in his soul. He was able to open up just enough to feel—to feel without being annihilated, without being swallowed up by the black hole of his horrific past or lost in the deep shadow of his immense grief and guilt about Paulo. Somehow, in this body-mindfulness, he was finding that there was a middle ground. He had uncovered a place

---

* Figure-ground shifting is often a general movement to fluidity and flow.

between being completely overwhelmed and flooded, on one hand, and shut down into a deadening depression on the other.

Adam later wrote to me that his experience of a tender, yet durable, middle ground allowed him to experience a new sense of hopefulness. From this place, he was able to feel compassion for himself as the orphaned Holocaust child. "It was also the beginning," he said, "of my being able to mourn for my beloved son and to find joyful pleasure with my family."

Discussion Points

I reflected on our session and on what might have brought Adam out of his immobilizing depression and into the stream of life. He was able to identify with the slum child's exuberance—an exuberance that transcended the child's deprived fate. Adam was able to feel, in his own body, the innocence, excitement and joy of a child flying a kite improvised from scraps of scavenged trash. In a similar way, Adam collected scraps from the trash heap of his devastating and dehumanizing past. This time, instead of collapsing under its weight, he marshaled a creative solution. By standing up (kinesthetically contradicting his habitual collapse) and physically grounding his pain, he mobilized his life force and joined with the transcendent flight of the kite. He could feel himself being drawn upward by the soaring image, and toward the possibility of authentic freedom and spontaneous play. Metaphorically, he reacquainted himself with the allegory of his namesake. Adam connected with the innocence of the biblical Adam—before the bitter fruit of terrible knowledge had singed his tongue with the bitter taste of man's cruel and evil inhumanity. This formerly broken man now had touched into the grounded embodiment and resilient self-compassion enough to begin grieving and thus initiate a movement back into life. I did not want to expose (and most certainly flood) him with the shock of seeing his son hanging in the bathroom. My main consideration, at this point, was to coax his nervous system out of the shutdown caused by the shock and to begin establishing a base of resilience and self-regulation.

I'd like to invite you, the reader, to ponder the following considerations. Were Paulo's inconsolable screaming episodes beginning at age four and his choice of hanging himself mere coincidences? (Remember, Adam's wife reported that her husband would also scream and cry during the night, just as his son had done). Or were these incidents some deep transgenerational reenactment of his father's unfelt experiences and unprocessed emotions? Such possibilities are among the mysteries of trauma and of the human spirit.

Certain authors discussing the Holocaust, such as Yael Danieli[103] and Robert Lifton,[104] have written groundbreaking analyses of the victims who lived through this horrific massacre. In working with Adam and a few other survivors of this kind of experience, I am personally confronted not only with the terrible knowledge of the cruelty that human beings are capable of, but also of the remarkable process by which the body is somehow able to compartmentalize the effects of this cruelty and go on with life. It maintains its tenuous hold, that is, until something is added to the unsustainable containment of their burden. Yet still, the smoldering flame of the deep self can miraculously reignite, given the right opportunity and carefully calibrated support.

Epilogue

After our session, Adam returned to the Polish town where he was born in search of any knowledge about his real mother, who had died during his birth. The Nazis had not destroyed the tombstone, and Adam replaced it with a new memorial stone because his heart "was so touched by knowing about her existence."

Vince: A Frozen Shoulder

The collision between the two contrary
processes, one of excitation and the other
of inhibition, which were difficult to
accommodate simultaneously, or too
unusual in duration or intensity, or both,
causes a breakdown of equilibrium.

—Ivan Pavlov

It is not uncommon, particularly for a fireman, to be reluctant to see a psychotherapist—a "mind doctor." This is especially true for a problem that is "obviously" physical. Vince was seeing a physical therapist for a frozen right shoulder. This disability was making it impossible for him to function in his job as a fireman. Treatment was not going well: after several sessions he was still barely able to move his arm from his trunk by more than a few inches. The consulting orthopedist had advised surgery: an operation in which the arm is "manipulated" (yanked violently) under general anesthesia in an attempt to free it. Such a surgery requires extensive and painful rehabilitation and often doesn't improve the situation very much.

Since there was no apparent physical injury, the therapist, in the hope of avoiding the difficult procedure, referred him to me. The symptoms had begun a couple of months before our appointment. He was working in his garage and picked up a starter motor to put into his car. As he lifted it, he felt "a twinge of something" in his arm. The next day his shoulder felt tight and sore. Over time, the pain became more acute, and his range of motion progressively worsened, becoming chronic. Not surprisingly, Vince attributed his shoulder "strain" to working on his car. This is somewhat like the person who reaches down and picks up a piece of paper, only to have their back go into spasm. Common sense, and the clinical observation of most chiropractors and massage therapists dictates that this was already a back primed—"an accident waiting to happen."

Vince is obviously confused about seeing a "mind doctor," and he is reluctant to engage with me. Sensing this, I reassure him that I will not be asking him personal questions, but would just focus on helping him get rid of his symptoms. "Yeah," he says, "my body sure is broke." I ask him to show me how far he can move it *before* it starts to hurt. He moves it a few of inches and then looks up at me: "That's about it."

"OK, now I want you to move it the same way, but *much* slower, like this." I show him with my arm.

"Huh," he replies as he glances at his arm. He is clearly surprised that he could move it a few inches farther without the pain.

"Even slower, this time, Vince … Let's see what happens this time … I want you to really give it your *full attention;* focus your mind into your arm now." Moving slowly allows awareness to be brought to the arm. Just moving it quickly, without mindfulness, is likely to re-create the protective holding pattern.

His hand begins to tremble, and he looks to me for some reassurance. "Yes, Vince, just let that happen. It's a good thing. It's your muscles starting to let go. Try to keep your mind focused there, with your arm and with the trembling. Just let your arm move the way it wants to." The trembling goes on for a while and then stops; Vince's forehead breaks out in sweat.

As Vince moves to the edge of the bracing pattern, some of the "energy" held in his muscular-defense pattern begins to release. This includes the involuntary autonomic nervous system reactions, such as shaking, trembling sweating and temperature changes.* Because these are subcortically based actions, the person does not have a feeling of control over their reactions. This may be quite unsettling. My function here is that of a coach and midwife, helping Vince to befriend these "ego alien" sensations, especially since he is wholly unaccustomed to involuntary reactions that he can't control.

"What is this, why is it happening?" Vince asks me in the voice of a frightened child.

---

* I believe that slow, mindful movements evoke the involuntary functions of the nervous system, particularly the extrapyramidal/gamma-efferent system.

"Vince, I'm going to ask you to just close your eyes for a minute now and go inside your body. I'll be right here if you need me." After some moments of silence his hands and arm begin to extend outward, his whole arm, shoulders and hands are now shaking more intensely. "It's OK for that to happen," I encourage; "just let it do what it needs to do and keep feeling your body."

"It feels cold then hot," he replies as he continues to reach out, moving now to about forty-five degrees. Then he halts abruptly. Amazed that he can reach out so far, his eyes open wide. At the same time, he seems agitated; his face suddenly turns pale. He complains of feeling sick.

Instead of backing off, I coach him to stay present with his physical sensations. He starts to breathe rapidly. "Oh my god, I know what this is."

"Yes, good," I interrupt, "but let's just stay with the sensations for a little longer, then we'll talk about it—is that OK?"* Vince nods and moves his arm back and forth from his shoulder as thought he were sawing a piece of wood in slow motion. In this slow movement, Vince is beginning to explore the inner movement held in check and locked in a bracing pattern. He is now separating two conflicting impulses, one involving reaching out and the other, pulling away in revulsion. (I observe the revulsion as a particular pattern involving the retraction of his lip to one side and the hint of his head slightly turning away.) The trembling increases and decreases again, then settles. Tears flow freely from his eyes. He takes a deep spontaneous breath and then reaches out, fully, in front. "It doesn't hurt at all!" This concurs with what I have found with chronic pain. There is generally an underlying bracing pattern, and when the bracing pattern resolves, the pain dissolves.

Vince opens his eyes and looks at me. Clearly complete with the bottom-up processing, he is now able to form new meanings. He tells me about the following event. About eight months earlier† he had gone

---

* I am interrupting the urge to seek temporary relief by finding an explanation for a sensation, rather than completing the frozen action and welcoming the formation of new meanings.

† Often there is a significant delay between a traumatizing event and when the symptoms present.

shopping for his wife. As he came out of the supermarket, he heard a loud crash. Across the street, a car had smashed into a light pole. He dropped his bag and ran to the accident. The driver, a woman, sat motionless in an apparent state of shock. The motor of the car was running, so he reached across her inert body to turn off the ignition, standard procedure to prevent fires or explosion. Just as he started to turn the key he saw a young child in the passenger seat, his head decapitated by an air bag. And then Vince *told me* why his shoulder got frozen: "I was fine before I saw the kid ... I'm used to doing things like that, things that are dangerous ... but when I saw the kid, part of me wanted to grab my arm back and turn away ... I felt like puking ... and the other part just stayed there and did what I had to do ... Sometimes it's really hard to do what you have to do." "Yes," I agreed, "it's hard and you and your buddies keep doing it anyway ... Thank you."

"Hmm," he added when he left, "I guess I have to learn to mind my body." Vince had learned that mind and body are not separate entities—that he was a whole person. He said he wanted to learn more about himself and came in for three more sessions. He learned how to better handle stressful and conflicting situations and, needless to say, didn't need the operation.

When we need to engage in life-saving actions, the amount of charge and adrenaline that floods our bodies is vast. When Vince attempted to save the passenger in the car wreck, there were two simultaneous, but opposing, survival actions: one to do whatever possible to save her life, and the other, to pull away from the horror. In this intense conflict, Vince's nervous system and muscles locked up; his shoulder froze. In being able to *"feel through" and separate out the conflicting impulses*, first to reach forward and then to pull away in horror, the vast survival energy,* instead of both acting against itself, was discharged in the waves of shaking sweating and nausea.

---

* In a different situation the urge might be to save one's own life, or to stay pinned down in a foxhole, as in the "fog of war."

Enter Dr. Pavlov

Ivan Pavlov, who was awarded the Nobel Prize in Physiology or Medicine in 1904 for his prodigious work on the conditioned reflex, was thrust into a study of experimental (traumatic) breakdown by a chance event. The great Leningrad flood of 1924 caused the water to rise in his basement laboratory, precipitously close to the level of his caged experimental dogs. This terrified them but left them physically uninjured. When he resumed his experiments, he was startled to find that they had lost their previously acquired conditioned reflexes. While this was of obvious interest to Pavlov, another set of observations altered the future of his investigatory work. A significant proportion of the animals, though physically unscathed, broke down emotionally, behaviorally and physiologically. This included cowering and shaking in the corner of their cages, while other previously tame animals struck out viciously at their handlers. In addition, physiological changes such as elevated and depressed heart rates under mild stress and full startle reactions to mild stimuli (such as to tones or to the approach of the experimenter) were observed.

The flood evoked two conflicting tendencies, as suggested in Pavlov's definition: "the collision between the two [intense] contrary processes, one of excitation and the other of inhibition." In another example, the simultaneous impulse to eat and to suffer an intense electrical shock (when the shock is paired with eating) results in breakdown for hungry animals. With the existence of two opposing impulses, one to stay and eat and the other to escape a highly noxious event, there will likely be breakdown.

In summary, the motor expression of two intense instinctual responses creates a conflict and results in frozen states, such as the stasis in Vince's shoulder. Normally, muscles that extend operate reciprocally with those that flex. In the traumatic state, however, agonist and antagonist operate against each other, creating frozen (immobility) states. This may lead to debilitating symptoms in almost any part of the body. The energy bound in inhibited (thwarted) responses is so powerful that it can cause an extreme bracing that often has profound effects. For example, when people jump from burning buildings to a trampoline net far below, the bones in their legs may actually fracture *during* the fall instead of on impact. This is because both the extensor and flexor muscles contract simultaneously, with inordinate intensity.

In times of war or natural disasters, the instinctual impulse for self-preservation often collides with those for the protection of one's comrades. In World War I the prevalence of shell shock was tremendously high in the trenches. The foot soldiers were literally trapped and barraged with loud explosives for days to weeks on end. Instinctually, they were "urged" to run wildly to escape or to stay under fire and fight for the preservation of the group. In fact many soldiers were killed by unwisely running to escape (or were shot for supposed cowardice). In the few motion pictures taken of shell-shocked soldiers from World War I, one sees the tortured, twisted, convulsive consequences of such chronic thwarting. One wonders how many soldiers developed trauma and enduring guilt symptoms *because* they chose to protect themselves by leaving the wounded to fend for themselves. In any case, courage is a more complex phenomenon than is generally appreciated.

Trauma through a Child's Eyes

In a lifelong career of working with adults, I have occasionally been asked to see the children of my clients. I was frequently astonished by how, with the briefest of interventions, children rebounded from what would otherwise have been a devastating lifelong debilitation. These children, unshackled from the yoke of trauma, were free to develop with confidence, resilience and joy. I have cowritten two books on the prevention and somatic treatment of childhood trauma. One of them is geared to therapists, medical personnel and teachers,[105] while the other is geared primarily toward teaching parents effective emotional first-aid tools.[106]

In this section, I offer the tender stories of three overwhelmed children: Anna, Alex and Sammy. Their vignettes illustrate the principle that less is more and speak to the innate resilience of the human spirit.

Anna and Alex: A Picnic Gone Wrong

Eight-year-old Anna has enormous brown eyes. She could have been a model for one of the popular Keane paintings of almond-eyed children. The school nurse has just brought her in to see me. Pale, head hanging and barely breathing, she is like a fawn frozen by the bright lights of an oncoming car. Her frail face is expressionless, and her right arm hangs limply, as if it were on the verge of detaching itself from her shoulder.

Two days earlier, Anna went on a school outing to the beach. She and a dozen of her classmates were frolicking in the water when a sudden riptide swept them swiftly out to sea. Anna was rescued, but Mary (one of the mothers who volunteered for the outing) drowned after courageously saving several of the children. Mary had been a surrogate mom to many of the neighborhood kids, including Anna, and the entire community was in shock from her tragic death. I had asked the school nurse to be on the lookout for children who displayed a sudden onset of symptoms (e.g., pain, head and tummy aches and colds). Anna had already been to see the nurse three times that morning, reporting severe pain in her right arm and shoulder.

One of the mistakes often made by trauma responders is to try to get children to talk about their feelings immediately following an event. Although it is rarely healthy to suppress feelings, this practice can be traumatizing. In these vulnerable moments, children (and adults as well) can easily be overwhelmed. Previous traumas can resurface in the aftermath of an overwhelming event, creating a complex situation that may involve deep secrets, untold shame, guilt feelings and rage. For this reason, my team sought out, and learned, some of Anna's history from several helpful elementary school teachers (and the nurse) prior to seeing the child. In this way, we could have information that either was consciously unknown to the child or might be dangerous to uncover given her fragile state.

We learned that at age two, Anna was present when her father shot her mother in the shoulder and then took his own life. An additional detail that compounded Anna's symptoms was provoked by an experience she had prior to the picnic. She had been infuriated when Mary's sixteen-year-old son Robert bullied her twelve-year-old brother. There was a strong possibility that Anna had been harboring ill will toward Robert before the drowning, and was seeking retribution at that time. This raised the likelihood that Anna might feel profound guilt about Mary's death—perhaps even believing (through magical thinking) that she was responsible for it.

I ask the female nurse to gently cradle and support Anna's injured arm. This could help Anna contain the frozen "shock energy" locked in her arm, as well as heighten the child's inner awareness. With this support, Anna would be able to slowly (i.e., gradually) thaw and access the feelings and responses that could help her come back to life.

"How does it feel to be inside of your arm, Anna?" I ask her softly.

"It hurts so much," she answers faintly.

Her eyes are downcast, and I say, "It hurts bad, huh?"

"Yeah."

"Where does it hurt? Can you show me with your finger?" She points to a place on her upper arm and says, "Everywhere, too." There's a little shudder in her right shoulder followed by a slight sigh of breath. Momentarily, her drawn face takes on a rosier hue.

"That's good, sweetheart. Does that feel a little better?" she nods, then takes another breath. After this slight relaxation, she immediately stiffens, pulling her arm protectively toward her body. I seize the moment.

"Where did your mommy get hurt?" She points to the same place on her arm and begins to tremble. I say nothing. The trembling intensifies, then moves down her arm and up into her neck. "Yes, Anna, just let that shaking happen, just like a bowl of Jell-O—would it be red, or green, or even bright yellow? Can you let it shake? Can you feel it tremble?"

"It's yellow," she says, "like the sun in the sky." She takes a full breath, then looks at me for the first time. I smile and nod. Her eyes grasp mine for a moment, then turn away.

"How does your arm feel now?"

"The pain is moving down to my fingers." Her fingers are trembling gently. I speak to her quietly, softly, rhythmically.

"You know, Anna, sweetheart . . . I don't think there is anybody in this whole town that doesn't feel that, in some way, it was their fault that Mary died." She briefly glances at me. I continue, "Now, of course that's not true . . . but that's how everybody feels . . . and that's because they all love her so much." She turns now and looks at me. There is a sense of self-recognition in her demeanor. With her eyes now glued on me, I continue, "Sometimes, the more we love someone, the more we think it was our fault." Two tears spill from the outside corners of each eye before she slowly turns her head away from me.

"And sometimes if we're really angry at someone, then when something bad happens to them, then we also think that it happened because we wanted it to happen." Anna looks me straight in the eye. I continue, "And you know, when a bad thing happens to someone we love or hate, it doesn't happen because of our feelings. Sometimes bad things just happen . . . and feelings, no matter how big they are, are only feelings." Anna's gaze is penetrating and grateful. I feel myself welling with tears. I ask her if she wants to go back to her class now. She nods, looks once more at the three of us, and then walks out the door, her arms swinging freely—in rhythm with her stride.

Alex, like several of the children who witnessed the tragedy from the beach, was having trouble sleeping and eating. His father brought him to us because the youngster had barely eaten in the last two days.

As we sit together, I ask him if he can feel the inside of his tummy. He places the hand gently on his belly and, with a sniffle, says, "Yes."

"What does it feel like in there?"

"It's all tight like a knot."

"Is there anything inside that knot?"

"Yeah. It's black ... and red ... I don't like it."

"It hurts, huh?"

"Yeah."

"You know, Alex, it's supposed to hurt because you love her ... but it won't hurt forever."

Tears cascade down the boy's cheeks, and color returns to his face and fingers. That evening, Alex eats a full meal. At Mary's funeral Alex weeps openly, smiles warmly and hugs his friends.

Sammy: Child's Play

You can discover more about a person in
an hour of play
than in a year of conversation.
—Plato

Just as neither Vince nor his medical practitioners were able to associate his persistent frozen shoulder with a horrific event, often, children's symptoms or changes in their behavior can present puzzling questions that baffle parents and pediatric professionals alike. This is especially true when the child has "good enough" parents that provide a stable and nurturing home environment. Sometimes the child's new actions, although anything but subtle, are a mystery. The bewildered family might not connect the child's conduct or other symptoms with the source of his terror.

Rather than expressing themselves in easily comprehensible ways, kids frequently show us that they are suffering inside in the most frustrating ways. They do this through their bodies. They may act bratty, clinging to parents or throwing tantrums. Or they might struggle with agitation, hyperactivity, nightmares or sleeplessness. Even, more troubling, they may act out their worries and hurts by steamrolling over a pet or a younger, weaker child. For other children, their distress may show up as head and tummy aches or bedwetting, or they may avoid people and things they used to enjoy in order to manage their unbearable anxiety. Parents ask where in the world these childhood symptoms can possibly come from?

The very emblem of youth—"ordinary" events, such as falls, accidents and medical procedures—when unresolved are suspects as hidden culprits that underlie a child's angst. This was certainly the case with the toddler Sammy.

Since children by their nature enjoy play, therapists and parents can help them to rebound, moving beyond their fears to gain mastery over their scariest moments through the vehicle of guided play. As children express their inner world through play, their bodies are directly communicating with us.

Here is the story of Sammy, a two-and-a-half-year-old boy, where setting up a play session led to a reparative experience with a victorious outcome. There are suggestions provided after this case story for therapists, medical professionals and parents. The following is an example of what can happen when an ordinary fall, requiring a visit to the emergency room for stitches, goes awry. It also shows how several months later, Sammy's terrifying experience was transformed through play into a renewed sense of confidence and joy.

Sammy has been spending the weekend with his grandparents, where I am their houseguest. He is being an impossible tyrant, aggressively and relentlessly trying to control his new environment. Nothing pleases him; he displays a foul temper every waking moment. When he is asleep, he tosses and turns as if wrestling with his bedclothes. This behavior is not entirely unexpected from a two-and-a-half-year-old whose parents have gone away for the weekend—children with separation anxiety often act it out. Sammy, however, has always enjoyed visiting his grandparents, and this behavior seemed extreme to them.

They confided to me that six months earlier, Sammy fell off his high chair and split his chin open. Bleeding heavily, he was taken to the local emergency room. When the nurse came to take his temperature and blood pressure, he was so frightened that she was unable to record his vital signs. This vulnerable little boy was then strapped down in a "pediatric papoose" (a board with flaps and Velcro straps). With his torso and legs immobilized, the only parts of his body he could move were his head and neck—which, naturally, he did, as energetically as he could. The doctors responded by tightening the restraint and immobilizing his head with their hands in order to suture his chin.

After this upsetting experience, mom and dad took Sammy out for a hamburger and then to the playground. His mother was very attentive and carefully validated his experience of being scared and hurt. Soon, all seemed forgotten. However, the boy's overbearing attitude began shortly after this event. Could Sammy's tantrums and controlling behavior be related to his perceived helplessness from this trauma?

When his parents returned, we agreed to explore whether there might be a traumatic charge still associated with this recent experience. We all gathered in the cabin where I was staying. With parents, grandparents and Sammy watching, I placed his stuffed Pooh Bear on the edge of a chair in such a way that it fell to the floor. Sammy shrieked, bolted for the door and ran across a footbridge and down a narrow path to the creek. Our suspicions were confirmed. His most recent visit to the hospital was neither harmless nor forgotten. Sammy's behavior told us that this game was potentially overwhelming for him.

Sammy's parents brought him back from the creek. He clung dearly to his mother as we prepared for another game. We reassured him that we would all be there to help protect Pooh Bear. Again he ran—but this time only into the next room. We followed him in there and waited to see what would happen next. Sammy ran to the bed and hit it with both arms while looking at me expectantly.

"Mad, huh?" I said. He gave me a look that confirmed my question. Interpreting his expression as a go-ahead sign, I put Pooh Bear under a blanket and placed Sammy on the bed next to him.

"Sammy, let's all help Pooh Bear."

I held Pooh Bear under the blanket and asked everyone to help. Sammy watched with interest but soon got up and ran to his mother. With his arms held tightly around her legs, he said, "Mommy, I'm scared."* Without pressuring him, we waited until Sammy was ready and willing to play the game again. The next time, grandma and Pooh Bear were held down together, and Sammy actively participated in their rescue. When Pooh Bear was freed, Sammy ran to his mother, clinging even more tightly than before. He began to tremble and shake in fear, and then, dramatically, his chest expanded in a growing sense of excitement and pride.

---

* This trust of safety would not happen without a solid attachment. Where healthy bonding is not the case, or where there is abuse, therapy is, of course much more complex and also generally involves therapy for the parents or caregivers.

Here we see the transition between traumatic reenactment and healing play. The next time he held on to his mommy, there was less clinging and more excited jumping. We waited until Sammy was ready to play again. Everyone except Sammy took a turn being rescued with Pooh Bear. Each time, Sammy became more vigorous as he pulled off the blanket and escaped into the safety of his mother's arms.

When it was Sammy's turn to be held under the blanket with Pooh Bear, he became quite agitated and fearful. He ran back to his mother's arms several times before he was able to accept the ultimate challenge. Bravely, he climbed under the blankets with Pooh Bear while I held the blanket gently down. I watched his eyes grow wide with fear, but only for a moment. Then he grabbed Pooh Bear, shoved the blanket away, and flung himself into his mother's arms. Sobbing and trembling, he screamed, "Mommy, get me out of here! Mommy, get this off of me!" His startled father told me that these were the same words Sammy screamed while imprisoned in the papoose at the hospital. He remembered this clearly because he had been quite surprised by his son's ability to make such a direct, well-spoken demand at just over two and a half years of age.

We went through the escape several more times. Each time, Sammy exhibited more power and more triumph. Instead of running fearfully to his mother, he jumped excitedly up and down. With every successful escape, we all clapped and danced together, cheering, "Yeah for Sammy, yeah! Yeah, Sammy saved Pooh Bear!" Two-and-a-half-year-old Sammy had achieved mastery over the experience that had shattered him a few months earlier. The trauma-driven aggressive, foul-tempered behavior used in an attempt to control his environment disappeared, while his "hyperactivity" and avoidance (which occurred during the reworking of his medical trauma) was transformed into triumphant play.

Five Principles to Guide Children's Play toward Resolution

The following analysis of Sammy's experience will help clarify and apply the following principles for working using pediatric therapeutic play.

1. Let the child control the pace of the game.

Healing takes place in a moment-by-moment slowing down of time. In order to help the child you are working with feel safe, follow her pace and rhythm. If you put yourself in the child's shoes (through careful observation of her behavior), you will learn quickly how to resonate with her. Let's return to the story to see exactly how we did that with Sammy:

By running out of the room when Pooh Bear fell off the chair, Sammy indicated loud and clear that he was not ready to engage in this new activating game. Sammy had to be rescued by his parents, comforted, and brought back to the scene before continuing. In order to make him feel safe, we all assured him that we would be there to protect Pooh Bear. By offering this support and reassurance, we help Sammy move closer to playing the game—*in his own time at his own pace.*

After this reassurance, Sammy ran into the bedroom instead of out the door. This was a clear signal that he felt less threatened and more confident of our support. Children may not state verbally whether they want to continue, so take cues from their behavior and responses. Respect their wishes in whatever way they choose to communicate them. Children should never be rushed to move through an episode too fast or forced to do more than they are willing and able to do. Just like with Sammy, it is important to slow down the process if you notice signs of fear, constricted breathing, stiffening or a dazed (dissociated) demeanor. These reactions will dissipate if you simply wait, quietly and patiently, while reassuring the child that you are still by his side and on his side. Usually, the youngster's eyes and breathing pattern will indicate when it's time to continue.

2. Distinguish between fear, terror and excitement.

Experiencing fear or terror for more than a brief moment during traumatic play will not help the child move through the trauma. Most children will take action to avoid it. Let them! At the same time, try and discern whether it is avoidance or escape. The following is a clear-cut example to help in developing the skill of "reading" when a break is needed and when it's time to guide the momentum forward.

When Sammy ran down to the creek, he was demonstrating avoidance behavior. In order to resolve his traumatic reaction, Sammy had to feel that he was in control of his actions rather than driven to act by his emotions. Avoidance behavior occurs when fear and terror threaten to overwhelm both children and adults. With kids this behavior is usually accompanied by some sign of emotional distress (crying, frightened eyes, screaming). Active escape, on the other hand, is exhilarating. Children become excited by their small triumphs and often show pleasure by glowing with smiles, clapping their hands or laughing heartily. Overall, the response is much different from avoidance behavior. Excitement is evidence of the child's successful discharge of emotions that accompanied the original experience. This is positive, desirable and necessary.

Trauma is transformed by changing intolerable feelings and sensations into desirable ones. This can only happen at a level of activation that is similar to the activation that led to the traumatic reaction in the first place.

If the child appears excited, it is OK to offer encouragement and continue as we did when we clapped and danced with Sammy.

However, if the child appears frightened or cowed, give reassurance, but don't encourage any further movement. Instead, be present with your full attention and support, waiting patiently until a substantial amount of the fear subsides. If the child shows signs of fatigue, take a rest break.

3. Take one small step at a time.

You can never move too slowly in renegotiating a traumatic event with anyone; this is especially true with a young child. Traumatic play is repetitious almost by definition. Make use of this cyclical characteristic.

The key difference between *renegotiation* and traumatic play (reenactment) is that in renegotiation there are incremental differences in the child's responses and behaviors in moving toward mastery and resolution. The following illustrates how I noticed these small changes with Sammy.

When Sammy ran into the bedroom instead of out the door, he was responding with a different behavior, indicative that progress had been made. No matter how many repetitions it takes, if the child you are helping is responding differently—such as with a slight increase in excitement, with more speech or with more spontaneous movements— he is moving through the trauma. If the child's responses appear to be moving in the direction of constriction or compulsive repetition instead of expansion and variety, you may be attempting to renegotiate the event with scenarios that involve too much arousal for the child to make progress. If you notice that your attempts at playful renegotiation are backfiring, ground yourself and pay attention to your sensations until your breathing brings a sense of calm, confidence and spontaneity. Then, slow down the rate of change by breaking the play into smaller increments. This may seem contradictory to what was stated earlier about following the child's pace. However, attuning to children's needs sometimes means setting limits to prevent them from getting wound up and collapsing in overwhelm. If the child appears tense or frightened, it's OK to invite some healing steps. For example, when renegotiating a medical trauma, you might say, "Let's see, I wonder what we can do so that Pooh Bear (Dolly, GI Joe, etc.) doesn't get so scared before you [the pretend doctor/nurse] give him the shot?" Often children will come up with creative solutions showing you exactly what they *needed—the missing ingredient* that would have helped them settle more during their experience.

Don't be concerned about how many times you have to go through what seems to be the "same old thing." (We engaged Sammy in playing the game with Pooh Bear at least ten times.) Sammy was able to renegotiate his traumatic responses fairly quickly. Another child in your care might require more time. You don't need to do it all in one day! Resting and time are needed to help internally reorganize the child's experience at subtle levels. Be assured that if the resolution is not complete, the child will return to a similar phase when given the opportunity to play during the next session.

4. Become a safe container.

Remember that biology is on your side. Perhaps the most difficult and important aspect of renegotiating a traumatic event with a child is maintaining your own belief that things will turn out OK. This feeling comes from inside you and is projected out to the child. It becomes a container that surrounds the child with a feeling of confidence. This may be particularly difficult if the child resists your attempts to renegotiate the trauma.

If the child resists, be patient and reassuring. The instinctive part of your child wants to rework this experience. All you have to do is wait for that part to feel confident and safe enough to assert itself. If you are excessively worried about whether the child's traumatic reaction can be transformed, you may inadvertently send a conflicting message. Adults with their own unresolved childhood trauma may be particularly susceptible to falling into this trap.

5. Stop if you feel that the child is genuinely not benefiting from the play.

In *Too Scared to Cry*, Lenore Terr,[107] the brilliant and esteemed child psychologist, warns clinicians about allowing children to engage in traumatic play "therapy" that reenacts the original horror. She describes the responses of three-and-a-half-year-old Lauren as she plays with toy cars. "The cars are going on the people," Lauren says as she zooms two racing cars toward some finger puppets. "They're pointing their pointy parts into the people. The people are scared. A pointy part will come on their tummies, and in their mouths, and on their ... [she points to her skirt]. My tummy hurts. I don't want to play anymore." Lauren stops herself as her bodily sensation of fear abruptly surfaces. This is a typical reaction. She may return over and over to the same play, each time stopping when the fearful sensations in her tummy become uncomfortable. Some therapists would say that Lauren is using her play as an attempt to gain some control over the situation that traumatized her. Her play does resemble "exposure" treatments used routinely to help adults overcome phobias. But Terr cautions that such play ordinarily doesn't yield much success. Even if it does serve to reduce a child's distress, this process is quite slow in producing results. Most often, the play is compulsively repeated without resolution. Unresolved, repetitious, traumatic play can reinforce the traumatic impact in the same way that reenactment and cathartic reliving of traumatic experiences can reinforce trauma in adults.

The reworking or renegotiation of a traumatic experience, as we saw with Sammy, represents a process that is fundamentally different from traumatic play or reenactment. Left to their own devices, most children, not unlike Lauren in the above example, will attempt to avoid the traumatic feelings that their play evokes. But with guided play, *Sammy was able to "live his feelings through" by gradually and sequentially mastering his fear.* Using this stepwise renegotiation of the traumatic event and Pooh Bear's companionship, Sammy was able to emerge as the victor and hero. A sense of triumph and heroism almost always signals the successful conclusion of a renegotiated traumatic event. By following Sammy's lead after setting up a potentially activating scene, joining in his play and making the game up as we went along, Sammy got to let go of his fear. It took minimal direction (30–45 minutes) and support to achieve the unspoken goal of aiding him to experience a corrective outcome.

CHAPTER 9

Annotation of Peter's Accident

For my final case example, I come full circle from where we began this undertaking, my experience on that sunny, beautiful day. I have chosen to recount my horrific accident detailed in Chapter 1, with a brief imbedded analysis **(in bold)**. This annotation serves not only as a review but also as a way to scrutinize the factors that prevented me from ending up with posttraumatic stress disorder (PTSD). The event itself— namely being struck by a car, smashed against a windshield, catapulted through the air and physically injured—certainly counts as a traumatic event. But why wasn't I traumatized?

As I walked along that fateful February day, absorbed in happy anticipation of seeing my dear friend Butch to celebrate his sixtieth birthday, I stepped out into a crosswalk ... The next moment, paralyzed and numb, I'm lying on the road, unable to move or breathe. I can't figure out what has just happened. How did I get here? Out of a swirling fog of confusion and disbelief, a crowd of people rushes toward me. **(1. Shock in my case was literally about having the wind knocked out of me. All traumas leave us breathless in some way. In the moment of shock people don't really know what happened to them; they are breathless with a loss of inner and outer orientation.)** They stop, aghast. Abruptly, they hover over me in a tightening circle, their staring eyes fixed on my limp and twisted body. From my helpless perspective they appear like a flock of carnivorous ravens, swooping down on an injured prey—me. Slowly I orient myself and identify the real attacker. As in an old-fashioned flashbulb photo, I see a beige car looming over me with its teeth-like grill and shattered windshield. **(2. In the shock state images become disparate and fragmentary, and are focused exclusively on the most salient threat features.)** The door suddenly jerks open. A wide-eyed teenager bursts out. She stares at me in dazed horror. In a strange way, I both know and don't know what has just happened. **(3. In one of the paradoxes of trauma, traumatized people have a split perception/reception. They are on autopilot, where they act calmly. They also enter into a dream/nightmare from which they cannot wake.)** As the various fragments begin to converge, they convey a horrible reality: *I must have been hit by this car as I entered the crosswalk.* In confused disbelief, I sink back into a hazy twilight. I find that I am unable to think clearly or to will myself awake from this nightmare.

A man rushes to my side and drops to his knees. He announces himself as an off-duty paramedic. When I try to see where the voice is coming from, **(4. This is an automatic, initial biological orienting response.)** he sternly orders, "Don't move your head." **(5. Now I am put in a double bind with two contradictory commands: one is the innate effort to orient; the other is a demand *not* to execute this compelling instinct. The result is a collision of opposing impulses. This results in a thwarting of the biological orienting impulse. This was also the case with Vince, the fireman with the frozen shoulder in Chapter 8.)** The contradiction between his sharp command and what my body naturally wants—to turn toward his voice—frightens and stuns me into a sort of paralysis. My awareness strangely splits, and I experience an uncanny "dislocation." It's as if I'm floating above my body, looking down on the unfolding scene. **(6. This description is a classic presentation of dissociation. However, dissociation takes many forms, including the panoply of psychological fragmentation and physical symptoms that can occur in the wake of trauma.)**

I am snapped back when he roughly grabs my wrist and takes my pulse. He then shifts his position, directly above me. Awkwardly, he grasps my head with both of his hands, trapping it and keeping it from moving. His abrupt actions and the stinging ring of his command panic me; they immobilize me further. **(7. This conflict deepens the thwarting and intensifies the immobility response by introducing more fear. This results in *fear-potentiated immobility*.)** Dread seeps into my dazed, foggy consciousness: *Maybe I have a broken neck,* I think. **(8. Dread and helplessness increase the depth and duration of immobility.)** I have a compelling impulse to find someone *else* to focus on. **(9. The need for human contact, when threatened, is a mammalian survival instinct— see Chapter 6.)** Simply, I need to have someone's comforting gaze, a lifeline to hold onto. But I'm too terrified to move and feel helplessly frozen. **(10. Due to the power of the shock and the immobilization response, there is a reduced ability to ask for help—that is, to engage that more recently developed mammalian social survival instinct.)**

The Good Samaritan fires off questions in rapid succession: "What is your name? Where are you? Where were you going? What is today's date?" But I can't connect with my mouth and make words. I don't have the energy to answer his questions. His manner of asking them makes me feel more disoriented and utterly confused. Finally, I manage to shape my words and speak. My voice is strained and tight. **(11. Voice-less terror is part of the immobility response and is seen in all species that normally vocalize.)** I ask him, both with my hands and words, "Please back off." **(12. This is the first time I am able to mobilize an effective defense against intrusion by beginning to establish a protec-tive boundary.)** He complies. As though a neutral observer, speaking about the person sprawled out on the blacktop, I assure him that I under-stand I am not to move my head, and that I will answer his questions later. **(13. As the shock is reduced by making an effective boundary, the communication centers in my brain—Broca's area—are coming online to further delineate and articulate my boundary.)**

The Power of Kindness

After a few minutes, a woman unobtrusively inserts herself and quietly sits by my side. "I'm a doctor, a pediatrician," she says. "Can I be of help?"

"Please just stay with me," I reply. Her simple, kind face seems sup-portive and calmly concerned. She takes my hand in hers, and I squeeze it. **(14. Her outreach and physical touch provide a source of orientation and help to enlist my diminished capacity for social engagement. The activation of the ventral vagal system—see Chapter 6—is helping to buffer me against being sucked down into the black hole of trauma.)**

She gently returns the gesture. As my eyes reach for hers, I feel a tear form. **(15. The eye-to-eye contact is integral to the social engagement system, as is touch. This physiological exchange, in which we are participating in each other's nervous systems, leads to stabilization and relief.)** The delicate and strangely familiar scent of her perfume tells me that I am not alone. I feel emotionally held by her encouraging presence. **(16. Through smell we have direct access to the limbic system— formerly called the olfactory-smell-brain—for this very reason.)** A trembling wave of release moves through me, and I take my first deep breath. **(17. This powerful moment is the first instance of physiological discharge and self-regulation.)** Then a jagged shudder of terror passes though my body. Tears are now streaming from my eyes. In my mind, I hear the words, *I can't believe this has happened to me; it's not possible; this is not what I planned for Butch's birthday tonight.* **(18. This is recognition of my own denial.)** I am sucked down by a deep undertow of unfathomable regret. **(19. In this moment I am contacting the deep emotional truth by acknowledging the loss. In therapy this frequently happens, gradually, over time.)** My body continues to shudder. Reality sets in.

In a little while, a softer trembling begins to replace the abrupt shudders. I feel alternating waves of fear and sorrow. **(20. This discharge in waves allows for the natural experience of pendulation—expansions/contraction as discussed in Step 3 in Chapter 5—and softens the feelings of sorrow and fear.)** It comes to me as a stark possibility that I may be seriously injured. **(21. It is part of a mammalian response to injury to scan the body and to assess the nature and level of the injury.)** Perhaps I will end up in a wheelchair, crippled and dependent. Again, deep waves of sorrow flood me. I'm afraid of being swallowed up by the sorrow and hold onto the woman's eyes. **(22. I am now actively engaging the woman as a resource.)** A slower breath brings me the scent of her perfume. Her continued presence sustains me. As I feel less overwhelmed, my fear softens and begins to subside. I feel a flicker of hope, then a rolling wave of rage. **(23. Rage is a strong defensive response—it is about the impulse to kill! Hence people become terrified by this impulse and try to suppress it. The pediatrician is helping me to contain this rage and** not be overwhelmed by it.) My body continues to shake and tremble. It is alternately icy cold and feverishly hot. **(24. This is indicative of a continued strong discharge.)** A burning red fury erupts from deep within my belly: *How could that stupid kid hit me in a crosswalk? Wasn't she paying attention? Damn her!* **(25. More rage—accompanied with the human neocortical tendency to blame.)**

A blast of shrill sirens and flashing red lights block out everything. My belly tightens, and my eyes again reach to find the woman's kind gaze. We squeeze hands, and the knot in my gut loosens.

I hear my shirt ripping. I am startled and again jump to the vantage of an observer hovering above my sprawling body. **(26. The abruptness with which the shirt is removed restimulates the dissociation.)** I watch uniformed strangers methodically attach electrodes to my chest. The Good Samaritan paramedic reports to someone that my pulse was 170. I hear my shirt ripping even more. **(27. As I notice that I'm dissociating, I am able to bring myself back to my body.)** I see the emergency team slip a collar onto my neck and then cautiously slide me onto a board. While they strap me down, I hear some garbled radio communication. The paramedics are requesting a full trauma team. Alarm jolts me. I ask to be taken to the nearest hospital only a mile away, but they tell me that my injuries may require the major trauma center in La Jolla, some thirty miles farther. My heart sinks. Surprisingly, though, the fear quickly subsides. **(28. The surging and receding of the emotional arousal is evidence of deepening self-regulation.)** As I am lifted into the ambulance, I close my eyes for the first time. A vague scent of the woman's perfume and the look of her quiet, kind eyes linger. Again, I have that comforting feeling of being held by her presence.

Opening my eyes in the ambulance, I feel a heightened alertness, as though I'm supercharged with adrenaline. **(29. I am adequately resourced now—enough to close my eyes and stay with the hyperarousal sensations in my body; the lingering scent of the woman's perfume helps calm my limbic system and body, providing additional support for exploring what's going inside of me.)** Though intense, this feeling does not overwhelm me. Even though my eyes want to dart around, to survey the unfamiliar and foreboding environment, I consciously direct myself to go inward. I begin to take stock of my body sensations. (**30. The perception of danger that my life is being threatened is receding, and the ability to access my body is increasing.**) This active focusing draws my attention to an intense, and uncomfortable, buzzing throughout my body.

Against this unpleasant sensation, I notice a peculiar tension in my left arm. I let this sensation come into the foreground of my consciousness and track the arm's tension as it builds and builds. Gradually, I recognize that *the arm wants* to flex and move up. (**31. I am now able to track my physical sensations. I am able to distinguish within the "noise" and buzzing of arousal a purposeful tension. This curiosity helps to reestablish present time orientation; trauma and curiosity are reciprocal psychophysiological functions and cannot coexist.**) As this inner impulse toward movement develops, the back of my hand also *wants to* rotate. Ever so slightly, I sense it moving toward the left side of my face—as though to protect it against a blow. (**32. This is the reassertion of an involuntary defensive response, a strong and protective response that was either inadequate or incomplete—its execution was interrupted by the clobbering impact of the window and the road.**) Suddenly, there passes before my eyes a fleeting image of the window of the beige car, and once again—as in a flashbulb snapshot—vacant eyes stare from behind the spiderweb of the shattered window. (**33. This image, associated with the original threat, reappears.**) I hear the momentary "chinging" thud of my left shoulder shattering the windshield. (**34. The sense impressions or images referred to in the SIBAM model, discussed in Chapter 7, are now expanding to include the auditory component of the impact, rather than only the visual.**) Then, unexpectedly, an enveloping sense of relief floods over me. I feel myself coming back into my body. The electric buzzing has retreated. The image of the blank eyes and shattered windshield recedes and seems to dissolve. In its place, I picture myself leaving my house, feeling the warm sun on my face, and being filled with gladness at the expectation of seeing Butch this evening. My eyes can relax as I focus outwardly. As I look around the ambulance, it somehow seems less alien and foreboding. I see more clearly and "softly." I have the deeply reassuring sense that I am no longer frozen, that time has started to move forward, that I am awakening from the nightmare. **(35. The image is continuing to expand, allowing a deeper level of completion with the detailed linking of the visual and auditory elements. I have now moved through the moment of impact, t = 0. I have gone from t – 1 (the moment before impact) to t = 0 (the moment of impact) to t + 1, the moment of time just after t = 0, exiting from the shock core—see Figure 9.1. I have emerged through the "eye of the needle," returning and orienting to present time and to the remembrances of that perfect winter morning.)** I gaze at the paramedic sitting by my side. Her calmness reassures me. **(36. This reassurance reinforces my felt experience that I have woken up from this nightmare and that I can extend my sense of resource and support to include the woman in the ambulance.)**

Reestablishing Continuity of Experience

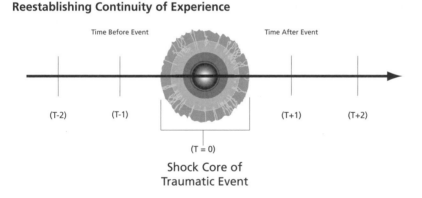

Figure 9.1 This shows movement toward, and then through, the core moment of shock. This dissolves immobility.

After a few bumpy miles, I feel another strong tension pattern developing from the spine in my upper back. I sense my right arm wanting to extend outward—I see a momentary flash; the black asphalt road rushes toward me. I hear my hand slapping the pavement and feel a raw burning sensation on the palm of my right hand. I associate this with the perception of my hand extending to protect my head from smashing onto the road. I feel tremendous relief, along with a deep sense of gratitude that my body did not betray me, knowing exactly what to do to guard my fragile brain from a potentially mortal injury. **(37. I am** now beginning to process the event in sequential time—from t – 1 to t + 1—and have a growing self-confidence in my body's ability to protect me.) As I continue to gently tremble, I sense a warm tingling wave along with an inner strength building up from deep within my body.

As the shrill siren blasts away, the ambulance paramedic takes my blood pressure and records my EKG. When I ask her to tell me my vital signs, she informs me in a gentle professional manner that she cannot give me that information. I feel a subtle urge to extend our contact, to engage with her as a person. Calmly, I tell her that I'm a doctor (a half-truth). There is the light quality of a shared joke. (38. This kind of playful social engagement is possible only when the ventral vagal system, discussed in Chapter 6, is online.) She fiddles with the equipment and then indicates that it might be a false reading. A minute or two later she tells me that my heart rate is 74 and my blood pressure is 125/70.

"What were my readings when you first hooked me up?" I ask.

"Well, your heart rate was 150. The guy who took it before we came said it was about 170."

I breathe a deep sigh of relief. "Thank you," I say, then add: "Thank God, I won't be getting PTSD."

"What do you mean?" she asks with genuine curiosity.

"Well, I mean that I probably won't be getting posttraumatic stress disorder." When she still looks perplexed, I explain how my shaking and following my self-protective responses had helped me to "reset" my nervous system and brought me back into my body.

"This way," I go on, "I am no longer in fight-or-flight mode."

"Hmm," she comments, "is that why accident victims sometimes struggle with us—are they still in fight-or-flight?"

"Yes, that's right."

"You know," she adds, "I've noticed that they often purposely stop people from shaking when we get them to the hospital. Sometimes they strap them down tight or give them a shot of Valium. Maybe that's not so good?"

"No, it's not," the teacher in me confirms. "It may give them temporary relief, but it just keeps them frozen and stuck."

She tells me that she recently took a course in "trauma first-aid" called Critical Incident Debriefing. "They tried it with us at the hospital. We had to talk about how we felt after an accident. But talking made me and the other paramedics feel worse. I couldn't sleep after we did it—but you weren't talking about what happened. You were, it seemed to me, just shaking. Is that what brought your heart rate and blood pressure down?"

"Yes," I told her and added that it was also the small protective spontaneous movements my arms were making.

"I'll bet," she mused, "that if the shaking that often occurs after surgery were allowed rather than suppressed, recovery would be quicker and maybe even postoperative pain would be reduced."

"That's right," I say, smiling in agreement. **(39. I am relieved at the restoration of my intellectual faculty and my "reserve capacity" when the going got rough.)**

And I leave you, dear reader, once again with the wise counsel of the ancient Chinese *Book of Changes:*

> When a man has learned within his heart
> what fear and trembling mean,
> he is safeguarded against any terror
> produced by outside influences.
> —*I Ching*, Hexagram #51 (circa 2000 BC)

PART III

Instinct in the Age of Reason

One does not meet oneself until one
catches the reflection from an eye
other than human.
—Loren Eiseley, *The Immense Journey*

We may be special animals,
we may be particular animals with
very special characteristics,
but we're animals nonetheless.
—Massimo Pigliucci

CHAPTER 10

We're Just a Bunch of Animals

My approach to healing trauma rests broadly on the premise that people are primarily instinctual in nature—that we are, at our very core, human animals. It is this relationship to our animal nature that both makes us susceptible to trauma and, at the same time, promotes a robust capacity to rebound in the aftermath of threat, safely returning us to equilibrium. More generally, I believe that to truly understand our body/mind, therapists must first learn about the animal body/mind because of the manner in which our nervous systems have evolved in an ever-changing and challenging environment.

Who are we? Where do we come from? How did we get here? These are the focal questions posed by theologians and biologists, by anarchists and zoologists, and by UFOlogists and psychologists. Each of these specialists postulates theories with diverse viewpoints of what stuff we are made of and who we really are. They all look at our humanity through very different lenses. But they're not necessarily overtly antagonistic. While all religions are organized around creation myths, there isn't, for example, a passionate rift between the big bang theory and the idea of biblical creation. Certainly, we do not hear of an active dissent and insistence calling loudly for the teaching of religious doctrine in place of physics and cosmography in our schools and universities. However, there is an almost violent schism lurking in our cultural zeitgeist. Let's face it: the fight against evolution by the proponents of "creationism" and "intelligent design" is not really about the professed gaps in the fossil records; rather, it's about whether or not we are basically animals.

Charles Darwin, in the publication of *The Descent of Man*, helped to locate our anatomical and physiological place among the animal kingdom. By doing this he become, today, an even more feared incarnation of what Kinsey represented more than half a century ago in his reports to puritan America. A throwback to the Scopes trial, the visceral fight against Darwinism by the American "religious right," is about the deeply rooted negation and fear of our animal nature. Such a disavowal reflects a fundamental disconnect between "higher man" (reason and morality) and "lower (sexual) animals." This denial of the instinctual life is also shared by strange bedfellows, many modern behavioral scientists.

The rejection of our animal nature is understandable as we have become (overly) socialized. This denial and its dehumanizing consequence, however, are summarized by the physician Max Plowman in his *Introduction to the Study of Blake:*

> In all cultivation, native instinct is the most difficult force to remember and take into account. Just because our civilization is old, our distance from the primal centers is as the distance of twigs upon an oak from the farthest contributory roots. We have become so cultivated that we do not know we have drains until they smell. We have become so confident in the mechanical use of intelligence that we take for granted the functioning of our instincts, even to the point of thinking it immaterial whether they can find true and natural expression or not. In time the instincts rebel against our want of care for them ... then there is consternation.

It seems that as we distance ourselves farther and farther from our instinctual roots, we have grown to be a species hell-bent on becoming better and better at making life worse and worse. We have been quite "successful" in distancing ourselves from our vital core. Instinct's role in guiding and informing that which makes us *both* animal and, in the finest way, most human is illustrated by the following vignette.

A nature photographer stood by in abject horror as he watched a wild elephant kicking, again and again, the lifeless body of its stillborn calf. As he continued observing and photographing this gruesome scene for three hours, something truly unexpected happened. The infant stirred. Remarkably, the mother had resuscitated the calf, bringing him back to life by stimulating his heart. It was instinct and instinct alone that accomplished this miraculous task; the mind would have been quite useless.

Swan Lake

Even in "lower" species, we are taken by the apparent intelligence of instincts in guiding complex behaviors we associate with mammals. Sitting by the edge of the emerald Vierwaldstättersee (the clear, glacial Lake Lucerne in Switzerland), the ducks and swans "proudly" parade their young chicks past the table where I am seated eating breakfast. A slight abrupt approach on my part toward the female would evoke frightening, hissing, aggressive reactions—unexpected for these otherwise staid and regal birds. As they drift peacefully by, I carefully toss out some small pieces of bread. It is curious to observe how the adults stand back, carefully monitoring their chicks while allowing them to peck and feast. Only after they have filled their fluffy bellies do the adults take some morsels for themselves. So it seems they not only ferociously protect their young from outside harm but with patient restraint show an uncharacteristic deference, protecting them from their own gluttony. When they are not parents, these gracious lily-white swans show their true colors as nasty aggressive beasts, jousting with one another for any crumbs thrown their way.

In mammalian development the instincts for protection and care were greatly extended and elaborated, flourishing with a wide range of nurturing behaviors. Then, in the evolution of primates and *Homo sapiens*, care of the young made a monumental jump; this involved paradigm shifts such as diverse altruistic and mutually supportive social behaviors. Then bonding, through direct physical touch and eye contact, promoted focus on one potential mating partner at a time. And that procreative connection between male and female—the one above all others—was cemented by the orgasm's commanding neurochemical surge.* We find ourselves, consequently, rising to the perennial saga of mustering the courage to love that which time will claim for its own; love, sexuality and loss were now forever and intrinsically entwined, becoming the broad business of the world's poetry, art, music and prose.

We humans do not hesitate to speak of the almost superhuman power of unconditional parental love; otherwise how could we explain the profound feelings and actions we take toward our newborns, with their slimy, wrinkled-prune bodies that know little else but to defecate, urinate and wail in ear-piercing shrieks of frantic discomfort? We gaze at them, listen, coo and smell; we hold and rock them; we become hopelessly and ridiculously smitten in love. And this, as any parent knows, is only just the beginning of trial by fire and infinite patience. Evolution has given us the most compelling of all feelings to direct and organize the critical acts of care and nurturance. The Darwinian emotions and behaviors of "love" have evolved, presumably, for the protection and care of the babies in a species bearing one offspring and compressing an eighteen-month gestation (arguably because of its large head) into nine. For these underdeveloped creatures to survive, special, extended, and therefore highly motivated caregiving behaviors were required. Such an enduring task demanded nothing short of love, perhaps the same emotion that drives soldiers in the heat of battle to rescue fallen comrades, pulling them to safety even at the supreme risk to their own lives. And love, in the final analysis, may be our collective antidote— the salvation for a species with such a penchant for senseless killing and carnage. Love is the glue that holds family, tribes, and—perhaps in times of need—even societies together. It is also the potion that binds the human animal to the divine through the highest religious and spiritual feelings of oneness and connection. Was I, at the lake's edge, witnessing an early precursor to that love supreme in the primitive instinctual programs that so nonchalantly inhibited the adult birds from exhibiting their normal voracious competitive appetites so that their young could fill their bellies first?

---

* Oxytocin and the endorphins have been implicated in this feel-good and trust-promoting chemical cascade.

An Open Window

Science is our new religion and its holy
water is disinfectant.

—George Bernard Shaw

In spite of persistent rejection of our animal nature, there was a vital
and rich window of time during the twentieth century when six Nobel
Prizes in Physiology or Medicine were awarded on the subject of
instincts.* Darwin, a century and a half ago, emphasized just how
nuanced and intelligent instincts are. In Notebook M (1838) Darwin
mused, "The origin of man is now proved. He who understands baboon
would do more towards metaphysics than Locke." In this regard it was
recently demonstrated that a mere one or two percentage points dif-
ferentiates the human and chimpanzee genomes (with not much more
distinguishing humans from other mammals). Indeed chimps can out-
perform college sophomores in a fairly sophisticated math exercise, and
yet psychology, purportedly a natural science, still seems to favor over-
looking the reality that we are, in the last analysis, animals.

Even our sense of wonder may be shared by our nearest cousins,
the apes. Jane Goodall, a leading primatologist, has suggested the existence of primal spiritual feelings in the chimps she had carefully studied over many years. Here she describes the behaviors of a troupe visiting
an especially beautiful place with a waterfall and river:

> For me, it is a magical place, and a spiritual one. And
> sometimes, as they approach, the chimpanzees display in
> slow, rhythmic motion along the river bed. They pick up
> and throw great rocks and branches. They leap to seize
> the hanging vines, and swing out over the stream in the
> spray-drenched wind until it seems the slender stems must
> snap or be torn from their lofty moorings. For ten minutes

---

* These include Ivan Pavlov, Sir Charles Sherrington, Nikolaas Tinbergen, Konrad Lorenz, Karl von Frisch and Roger W. Sperry.

or more they may perform this magnificent "dance." Why?
Is it not possible that the chimpanzees are responding to
some feeling like awe? A feeling generated by the mystery of the water; water that seems alive, always rushing
past yet never going, always the same yet ever different.
Was it perhaps similar feelings of awe that gave rise to the
first animistic religions, the worship of elements and the
mysteries of nature over which there was no control?[108]

Ironically, despite the creationists' rejection of their animal roots, religious awe may be yet another confirmation of the Darwinian continuity of the species and of our profound instinctual heritage.

To many reasonable scientists, the attribution of "religious awe" to
nonhuman primates would seem a stretch at best. At the very worst, it
could be seen as an extreme case of anthropomorphism gone amok.
However, there is a solid, empirically based tradition of studying the
behaviors and emotions in chimpanzees as evolutionary antecedents to
human morality. Beginning with Eibl-Eibesfeldt's seminal work, *Love
and Hate: The Natural History of Behavior Patterns*,[109] and recently cul-
minating in Frans de Waal's beautifully written *Our Inner Ape*,[110] a compelling case is made for certain social behaviors of monkeys and apes
as precursors for various human moral behaviors, including highly
refined deportment such as peacemaking. These forerunners include
reciprocity of grooming, maintenance of social ranking and violence
attenuation. Easy to appreciate are clear examples such as an adult chimp
helping a juvenile climb a tree or zoo-confined chimps (who are known
to be unable to swim) jumping into the moat in a futile attempt to rescue
a drowning chimp. Such altruistic behaviors conjure images of fireman
entering buildings engulfed in flames to rescue trapped families or soldiers running directly into the line of fire to rescue a fallen comrade.

De Waal's views are based on many decades of observing aggression
in primate societies. He noticed that after fights between two chimps,
other chimpanzees would appear to console the loser—a behavior

requiring both the capacity for empathy and a significant level of self-awareness. De Waal also describes female chimpanzees poignantly removing stones from the hands of males readying to fight so as to head off the brawl or at least to prevent them from inflicting mortal harm. Such "reconciliation" efforts may preserve group solidarity, thus diminishing vulnerability from outside attackers.

Human morality organizes around questions of right, wrong and justice. According to de Waal and others,[111] it originates with concern for others and in understanding and respecting social rules. This is seen in a multitude of mammalian groups. The orchestration of such pre-moral behaviors requires a highly sophisticated level of emotional and social functioning. Marc Hauser, an evolutionary biologist working at Harvard University, has extended these notions and regards the brain as having genetically shaped mechanisms whose function is the acquisition of moral rules based in complex feeling states.[112]

In the face of such robust observations, the social sciences often appear to manifest their distaste for the human-as-animal supposition, most notably by sanitizing their terminology around the concepts of instinctual behavior. In fact, the word *instinct* is rarely found in modern psychological literature. Rather it is purged and replaced with terms such as *drives, motivations* and *needs*. While instincts are still routinely drawn upon to explain animal behaviors, we have somehow lost sight of how many human behavior patterns (though modifiable) are primal, automatic, universal and predictable. For example, as the World Trade Center towers crashed to the ground, instinctually driven people ran until their feet were bleeding. They ran for their lives like their ancestors who were chased by the predatory cats on the ancient Serengeti. They then regrouped, seeking the safety of their dens and communities, as they walked in an orderly fashion, over bridges leading to each of the five boroughs.

When we collapse in grief at the death of a loved one, we share this innate response to loss with the other highly developed mammals. Jane Goodall's description of the matriarch Flo's death and the subsequent self-starvation of her young male offspring in the tree above her corpse is one such example.* Yet another comparable instance of a grief response comes to mind with the listless pets we frequently return to after what seemed to us a short weekend away from home. Road rage and sexual fixations are disturbing manifestations of other instincts—in these cases, instincts gone awry. Grief, anger, fear, disgust, lust, mating, nurturing of young and even love (as well as all the *action patterns* that go with them) are universals among humans. All bear a remarkable resemblance to similar behaviors in mammals.

Charles Darwin, more than any other human being, clarified the essential connections between the human and other animal species. Aside from discovering the evolution of form and function, he further recognized the similarities of movements, action patterns, emotions and facial expressions shared by mankind and animals. Darwin's masterworks addressed the continuity of emotional expressions among mammalian species. He was struck not only by the similarities in physiological and anatomical structures, but also by inborn, instinctive behaviors and emotions across species. In *The Descent of Man* Darwin writes,

> Man and the higher animals ... have ... instincts in common. All have the same senses, intuition, sensation, passions, affections and emotions, even the more complex

* Jim Anderson, a psychologist and primate researcher at the University of Stirling, in Scotland, described a recent videoing of the death of Chimp and the reaction of others in the same pen (*BBC News*, April 26, 2010): "As the breathing of the old female chimp slowed, and finally stopped, the others bent down to look intently into her face ... We had never seen that before." They poked and gently shook her body for 30 or 40 seconds. They looked puzzled, Anderson reported, and slept more fitfully that night than usual. The dead chimp's adult daughter slept on the platform where her mother's body lay—close but not touching or inspecting it. Reporting in the April 27, 2010, issue of the scientific journal *Current Biology*, Anderson said that these observations add to the growing body of evidence suggesting that chimps have a rich emotional life. "It might well be that they do have some awareness of death. We know from other work that chimpanzees, more than monkeys, are capable of showing empathy toward others who have a problem, or have been attacked. We see consolation behavior." Chimps clearly have a sense of self, Anderson said, and some sense of future and past.

ones such as jealously, suspicion, emulation, gratitude and magnanimity; they practice deceit and are revengeful; they are sometimes susceptible to ridicule, and even have a sense of humor; they feel wonder and curiosity; they possess the same faculties of imitation, attention, deliberation, choice, memory, imagination, the association of ideas, and reason ... though in very different degrees.[113]

The omnipresence of instincts dazzles us in mating rituals such as the stunning display of feathers by the male peacock. This provocative announcement is as successful in attracting mates as it is beautiful. These two outcomes are, arguably, one and the same. Most mating rituals begin with an initial phase of "flirting," followed by a sequence of strutting. This strutting demonstrates not only the male's physical prowess, but also something less tangible. For example, in certain bird species it is the male's unique and creative use of notes, rhythm and phrasing that the female finds attractive.* On the other hand, the defense of territories also can involve combat and killing. In fact, 70% of male monkeys in a monkey troupe never get to mate, and they die in isolation.[114] Evolution is about life or death; if love fits in there, so much the better (for us).

The combination of raw instinct and artful shaping is also found in human mating rituals. Clearly, however, one must beware of what has been called "zoomorphism"—the uncritical extension of conclusions drawn from animal behavior to humans. Having said this, anyone who has seen a well-executed rendering of a dance such as the tango or samba has witnessed an exquisitely instinct-rooted mating ritual. Seen simply as formalized movements, devoid of their primal sexual rooting, the steps lose their vitality and credibility. Equally important

---

* In the tradition of St. Francis of Assisi, both David Rothenberg, in *Why Birds Sing*, and Maya Angelou, in *I Know Why the Caged Bird Sings*, write about this creative core in birdsong. Rothenberg asks the question of why birdsong sounds so musical, and after earlier "duets" with birds and cello and flute, he has recorded a series of live duets between bird and clarinet.

are the unexpected and creative variations as well as the partner's response to those surprises that make the dance simultaneously instinctual and artistic. I once watched the mating dance of two scorpions, and had to laugh at just how it resembled (including the gift of a rose—in the form of a twig) the tango in its basic structure. Imagine seeing, in a split screen, a couple passionately engaged in a tango, along with two scorpions coupled in the fervor of their mating dance. One would be struck both by the unexpected, almost bizarre, similarity as well as by the difference in the sense of nuance and variation. Let us not forget the millions of lovers the world over who, at this very moment, are gazing into each other's eyes. With their enchantment, originality, creativity and perfection ignited, they are engaging the instinctual stepping-stones for an entire life together. Unfortunately, when this dance goes awry, there are also the instincts that drive the jealous rage of broken-hearted lovers.

For most of us, the multitude of primal impulses is generally hidden from our rational appreciation. Yet, in sharpening our focus, we can begin to discern an internal savannah, one populated by ancient instincts that manifest as coherent behaviors, sensations, feelings and thoughts. These primal reactions and responses are organized and orchestrated by "hardwired" neurological mechanisms. The assemblage of physiological processes, known as "fixed action patterns" and "domain-specific programs" (and the stimuli that release them, the so-called innate releasing mechanisms, or IRMs), are the legacy of our long evolutionary past. It is worth mentioning that the term *fixed* makes these behaviors seem more rigid than they really are. This is probably due to a mistranslation of the original German word for these responses, *Erbkoordination*, which translates, descriptively, as "legacy coordination." This latter term infers a strong genetic component but one that is not fully determined and is subject to modification.

According to Darwin,[115] emotions are accompanied by bodily changes and by "incipient" bodily action. He describes, for example, the typical bodily action that accompanies rage:

The body is commonly held erect; ready for instant action ... The teeth are clenched or ground together ... Few men in a great passion ... can resist acting as if they intended to strike or push the man [with whom they are enraged] violently away. The desire, indeed, to strike often becomes so intolerably strong that inanimate objects are struck or dashed to the ground.[116]

However, Lorenz modified this view of instinctive action patterns by pointing out that "even highly irascible people will refrain from smashing really valuable objects, preferring cheaper crockery."[117] Emotion thus is associated with a *tendency* to specific action, a *readiness* for that action—but the action may be restrained, moderated or modified.

Instincts, in essence, are expressed as actions—that is to say, as physical urges and movements. In early evolution, instinctual programs were "written" primarily for the action system. Instincts, therefore, are about movement—how to find food, shelter and a mate, as well as how to protect ourselves. These responses need no learning. They are hardwired in the service of our survival. One of the most basic instincts is our reaction to large looming shadows; another, which we share with even the smallest of creatures including mammals, birds, and possibly even moths, is our innate fear of eyes swooping down from above (presumably those of an avian predator).* Arguably, this may be the genesis of our fear of the "evil eye," expressed in many cultures in talisman, ritual and art.[118] An example of these innate reactions was sent to me by a friend concerning an episode with their young son:

Aleksander, a usually calm, happy and peaceful child, was sixteen months old and still only crawling and standing, not yet walking. (He would start to walk at eighteen months.) He and his father went to a friend's house to play. An adult friend was holding Aleksander on his lap and showed him a bag of rubbery or gelatinous eyeballs (the kind that that if you squeeze them, one will pop out). Aleksander did not seem to like the toy; he showed this by sharply turning away and making

---

* Note that one of the moth's camouflages is an eye on its wings.

faces. Later, when Aleksander was sitting on the floor, a friend showed him the toy again, this time standing and squeezing the eye from above. The distance between the child and the popped eye was about four or five feet. Aleksander, in a fraction of a second, turned 180 degrees and catapulted backward, screaming and waving his hands and legs. He landed on the opposite wall crouched in the corner. Both adults were startled by the reaction and immediately went to the child. His father held him in his arms, and after a short time Aleksander calmed down.

Instinctive movements may be large and powerful like Aleksander's reaction to the "evil eye" of a bird of prey and the other fight/flight responses. Or they can be subtler, as in the small gasping when one cries inside. Instinctual movements can also be delicate, such as in the tiny throat movements that generate our most tender murmurs and whispers for our babies and lovers.

In the Beginning, before the Word, Was Consciousness

The primal consciousness in man is pre-mental,
and has nothing to do with cognition.
It is the same as in the animals.
And this pre-mental consciousness remains
as long as we live the powerful root
and body of our consciousness.
The mind is but the last flower, the cul-de-sac.

—D. H. Lawrence, *Psychoanalysis and the Unconscious*

Why did consciousness ever evolve in the first place? Why aren't we, and all other animals, just going about our business without an inkling of our internal experience? After all, who needs all the feeling and suffering that goes along with consciousness? Without a satisfactory answer, we are left with a hole in the whole Darwinian argument. Wouldn't any behaviors or functions that are so widespread throughout the kingdoms of man and beast be there because they are a requisite of survival? To begin to address this question we need first to inquire, simply, about the presumed function of consciousness.

The Darwinian struggle for survival manifests as a continual arms race between predator and prey. The capacity for successful predation and clever evasion is a constantly evolving process. Combatants try out and refine (through genetic selection as well as through learning) diverse strategies enhancing strike capacity, camouflage and flight. They do this to ensure the right to eat and avoid being eaten. Anything that will help in maintaining an edge in the food supply war would generally be incorporated into the evolving scheme of brain and body.

Even by the Cambrian period (some 500-plus million years ago) the fossils that have been preserved paint a picture of lethal jaws by which predators could dismember their prey, as well as exoskeletons that served as protection against attack from their enemies.* In addition, the creatures of this period had prehensile limbs and appendages by which they could pursue their prey and escape from their predators. Thus the typical modus operandi of this epoch became one of predatory/prey struggle for survival.

Then, for about 280 million years, animals had begun to move in relation to physical space and gravity. Terrestrial adaptation demanded the addition of more complex behavioral repertoires. The navigation of new and unpredictable environments required creatures to incorporate and integrate external sense perception (such as sight, hearing, touch, taste and smell) so as to be able to survey the environment for obstacles and threat, as well as to acquire the basic necessities of life. At the same time, the instinctual programs required interoceptive (internal) feedback from muscles and joints to signal tension and position, more precisely allowing animals to know where they were in space at any given moment.

---

* There may, of course, have been multitudes of soft-bodied creatures that are not preserved in the fossil records. See Richard Dawkins, *The Ancestor's Tale: A Pilgrimage to the Dawn of Evolution* (New York: Houghton Mifflin, 2005).

The predator/prey struggle demanded the capacity to *plan ahead*, both for attack and for evasion. The inhabitants of this period had to be able to solve the complex Newtonian physics problem of two moving bodies—that of its prey (or stalking predator) and that of itself. They had, in other words, to anticipate the future in a terrain that was uncertain and difficult to predict. The only way to accomplish this was to have awareness of *five* dimensions, three in space, one in gravity and one in *time*. Accurate timing required the integration of events in the recent past with those in the present moment. Extrapolation into the future then became the sought-after "fittest" pièce de résistance for survival.

In the absence of clairvoyance or telepathy, the future can only be anticipated through the permutation and recombination of "recollected" (implicit) past experiences. Nature seems to have arrived at a grand solution to the complex calculus of prediction. Her name is *consciousness*. Such a "device" (i.e., mechanism) facilitates this game of "take-and-put." In other words, if I take this *present* situation and, based upon past experience, place it (in the body/mind's eye) there; then such and such is likely to occur in the future. The capacity to anticipate and predict movement is the basis of what consciousness is all about. Consciousness at its very most basic level is a strategy, simply an evolutionary invention that allows an animal to better *predict* its trajectory (in space, gravity and time). It does this in relation to potential sources of food, shelter and threat. This is the role that consciousness "plays"—or that plays itself in consciousness. The "game" of driving a car, sailing a boat, skiing, playing tennis or dancing could not occur without consciousness. And then, abstractly, consciousness is played out in the symbolic logic of checkers, chess, letters, words and mathematical relationships. In this sense, the modern-day chimpanzee rates as a novice in consciousness, while the dog, cat, pig and rat, in diminishing order, demonstrate a nascent capacity for consciousness. However, any animal that is able to modify its behaviors (in response to changes in its situation) is imbued with some form of consciousness.

In this way "mindedness" derives directly from improved organization and execution of bodily movement in space and time.[119] Without predictive consciousness, we could not grasp and remove a carton of milk from the refrigerator or make a sandwich and eat it. We could not solve a quadratic equation or write a book. All of these wonderful talents have evolved, however, because an archaic consciousness helped us to avoid being eaten by a stalking predator and to be cunning in pursuit of our prey. With crisp parsimony, the father of modern neurophysiology, Sir Charles Sherrington, a gentleman of few words, put it this way: *"The motor act is the cradle of the mind."*

Our basic survival instincts are the evolutionary engine upon which the castle of consciousness was built. While consciousness is not a uniquely human attribute, conscious awareness varies in quality and quantity in relationship to the complexity of each organism's nervous system, but not in the essential phenomenon itself. I am reminded of a "trick" performed by my dog, Pouncer (an exceptionally bright dingo–Australian shepherd mix), suggesting a fairly sophisticated form of conscious awareness. I shall use him as an example:

Pouncer loved to go cross-country skiing with me and resembled a snow-dolphin as he joyfully leaped through the flaky white mounds by my side. However, when I chose downhill skiing, he would have to spend most of the time in my truck with only an occasional run around the parking lot. One morning, ready for a downhill day on new powder, I brought my downhill boots and skis up from the basement. Resigned, Pouncer flopped to the floor in apparent disappointment. However, after a bit, he got up, marched out of the room and returned a few moments later from the basement with one of my cross-country shoes gripped firmly in his mouth. He shook it in front of my face as though to tell me he had a different plan for the day. His point was so well made, and I was so touched, that I couldn't help but change my course of action accordingly. Had Pouncer possessed full linguistic capability, words couldn't have made his point any more clear than did his disarming unspoken response. As evidenced by Pouncer's response, the give-and-take game of predictive consciousness does not involve symbols or abstractions but, rather, has its elementary roots with "plus-and-minus" values and purposive action; or, how do I get from here to there in a way that imparts an overall positive outcome?

Both successful attack and escape are promoted by a basic strategy that incorporates *past experience* in the service of imagining ("image-ing") future outcomes. The spanning of time allows choice of the imagined options. This strategy, however, is only effective when the organism is fully present in the *now*. If, on the other hand, we view the future solely in terms of the past—without a robust anchoring in the present—then, in the words of the country-and-western singer Michael Martin Murphy, "There ain't no future in the past." In other words, a future that is overly determined by the past ain't no future at all. This fixation, set in the past, with no sense of a future that is different, is precisely what happens in trauma. If Pouncer couldn't have imagined in the present, he most likely would have stayed resigned, and therefore a bit depressed. Unfortunately, unlike our animal friends, humans have a tendency, when under stress, to be pinned to the past. Only man routinely becomes lost in regret for the past and fearful of what will happen in the future, causing us to be disconnected and adrift from the now. One might even call this lack of living in the present moment a modern-day malady. It appears to be a by-product of a loss of connection with our instinctual animal nature.

Finding our Way in the World: The Instinct of Purpose

The "job" for each species is to adapt and maintain a place for itself in a very complex ecosystem. Evolution's winnowing-out process has produced, for all species, a means of coping, through complex sets of *actions*, even in the most extreme situations. Whether we are frozen in terror, overwhelmed and collapsed or remain mobilized and engaged is determined largely by our ability to navigate the complex instinctual action patterns described by Darwin and elaborated by his followers. These complex organismic responses depend, in a context of social collaboration, on harmonious teamwork between chemicals, hormones, neurons and muscles. It is this complex coordination that allows animals to orient and to take the right actions to ensure the reestablishment of control and safety. When all of these intricate systems are working together coherently, we humans have the felt-sense recognition that we "belong" in the world, that our consciousness is expanded and that we are capable of coping with whatever challenges life brings our way. When these systems are not operating smoothly, we feel insecure and out of sorts. So while our literal survival in a postmodern (actual predator-sparse) environment does not so much depend upon expanded consciousness, the very survival of our sanity and selfhood does.

Let's take a step back to the beginnings of life to glean a deeper understanding of the concepts we have been exploring. A single-cell organism, like the amoeba, retracts when poked by a sharp object or withdraws from toxic substances. On the other hand, it propels itself toward a source of food by following along chemical nutrient gradients in the water. The totality of its behaviors involves *approach and avoidance*. It moves toward sources of nourishment and away from noxious stimuli. Later, as cells formed into colonies and neural nets developed to electrically communicate, movements became more organized and "purposeful." The highly coordinated pulsing rhythm of the jellyfish, navigating in the surging sea, is an example of this coherent functioning. As organisms became increasingly differentiated and complex, first as fish and later as reptiles and mammals, the motor systems were fundamentally refined, and the organization gradually became more social in mammalian development.

Our early hominid ancestors were social creatures who needed to be able to rapidly alert each other about novelty, danger and other emergencies. In addition, they needed to be able to predict each other's behaviors, to establish hierarchies and to facilitate deception. The best way to hone those skills was by observing, and trusting, their own inner processes. In "Cells That Read Minds," Sandra Blakeslee quotes the neurophysiologist Giacomo Rizzolatti:[120]

> "We are exquisitely social creatures. Our survival depends on understanding the actions, intentions and emotions of others. Mirror neurons allow us to grasp the minds of others not through conceptual reasoning but through direct simulation. By feeling—not by thinking."

To facilitate survival in an increasingly complex and socially medi-ated world, a new mammalian adaptation evolved: feeling states. Feel-ings are never neutral; they exist along what is called a "hedonic continuum" designating affective spectrum from unpleasant to pleas-ant. We *never* feel a neutral emotion. Whereas the amoeba either reflex-ively retracts when poked (avoidance) or moves toward something nourishing (approach), higher animals "feel into" such movements as being either pleasurable or painful. External sense organs transmute physical stimuli and convert them into nerve impulses registering sight, hearing, touch, taste and smell. Ubiquitous internal sensors monitor a multitude of physiological and visceral processes and sort them into comfortable and uncomfortable. Such was the wisdom imparted by William James—that it is the scanning of our internal sensations that becomes the crucible of feeling.

A mammal baby does not have to learn that the taste of sugar is "good" and a hard pinch or a tummy ache is "bad." The ingestion of sugar is necessary for energy production, hence the pleasure attraction; while the pinch can cause tissue damage, feels painful and is, therefore, to be avoided. Similarly, a very light touch can give us an uncomfort-able creepy feeling simply because crawly things, in the evolutionary past, were likely to be poisonous. Our most compelling feelings of bad-ness (avoidance) and goodness (approach) derive from visceral sensa-tions such as nausea or belly warmth.

Hedonic feelings are also important for group cohesion and, there-fore, for survival. As an example, when we exhibit behaviors that are beneficial to the group, such as nurturance and cooperation, we are rewarded by feeling good. We may even rescue someone (or give them one of our kidneys) even though it may put our own life at risk. On the other hand, when we do something that may endanger the group, such as coveting another's mate or possessions, or endangering one's chil-dren, we are shamed and shunned. These feelings can be so distressing as to cause illness or even death.[121] In fact as studies have shown, those individuals who experience the greatest health and positive self-regard, throughout the world and in all socioeconomic levels, are those with strong group affiliations.

Feelings and emotions have evolved, at least in part, to amplify the hedonic sensations of approach and avoidance. When, for example, we taste something that is mildly bitter, sensations of "distaste" are registered upon our consciousness. However, when something tastes extremely bitter (and therefore, likely to be toxic), we are more apt to have the compelling emotion of disgust, with the associated sensation of nausea. With this emotional red flag (disgust), we are very likely to avoid such substances (or those that taste, smell or look like them) in the future. In addition, other members of the group who see our reaction will be less likely to ingest the same substance. Because we may not get the chance to avoid a poison (such as a rancid carcass) more than once, these emotional signaling reactions are meant to be compelling to us and others, making a long-lasting survival imprint. This is why if you get violently ill after eating steak béarnaise at your favorite restaurant, you are likely to avoid this particular dish and even that restaurant for years—if not going to the extreme of becoming a vegetarian.

By being able to *feel things out*, we are afforded the precision and overall adaptability that have put us at the top of the heap. There is a significant downside to this solution of imparting to feelings such a kingly executive function. If the emotional feeling systems were to fail and become disordered, as they do in stress and trauma, this disarray would reflect throughout the myriad of the physiological, behavioral and perceptual subsystems. This leaves us susceptible to fundamental misperceptions. A disturbing example of this flaw is when we detect danger where it does not exist—and, on the flip side, when we fail to detect it when it's actually in our face. Another poignant example of our "feeling system" gone awry is the presence of every sort of stress, autoimmune illness and "psychosomatic" disease, which have been the bane of modern medicine. It has been estimated, for example, that between 75 to 90% or more of all visits to the doctor's office are stress related. Fortunately, the evolution of conscious emotional feeling states provides, in itself, a remarkable solution *if* we can learn to register and respond to the inner promptings of our bodies.

Our instinctual feeling-programs are the foundation for what allows us to plan and move ahead with purpose and direction. It is the fabric of what connects us to one another. When this critical map becomes disordered and maladaptive with trauma or protracted stress, as a consequence, we simply become lost.

Losing our Way in the World: Serendipity Gained

Ivan Pavlov was born in a small village in central Russia. His family, wanting him to become a priest, enrolled him in a theological seminary. After reading the revolutionary Charles Darwin, however, he dropped out, leaving the seminary for the University of St. Petersburg, where he pursued a scientific career studying chemistry and physiology. He received his doctorate in 1879. In 1904 he was awarded the Nobel Prize in Physiology or Medicine for his prodigious research on the conditioned reflex. Pavlov is most well known for his methodically controlled conditioning studies. Yet his pivotal contribution to the understanding of trauma was spontaneously provoked by an unexpected and uncontrolled experiment, a natural disaster that disrupted his rigidly structured laboratory protocols. He had been resting on his Nobel laurels for almost two decades when a chance occurrence opened a new vista—a discovery that is little appreciated as *the first*, and arguably the single most critical, experimental antecedent for understanding the physiology and behaviors of trauma.

The great Leningrad flood of 1924 caused the water to rise in Pavlov's basement laboratory precipitously close to the level of his caged experimental dogs. Fortunately, his assistant rescued the dogs from their cages and carried them to safety. While the animals had suffered no physical harm, and looked from all outward appearances to be completely normal, very strange changes had come over them. First of all, these terrorized animals had "forgotten" or had reversed the conditioning that they had learned prior to the event. Secondly, some of the dogs that were previously docile in nature attacked anyone who approached them, while those with previous aggressive tendencies often shook and cowered in their cages. In addition, Pavlov observed physiological changes such as elevated and depressed heart rates under mild stress and full startle reactions to mild stimuli, such as tones or the sounds and movements of an approaching experimenter. Embarking (no pun intended) on his new career, Pavlov began to systematically study these phenomena with his dogs. He must have been aware of the traumatic breakdown of soldiers and the salient need for treatment considering that Russian military losses in October 1916 were between 1.6 and 1.8 million killed and another two million held as prisoners of war.

Pavlov remained focused on his experimental study of animals breaking down under stress during this epoch. He formulated the following sequence by which his dogs (and presumably humans) break down under extreme or protracted stress, thereby losing our sense of direction and purpose.

In the first stage, the *equivalent* phase, the animal gives the same response to both weak and strong stimuli. This can be observed in humans who are deprived of sleep for even a couple of days. Under this type of stress, people may react to an innocuous question with the same degree of irritability and confusion as when they are exposed to a significant provocation. One wonders how many domestic arguments, often around trite frictions, arise out of simple sleep deprivation.

In the *paradoxical* phase, or Pavlov's second reaction to protracted stress, the animals exhibited a *reversal* of their conditioned responses. Something had happened in their brains that made the dogs respond more actively to weak stimuli than to strong ones. This is something that does not normally happen to individuals unless they have been traumatized. The Vietnam veteran who ducks for cover when a distant car backfires, but spends his afternoon at the firing range, demonstrates this phase of breakdown. Another example might be the rape victim who startles to every passing shadow yet hangs out in seedy bars.

Pavlov named the third and final chapter in the breakdown saga following unmitigated stress *ultra-paradoxical* but also referred to it as the *transmarginal* phase. In this final phase of "supramaximal" stimulation, a critical point was reached. Going beyond this apex would cause many of his dogs to just shut down; they became unresponsive for an extended period of time. Pavlov believed that this shutdown was a biological defense against neural overload. (In this way Pavlov set the stage for the study of conservation-withdrawal as investigated by Engle and later by Porges with the formation of his polyvagal theory.) In addition, as his animals "recovered" from being stunned, they exhibited extremely odd and inexplicable behaviors. The aggressive dogs became docile while the timid ones turned hyper-aggressive, as mentioned earlier. Similarly, trainers for whom the dogs had shown affection prior to the flood were now confronted with aggressive snarls and lunges. Other dogs, who had previously disliked their handlers, greeted them with showers of tail wagging and affection.

These about-face counterintuitive behaviors are analogous to those of highly traumatized humans. The loving husband who attacks his wife upon returning from the Iraq War is one such possible example. Another involves hostages who exhibit the Stockholm syndrome. They are not only compliant but may behave as though they have fallen in love with their captors, even refusing to leave when their rescuers arrive. There are a multitude of examples where victims of kidnapping have regularly visited their previous attackers in prison for years and have even married them. Jill Carroll, the *Christian Science Monitor* reporter, described her Iraq abduction in almost cheerful terms but then, a day or two later, talked about being in seclusion because of her trauma. And then, hopefully back to equilibrium, she made the statement, "I finally feel like I am alive again."

In addition, traumatized individuals generally find themselves, as with Pavlov's transmarginal phase, swinging wildly and unpredictably between being numb and shut down on the one hand and being flooded by emotions, including terror and rage, on the other. These bipolar swings are often erratic and capricious. With human posttraumatic stress disorder, chronic sufferers tend to gravitate, over time, toward shutdown. This shows up as symptoms of alexithymia (the inability to describe or elaborate feelings due to a deficiency in emotional awareness), depression and somatization.

Pavlov, observing his dogs suffering with their debilitating and intractable symptoms, concluded that they had lost their capacity to make adaptive approach/avoidance responses; they had essentially "lost their purpose." In summarizing the plight of these poor creatures, he remarked that they had lost the "reflex" or *instinct of purpose*; they had lost their way. A similar example of breakdown comes from nature. A Galapagos Island guide told the following story to one of my students: "When a volcano erupts, the animals frequently lose their survival instincts, get confused, and some walk straight into the oncoming lava. This includes sea lions and marine iguanas capable of swimming to another island." It appears that under this form of extreme duress, even animals in the wild may lose their bearings in the chaos. With a rare prescience Pavlov also inferred the natural, instinctive mechanisms by which traumatized organisms could regain their purpose and will to live. In particular he realized that approach and avoidance were aligned with what he called the *defensive and orienting response*. In his further study of the orientation responses (approach) and defensive responses (avoidance), Pavlov provided us with the key to establishing a healthy encounter between an organism and its environment: an optimal balance between curiosity and the need to defend and protect oneself.

Pavlov discovered that when animals are exposed to something novel in their environment, they first arrest their movement. Next they direct their eyes, head and neck in the direction of a momentary sound, fleeting shadow or novel scent (or follow the lead of other members of the group as they go into an arrest and alert response.). During arrest there is a brief deceleration of the heart rate, which apparently "tunes" and opens sensory perception.[122]

Pavlov discovered that these *orienting responses* served the function of both locating a source of novelty as well as accessing its meaning (i.e., is it a source of threat, mating, food or shelter?). It was likely that Pavlov was aware of this dual function. He called the innate characteristic of the orienting response the *chto eta takoe* reflex (instead of the simpler *chto eta*). Attempts at a literal translation have resulted in its being called the "What is it?" reflex. A more exact translation, however, suggests something closer to "What is that?" or "What is going on here?" or "Hey man, what's happening?!?"* This labelling emphasizes the amazement and curiosity inherent in the response. This dual

---

* I recently spoke to the Russian translator for my first book, *Waking the Tiger: Healing Trauma*, and she confirmed this analysis.

response (reacting plus inquiring) is the dominant feature of orienting behaviors. For humans, as well as other animals, this includes expectancy, surprise, alertness and curiosity.

Let's end this chapter by tracking what Pavlov taught us back to its therapeutic application with clients: In virtually every session, as (formally) traumatized individuals emerge from immobility and shutdown, they are biologically wired to have the nascent impulse to orient to the room, to the therapist and others (as in group sessions) and to the here and now. So as Pavlov showed us how we lose our way, he also illuminated the way back. Recall for a moment an example of this during the session with Adam (the Holocaust survivor in Chapter 8). By embodying the image of the slum children joyfully flying their kites, Adam was able to emerge from his profound shutdown and began to orient to the various objects in the room and, then, to engage with me in a fresh and vital way. In that moment he came back into life long enough to embody new possibilities.

So you see, we are, in the final analysis, just a bunch of animals—instinctive, feeling and reasoning. In closing, I would like to repeat the quote from Massimo Pigliucci that opened this chapter because it seems to sum it all up succinctly: "We may be special animals, we may be particular animals with very special characteristics, but we're animals nonetheless."

CHAPTER 11

Bottoms-Up

Three Brains, One Mind

Understanding the laws of gravity does
not make us free of gravity ... it means we
can use it to do other things. Until we
have informed mankind about the way our
brains function, of the way we use them ...
until we acknowledge that it has been to
dominate others, there's little chance
anything will change.

—Henri Laborit *(Mon oncle d'Amérique)*

Give me a place to put my lever and I will
move the world.

—Archimedes

Surely, no one would reasonably dispute that we are the product of how our brains and bodies operate. While this may not be the whole story, it is a reasonable working approximation. However, at the same time it would be hubris to say that all of subjective experience is precisely explained by the anatomy and physiology of the brain, just as it would be absurd to believe that everything we feel and know is understandable by how the brain functions. In the final analysis, for better or for worse, we cannot escape the fact that we are constrained by the brain's influences and operations on our bodies. To know ourselves is to know our brains, and to know our brains is to know ourselves—more or less.

Following the visionary and experiential work of William James in the early twentieth century, there followed a shift in emphasis on the study of brain function. While James focused on the subjective experience of emotion, the research that followed involved stimulating and excising animal brain tissue and then correlating those sites with *observed* emotional behaviors (such as rage and fear). First, Walter B. Cannon, the preeminent physiologist of his times (1920s–40s), along with William Bard, underscored the control of emotion in the brain rather than (its experience in) the body.* Their central theory was furthered by James Papez, an obscure physician and neuroanatomist working independently in his small-town office in upstate New York. In his landmark 1937 article titled "A Proposed Mechanism of Emotion,"[123] Papez described an "emotional circuit" that was centered upon the upper part of the brain stem, the thalamus. Surrounding the thalamus was a circle, or "limbus," of nuclei including the hippocampus, hypothalamus and cingulate. The cingulate is an important intermediary, as we shall see, between emotion and reason. Notably, Papez did not include the amygdala (now recognized as an important mediator of emotions, particularly those associated with novelty and threat) in his papers on emotional circuitry.

Papez gave his circuit the catchy title, "the stream of feeling." Today this region is known as the limbic system, or the emotional brain. The latter descriptive title was coined by the well-known brain researcher Joseph LeDoux. It should be noted that these twentieth-century students of the brain concerned themselves exclusively with the *expression* of emotion while ignoring subjective emotional *experience* altogether. Freud's metaphoric framework and James's introspective focus on sensations and feelings had been eclipsed by research technology and a fascination with the concrete neural mechanisms and behavioral components of emotional expression. And yet, one might take the liberty here to speculate that Freud (originally a neurologist) would have been

---

* Cannon also mounted a well-reasoned critique of James's theory by arguing that feedback from the viscera would be too slow and not specific enough to account for different emotions. (These questions will be addressed in Chapter 13.)

delighted, at least, with the locus of emotions. After all, it sat at the core of the brain where he believed that the instincts (or what he dubbed the "id") resided, well out of range of the "ego" and deliberate consciousness. However, as we shall see, while there may be no direct connection between the instincts (id) and rational consciousness (ego), there are *vitally important* two-way conduits between the id (instincts) and self-awareness.

Our most primitive instincts reside at the root of the limbic system, in the most ancient, no-frills portion of the brain. There a core of barbed neurons meanders along the brain stem. It is this archaic system that serves the functions of maintaining constancy in the internal milieu and modulating states of arousal. One little nick in this sloppy web of twisted barbed wire, and we find ourselves in an irreversible coma. When it was announced that President Kennedy had been shot and had sustained an injury to his brain stem, my group of research assistant colleagues in James Old's neurophysiology lab wept as we sat by the television in the University of Michigan student union, realizing that the end had come to our Prince of Camelot.

The neuroanatomist Walle Nauta aptly called the primal brain stem regulation of arousal "the posture of the internal milieu." With this descriptive connotation, he acknowledged, validated and updated the prophetic work from the previous century of the father of modern physiology, Claude Bernard. Bernard had shown how the primary requirement of all life is the maintenance of a stable internal environment. Whether one is considering a cell, an amoeba, a rock star, a custodian, a king, an astronaut or a president, without this dynamic internal stability in the face of an ever-changing external environment, we would all perish. For example, the oxygen levels and ph (acidity) of the blood must be kept within a *very* narrow range for life to remain viable. It is the brain stem, through a myriad of complex reflexes, that is "control central" responsible for the minutiae of constant adjustments that are required for the basic maintenance of life. This also includes the regulation of our basic states of arousal, wakefulness and activity. And as messy and primitive as the brain stem reticular activating system is, it does its assigned job of preserving life *magnificently*.

When compared with the obsessively neat, six-layered columnar organization of the grand cerebral cortex, the brain stem appears a lowly chaotic mess. However, it is just this primitive organization that allows it to carry out its assigned function. It quickly and efficiently gathers diverse sensory data from both inside and outside of the body and keeps the inside relatively stable in the face of a restless and capricious external milieu. At the same time, it collects and summates these various sensory channels to augment the overall state of arousal. This is why the noise of a passing truck can abruptly rouse us from slumber, or why stimulating a comatose patient with music, smells and touch may help return him to the land of the living. Nature has discovered that the modulation of arousal is best served through the nonspecific synesthesia of sights, sounds, smells and tastes in addition to the specific function of the various sensory channels.

As Below, So Above

Pre-mental consciousness remains as long
as we live the powerful root and body of
our consciousness. The mind is but the
last flower, the cul-de-sac.

—D. H. Lawrence, *Psychoanalysis and the
Unconscious*

The apparent opposition and dominance by the military order of the intricate six-layer cerebral cortex, over the messy anarchistic networks of the "simple- minded" brain stem, was upset by the great Russian-born neuropathologist Paul Ivan Yakovlev. In a seminal 1948 paper, this protégé of Ivan Pavlov challenged the hierarchical (top-down) Cartesian worldview and proposed that just as phylogeny begets ontology, the central nervous system structures, and by implication our increasingly complex behaviors, have evolved *from within to outward, from below to above.*

The innermost and evolutionarily most primitive brain structures in the brain stem and hypothalamus (the archipallium) are those that regulate the internal states through autonomic control of the viscera and blood vessels. This most primitive system, Yakovlev argued, forms *the matrix upon which the remainder of the brain, as well as behavior, is elaborated.*

The next level, the limbic system (the paleopallium or paleomammalian brain in terms of evolution and location), is a system related to posture, locomotion and external (i.e., facial) *expression of the internal visceral states.* This stratum manifests in the form of *emotional drives* and affects. Finally, the outermost development (the neopallium or neocortex), an outgrowth of the middle system in Yakovlev's schema, allows for control, perception, symbolization, language and manipulation of the external environment.

Though we identify primarily with the later, more sophisticated elaboration, Yakovlev emphasized that these brain strata (residing concentrically one within the other—much like Russian nesting dolls) are not functionally independent. Rather, they are overlapping and integrated parts that contribute to the organism's total behavior. The limbic system and neocortex are rooted in the primitive (visceral) brain stem and are elaborations of its function. It was Yakovlev's contention that the appearance of the more complex and highly ordered cerebral cortex is an evolutionary *refinement*—ultimately derived from emotional and visceral functions including ingestion, digestion and elimination. One could say that the brain is a gadget evolved by the stomach to serve its purposes of securing food. Of course one could also argue that the stomach is a device invented by the brain to provide it with the energy and raw materials it needs to function and stay alive. So whose game is it, body or brain? Of course, both arguments are equally true, and this is how *organisms* function. The brain implies the stomach and the stomach implies the brain; they are mutually intertwined in this democratic web of reciprocity. This organismic view turns on its head the Cartesian, top-down model where the "higher" brain controls the "lower" functions of the body, such as the digestive system. This difference in perspective is not just wordplay; it is rather a wholly different worldview, an entirely different outlook on how the organism works. It is here that Yakovlev has provided a map that modern-day neuroscientists could do well to incorporate into their thinking—that of a deeper appreciation for the organismic welding of a body-brain.

In summary, then, the tendency toward encephalization (according to Yakovlev) is a refinement of the evolutionarily primitive needs of visceral function. Thoughts and feelings are not new and independent processes divorced from visceral activity; we feel and think with our guts. The digestive process, for example, is originally experienced as physical sensations (pure hunger), then as emotional feelings (e.g., hunger as aggression) and finally as cortical refinements in the form of assimilating new perceptions and concepts (as in the hunger for and the digestion of new knowledge). Less flattering to our egocentrism, this (r)evolutionary "bottom-up" perspective focuses on an archaic, homeostatic, survival function as the template of neural organization and consciousness. Our so-called higher thought processes, of which we have become so enamored, are servants rather than masters.

The matrix of function and consciousness, Yakovlev's sphere of visceration, is in the primitive reticular formation. His methodical analysis of thousands of slices of brain tissue (histology) yielded a poetic vision in the great traditions of his countrymen, Tolstoy and Dostoyevsky. Yakovlev delicately summarized his meticulous, lifelong investigations with the single encompassing statement, *"Out of the swamp of the reticular system, the cerebral cortex arose, like a sinful orchid, beautiful and guilty."* Wow ... wow ... wow!

A Personal Pilgrimage

When I first encountered the ideas of Yakovlev, I registered the truth of his hypothesis viscerally. My gut rumbled in recognition; my emotions soared in excitement. And intellectually, I yearned to digest and savor the exquisite essence of this man's genius.* I wanted to devour him alive—that is, if he was still alive. It took several days of persistent phone calls to locate him. He was indeed alive and well. This coming-of-age odyssey mutated to locating and meeting with some of my other key

---

* In psychology, *appetitive* means acquiring.

intellectual heroes. After finally receiving my doctorate from University of California–Berkeley in 1977, I sent copies of my thesis on stress to several scientists who were my intellectual mentors. This list included Nikolaas Tinbergen, Raymond Dart, Carl Richter, Hans Selye, Ernst Gellhorn, Paul MacLean and Yakovlev himself. I was on my way …

Yakovlev's lab was in the basement of a dark cavernous building belonging (I believe) to the National Institutes of Health. I proceeded toward the door described to me by the receptionist. It was ever so slightly ajar. As I poked my head in, I was startled by the panoramic vision of shelf after shelf filled with bottles of pickled brains. An impish figure called out, motioning me to his desk. This octogenarian of small stature had a quiet and gentle presence belying his truly expansive character. With twinkling blue eyes and genuine enthusiasm, Yakovlev warmly invited me to sit down. He proceeded to ask me about my interests and was curious why I might have chosen to come so far to visit him.

When I told him about my interest in instincts and about my ideas concerning mind-body healing, stress and self-regulation, he jumped up, grabbed my arm excitedly and took me from jar to jar sharing with me his vast variety of specimens, demonstrating the basic anatomical building blocks of the brain. From there he led me back to his desk and microscope; together we looked at slides of minutely thin slices of brain tissue. He narrated this viewing, waxing lyrical in his elaborate reasoning, as I imagined Darwin might have done in his laboratory a mere hundred or so years earlier. For me, the thrill was so intense that I felt as though I could not contain my pressing urge to jump up and shout, "Yes!" I knew that I was on the right track, that we truly are, to the last of our neurons, just a bunch of animals—and that's really not so bad.

At one o'clock, after sharing an egg salad sandwich, Yakovlev drew me an intricate map to guide me to my next appointment, which was about forty miles into the Maryland countryside. He did this task in anatomical detail, meticulously employing a set of brightly colored pencils and dissecting, with exacting precision, the best route and its distinguishing landmarks. He offered that if I had time at the end of the day, I was welcome to return by the same route.

I arrived at my destination right on schedule. Paul MacLean greeted me politely but without the exuberant warmth that had been lavished upon me at my prior appointment. He did, however, ask me the very same question—why I had come so far to see him. I repeated the same answer. MacLean looked at me with a puzzled expression, combining both curiosity and a seemingly paternal concern. "That's all very interesting, young man," he offered, "but how do you expect to support yourself?" Feeling somewhat dejected, I asked him many questions about his twenty years of rigorous experimental study of what is now called the triune brain theory. MacLean had associated many specific behaviors suggested by the neuroanatomical pathways laid down by Yakovlev, Nauta and Papez. Although these fundamental brain types show great differences in structure and chemistry, all three intermesh and are meant to function together as a unitary ("triune") brain. MacLean demonstrated methodically that not only did our neuroanatomy evolve as an elaboration, from the most primitive to the most refined and sophisticated, but (as Darwin would have predicted) so did our behaviors. The implications of this are beyond profound. They tell us that as much as we may not want to admit it, most primitive forms of our ancestral past dwell, latently, deep within us today (see Figure 11.1).[124]

The Paul MacLean Triune Brain Model

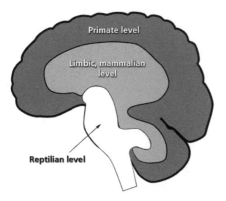

PRIMATE LEVEL:
Thinking, conscious memory, symbols, planning and inhibition of impulses

LIMBIC, MAMMALIAN LEVEL:
Feelings, motivation, interaction and relationship

REPTILIAN LEVEL:
Sensation, arousal-regulation (homeostasis) and initiation of movement impulses

Figure 11.1 This figure illustrates the basic functions of the reptilian (brain stem), paleomammalian (limbic) and primate (neocortex) levels.

The eminent psychiatrist Carl G. Jung presciently recognized the need for the integration of our instinctual layering through the process of *psychological individuation*. He believed that in the assimilation of what he called the collective unconscious, each person moves toward wholeness. Jung understood that this collective unconscious was not an abstract and symbolic notion, but rather a concrete physical/biological reality:

> This whole psychic organism corresponds exactly to the body, which, though individually varied, is in all essential features the specifically human body [and mind] which all men have. In its development and structure, it still pre-serves elements that connect it with the invertebrates and ultimately with the protozoa. Theoretically, it should be possible to "peel" the collective unconscious, layer by layer, until we came to the psychology of the worm, and even of the amoeba.[125]

Jung's mentor, Sigmund Freud, also struggled with the implications of our phylogenetic roots in his seminal work, *The Ego and the Id*. With disarming honesty and ruthless self-examination, he challenges the basic assumptions of his life's work. He states that "with the mention of phylogenesis, fresh problems arise, from which one is tempted to draw cautiously back ... But there is no help for it," he bemoans. "The attempt must be made—in spite of the fact that it will lay bare the inadequacy of our whole effort." Clearly, Freud was questioning the basic validity and premise of his entire psychoanalytic foundation in the light of our phylogenetic heritage. Here he acknowledges the need to incorporate an understanding of our animal roots into the therapeutic process—but how? Yakovlev and MacLean give us just this underpinning.

As did Yakovlev before him, MacLean divided the mammalian brain into three distinctly organized strata, corresponding roughly to the reptilian archipallium, the paleomammalian and the neomammalian epochs of evolutionary development. MacLean developed this map to include the hypothalamus as nodal in the relations between the three brain regions—a driver at the wheel of the brain stem, regulating autonomic nervous system outflow. Drawing on the earlier work of W. R. Hess[126] (who shared the 1949 Nobel Prize in Physiology or Medicine with the Portuguese neurologist, and ambassador to Spain, Egas Moniz), MacLean and Ernst Gellhorn[127] argued that this primitive, pea-sized organ, the hypothalamus, organizes alternative courses of behavior. It directs the behavior of the organism as a whole, a job conventionally ascribed to the neocortex. As we shall see, the control of behavior is shared by various systems throughout the brain—there being no single locus of control. We have not a *tripartite brain* (containing three separate parts) but a *triune brain*, as MacLean called it, emphasizing the holistic integration of its parts. With our three brains (actually four if you include the aquatic—homeostatic—component we share with fish), we are presented with the Herculean task of being "of one mind," a challenge that is both confining and liberating.

Three Brains; One Mind

The striving and territorial protectiveness
    of the reptile,
the nurturing and family orientation of
    the early mammal,
the symbolic and linguistic capacities of
    the neo-cortex
may multiply our damnation or grace our
    salvation.

—Jean Houston *(The Possible Human)*

MacLean's triune brain has a delicate balancing act to navigate in its triune rather than tripartite role. If you were to face the side of the head and slice the brain in half (providing what is known as the midsagittal view), you would observe a "mind be-lowing" fact. The very front of the brain, the prefrontal cortex, responsible for the most complex functions of human behavior and consciousness, curves all the way around the cranium, making a near U-turn and abutting, with intimate proximity, the most archaic parts of the brain stem, hypothalamus and limbic system. Neuroscience teaches that generally when two parts of the brain are in close anatomical closeness, it is because they are meant to function together. This makes it even more likely that the electro-chemical signals will be reliably transmitted.

Descartes might have been utterly flabbergasted at such an intimate relationship between the most primitive and the most refined portions of the brain. Here we have the highest pinnacle of what it is to be human "in bed" (cheek to cheek) with the most primal and archaic vestiges of our animal ancestry. Descartes would have found no rhyme or reason to this physical arrangement. Had he ever speculated in real estate, where value is all about "location, location, location," he might have been even more perplexed. In addition, as next-door neighbors, brain stem, emotional brain and neocortex must find a common language with which to communicate. Maintaining such an intimate relationship is analogous to the task of interfacing a Craig or IBM supercomputer at MIT with an ancient abacus at the Chinese grocery so that they oper-ate together as one unit. Likewise, the lizard's rudimentary brain and Einstein's genius brain (the neocortex) must cohabitate and communi-cate in a coherent harmony. But what happens when this coexistence between instinct, feeling and reason becomes disrupted?

Phineas Gage, a railroad supervisor in 1848, was the first well-documented case of such a violent divorce. While he was blasting a tun-nel near Burlington, Vermont, a three-foot-long spike called a tamping iron was propelled, bullet-like, through his skull. It entered near his eye socket, penetrating his brain, and exited through the crown on the opposite side of his head. To everyone's amazement, Mr. Gage, minus one eye, "recovered fully." Well, not quite ... While his intellect func-tioned normally, the injury altered his basic personality. Before the acci-dent, he was well liked by his employers and employees (the ideal middleman). However, the "new" Mr. Gage "was arbitrary, capricious, unstable and considered by those who knew him to be a foul-mouthed boor." Lacking in motivation, he was unable to hold down a job and ended up drifting, including time spent in a carnival sideshow.* One longtime associate observed that "Gage was no longer Gage." In addition, a Dr. John Harlow, his physician, poignantly, described him in this manner: *"Gage has lost the equilibrium or balance between his intellectual faculty and [his] animal propensities."*

Fast-forward one hundred and forty years to Elliot, a patient of the eminent neurologist Antonio Damasio.[128] This poor man was at the end of his rope, having burned bridge after bridge in his personal and professional life. Unable to hold a job, bankrupted by various business ventures with disreputable partners and slammed by a rapid succession of divorces, Elliot had sought psychiatric help. His referral to Damasio provided the opportunity for a thorough neurological workup. He passed one cognitive/intellectual test after another and even scored normal on a standard personality inventory. Even on a test purporting to measure moral development, he scored high and was still able to reason through a variety of complex ethical questions. However, something was clearly *not* "normal" with this man. Yet in his own words Elliot said, "And after all of this I still wouldn't know what to do." While being able to "think through" all manner of complex intellectual and moral dilemmas, he was unable to make choices and act accordingly. His moral computers were working, but his moral compass was not.

Eventually, Damasio designed some clever tests that were able to pinpoint Elliot's deficit and provide clues as to why his life was such a disaster. One of these tests was a type of card game where strategies of risk and gain were played off against one another. When needing to shift his strategy from high risk–high gain (with a probable overall loss) to moderate risk–modest gain (with ultimate gain), Elliott was unable to learn and sustain the transition. Just like the overall outcome in his life, Elliot was an abject failure; he simply could not learn when it mattered. Damasio speculated that his patient was unable to emotionally experience the consequences of his decisions or acts. He could reason

---

* For an authoritative memoir see M. Macmillan, "Restoring Phineas Gage: A 150th Retrospective," *Journal of the History of the Neurosciences* (2000), 9, 42–62.

perfectly well, except when something of importance was at stake. Essentially, Damasio reasoned that Elliot had lost the ability to feel and to care. He was therefore unable to make (e)valuations, integrate them into meaningful consequences and then act upon them. He was emotionally rudderless.

Damasio puzzled about the possibility that Elliot was a contemporary Phineas Gage. Both physicians, Harlow and Damasio, though separated by more than a century, speculated that their patients had lost their capability to balance instinct and intellect. However, rather than idly pondering this possibility, Damasio and his wife, Hannah, set out on a medically oriented archeological expedition. They located Gage's preserved skull, ignominiously gathering dust on a shelf in an obscure museum at Harvard Medical School. In a study more like a suspenseful TV crime scene investigation replete with dramatic forensic analysis than a stodgy academic experiment, the Damasios were able to borrow the pierced skull and subject it to sophisticated computer-driven analysis. Using powerful imaging techniques, they were able to predict precisely where the wayward projectile would have ripped through his brain, throwing him to the ground and forever mutilating his personality. With breathtaking anticipation, Gage's resurrected "virtual brain" revealed devastating destruction of the same tract of nerve cells as were malfunctioning in Elliot's brain. The mystery was solved! The severing of the brain pathway between the emotional circuits and reason, though extreme in one case and apparently more subtle in the other, was dreadfully injurious to the person's function and spirit, turning them into wastrels. Their brains were no longer *triune* but rather tripartite, cut off from the vital communication networks that link up the brains into a coherent whole.

Sandwiched between the frontal lobes and the adjacent limbic regions (the site of both Gage's violent lobotomy and Elliot's dysfunctioning neurons) is a folded structure called the cingulate gyrus. This region is pivotal in the integration of thought and feeling.[129] Said another way, it is the structure that connects the primitive, rough, raw and instinctual underbelly with the most complex, refined, computational lobes of the neocortex. The cingulate and its associated structures, such as the insula, are what may hold the key to being a fully human animal—in being of one mind, though with three brains.

Both Gage and Elliot lacked a functioning connection between their instinctual and their rational brains. As a consequence of this, they were both lost. Without instinct and reason (warp and weft) woven together on the enchanted loom of the brain, they lacked what it means to be a wholly human being.

The picture of Gage, painted by Harlow, was of a man enslaved by his instinctual whims, "at the same time both animal and childlike." Then, in 1879, a neurologist named David Ferrier added an experimental perspective to this condition by removing the frontal lobes of monkeys. He discovered that "instead of showing interest and actively exploring their surroundings [as before], curiously prying into all that came within the field of their observation, they remained apathetic, dull, or dozed off to sleep."[130]

Unfortunately, Ferrier's primate research was not headed by the Portuguese neurologist Egas Moniz, who later devised a similar operation on humans, which he called a prefrontal leucotomy. With the advent of this procedure, the scandalous field of "psychosurgery" was birthed. However, these "cures" were usually worse, far worse than the "disease." And this procedure created multitudes of irreversible zombies. Moniz, as I mentioned earlier, shared the Noble Prize for his horrendous and blatantly pseudo-scientific, freakish work, which "docilized" tens of thousands of patients worldwide. The procedure was most popular in the United States, where Walter Freeman (ironically, the father of one of my graduate advisors, Walter B. Freeman Jr.) invented a procedure called a prefrontal lobotomy. Bizarrely, this treatment, according to the senior Freeman, "was simple enough to be conducted in the offices of any general physician." Basically, in his own words, his method consisted of "knocking them out with an electric shock" and then (in a "medical procedure" reminiscent of Phineas Gage's accidental lobotomy by tamping iron) "thrusting an ice pick into the crease of the eyelid and into the frontal lobe of the brain and making the lateral cut by swinging the thing from side to side ... an easy procedure, though definitely a disagreeable thing to watch." (Note Freeman's curious and callous use of "them" and "thing," as well as his choice of "surgical instrument"—an *ice pick*!)

It may seem contradictory that this procedure can produce, as in the case of Phineas Gage, "an individual both animal and childlike"; while Ferrier's monkeys lacked curiosity and exploration; and, with Damasio's patient Elliot, the capacity to make valuations and to choose appropriate options was permanently destroyed. Unfortunately, the trend that followed created a Frankensteinian group of tens of thousands of lobotomized patients (and hundreds of thousands more who were zoned out on doctor-prescribed Thorazine and Hadol). Without the animal in the human and without the human in the animal, there is little we can recognize as being a vitally engaged and alive person. It is interesting that many people struggling with attention-deficit/hyperactivity disorder (ADHD), as well as many violent offenders, appear to exhibit hypo-arousal of their instinctual brains, together with a shutdown in their prefrontal cortex. In this regard the maladaptive behaviors associated with both may be attempts to stimulate themselves in order to feel more human. Unfortunately, the cost of these impulse disorders may be disastrous to both the individual and society.

On the other hand, people who are chronically flooded by emotional eruptions can be just as limited in life. While they are less inhuman (like the Gage-Elliot zombie "body-snatchers"), their explosions can be just as corrosive to the maintenance of intimate and professional relationships, and—it goes without saying—to a coherent sense of self. Traumatized individuals are imprisoned with the proverbial worst of both worlds. At one moment, they are flooded with intrusive emotions like terror, rage and shame, while alternately being shut down, alienating them from feeling-based instinctual grounding, rendering them incapable of a sense of purpose and inept in finding a direction. These may be our clients, relatives, friends or acquaintances who are caught in either extreme, endlessly swinging between emotional convulsion and coma (blandness/shutdown). As such, they are unable to make use of their emotional intelligence. To some degree they represent, when we are under the influence of chronic stress or trauma, the Phineas Gages in all of us.

Wholeness as Balance

As above, so below. As below, so above.
—*Kybalion*

We are more than speaking animals; we are language creatures. However, whether we are confined by the tyranny of language, or liberated by it, is a question that is up for grabs. How we use, or abuse, language has a good deal to do with how we live our lives. Words, in and of themselves, are of little importance to an infant when it is upset. Language needs to be accompanied by *close physical soothing* in the form of holding, rocking and gentle sounds such as coos and ahs. It is our use of nonverbal tone and cadence that gives language its power to calm and dulcify a baby's upset. As children develop, they begin both to understand the actual words and to be soothed by the mode in which they are uttered.

However, words must still have a physical context in order for them to be healing and salubrious. You may recall a young boy named Elian Gonzalez, who became the pawn in an outrageous political battle in the state of Florida. Elian's distant cousins (Cuban exiles living in Miami), supposedly concerned for the boy's welfare, fought vehemently against Elian's own father (who was living in Cuba) for custody of this young child. As in Bertolt Brecht's play *The Caucasian Chalk Circle*, they were literally pulling this bewildered six-year-old child apart. Eventually, the Supreme Court interceded and blocked Governor Jeb Bush's efforts to keep Elian in the United States as a "model anti-Castro citizen" and returned him to the custody of his father.

National Guard soldiers were ordered to remove and guard Elian against a hostile, placard-wielding mob as a female federal agent snatched him from the cousins and angry onlookers, holding him securely to her body. Clearly, this unexpected and unwanted embrace from a stranger terrified the already frightened, disoriented and brainwashed child. But then something quite remarkable happened. The agent held him firmly enough to not be ripped away by the angry mob, yet gently enough for her embrace to match the words she calmly recited in Spanish: "Elian, this may seem scary to you right now, but it soon will be better. We're taking you to see your papa ... You will not be taken back to Cuba [which was true for the time being] ... You will not be put on a boat again [he had been brought to Miami on a treacherous boat ride]. You are with people who care for you and are going to take care of you."

These words were carefully scripted, as you might have suspected, by a child psychiatrist who had known of Elian's history and plight. They were designed to alleviate the boy's uncertainty and terror. It worked. However, the words alone would not have sufficed without what was obvious in the body language, presence and tone of the female FBI agent. She either instinctively knew (and/or was perhaps coached) how to hold Elian only as tightly as was necessary to protect him but loosely enough so that he wouldn't feel trapped. With a very gentle rocking, brief eye contact and a gentle calm equipoise, she spoke—with one voice—to Elian's reptilian, emotional and frontal brain, all at the same time. This unity of voice and holding most likely helped to prevent excessive traumatization and scarring to this child's delicate and vulnerable psyche. In different ways and in various forms, this is what good trauma therapy does, as we saw in Chapter 8.

Some years ago, I witnessed another example of the instinctive use of human touch with soothing words to ameliorate suffering. I was in the Copenhagen flat of my friend, Inger Agger. Inger had been the chief of psychosocial services for the European Union during the carnage in the former Yugoslavia and was no stranger to trauma and humanitarian catastrophe. So, when the BBC World News, which was on in the background, announced coverage of the East Timor conflagration, we turned to see images of refugees who were clearly dazed and disoriented as they wandered aimlessly into a refugee camp. Posted at the entrance to the camp were a group of rotund Portuguese nuns dressed in white habits.

It was clear to both Inger and me that the alert nuns were instinctively scanning and "triaging" for the refugees, particularly children, who were the most disoriented and in shock. The nun closest to that person would move swiftly, though noninvasively, to that dazed individual and take him into her arms. We watched, with tears streaming down our faces, as the nuns gently held and rocked each one, seemingly whispering something into their ears. And we imagined what they might have been saying—in all likelihood something similar to what the FBI agent had told Elian. However, in stark contrast to what these images were portraying, the BBC commentator pronounced that "these unfortunate souls would be scarred for life," implying that they would be sentenced to live forever with their traumatic experience. He was missing the point graphically being made by the body language of the nuns and the refugees who were fortunate enough to be enfolded in the goodness of these compassionate women.

This powerful scene illustrates just what it takes to help people thaw, come out of shock and return to life—to set them on their journey of recovering and coping with their misfortune. The work of my non-profit organization, the Foundation for Human Enrichment, whose volunteers responded in the aftermath of the devastating tsunami in Southeast Asia and Hurricanes Katrina and Rita in the United States, was a more immediate and personal example.[131] Here again, it was the weaving of the most immediate and direct physical contact, together with the simplest of words spoken at the right moment, that helped people move out of shock and terror so that they could retain their sense of self, thereby beginning the process of dealing with their terrible losses.

In all of these examples, the brain stem's reptilian and rhythmic needs, the limbic system's need for emotional connection, and the neocortex's need to hear consistent calming words converge were all met. We are reassured that whatever we are feeling now, it will pass.

A counterexample was clearly illustrated when the world saw graphic images of dozens of dead and mutilated women's and children's bodies carried out of bombed Beirut buildings in the dreadful 2006 Israel-Hezbollah war. Following the televised photos, U.S. Secretary of State Condoleezza Rice spoke mechanically in legalese, instead of words of compassion and sorrow, only compounding an already dreadful report. With these visual and auditory images, a metaphorical metal spike is launched, searing through the cingulate gyrus, splitting the (once) triune brain into contradictory shards reminiscent of Phineas Gage. What a pity, when gentle, kindhearted words could have been offered instead, imparting a sense of hope and help unknown already on its way.

The preceding chapters have all skirted around the phenomenon of instinct. However, in this chapter, we have no longer neglected this lodestar, finally giving instinct its due.

PART IV

Embodiment, Emotion and Spirituality: Restoring Goodness

My belief is in the blood and flesh as being wiser than the intellect. The body-unconscious is where life bubbles up in us. It is how we know that we are alive, alive to the depths of our souls and in touch somewhere with the vivid reaches of the cosmos.

—D. H. Lawrence

CHAPTER 12

The Embodied Self

The Body is the Shore
on the Ocean of Being.

—Sufi saying

Let's now return for a moment to my personal story of being struck by the teenager's car. The outcome of my accident could easily have been horrific, utterly devastating. Instead it turned out to be transformative. Despite having been acutely terrified, disoriented and dissociated, I was spared the dreadful repercussions of PTSD. What saved me from succumbing to prolonged trauma symptoms? Along with the method I have described throughout this book were the conjoined twin sisters of *embodiment* and *awareness*. This asset, even beyond its crucial role in regulating stress and healing trauma, is a master tool for personal enrichment and self-discovery. My job here is to entice you to take your body seriously enough to learn a bit more about its promptings. Yet I also want to encourage you to hold it lightly enough to engage it as a powerful ally in transforming intense "negative" or uncomfortable emotions—and so to experience what it's like to truly embody goodness and joy.

Since these twin sisters of mercy are so essential to the prevention and healing of trauma, let's consider what embodied awareness looks like and feels like. Though we don't usually bring conscious awareness to the multitude of internal bodily sensations happening moment by moment, these experiences are frequently referred to in common parlance. We "bite into and chew on" tough issues. There are things that we cannot "swallow or stomach," while others make us "want to puke."

271

And of course most of us have experienced "butterflies in our stomachs." Surely the sensation of being bloated, constricted or "tight-assed" catches our awareness and has its emotional meaning. We may be "tight-lipped" on one occasion and "loose-lipped" on another. Or we may just feel open in our bellies and chest or even "breathless with excitement." Such are the poignant messages from our muscles and viscera.

All human experience is incarnate, that is to say, "of the body." Our thoughts are guided by our sensations and emotions. But *how* you know when you are angry? Or, do you know *how* you know when you are happy? Typically, people tend to ascribe a mental causation to an emotion; for example, I am feeling (angry, sad, etc.) *because* he/she did this (said this, forgot to do this, etc.). However, when people learn to focus on what is going on in their bodies in the here and now, they typically report, "My stomach is tight," or "My chest feels bigger—my heart is more relaxed and open." These physical cues let us know not only what we are feeling but also what to do to remedy difficult sensations and emotions. They also inform us that we are alive and real.

All of our experiences (tracing back as early as growing in our mother's womb), all of the stresses, injuries and traumas, as well as the feelings of safety, joy, grace and goodness that have affected our lives— all of these change the shape of our bodies. Sometimes these changes are obvious, such as tightly folded arms, a stiff spine, slumped shoulders or a caved-in chest. Others are subtle, such as a slight asymmetry of the shoulders, a seemingly insignificant turning to one side, arms or legs that seem small in relation to the trunk, a retraction of the pelvis or an uneven skin coloration indicating coldness and warmth. These form the bedrock of who we have become. They are a starting point of who we are becoming.

We take in information from the world through our external sense organs, those of sight, sound, touch, smell and taste. Most of us rely primarily on the first two. However, we are receiving crucial information from all of our senses. Of equal, if not greater, importance than the information from our external senses are the vast streams of information that we register from our *internal* sense organs. We receive this information from our muscles, joints, gravity receptors and visceral organs (see the discussion of SIBAM in Chapter 7). In fact, without this *interoceptive* sensory information, we would be fundamentally lost—more so even than an individual who is both blind and deaf.* Without internal information we would not be able to walk on the earth or know our emotions and our desires. Our relationship with others is utterly dependent upon a mutual exchange of sensory data, both external and internal. We gaze, touch and speak, and through a *resonance* of our sensations, know ourselves and each other. The overall sense when this process is in sync is one of belonging and goodness. Without access to the feeling sense, through bodily sensations, our lives would be one-dimensional, black and white. Both our physical life and feeling life, from our most primal cravings to the loftiest artistic creations, depend upon embodiment. And while most of this book is theoretical and didactic, I invite you, the reader, to participate in brief awareness encounters in this chapter. The reason for these "interruptions" is to encourage you to participate and actively engage in this material—making direct personal contact with the essence of the body's innate capacity to feel, to heal and to know.

A Basic Awareness Encounter

Look at your right hand with the palm facing you. Observe it with your eyes. Now close your hand into a fist. Watch the movement and visually note the end position. Open the hand and look at it again. Now, close your eyes and feel the physical sensation of your open hand. While keeping your eyes closed, slowly contract the hand again into a fist; then once again open it. With the eyes still closed, focus all of your attention on this opening and closing as you repeat the movement. Notice how your awareness changes as you continue to be mindful of the sensations of this seemingly simple body activity.

---

* Rare neurological conditions have been documented where the patient's entire internal sensory nerves are not functioning. These unfortunate individuals can barely navigate and would fall over the moment they close their eyes.

This little exercise may seem banal. However, to actually become aware of our body without being distracted by what's going on around us or by our thoughts and images (about the action) can be truly a Herculean task. Yet it is a task with rich rewards. Our tendency is to identify with our thoughts to such an extent that we confuse them with reality; we believe that we *are* our thoughts. With this exercise you can detect the fundamental difference between your visual image of your body and your actual "interoceptive" experience. Body awareness helps us get some distance from our negative emotions and belief systems as well as contacting those of goodness. In discovering that we are not just our thoughts and images, we begin a journey to fullness as living, participating, sentient, embodied creatures.

In the Beginning

What follows is a brief review of humanity's experience with embodiment and awareness. This admittedly speculative exploration is offered in the hope that it will better illustrate how the two important concepts of embodiment and awareness have been perceived and have developed over the ages.

Biologically, we have evolved powerful movement systems designed for protection, hunting and avoiding being hunted. These automatic (instinctual) *action systems*—things that the body does to protect itself— were designed for rapid response when we come upon a snake or tiger. Without thinking we immediately react—escaping, fighting or freezing. For our earliest ancestors, physical readiness was a basic survival requirement. They had to be in the "here and now" every single moment of every single day. They were prepared to respond instantaneously and meaningfully to a few molecules of a novel scent or to the sound of a twig snapping in the distance. Simply put, they had to react from their guts. Without these compelling sensory prompts, our hunter-gatherer forbearers would not have lived to tell the tale. The degree to which they were "self-aware" of their instinctual responses remains, however, an unanswered question.

Instincts, at their archaic roots, are compelled *actions*. They are movements that the body does or postural adjustments that prepare us for those actions. For this reason, physical sensations that guide these actions are the vehicle for direct knowledge of our instinctual selves. The advent of tools, symbols and then a rudimentary language allowed our ancestors to communicate with each other, sharing which action patterns worked and which didn't, thereby refining their collective behaviors. To this end, one might speculate that they embraced art, dance and storytelling—and in the process attained, cultivated and developed, over time, reflective self-awareness. Cave paintings and other archaeological evidence record the saga of the evolution of embodied human consciousness as it blossomed in self-knowledge, in abstract symbols and finally in written language.

As individuals congregated in populated communities, their survival need for constant environmental vigilance waned. Their awareness of bodily sensation took on more of a social function—what is now termed social and emotional intelligence. Survival no longer depended solely on the urgency of fight, flight or freeze. Rather, as society became more and more complex, the need for greater mental capacity to navigate our position within the group increased. Nuanced body language—the reading of facial and postural cues (the unspoken language of the body)— gave way to establishing impulse control, which propelled our progenitors toward an increasingly mental framework.

By the so-called age of reason, in the mid-seventeenth century, the importance of rationality ascended to new heights. Disembodiment, in the alleged service of this rationality, had become the norm. Instincts and the immediacy of physical drives (such as sex) had become an embarrassment or worse. The subjugating power of the church reinforced this deepening split between mind and body. Finally, the supremacy of rationality congealed in Descartes' "I think; therefore I am," an iconic statement for modernity. The rest is history, for better and for worse.

However, while apparently disengaged, our compelling instincts remain coiled, waiting to ignite and reunite body and mind into effective coordinated action. If, for example, we become stranded in the wilderness, our instincts for predation, protection and shelter will click into sharp focus. If not we will surely die. Additionally, the full power of our intellects will be enrolled to service these bodily instincts. The snapping twig, a novel scent or a fleeting shadow will arouse us to a heightened alert readiness. Sticks, leaves and mud will present themselves as precious building material and protection from the elements. When death looms, rumination is worthless, while body engagement in the here and now is invaluable.

Mostly, though, our gripping survival instincts seem largely useless; in fact, in day-to-day life they are frequently detrimental. We expend an enormous amount of energy suppressing our instinctual eruptions. For example, when our boss passes over us and promotes a less experienced rival, we (*perceiving* actual threat) momentarily explode, then stuff our murderous rage back into our bodies from whence it came— almost before we can feel it. The cumulative consequences of suppressing such powerful impulses, however, takes its toll in the form of back pain, headaches, high blood pressure, heart disease and gastrointestinal disorders, just to mention a few.

Today our survival depends very little on actually executing our basic instincts. Rather, our physical and psychological health depends on having deliberate and nonreactive access to them. Because our ancient design plan remains intact, it is our legacy to *feel really alive only* when our survival instincts are fully engaged. However, and this is the rub, modern life rarely provides the opportunity for that kind of raw and powerful expression. And when we are called to action, being swept away with a fight-or-flight response is rarely appropriate to the social context in which we find ourselves. As such, we are damned if we do and damned if we don't.

Unable to feel our instinctual aliveness, we are left with certain cravings. These impulses generally revolve around two of our primary instincts: those for self-survival (threat) and those for species survival (sex). Furthermore, if we cannot find a "real" situation to evoke these instincts, we manufacture one. For example, we may engage in inappropriate and dangerous sexual liaisons or jump off cliffs with our ankles attached to bungee cords. These temporary fixes don't satisfy our yearnings. Most of the time we have solely our thoughts as meager substitutes for our instinctual drives. We not only put a lot of energy into our thoughts, but we also frequently confuse them with reality; we come to believe erroneously, as did Descartes, that we *are* our thoughts. Thoughts, unfortunately, are poor surrogates for experienced aliveness, and when disconnected from feelings, they result in corrosive rumination, fantasy, delusion and excessive worry. Such perseveration is not really surprising, as the paranoid tendency toward concern for potential threat in the face of ambiguity might have had a significant adaptive advantage in earlier times. Now, however, it is the currency of our judgmental, negativistic "superegos." On the other hand, when we are informed by clear body sensations and feelings, worry is diminished, while creativity and a sense of purpose are enhanced.

The poet David Budbill, working in his Vermont garden, speaks to this very human condition in his relevant verse, "This Shining Moment in the Now":[132]

> When I am every day all day all body and no mind, when
> I am physically, wholly and completely, in this world with
> the birds, the deer, the sky, the wind, the trees ... this
> shining moment in the now, devoid of mental rumination.

And in another sort of garden, a young woman expresses the following sentiment in a sexuality seminar, "I feel like the most important thing is being there, in my body, with my husband and not inside of my head." The poet Budbill finds relief from the tyranny of his mind through methodical physical work. Many urban dwellers use jogging to tame their minds. However, such respite is usually temporary and can quickly transition to excess and then become a way of avoiding uncomfortable sensations and feelings.

We all ruminate on the undigested cud of unresolved problems, whether or not this helps us to solve them. "Unnecessary suffering," through repetitive negative thinking, is well known to practitioners of meditation, Buddhism, Taoism and other spiritual traditions. It is also the impetus for cognitive-behavioral therapies. These practices, traditions and therapies point to a common solution: defeating the tyranny of obsessive thinking before it spews its toxic emissions into the body. However, approaches that attempt to tame the restless mind may not be nearly as accessible or effective as those that help us return to our bodies in a sustaining way. The poet Budbill discovered that when he fully engaged his body in purposeful activity, his mind finally rested. The immersion in his body is what allowed him to directly encounter the nitty-gritty, moment-to-moment experience of being alive. Rather than obsessive worry or regret, he opened to the experience of appreciation and gratitude in the "shining moment in the now."

For our distant forbearers, survival was the only game in town. This put them in a perpetually reactive mode—surviving from threat to threat, triggering one protective instinct after another. While we are under the domination of these same instincts, saddled with the reflexive reactions to perceived threat, we possess the opportunity to recognize them, stand back, observe and befriend these powerful sensations and drives, without necessarily acting on them. The conscious containment and reflection upon our wild and primal urges enlivens us and keeps us focused on actively pursuing our needs and desires. It is the basis for reflective self-awareness. Rather than automatically reacting to (or suppressing) our instincts, we can explore them mindfully, through the vehicle of sensate awareness. *To be embodied* (as I will use the term in referring to our contemporary experience) *means that we are guided by our instincts, while simultaneously having the opportunity to be self-aware of that guidance.* This self-awareness requires us to recognize and track our sensations and feelings. We unveil our instincts as they live within us, rather than being alienated from them or forcibly driven by them.

These facts of life make living in the *now*, free of ruminative thoughts, a formidable task. When embodied, we linger longer in the lush landscape of the present moment. Even though we live in a world where bad things can and do happen, where unseen dangers nip at our heels, we can still live in the now. When we are able to be fully present, we can thrive with more pleasure, wonder and wisdom then we could have imagined.

"Embodiment" is a personal-evolutionary solution to the tyranny of the yapping "monkey mind." It is one that paradoxically allows instinct and reason to be held together, fused in joyful participation and flow.* *Embodiment is about gaining, through the vehicle of awareness, the capacity to feel the ambient physical sensations of unfettered energy and aliveness as they pulse through our bodies.* It is here that mind and body, thought and feeling, psyche and spirit, are held together, welded in an undifferentiated unity of experience. Through embodiment we gain a unique way to touch into our darkest primitive instincts and to experience them as they play into the daylight dance of consciousness; and in so doing to know ourselves as though for the first time—in a way that imparts vitality, flow, color, hue and creativity to our lives.

The poet laureate T. S. Elliot seems to have grasped the paradox of such evolving consciousness in "Little Gidding," the fourth quartet of his epic poem *Four Quartets:*

> We shall not cease from exploration
> And the end of all our exploring
> Will be to arrive where we started
> And know the place for the first time.

Embodiment and Creativity

It is well known that Albert Einstein thought in images. His theories reflect this processing, as do his own metaphors. For example, pictures of elevators and trains moving past each other are indelibly etched in our understanding of the theory of relativity. It is much less known that he also thought with his body. He reveals, in his biography, how some of his greatest discoveries appeared to come first from his body in the form of tingling, vibrating and other enlivening physical sensations. In a process that appears to have been mysterious, even to him, his bodily

---

* I do have my own personal impression (based on an admittedly meager knowledge of art history) that the age of embodiment in the West peaked around the late Egyptian and early Cycladic period of Greece, some five thousand years ago.

sensations informed the images and insights that led him to his great discoveries.

Decades later, when Einstein's brain was dissected and studied for medical research, the *only* distinguishing feature was the size and structure of his parietal lobes, the region of the brain where information from the body is integrated for orientation in space and time.* There is another revealing story about this great man. When asked by a reporter what he thought would be the next great breakthrough in science, Einstein pondered for a moment and then replied, "To prove that the universe is friendly." He did not mean, I believe, that there would not ever be pain and suffering in life, but that the universe was, well ... playful, wonderful and fascinating. Such was his delight in the inner universe of his body. The Tibetan lama Dr. Tsamp Ngawang taught that "the body is a mandala. If you look inside it is an endless source of revelation."

I do not mean to give the impression that Einstein was the exemplar of a fully embodied man. Certainly, this was not the case. However, in this particular way, I believe he was. And it was this attunement that (arguably) allowed him to think outside of the box—far beyond its perimeters. Clearly, this is a mark of genius. Partaking in great intellectual discovery and engaging with the sensations of the body are not mutually exclusive experiences. In fact, for the human animal, this may be what "wholeness" is all about. In the philosopher Nietzsche's words, "I am body through and through, nothing more; and the soul is just a word for something in the body." The great American bard Ralph Waldo Emerson sums this all up: "What lies behind us and what lies before us are tiny matters compared to what lies *within* us."

---

* The parietal lobes are divided into two functional regions. One involves sensation and perception, and the other is concerned with integrating sensory input, primarily with the visual system. The first function integrates sensory information, coming from inside and outside of the body, to form a single percept. The second function constructs a spatial coordinate system to represent the world around us. Individuals with damage to the parietal lobes often show striking deficits, such as abnormalities in body image and spatial relations (Kandel, J., Schwartz, J., & Jessell, T.; *Principles of Neural Science*, 3rd ed.; New York: Elsevier, 1991).

In a more psychological vein, Eugene Gendlin remarks that "the door into the bodily living of our situations is right in the center of our very ordinary body." However, this "ordinary" is also the extraordinary. As the Kum Nye tradition of Tibetan Buddhism teaches, "the space outside the body though vast is finite, while the space inside of the body is infinite." This application ignites a wonder and delight that delivers enlightenment in Tantric Buddhism.[133] This is not just an "Eastern" notion. Dr. Daniel Brown, Department of Psychiatry at Harvard Medical School, adds that "focusing helps to cultivate a kind of internal bodily awareness that is so much the foundation of spiritual practice." R. D. Laing adds that "without the inner world the outer loses its meaning, and without the outer the inner loses its substance."

We have all had the experience, at some time in our lives, of just "knowing something in our guts." Without it making "logical" sense, and often to the contrary of "logic," we just "knew it was right." And when we did not follow this gut instinct, there were often harsh consequences. We label this kind of precognition as "intuition." I believe intuition emerges from the seamless joining of instinctual bodily reactions with thoughts, inner pictures and perceptions. How this holistic "thinking" works remains somewhat of a mystery (though speculation abounds), as is evidenced by the writings of the homeopathic physician, Dr. Rajan Sankaran: "Sensation is the connecting point between the mind and the body, the point at which physical and mental phenomena are spoken in the same language, where the boundaries between these two realms disappear and one can actually perceive what is true for the whole being." Such is the essence of deep intuition.

Intuition is an example of bottom-up processing. This is in contrast to the top-down processing reflected in Descartes' "I think; therefore I am." Bottom-up processing is more potent than top-down processing in altering our basic perceptions of the world. This potency derives from the fact that we are first and foremost *motor creatures. Secondarily*, we employ and engage our observing/perceiving/thinking minds. We think because we are, rather than existing because we think. When asked in a pub whether he wanted another beer, Descartes responded, "I think not." But did he disappear? Descartes' theorem might be updated to reflect bottom-up processing as follows: "I sense, I act, I feel, I perceive, I reflect, I think and I reason; therefore I know I am."

It has been implicitly assumed that psychological change occurs, primarily, through the vehicle of insight and understanding or through behavior modification. The study of mental processes has, however, proven to be of only limited value in helping people transform in the aftermath of trauma. Often people are left besieged with distressing symptoms for years. Lasting change, rather than being primarily a psychological, top-down process (i.e., starting from our rational thoughts, perceptions and disciplined behavior choices), occurs principally through bottom-up processing (where we learn to focus on physical/physiological sensations as they continuously evolve into perceptions, cognitions and decisions). Transformation occurs in the mutual relationship between top-down and bottom-up processing. As sentient beings, we own the latent capacity for a vital balance between instinct and reason. From this confluence, aliveness, flow, connection and self-determination come to pass.

Trauma and Disembodiment

Traumatized individuals are disembodied and "disemboweled." They are either overwhelmed by their bodily sensations or massively shut down against them. In either case, they are unable to differentiate between various sensations, as well as unable to determine appropriate actions. Sensations are constricted and disorganized. When overwhelmed, they cannot discern nuances and generally overreact. When shut down, they are numb and become mired in inertia. With this habitual deadening, they chronically underreact even when actually threatened and are thus likely to be harmed multiple times. In addition, they may actually harm themselves in order to feel something—even if that something is pain. In the poignant 1965 film *The Pawnbroker*, Rod Steiger plays Sol Nazerman, an emotionally deadened Jewish Holocaust survivor who, despite his prejudice, develops affection for a young black man who works for him. When, in the last scene, the boy is killed,

Sol impales his own hand on the sharp memo spindle that holds the bills so that he feels something, anything!*

The constriction of sensation obliterates shades and textures in our feelings. It is the unspoken hell of traumatization. In order to intimately relate to others and to feel that we are vital, alive beings, these subtleties are essential. And sadly, it is not just acutely traumatized individuals who are disembodied; most Westerners share a less dramatic, but still impairing disconnection from their inner sensate compasses. In contrast, various eastern spiritual traditions have acknowledged the "baser instincts" not as something to be eliminated, but rather as a force available for transformation. In one book describing Vipassana meditation, a quote reads that the goal is in "purifying the mind of its baser instincts so that one begins to manifest the truly human spiritual qualities of universal goodwill, kindness, humility, love, equanimity and so on."[134] What I believe the author means is that rather than renouncing the body, spiritual transformation emerges from a "refining" of the instincts. The essence of embodiment is not in repudiation, but in living the instincts fully, while at the same time harnessing their primordial raw energies to promote increasingly subtle qualities of experience. In the book of Job it is said, "For in my flesh I shall see God."

The degree to which we cannot deeply feel our body's interior is the degree to which we crave excessive external stimulation. We seek titillation, overexertion, drugs and sensory overload. It is difficult to find a movie these days that is without over-the-top special effects and multiple car crashes. As a culture, we have so negated the capacity to feel the subtlety of the life of the body that we have become habituated to a seemingly endless barrage of violence, horror and explosive, body-vibrating noise. On the wane are films of engaging dialogue and affective nuance. Instead, we are continually bombarded with jumbles of disconnected, incoherent and meaningless images or sentimental mush. There is the paucity of time we have for ourselves to quietly reflect.

---

*Paradoxically, as some "cutters" know, inflicting self-harm also releases endorphins, which deaden pain.

Rather, these precious free moments we have are spent online, in chat rooms substituting for real human contact, creating avatars in virtual space or watching TV on our cell phones. I'm not against having a good time or unappreciative of our technological strides. It is simply that while the media reflects our sorry state of insensitivity, it is also contributing, in a significant fashion, to our addiction to overstimulation.

To the degree that we are not embodied, our basic instincts—survival and sexuality—become distorted. Distortion of self-survival leaves us fearful, angry and anxious. Disembodied sexuality and a lack of the capacity for self-regulation produce the starkly barren landscape of pornography, as well as such disorders as anorexia and bulimia. Notwithstanding the complex psychodynamic, social and media factors (with its airbrushed barrage of models with "ideal" bodies), disembodiment promotes and fosters many of the eating disorders. Just like pornography, these disorders have their existential origins in alienation from the living-sensing-feeling body. For disembodied men, *images* of the female body become titillating, rather than experienced as joyful. They evoke a craven drive, rather than inviting playful flirtation, enjoyment, surrender and deep appreciation. In this way, disembodied men (who tend, by their nature, to be visual) contribute to women's anorexia because of their disembodied pseudo-need for the "idealized" female body. Hence, women's bodies become objectified both in the eyes of the other and in their own eyes. Young woman who have exchanged their bodily sense for body image are susceptible to seeking breast implants that sever sensation or super "slimness" as in anorexia. In the latter case, they are drawn to identify with grotesque, culturally reinforced, Biafra-like body *images*, rendering them barely able to sustain life or procreate instead of feeling body sensations. The compulsions of binging and purging (as in bulimia) are a futile attempt to control their body sensations—which are either chaotic and overwhelming or shutdown and numb. Some bulimics report that sex makes them want to vomit and vomiting, for them, is like having an orgasm. In addition, bulimia is an ineffective attempt to rid the body of something that is not-body; something that was forced onto or into the person's body. For men, it is pornography that fills the void of disembodiment, alienating men from their own sexuality.

There are plentiful other disembodying methods, other compulsions. These include the addictions to overwork, sex, drugs, drinking or compulsive eating. All are ways to suppress, numb or control the body—or are, ironically, misdirected attempts to feel it. However, without embracing bodily experience, we are left with an empty shell, a narcissistic *image* of who we think we are. We are unable to really feel the fullness of ourselves, a fullness formed from a continuous flux of experience. Pornography and eating disorders are two sides of the same coin—disembodiment and objectification. The less the body is experienced as a living entity, the more it becomes an object. The less it is owned, the further it is divorced from anything having to do with one's core sense of self.

A visit to the gym reveals a similar story. Lines of people are robotically pumping iron in an attempt to buff their bodies, but with little internal feeling or awareness of their actions. There is a great deal to be said about the clear benefits of cardiovascular fitness and challenging the power function of muscles. However, there is something beyond endurance and body mechanics. It is the kinesthetic sense, which can be awakened and developed in any movements we make and in the very sensations that prefigure any movement. This is the difference between *willing* a movement and *being* the movement.

On returning to my local YMCA from a trip abroad, I was startled to see that in front of virtually every work-out station there was a brand-new flat-screen TV! It's as though these individuals had temporarily parked their bodies, only to pick them up like the dry cleaning, after they had been exercised by the machines. In this regard, there is a distinction made in the German language between the word *Körper*, meaning a physical body, and *Leib*, which translates to English as the "lived (or living) body." The term *Leib* reveals a much deeper generative meaning compared with the purely physical/anatomical *Körper* (not unlike "corpse").

As a society, we have largely abandoned our living, sensing, knowing bodies in the search for rationality and stories about ourselves. Much of what we do in our lives is based on this preoccupation. We certainly wouldn't have computers or airplanes, cell phones or video games—

not to mention even bicycles or clocks—without the vast power of our rational minds. However, like Narcissus, who fell in love with his reflection in a pond, we have become enamored by our own thoughts, self-importance and idealized self-images. Have we fallen in love with a pale *reflection* of ourselves? In gazing adoringly at his reflection, Narcissus lost his place in nature. Without access to the sentient body, nature becomes something out there to be controlled and dominated. Disembodied, we are not a part of nature, graciously finding our humble place within its embrace. After Darwin, Freud was one of the first thinkers in modern (psychological) times to insist that we are part of nature, that nature—in the form of instincts and drives—lies within us. "The mind may have forgotten," Freud says, "but the body has not—*thankfully*." The explosion of people now attending yoga and dance classes, or receiving bodywork, are clues of our attempts at reviving a deep, unmet yearning. Could it be we are finally trying to "re-member" and listen to the unspoken voice of our bodies?

Ripped from the enlivening womb of interior experience, we then see the body as a thing, as an objective biochemical assemblage. However, in his lovely essay "What Is Life?" the eminent physicist Erwin Schrodinger concluded that life cannot be explained through reduction to its chemical elements. The human organism is not like a watch that can be made to function by putting together the components, springs, gears, stems and so on. Paradoxically, while not violating the laws of physics, life, he says, goes beyond them. Schrodinger speculated how this might happen and prefigured the field of what would later be called "self-organizing" systems. However, it doesn't take a Nobel Prize-- winning physicist's explanation to recognize that when we see innocent children joyfully playing together, or when we gaze upon a bead of morning dew gracing a blade of grass, that life is not just the sum total of its chemistry and physics. But *how* do we know that? We know it because we feel it. We feel what it is like to be alive and real in a vital, sensing, streaming, knowing body. We know ourselves as living organisms.

Most people, if asked the question, "How do you know that you're alive?" would speculate with something like, "Well, because ..." But that just isn't the answer; it can't be. The way we *know* we're alive is rooted in our capacity *to feel*, to our depths, the physical reality of aliveness embedded within our bodily sensations—through direct experience. This, in short, is embodiment.

Awareness

The precursor and twin sister of embodiment, awareness, is the 800-pound gorilla perched quietly on a solitary rock that is difficult to overlook yet unwittingly ignored. As with many mercurial archetypes, the presence of this primal diva is confounding—enormous yet elusive. Lady awareness sits in wait, yet slips away, when we attempt to grasp for her.

No one has been able to demonstrate an independent, fixed or unitary self. The philosopher David Hume wrote that "when I enter most intimately into what I call 'myself,' I always stumble on some particular perception or another; heat or cold, light or shade, love or hatred, pain or pleasure. I can never catch 'myself' without a perception, and can never observe anything but the perception."[135] The existential philosopher Sartre seems also to have thrown his hands in the air with his musing that "we are condemned to a belief in the self," even if it is a fallacy of (mis-) perception. Paradoxically, the only way that we can know ourselves is in learning to be mindfully aware of the moment-to-moment goings-on of our body and mind as they exist through various situations occurring in time. We have no experience of anything that is permanent and independent of this. Thus there is no ego or self, just a counterfeit construction. While counterintuitive to most of us, this is common "knowledge" to highly experienced meditators.

Awareness (like consciousness) is a relative concept. An animal may, for example, be partially aware, may be subconsciously aware or may be acutely aware of an event. Many biological and psychological scientists, however, are uncomfortable with ascribing awareness to animals and choose to differentiate between awareness and *self-awareness*, the latter being attributed only to humans. Self-awareness is the explicit understanding that one exists, and that one exists as an individual (separate from other people) with her own private feelings and thoughts.

However, recent investigations have demonstrated something akin to self-awareness in chimps and even in elephants. I have elected, along with others, to view awareness as occurring along a continuum, with so-called self-awareness at the upper end.

Awareness, whether in mankind or in the animal kingdom, may emanate from an internal state, such as a visceral feeling, or through external events by way of sensory perception. Awareness provides the raw material from which animals (including humans) develop qualia or subjective meanings about their experience.

Awareness of our internal milieu lets us know when we are hungry or horny, thirsty or tired, happy or sad, distressed or at peace; and this awareness facilitates what we do to address these internal states. With awareness of discomforts or imbalances, and with determination and will, we can set out to meet these needs. For example, when we experience hunger pangs, we set out to find food. When the rain starts to drench us, we seek shelter; and when we are sexually primed, we seek out a mate, court and procreate. Awareness, most simply stated, derives from the *moment-to-moment* sensing of internal and external environments in the service of satisfying organismic needs and reestablishing "self-regulation."

Unfortunately, most all of us have misplaced the capacity for awareness for a multitude of reasons. Tuning out begins at the earliest stages of life. As infants, all of our basic needs must be met by the ministrations of a caregiver—when we get fed, held, rocked and soothed; when our uncomfortable diapers are changed and when we are too hot or cold. All of these primitive needs must be met by "the other." When they are not, we protest, escalating to a cacophony of screaming, wailing and the flailing of our limbs. Moreover, when our needs are repeatedly not met in a timely and consistent fashion, the sensations of distress become so intense and unbearable that shutting down is the final option for the infant. This is the only semblance of agency left to the baby. As we grow and mature, we learn to actively suppress our instinctual impulses, needs and emotions in fear of retribution from our parents. Implicitly, we can sense their subtle disapproval and discomfort, turning away from this invalidation and further shutting down nascent awareness.

In immediately offering to buy a new "replacement" puppy to extinguish a child's shock, grief, horror and rage at witnessing his beloved pet getting run over, the parent teaches the child not only that his emotions do not matter but also, essentially, that they don't even exist. Is it any surprise that as adults our capacity for awareness is so blunted and diminished?

Awareness and Introspection

Though frequently used interchangeably, awareness and introspection are two very different creatures. Stated simply: *awareness is the spontaneous, and creatively neutral, experiencing of whatever arises in the present moment—whether sensation, feeling, perception, thought or action.* In contrast, *introspection is a directing of our attention in a deliberate, evaluating, controlling and, not infrequently, judgmental way.* Introspection, while often valuable (and the essence of many talk therapies) can in itself become interfering, taking us far away from the here and now. The unexamined life, according to Thoreau, may not be worth living. However, introspective examination can become pathological, contributing to increased rumination, inhibition, self-consciousness and excessive self-criticism.

Awareness might be likened to seeing a glowing ember emanating the light of its own internal combustion. Introspection, on the other hand, is like viewing an object illuminated by an external light source, such as a flashlight. With awareness one directly experiences one's life energy as it pulsates and glows. In introspection, one sees only a reflection of the contents of one's life. Confusing thought and awareness, of equating them, is at the root of so much unnecessary human suffering.[136] Insight, while important, has rarely cured a neurosis or healed a trauma. In fact, it often makes matters worse. After all, knowing *why* one reacts to a person, place or thing is not, *in itself*, helpful. Indeed, it is potentially harmful. For example, breaking out in a cold sweat when your lover touches you is distressing enough. Yet, having this same reaction, over and over, even after understanding why it occurs, can be further demoralizing. Comprehending that what happened was merely triggered by an earlier event, while repeatedly having to endure its uninvited intrusion, can add crippling feelings of failure, shame and helplessness.

On the other hand, "simple" awareness, along with a fortified tolerance for bewildering and frightening physical body sensations, can seemingly, as if by magic, prevent or dissolve entrenched emotional and physical symptoms. A deeply focused awareness is what allowed me to survive my accident without being emotionally scarred. It is also what allowed the young samurai to find peace in the midst of his emotional hell. However, let it be said that in actuality, it may not be so easy to experience the potent simplicity of awareness—especially in the beginning.

This trial is described by one young man learning to contact the essence of awareness:

> Deepening awareness is a challenge. It isn't a challenge because my parents didn't love me enough. It's a challenge because it's a challenge. I don't need to take it personally. I've spent years excavating my past, sorting and cataloguing the wreckage. But who I really am, the essential truth of my being, can't be grasped by the mind, no matter how acute my insights. I've confused introspection with awareness, but they're not the same. Becoming the world's leading expert on myself has nothing to do with being fully present.[137]

Beginning meditators are often painfully surprised at the tumultuous activity of their minds. Thoughts, sensations, feelings, fears and desires chaotically pursue each other like dogs obsessively chasing their tails. However, as they gain some steadiness in awareness, practiced meditators start taming their restless minds. They begin having extended periods when they are not sucked into the endless swirling vortex of their frenzied thoughts and emotions. In place of this turbulent state a sublime inquisitiveness about moment-to-moment experience begins to develop. They start to investigate the "how" of each arising moment, as well as their *reactivity* to various thoughts, sensations, feelings and situations. They settle into the mysterium tremendum of "no-self." In the words of the meditator, "One must be present, and it is not always useful to begin the past all over in order to live in the present."

One of the greatest barriers to being fully present is the habit of accepting what one does deliberately (i.e., "on purpose") "as the last word" instead of only one mode, rather than including what occurs spontaneously. For growth and development, any live organism and its supporting environment must be in intimate contact. However, because of our cultural conditioning, as well as frightening and aversive events from the past, we have learned to block this organic flow.

Perhaps the most concrete reason to pay attention to your body is that it is a ready tool to resolve various physical, emotional and psychological symptoms. However, such a "cure" is not a treatment in the traditional sense. It is not a mere alleviation of symptoms. Rather, it is a descent into the parts of our being that are alien, that we might prefer not to deal with—the parts of ourselves that we have split off from and, at one point, "chosen" to deposit out of sight and touch. They are concealed in the world of "non-experience."

Absent Body, Present Body

You walk into the kitchen. There, sitting in a bowl on the kitchen table, is the "perfect" apple. Its color, shape and size make you want to reach out and hold it in your hands. You do just that, and then notice its solid weight, fragrant smell and smooth texture. Already saliva begins to form in your mouth, and your viscera gently gurgle. You bring the apple to your mouth, open your jaws and take a powerful bite. As you start to chew, saliva flows copiously from your glands. The sweet and tangy taste is almost orgasmic. You continue to chew. The apple liquefies, and you acquiesce to the reflex to swallow. When the fruit moves through the throat, and begins its slide down the esophagus, perhaps you have the physical sensations of food in free fall, followed by a gentle dropping sensation in your stomach. Then nothing—that is, nothing until much later when you feel the urge in your bowels for evacuation.

Let's go back to the beginning of this mini exercise and follow the train of body sensibility as it leads from eyes to mouth to rectum. The visual impression of the apple, before registering in the conscious regions of the brain, already stimulates subconscious portions of the brain and generates small gentle movements in your viscera. The arm begins to move at the bidding of those physical sensations in your guts and salivary glands—sensations that probably have eluded our awareness. As you are making the motion of reaching out with your hands, your eyes direct the action. The motion is executed and orchestrated by our motor (muscular) system. The impulse to reach is guided by feedback to our brains from tension receptors in the muscles and positional receptors in the joints (the kinesthetic and proprioceptive senses, respectively). Theses senses guide our hand as it grabs the apple and moves it toward the mouth. The eyes could just as easily be closed, and the proprioceptive and kinesthetic senses would have accurately guided the arm and hand touching a finger, precisely, on our nose. We are generally not aware of this guidance—and we do not specifically notice the muscle tension or joint position. Nonetheless, they guide the sumptuous morsel precisely to its intended target.

If, as the morsel is chewed, savored and swallowed, we happen to pick up and read the Sunday paper, we might easily lose conscious awareness of the sequence of sensations. And later in the day, as our large intestine fills and calls for evacuation, we might still choose to ignore it, being preoccupied with completing a task at hand. However, by busying ourselves, by withdrawing awareness, our inner sensations recede into the shadow of absence. There will come a time, however, when we can no longer suppress the urgency and must let nature take its course.

Back to the apple: We can be more or less oblivious to the whole sequence: apple to eyes, eyes to brain, brain to viscera, viscera to arm and hand to mouth, mouth to stomach, stomach to small intestines, small intestines to colon and colon to anus. Functionally, we are able to carry out such operations with little conscious awareness. In that sense, we are akin to a machine, a complex servo system with multiple feedback loops. However, when we take the time to invite awareness, a whole new world of experience begins to open up ... one that we might never have even imagined existed!

Similarly, in deep sleep, we surrender ourselves profoundly to the interoceptive world. Automatic visceral activities regulate and sustain life far outside our realm of awareness. Respiration, heartbeat, temperature and blood chemistry are all maintained within the narrow range that supports life. This internal world usually resides at or beyond the outer reaches of conscious awareness. While awake we may not be aware of this inner world, but it is possible to entice it from far background to near background and then gently seduce it, if only fleetingly, into the foreground of our awareness. Let us proceed.

Going Inside: Adventures in Interoception

Preface

It takes one to stand in the dark alone.
It takes two to let the light shine through.
—Motown song

The following few exercises can be done alone, but as mammals the very stability of our nervous systems depends on the support from a safe other. This was the case of the pediatrician attending to my desperate need right after my grave misfortune described in Chapter 1. By myself, I could have possibly done some of what I did to recover my equilibrium after the accident, but it made an enormous difference to have her sitting quietly by my side. Her stable presence made it more possible for me to stay focused and not swallowed in fear, bereft in sorrow and utterly alone. The following exercises can be practiced alone but are more fruitfully practiced in the presence of another person.

Exercise 1: Wandering Inward

Awareness on the body as a whole is the object of this initial exercise. Let your attention leisurely wander through every part of your body. Without judgment of good/bad or right/wrong, simply note what parts you are able to feel. To what degree does your body exist for you? Initially, you may be surprised that you do not actually feel a part of your body, even an area as large as your pelvis or legs. Of the parts of the body that you do feel, you will, at first, probably be mostly aware of uncomfortable, tight and painful areas. You may also feel twinges and twitches; these uncomfortable feelings may turn out to be an entry to the deeper sensing of your body.

Next bring your attention to muscular tensions. Attend to them without trying to do something with them. You may want to try and relax them prematurely. It is important, rather, to just let the tensions remain and follow them as they change spontaneously. *Notice*, now, your skin sensations: can you feel your body as a whole? Can you feel where your head is in relation to your neck and shoulders? Can you feel your chest—from front to back, how does your breathing feel? Can you sense whether it feels full and easy or whether it may get "stuck" in your chest, throat or belly? Do you sense your ribs expanding and contracting with your breath? Can you feel your legs—or at least part of them? Next try to locate your genitals. Note what happens as you focus upon them.

Discussion

If you have the notion that this exercise was a piece of cake or you believe that you have observed everything that lies within the boundary of your body in this first experiment, then you are almost certainly mistaken. You probably have begun to notice just how difficult it is to "simply" observe experience without judgment and evaluation. Body awareness is a skill that needs to build gradually over time. If we experience things too quickly and deeply, we might be overwhelmed, leading us to further suppress or dissociate. Most of the time, we substitute an idea or picture for actual direct experience. Until we become aware of these counterfeits for actual sensate feelings, it is hard to tune in to the wonderland below our skin. How can we know what we are missing if we never knew it existed in the first place? That is why we only gradually begin to experience the body directly. Although we may "know" where the parts of our bodies are, it may take some time to actually feel them. Even many dancers and athletes have trouble with this. For free, unforced, spontaneous functioning of your legs—and other parts of your body—you must have a direct felt experience of their tensions and position in relation to the rest of the body. I have worked with a number of professional dancers who, at first, find this extremely difficult; so please don't be discouraged. If you practice this exercise daily in *moderate* amounts, skillfulness in sensory awareness will eventually come.

It may be beneficial to understand that there is a fundamental difference between your mental image of yourself and your actual physical/bodily sense of yourself. Of course, some discrepancy is true for all of us. But, the "neurotic" personality creates and perpetuates its symptoms through an unconscious constricting (hypertonicity) or collapsing (hypotonicity) of the musculature.* It is only through building a refined awareness and allowing the muscles and viscera spontaneous expression that we can begin to dissolve the "neurotic" and traumatic (split off) parts of ourselves and lay claim to a deeper, more authentic self.

Because developing the capacity for awareness is tricky at first, it would be good for you to appreciate how universally difficult body sensing is and be both determined and patient. These exercises are worth spending hours on. But please don't overdue it; fifteen or twenty minutes at a time is more than sufficient when you are beginning. Also, mini awareness excursions as you go about your day can be particularly revealing. You may find how everyday activities and routines affect your muscles, posture and breathing. You may begin to discover how dif-

---

* This area has been extensively studied by people like Wilhelm Reich, Else Gindler, Else Mittendorf, Charlotte Selvers, Lilimor Johnson, Frits Perls, Magda Proskauer and a handful of others. See: Heller, M. (2007). The Golden Age of Body Psychotherapy in Oslo I: From Gymnastics to Psychoanalysis. *Journal of Body, Movement and Dance in Psychotherapy, 2* (1), 5–16. Heller, M. (2007). The Golden Age of Body Psychotherapy in Oslo II: From Vegetotherapy to Nonverbal Communication. *Journal of Body, Movement and Dance in Psychotherapy, 2* (2), 81–94. Also see Perls, F. S., Hefferline, R. F., & Goodman, P. (1994). *Gestalt Therapy: Excitement and Growth in the Human Personality.* London: Souvenir Press.

ferently your whole body acts and reacts, for example, while walking, talking, driving, working on the computer and standing in line at the grocery store. There is no winning or losing, success or failure, with these brief daytime trips into the body consciousness. The only objective is to continue the journey, exploring a little further each time with a sense of wonder.

Try to keep yourself in the frame of mind that it is *you* that is living the experiences no matter how it feels. Try to accept blockages and resistances as part of the experience without holding on, censoring, forcing or pushing them away. With each and every experience, preface your observation with the words, "Now I am aware of ..." or "Now I am experiencing ..." This may seem silly and repetitious, but it is useful in establishing an attitude of exploration and self-acceptance. There is no need for struggle or change. Observation of what you are sensing is the ticket.

Exercise 2: Differentiating Sensations, Images and Thoughts

Find a comfortable place to sit or lie down, but not on a surface that is too soft or where your head is too elevated if you decide to recline. First attend to what you see, hear and smell in the external environment. Use the words, "Now I am aware of this or that ..." Then softly invite your focus inward to the surface and interiors of your experiencing. Note any images (pictures), muscular tensions, visceral sensations or emotional feelings. Allow yourself to become aware of when you switch from feeling or sensing to thinking, and then gently draw yourself back to inner sensing. You might say to yourself something like, "And when I have the thought that ... what I notice in my body is ..." At first you may find it difficult to differentiate between sensations, emotions and thoughts. Give yourself time as you accept the perplexity of this challenge. With practice you will become much more clear and adept at untangling the various aspects of body/mind. Trust that over time your steadfastness will bring with it, potentially, rich opportunities for extending your experiential edge.

Exercise 3: Focusing on One Element of Experience

This time as you explore your experience, notice and label your sensations, images and thoughts as they come into your awareness. When you peek inside, notice which of these three elements appears to be most salient. Then, one by one, shift your attention by focusing exclusively on images, then on physical sensations, next on feelings, and finally on thoughts. It is possible that certain experiences will just pop up into awareness from seemingly out of nowhere. This may surprise or even startle you and cause your "thinking mind" to jump in and try to understand what is going on. Resist this habit. It will take you away from the developing focal experience. Such seduction by the mind is to be expected. Each time this happens, simply and gently remind yourself, "This is what I am experiencing *now*," and then bring yourself back to the picture, sensation or feeling that you were experiencing before you were lured into thought. As you continue focusing, your images, sensations or feelings may expand, deepen or change. Softly say to yourself, "Now I am aware that . . ."

You are likely to try to figure out what is going on or try to remember what you *think* may be a memory from the past. The idea is not to try to "remember" anything (repressed or otherwise); though it is entirely possible that some sort of "revivification" may occur *spontaneously*. The key is to bring yourself back to the present with the gentle words, "Now I am aware that . . ." as you continue to *follow* your internal experience in the *here and now*. The tendency is to be drawn to the revivification, especially when traumatic material is involved. It turns out, however, that a key to processing traumatic material successfully (as well as avoiding the pitfalls of so-called false memories) is in cultivating the ability to hold a dual consciousness with an emphasis on the sensations, feelings, images and thoughts that are unfolding in the *here and now*. When this is done, fragmented sensory elements, which make up the core of trauma, become gradually integrated into a coherent experience. It is this transformation that healing trauma is all about; it is not about

"remembering" per se, but gradually moving out of fixity and fragmentation into flow and wholeness.

Discussion

You may (unless you are extremely obsessive) have found it madden-
ingly difficult to stay focused on a sensation (or image) without drifting off into thought. For these exercises to take hold, you will need to
regularly set some time to practice (generally from five or ten minutes
to an hour). You will encounter a myriad of possible resistances ranging from drifting into thought to "spacing out" entirely or having the
urge to go to the refrigerator to eat. Another kind of avoidance occurs
when a sensation or image somehow reminds you of a past event, as in
the experience of déjà vu. In "grabbing" prematurely for a meaning or
understanding, you will almost certainly abort the developing internal
process. Recall Miriam's session (in Chapter 8), where she learned to
trust the spontaneous happenings in her body by suspending her inclination to interpret, judge or understand. With practice she came to
deepen her experience, notice her boundaries, heal her unresolved grief
from her first marriage and physically open to her suppressed sexuality.

The capacity to stay focused and deepen, focally, is a magnificent
skill with great rewards, but it is stepwise and frustrating. Generally,
when people are able to get in touch with their bodies, they are drawn
first to a painful area. This is OK; in fact, pain (not due to a medical
reason) is generally *blocked sensation*, indicating an area of conflict.* You
will gradually learn to tease out these places of discord and progressively resolve them. But *first and foremost* you must learn to maintain
focus and differentiate various *spontaneous* bodily (muscular and visceral) sensations.

The term *spontaneous* is central here. Our limited acquaintance with
our body is primarily with doing—namely, how we use our bodies to
do what we want. If you observe the goings-on in any gym or health

---

* The bases of conflict are oppositional or incomplete motor patterns. The significance of this for the practice of therapy (and life) is monumental.

club, you will note that most people are not having an intimate relationship with their bodies. Rather, they are burning calories or building what they perceive to be an attractive shape. Even athletes (with the exception of some gymnasts, dancers and graceful individuals), more often than not, have very limited body awareness. To burrow into the world of spontaneous sensations and feelings takes a radically different approach than merely feeling the form and function of our bodies.

Review: Interoception, Contacting the Internal Self

The most intimate sense we have of ourselves is through *proprioception, kinesthesia and visceral sensation*. Proprioception is afforded through special sensory receptors in the joints that signal the *position* of all the parts of the body with respect to gravity. Kinesthesia is the sense of the *degree of tension* in your muscles. And the visceral sense arises through receptors in the gut that are integrated by the enteric nervous system (a neuronal system in our gut with more nerve cells and complexity than the entire brain of a cat has, as you'll recall from Chapter 6). Without these internal senses and without an expanded, "non-trance" perception of the external world, we simply are unable to know ourselves and realize that it *is you* who is focusing on these events whether they are interesting, pleasant, beautiful, ugly, dangerous, dull and so on. Without the unimpeded perceiving of these sensations, it simply is not possible to know *who* you are and what you want and need in life. This is a strong statement, admittedly, but hopefully you will become convinced about its veracity through experiencing the following exercises yourselves.

Internal bodily sensations are what allows you, eyes closed, to wave your arms and then touch your index finger to the tip of your nose with remarkable accuracy (at least if you are not inebriated; if suspect, a policeman may ask you to accomplish that task to establish your level of sobriety). The *visceral* sense is our capacity to directly perceive our gut sensations and those of other organs, including our heart and blood vessels. Most medical texts state that a refined visceral sense is not possible, that "gut feelings" are just a metaphor and that we are only able to feel pain "referred" from the viscera to more superficial body regions.

This is dead wrong; in fact, without the visceral sense we literally are without the vital feelings that let us know we are alive; it's our guts that allow us to perceive our deepest needs and longings.

Sensation Patterns

The next task is to begin to recognize and work with patterned responses of sensation. In particular, you will begin to notice what various sensations (i.e., tensions, contractions, aches, pains, etc.) tend to emerge in sequences or in groups. For example, you may notice that a "knot" in the belly or tightening of the anus is associated with a suppression or holding of breath. At first this additional task may increase frustration and even stir up fear. It may seem excessively difficult to follow so many sensations (a task initially difficult for single focus), and as they connect with each other, there will be the possibility of becoming overwhelmed or "stuck with them forever."

These concerns are legitimate. However, as you begin to gain mastery through practice, rather extraordinary things may begin to happen. You will be moving toward some of the root causes of these tension patterns. These stale constellations of habitual discomfort form the underlying maladaptive organization of all conflicts and unresolved traumatic residue. Through the following experiential exercises you have the opportunity to "see" for yourself, rather than believe on my word alone, the hypothesis that is spelled out in this text. Although it may take persistence and dealing with an intensification of the resistance associated with these complexes, the potential benefits range from greater relaxation and alertness and deeper sleep to more vitality and aliveness. It is also possible to eliminate, sometimes instantaneously, psychosomatic, emotional and psychological symptoms that may have plagued you for decades.

One of the keys in this process is to eliminate the idea that any of these sensations are insignificant. While they may appear that way to you, labeling them as such interferes with their advancing in a manner that reveals their significance. Secondly, as you begin to notice the increasing amount and intensity of aches, pains and other disturbing sensations, you might be worried that they will interfere with your daily functioning and that you will become more symptomatic. Though this might be a fear of yours, it is highly unlikely. If you do feel overwhelmed or "stuck," please enlist the help of a competent therapist trained in body-oriented therapy.*

It is hardly my intention to just open you up to the malfunctioning of your organism and leave you stuck there without an effective course of action or without a way even to retreat. Specifically, it is the purpose of this phase of the experiment to have you explore the chronic patterns of seemingly meaningless tensions and sensations that have become all-too-familiar features. Realize that these sensations were there long before you became deliberately aware of them. Furthermore, you will find that continuing application of directed awareness is exactly what will allow for "corrective procedures"—not so much by doing anything but by standing out of the way of your own organism's innate capacity for self-regulation.

The Continuity of Experience

The previous explorations involved proprioception and kinesthesia as the basis for awareness of the body's tendency toward action. In this exercise we now begin to explore the fusion of internal with external experience. This processing of the organism/environmental field is what steers our forward course.

Feeling is a continuous process involving varying degrees of pleasantness and unpleasantness. Feeling tones (based on physical sensations) are unique registrars of experience. They are the way that we become aware of our concerns and how we can go about satisfying them. These contours of feeling, however, are often unnoticed. This is in large part because of our lack of sensitivity to inner experiencing or because sensations are often hidden in the shadow of the more intense emotions. Most people are unaware of these nuances that are overshadowed by the periodic upheaval of discontinuous intense emotions that appear to come from nowhere. They may seem wholly irrational and even

---

*A list of practitioners trained in Somatic Experiencing®, my approach, can be found on the website www.traumahealing.com.

"dangerous," leading to suppression. This only further deadens the subtlety of the continuous feeling tones ... which in turn leads to the eruption of more overbearing emotional states punctuating those by increasing the flattening and deadness ... and so on. This is how various feeling tones become stifled before they are born into awareness. They are aborted during gestation, never completing what they were designed for: namely, directing action. The consequence of this lack is the evoking of "secondary emotions." These spurious emotions override (and are, unfortunately, often confused with) the spontaneously arising ones.

Exercise 4: Mindful Chewing

The jaw is one of the places that most people carry considerable tension. There are reasons for this. The following exercise may serve to illuminate both reasons for this typical "holding pattern" and what may lie on the other side of it, as it dissolves:

At your next meal, or with a crisp apple in hand, take a good "aggressive" bite into a food that you desire. Really, take a good bite out of it and then begin chewing deliberately. Continue chewing, slowly, mindfully, until the food turns to liquid. As you do this, become aware of other sensations and reactions in your body. If you feel the urge to swallow, try to restrain it—to "play the edge" of feeling the urge to swallow, when it arises, and continue to focus on gently chewing. This may be difficult and uncomfortable, so be patient. Note any impulses you might have such as the urge to swallow, tear, vomit, or associations to things going on in your life—present or past. If reactions such as nausea or anxiety become too strong, please don't push yourself. Make written notes of your reactions.

Exercise 5: Goldfish Jaw

Attend to the tension in your jaw and mouth. Notice whether your lips and teeth are touching. Slowly begin to part your lips and slightly drop your chin and lower jaw. Notice any impulses or urges. Next, infinitesimally slowly, begin opening and closing your mouth as though you were a goldfish. Gradually, almost imperceptibly, increase the range of your opening and closing. When you come to a point of resistance, gently back off and then slowly move back into the resistance. Do this several times, finding a rhythm. Likely, you will have a strong urge to yawn. Gently try to resist this and move into the feeling of yawing without actually giving into a full yawn. This process will almost surely be maddening, but try to stay with it as best as you can. Note times when you have an urge to shake or tremble or if it brings up emotional feelings or images. Note also if you seem to be fighting or bracing against it or to surrender into it. Again record your experience and compare it as you repeat this exercise over time.

Exercise 6: Shoulders

Most people also carry considerable tension in their shoulders. Here is a simple exercise to explore the nature of these tensions:

Take some time to explore the sense of tension in your shoulders. Note which shoulder is more tense. Now, keep your awareness on that tension. Then imagine that this tension is increasing. As it increases, note how that tension would "want to move" the shoulder. Allow the shoulder to move ... very slowly so that it feels like it is moving on its own. It may take ten minutes to do this. Does it seem like it's moving upward toward your ear? Do the ear and shoulder want to move toward each other? Do you have the sense that your shoulder is somehow protecting you? If so, what might it be protecting you from? Do you notice your head, neck and eyes wanting to turn (and orient) in a particular direction? How does this feel? When you open your eyes, let them look outside the window at a tree or around the room and focus on different objects.

Enjoy!

CHAPTER 13

Emotion, the Body and Change

If your everyday practice is to open to
your emotions, to all the people you meet,
to all the situations you encounter,
without closing down, trusting that you
can do that—then that will take you as far
as you can go. And then you'll understand
all the teachings that anyone has ever taught.

—Pema Chödrön (Buddhist teacher)

How Do People Change?

Neuroscientists can tell us where in the brain various emotions reside. However, they tell us precious little about how we can change "undesirable" emotions such as sadness, anger and fear. Nor do they shed much light on how people change in general.

Whether we admit it or not, we all want to change something fundamental about ourselves. Most likely though, being human, our first effort may be targeted at changing whoever is in our line of sight. We look for ways to get others to change—be they our spouses, employers, children or parents—and search out ways to cajole or coerce them to get with the program. With a modicum of insight, however, we will probably recognize that deep change must occur first within ourselves. Yet, just how this long-term change process occurs remains elusive.

In the attempt to improve our lives, we may urge ourselves with the familiar refrains: "Just apply yourself ... Start exercising tomorrow ... Cut down on the sweets, booze, shopping ... Pull yourself together ...

Come on, shape up, work out ... You can do it if you really want." And so it goes over and again. These exhortations and good intentions are all admirable efforts at what we call self-control. While this ability is an important life skill, it is often modest in what it can accomplish and is fraught with obvious shortcomings. Frequently, this strategy only works in the short run, leading us blindly into the quicksand of guilt and self-recrimination. Ironically, there are some days when it is no simple matter just to schedule a dental appointment or arrange for an annual medical exam.

Consider the following snapshot of goal setting: On Monday, John and his wife conclude that they could use some extra income for their daughter's dental braces. John, seeking a raise, summons his capacity for self-control. While keeping in mind his value to the firm, he awaits a strategically opportune moment. When he receives a generous compliment from his boss during their routine Friday meeting, he is cued to delicately broach the topic of the raise. In order to hold all of this information in check, until the ripe moment, his brain must employ volitional memory. John's voluntary memory has to keep his clandestine intentions intact for four days. That's not too hard, but not simple either. Anyone who has ever said to herself, midweek, "This weekend I will go the gym and work out," knows how elusive it can be to keep that intention fresh. To get up on Saturday, pull the jogging shoes out of the closet and go to the gym before family responsibilities crowd out precious personal time is no small achievement.

Accomplishing the larger, longer-range goals, such as losing weight, "making ourselves" more attractive or creating more freedom in our lives, can be so intimidating that we may give up early or never approach them at all—even at serious costs to our health and well-being. This is where self-control falls short. Resolutions falter as soon as we are under stress or get distracted by the myriad of day-to-day tasks. For more sustained and meaningful goals, volitional memory is inadequate. Self-control is not able to support enough sustained (retained, i.e., remembered) motivation to achieve our big plans over the long haul. For those grand projects and aspirations we need to access a deeper, more intrinsic, memory system, one that engages our *emotional* compass and guides our responses without overt conscious directives.

For long-term goals (e.g., losing weight, changing careers, getting in shape or forming intimate enduring relationships), *emotional-experiential memory* must be evoked. This type of involuntary memory grabs our attention and continuously motivates us through emotional signals well after declarative (laundry list) memory is completely forgotten. Long after the health goals we set for ourselves some months ago have evaporated, emotional memory comes to our aid when we least expect it. It may visit us in the form of an especially vivid dream or an unexpected attraction. For example, casually walking through a farmers market, a display of brightly colored fruits and vegetables may catch our eye. As our senses absorb this yummy array of healthy foods, we begin selecting some of the produce. This beckoning is not due to our conscious determination to lose weight, but rather because the signals from the primitive instinctual regions in our brains (programmed for nutrient-seeking behaviors) are no longer overridden. These brain mechanisms signal positive nutritive choices by evoking certain subjective feeling states that guide what we pick—those of attraction and avoidance. Similarly, our sexual partner selections, which may have been previously driven by compulsions and risky flirtations, will be guided by affinities for soft nurturing feelings, erotic tenderness, goodness and safety.

In contrast to volitional memory, feeling-based memory function stores all experiences *implicitly* (like learning how to ride a bike) and evaluates them from the emotional tone they evoke. It is this attention-grabbing reaction that prompts us to retain or reactivate our motivation and sustain determination to go the distance required for substantive change. One example is the woman who wants to lose weight for health reasons (a mental idea—unable to sustain the goal) and adapts the (emotional) strategy of imaging herself, in a sexy dress, walking into a party and turning heads. Leaving aside the possibility that one of the reasons for the woman's excessive weight might have been a desire to not have just such attention called to her body, the imaging strategy is a reasonable one. The point here is that conscious deliberation is easily forgotten and buried among the flotsam and jetsam of our daily lives. However, this frailty is sidestepped when sensations and feelings are evoked. Perhaps the reason that "the elephant never forgets" is because her memories are emotional ones.

In contrast to volitional memory, emotional memory often operates outside the range of conscious awareness. Rather than holding a verbal idea in our conscious minds ("I have to wait until the meeting on Friday" or "Remember to eat salads for lunch to lose weight"), experiential memory makes use of what have been called *somatic markers*.[138] These are emotions or physical sensations that inform us about a situation based on past experiences or feelings. Somatic markers might be the fluttering butterflies in our stomachs when we are anxious, the flushing of our cheeks when we are embarrassed, wide-open eyes when we hear an idea that excites us, the relaxation of our body muscles signaling the relief we feel when we complete a crucial task or the lightness and easy breathing we notice when we get something important off our chest.

The reason the bodily felt sense has the power to creatively influence our behaviors is precisely because it is involuntary; feelings are not evoked through acts of will. They give us information that does not come from the conscious mind. "Emotional intelligence" and "emotional literacy" communicate through the felt-sense/somatic markers and are vitally important to the conduct of our lives. Indeed, the writer Daniel Goleman[139] claims that it accounts for eighty% of our success in life. However, emotions can also lead us astray.

The Merry-Go-Round of Therapy

When psychologists talk about change, they often equate it with insight. This assumption, though often subliminal, has had a profound influence on theories and therapies purported to help people deal with "mental" and "emotional" disorders. However, when we investigate this further, we see that understanding, talk and change frequently have little relationship to one other. Woody Allen, asked if he still had his same symptoms, quipped that he was *only* on his "fifteenth year" of psychoanalysis. If only he had known that the process of change has to do primarily with being able to alter one's internal feeling states, and that "psychological" problems arise when these states have become habitual or "stuck." These chronic emotional states in turn dominate our ways of thinking, imagining and behaving. An understanding of how deeply rooted feelings can change is at the core of any effective therapy. It is particularly germane to how traumatized individuals can begin to free themselves from the many behavioral reenactments and repetitive feelings of fear, numbness, rage, terror, helplessness and despair.

The disparate roles of sensation, feeling and cognition in therapy have followed a convoluted and confounding path. At times emotions have been neglected, while cognition was esteemed. At other times, cognition has been dismissed, while emotions were practically worshiped. And most of the time, with very few exceptions, the therapeutic role of sensations has remained unknown. The balanced attention to sensation, feeling, cognition and élan vital (life-energy) remains the emergent therapeutic future for transforming the whole person.

Freud, following his gifted teacher Charcot, initially believed that to cure neurosis, the patient must "relive" the painful (traumatic) memories that she had "repressed." In addition, this reliving had to include a strong emotional component, a dramatic catharsis associated with the precipitating event. Employing this method, Freud came to believe that the precipitating event was frequently childhood molestation, usually perpetrated by the father on his daughter. (The vast majority of Freud's patients were so-called hysterical women).

Needless to say, Freud's theory was not well received by the professional community, many of them doctors, bankers and lawyers. Most of them were fathers as well. From what is now known about the prevalence of sexual abuse, some of them almost certainly had been guilty of incest themselves. For this and other reasons, Freud backed away both from the seduction theory (as it was ironically labeled) as well as from his therapeutic method of uncovering repressed memories in order to relive them through strong emotional catharsis. In what must have been a profound betrayal to many of his patients, Freud began to interpret their symptoms not as deriving from sexual violation, but as being rooted instead in their childhood "oedipal" wishes, fantasies to have sex with the parent of the opposite gender. Freud may have also been unnerved when, during the intense cathartic reliving, patients would frequently transfer those (alleged) oedipal lusts onto him. Freud, with a discomfort in his own sexuality, appears to have shrunk from staying present with his patients' confused, volatile sexuality and, thusly, betrayed them in yet another way. For these and other reasons, it appears that Freud abandoned the "hypno-abreactive" techniques in favor of free association to "help" the patient become conscious of their oedipal wishes and then to (somehow) sublimate these infantile "lusts." In this way, Freud believed that by recognizing their fantasies, his patients' neuroses could be transformed to "ordinary suffering." A contemporary (Pierre Janet[140]) and a student (Wilhelm Reich) of Freud saw things differently.

The Austrian-born psychiatrist Wilhelm Reich was convinced that his teacher had made a terrible mistake on two accounts. First, Reich believed that neurosis arose *both* from real events as well as from deep conflicts. Secondly, he was adamant that cure could only be realized when there was a powerful emotional release at the same time as the patient remembered a traumatic event. However, Reich went further than Freud in his treatment. He clearly recognized that the painful emotions evoked in reliving traumas had to be replaced (in the course of treatment) with deeply pleasurable sensations in order for health to be restored and maintained. Reich also believed that repression, of both the negative emotions as well as the pleasurable ones, was a physical reality, manifest in chronically tight and spastic muscles. These bodily restrictions caused constrained breathing and awkward, uncoordinated or robotic movements. He named this muscular rigidity *character armor* and perceived it as a mechanism having two unitary functions. While enabling the emotional component of the memory to be repressed, it also stifled the capacity to feel pleasurable sensations.

Reich had a further conceptual breakthrough with the realization that one did not have to dig for traumatic memories as Freud believed. (This excavation was a central part of Freud's free association treatment.) Rather, Reich's therapy addressed the "body/character-armoring," which had the function of freezing the emotions while maintaining the neurotic symptoms in the present. His therapy worked aggressively on two fronts. First, he brought the patient's characterological defenses to their awareness by confronting their behaviors such as obsequious politeness or passive-aggressive hostility. In addition, he "attacked" the muscular armoring, directly, through vigorous manipulation and massage of the tight muscles. Reich also believed that the repression (the damming up) of adult sexuality was in itself one of the main causes of the neurosis. This is not dissimilar to Freud's very early belief that "aktuelle" neurosis was the result of certain sexual aberrations such as masturbation and "coitus interruptus."

The end of Reich's life was truly a national disgrace. In the sulfurous cloud of the McCarthy era, his books were burned by the FBI. Because of his radical ideas about sexuality, Reich was imprisoned for the trumped-up charge of violating interstate commerce laws. He died, in 1957, in the Pennsylvania federal penitentiary, an embittered visionary. With his death and Freud's abandonment of both "real" trauma and emotional catharsis, the therapeutic interest in emotionality waned. Meanwhile, the movement toward behaviorism and rationality came into its ascendance. By the 1950s, such therapies as Skinnerian conditioning and Albert Ellis's rational emotive therapy (RET) were dominating psychotherapy. (Incidentally, this therapy had very little to do with emotions.) The synergism of these approaches is now generally known as cognitive behavioral therapy (CBT). However, by the 1960s, the pendulum had begun to swing in the opposite direction. Emotions were finding their way back into the therapeutic community.

Two of Reich's patients (who later became his students) were Alexander Lowen and Fritz Perls. The first he referred to as the "uppity uptown tailor," while the other he contrasted as "the dirty old man from the Bowery."[141] Both developed parallel extensions of Reich's work, incorporating various aspects of his ideas and methods. While Lowen continued to emphasize emotional expression, and added the function of the legs in "grounding" emotions, Perls held to a more complex view of the organism. His therapeutic approach incorporated many ideas taken from the gestalt psychologies of the 1930s, 1940s and 1950s, including those of Wolfgang Kohler and Kurt Goldstein. However, in the anarchy of the 1960s, with its revolutionary disregard for rationality and the status quo, emotional catharsis was resurrected as a sure path to "liberation" and "freedom."

However, this process of emotional abreaction can become a self-perpetuating mechanism by which patients crave further "emotional release." Unfortunately, this process moves into an ever-tightening spiral that frequently culminates in a therapeutic dead end. Such was the case, for example, in the 1970s, when Arthur Janov promoted his primal therapy. (Reich had warned his contemporaries about mindlessly using emotional catharsis, pejoratively calling its promoters "freedom peddlers.") "Neo-Reichian release," "encounter groups," "primal therapy," "rebirthing" and other dramatic therapies co-opted the staid preeminence of the "talking cure" with an exuberant expressive zeal. Presently, at the beginning of the third millennium, we are seeing an emerging synthesis, a movement toward a more balanced emphasis on emotion and reason. In particular, experiential therapies are emerging, such as those described by Diana Fosha and others.[142] These include dialectical behavior therapy and acceptance and commitment therapy (ACT).

The ability to effectively contain and process extreme emotional states is one of the linchpins both of effective, truly dynamical trauma therapy and of living a vital, robust life. While love can sway us off our feet, powerful emotions like rage, fear and sorrow can pull our legs out from under us. We can be driven nearly insane by rage, paralyzed by fear and drowned by sorrow. Once triggered, such violent emotions can take over our existence. Rather than feeling our emotions, we become them; we are swallowed up by these emotions. This can be quite a dilemma because being *informed* by our emotions, not domineered by them, is crucial in directing our lives. We may have too much or too little; they may come upon us like a torrential flood or leave us dry like a parched desert. They may lead us in a positive direction or cause us untold suffering. They may prompt creative exultation or may provoke disastrous actions and poor decisions. They can lift us up or tear us down. No matter what the case, most of us realize that emotions (whatever they are) play a central role in the conduct of our lives.

The key to not being swept away by intense emotional states is to catch them before they ignite and inflame us. The Buddhists have an expression for this: to "cool and extinguish the glowing embers *before* they ignite into a consuming flame." Constraint allows us to tame and befriend emotions so that we may be guided by them. It is the way we can become aware of our emotional undercurrent before it becomes an out-of-control emotion. The tools that allow us to do this are the twin sisters of awareness and embodiment.

As people learn to master their emotions, they also begin to harness the underlying impulses to action. For example, underneath the emotions of rage and anger are the impulses of aggression. Healthy aggression is about protecting ourselves and those who are close to us. It is also about setting clear boundaries and getting the things we need, including food, shelter and mating partners. It is what empowers our lust for life. This passion for life must be supported by a capacity to embody a range of purposeful emotions. For now, let us back off and ask the following question: What is an emotion, anyway?

"Qu'est ce qu'une émotion?"

Binet posed this very provocative question at the dawn of the twentieth century.[143] He opened the debate with a salvo that eludes a solution even to this day, despite the most vigorous of arguments. Simple to ask, though difficult to answer, the question remains: What the heck is an emotion?

Theories of emotion, abundant and diverse, have had a long, twisted, confounding and often-contradictory history. They have been grappled with in turn by philosophy, psychology and evolutionary biology. Each of these disciplines has attempted to define, refine or, simply, understand emotion.

"Emotion as a scientific concept," wrote Elizabeth Duffy, the matriarch of modern psychophysiology, "is worse than useless." On the basis of extensive physiological recording, she felt that there was no way of differentiating one emotional state from another. In other words, distinguishing an emotion solely on the basis of physiological measurements (e.g., heart rate, blood pressure, respiration, temperature, skin conductance, etc.) seemed impossible. Thus, emotions, from her vantage point in 1936, were unworthy of scientific study. Yet recently there has been a rich vein of inquiry and grounding in the emerging field of the "affective neurosciences,"[144] demonstrating distinct brain *systems* involved in the *expression* of various emotions (e.g., fear, anger and sadness). However, the question of *felt (as opposed to expressed) emotional experience* has been all but neglected. Psychology, questing for objective respectability, has attempted to purge subjectivity from its midst. It has, in the process, unwittingly thrown out the proverbial baby (the subjective feeling experience) with the bathwater by studying primarily the *expression* of emotion.

Much of philosophy and early psychology were of the logical, "common-sense" conviction regarding the sequence by which an emotion was generated. Today, like the early philosophers, we resort to similar explanations. For example, when something provocative happened to René Descartes (perhaps someone raised his fist and called him a jerk or alternatively patted him and told him, "You're a great guy"), he might have believed that his brain recognized this provocation as being worthy of an emotional response—anger, fear, sadness or elation. Had the physiology of his times been more advanced, he would have interpreted the next step as his brain telling his body what to do: increase your heart rate, blood pressure and breathing; tense your muscles, secrete sweat and/or make goose bumps. These are responses controlled by the autonomic (involuntary) nervous system, preparing the organism for various actions related to fight or flight. For Descartes, and for most of us, this sequence makes perfectly logical sense and seems to describe how we experience emotion.

At the turn of the nineteenth century, however, William James, who had studied with the experimental psychologists of his time, took an experiential, rather than philosophical and speculative, approach to the study of emotions. James would set up imagined situations, such as being chased by a bear, and then through experiential introspection would attempt to infer the chain of events by which an emotion, such as fear, was generated. In these subjective experiments he would sense into the interior of his body, as well as noting his thoughts and internal images. Ultimately, he arrived at a rather unexpected conclusion. Common sense dictates that when we see a bear, we are frightened, and then motivated by fear, we flee. However, in his careful, reflective observations, *James concluded that rather than running because we are afraid, we are afraid because we are running (from the bear)*. In James's words,

> My theory ... is that the bodily changes follow *directly* the perception of the exciting fact, and that our feeling of the same changes as they occur *is* the emotion. "Common sense" says we lose our fortune, are sorry and weep; we meet a bear, are frightened and run; we are insulted by a rival, are angry and strike. The hypothesis here to be defended says that this *order of sequence* is incorrect, that the one mental state is not immediately induced by the other, that the bodily manifestations may first be interposed between, and the more rational (accurate) statement is that we feel sorry *because* we cry, angry because we strike, afraid because we tremble.[145]

This counterintuitive (bottom-up) view challenged the Cartesian/cognitive (top-down) paradigm where the conscious mind first recognizes the source of threat and then commands the body to respond: to flee, to fight or to fold. James's bottom-up perception—that we feel fear *because* we are running away from the threat—while only partially correct, does make a crucial point about the illusory nature of perception. We commonly believe, for example, that when we touch a hot object, we draw our hand away *because* of the pain. However, the reality is that if we were to wait until we experienced pain in order to withdraw our hand, we might damage it beyond repair. Every student of elementary physiology learns that there is *first* a reflex withdrawal of the hand, which is only then *followed* by the sensation of pain. The pain might well serve the function of reminding us not to pick up a potentially hot stone from the fire pit a second time, but it has little to do with our hand withdrawing when it is first burned. Similarly, every student of basic chemistry learns, hopefully after the first encounter, that hot test tubes look just like cold ones. However, what we *falsely perceive*, and believe as fact, is that the pain causes us to withdraw our hand. James was able to perceive that fear was not a primarily cognitive affair, that there was a muscular and visceral reaction in his body *first*, and that it was *the perception of this body reaction* that then generated the emotion of fear. What James observed was that, yes, when the brain calculates that there is danger, it makes this assessment so quickly that there isn't enough time for the person to become consciously aware of it. What happens instead, according to James, is that the brain canvases the body to see how it is reacting in the moment. In what was a revelatory revision, James relocated the consciousness of feeling from mind to body. In doing this he demonstrated a rare prescience about what neuroscience was only to begin to discover a hundred years later.

Ben Libet,[146] neurosurgeon and neurophysiologist at the University of California–San Francisco's Medical School, conducted a revealing, but little known, series of studies over thirty years ago. He essentially confirmed James's observational chain. Here's a little experiment that you can do right now. Hold one of your arms out in front of you with your hand facing upward. Then, whenever you feel like it (of your own "free will"), flex your wrist. Do this several times and watch what happens in your mind. You probably felt as though you first consciously decided to move and then, following your intention, you moved it. It feels to you as though the conscious decision *caused* the action.

Libet asked experimental subjects to do just this while he systematically measured the timing of three things: (1) The subjects "conscious" decision to move was marked on a special clock. (2) The beginning of (what is called) the readiness potential in the motor cortex was measured using EEG electrodes on the scalp. (3) The start of the actual action was measured using electrodes on the wrist. So which do you think (based on your experience in the preceding experiment) came first? Was it the decision to move, activity in the motor cortex, or the actual movement? The answer, defying credulity, dramatically contradicted common sense. The brain's activity began about 500 milliseconds (half a second!) *before* the person was aware of deciding to act. *The conscious decision came far too late to be the cause of the action.* It was as though consciousness was a mere afterthought—a way of "explaining to ourselves," an action not evoked by consciousness. As peculiar as this might seem, it fits in with previous experiments that Libet did on exposed brains as part of a neurosurgical procedure. Here, Libet had demonstrated that about half a second of continuous activity of stimulation in the sensory cortex is needed for a person to become aware of a sensory stimulus.[147] I had the opportunity to watch one of these procedures, and it was jaw-dropping to see it on the oscilloscope.

In summary, Libet found that the "conscious" decision to perform a simple action (such as pushing a button) preceded the action. This conscious decision, however, occurred only *after* the "premotor" area in the brain first fired with a burst of electrical activity. In other words, people decide to act only after their brain *unconsciously prepares* them to do so.

Daniel Wegner, at Harvard University, recently advanced and refined this proposition.[148] In one of his studies, an illusion was created by a series of mirrors. Subjects, thinking that they were looking at their own arms, were actually seeing (in the mirror) the movements of an experimenter's arm. When the experimenter's arms moved (according to the instructions of another researcher), the subjects reported that *they* had made and therefore willed the movements (when, in fact, they had not even moved their arms)!

Wilhelm Wundt (considered one of the founders of experimental psychology) expands on our attachment to the notion of free will: "Nothing seems to us to belong so closely to our personality, to be so completely our property as our will." Yet, the results of Libet and Wegner, taken together, seriously challenge (if not put to rest) our commonsense understanding of consciousness and our love affair with free will. The annihilation of free will, suggested in Wegner's book,[149] goes against what we believe is the very core of our existence as autonomous human beings. It challenges such cherished beliefs as the capacity for planning, foresight and responsible action. Who or what are we without the power of free will? This dispute of free will, which has been revered in Western thought for three thousand years, is not just another philosopher's opinion, but rather stems from a variety of dispassionate laboratory research. Einstein, in paraphrasing the philosopher Schopenhauer, restated the conundrum of free will with his characteristic understated wisdom: "A human can very well do what he wants but cannot will what he wants."

William James, a century ago, had argued that a person's passing states of consciousness create a false sense that an 'I' or ego runs the show. Neuroscientist Wegner took this further, adding that the average people's belief that they even have a self that consciously controls their actions is simply an *illusion*. Is this a farewell to Freud's ego and Descartes' *cogito ergo sum*? Although this new credo, "I think; therefore I am," was an important start in freeing people from the rigidity of church doctrine, it's in great need of revision.[150] Today's credo should be more like, "I prepare to move, I act, I sense, I feel, I perceive, I reflect, I think *and* therefore I am." So what might actually be going on in consciousness? And can the idea of free will be somehow reformulated?

Together, the studies of James, Libet and Wegner suggest that before a "voluntary" movement is made, there is an *unconscious premovement*. Because we are generally not conscious of this premovement impulse (analogous to our withdrawing of our hand from a hot object *before* we feel the pain), we falsely believe that we (our egos) are directly willing the movement. So where does movement originate from?

Let us consider the following experiment provided by a capricious Mother Nature that will allow us to explore the blurred border between conscious and unconscious stimulus and response. It is now known that there are multiple visual (and other sensory) systems that register nerve impulses in areas of the brain that are primarily nonconscious. These brain stem areas are in addition to the conscious one in the back (occipital region) of our cerebral cortex—known dispassionately as *area 17*. There is a revealing condition called *blindsight*.[151] This strange affliction is due to damage to a part of the visual cortex on one side of the brain. This causes a blind region on the opposite side of the visual field. If an object is presented in this part of the visual field, patients are unaware of seeing anything at all. Lights can be flashed, objects moved or even writing displayed, and these patients will insist, unequivocally, that they see absolutely nothing. Yet detailed experiments show that *while denying all visual experience*, they can nevertheless point to the location of a flashed light, or discriminate between upward and downward movement, between vertical or horizontal stripes and between various different objects. Oliver Sacks, from his many moving and wise vignettes about the tragic, yet compelling, consequences of neurological disorders, describes the case of Virgil.[152] Virgil's entire visual cortex was knocked out by oxygen deprivation, rendering him completely blind, yet Sacks describes Virgil's wife's inexplicable observations: "Virgil had told her that he was completely blind, yet she observed that he would reach for objects, avoid obstacles and *behave* as though he were seeing." Such is the enigma of this type of "implicit" information processing.

The explanation that is generally accepted for this phenomenon is that destruction of the visual cortex still leaves several other (primitive, subcortical) visual pathways intact. Sensory information to these somehow registers basic information that normally has the function of directing eye movements to garner more data. These data, however, also render a flimsy sketch of which we are largely unconscious. It is this unconscious information that evokes the readiness for movement (i.e., premovement). It is also this primitive circuitry that makes possible the reasonably accurate "guesses" that are observed in people with blindsight disorder. Hence, we are once again appreciative of the prompting to respond to events before we become overtly aware of them. Consider your response to the fleeting shadow, the subtle gesture of another person or a distant sound. Each of these events can evoke in us survival-bound responses without our ever being aware that something in our environment has triggered them. Notably, when we have been traumatized, we are particularly sensitized to (and hyperaroused by) these fleeting stimuli. Our senses of seeing, hearing and smell provide countless stimuli that cause us to overreact, even though we may be unaware of the presence of those subliminal stimuli and our premotor responses to them. As a result we may, and often do, *attribute* our actions to irrelevant or manufactured causes. This attribution of causation is like the subjects in Wegner's experiments who falsely believed that they had willed the movement of the experimenter's arms.

It is specifically because we are unaware of our environmentally triggered premovement that we falsely believe we are consciously initiating and constructing the movement. Furthermore, when the (unacknowledged) premovement drive is strong, we may feel compelled to fully enact the entire movement sequence. Two confusions of causality occur for traumatized individuals. The first one is the unawareness of the premovement trigger. The second is the extent of the response. Imagine the consternation of an individual trapped in the full-blown, ferocious reenactment of a survival-bound response. Take for instance the Vietnam vet who wakes up to find himself strangling his terrified wife, unaware that it was the backfiring of a distant car, or even the light footsteps of their young child in the hallway, that provoked his freakish behavior and grossly exaggerated reaction. However, years earlier, when sleeping in a bamboo thicket, under fire from the Vietcong, his immediate kill-response was an essential, life-preserving action. It may only take a very mild stimulus to abruptly trigger the tightly coiled spring (the kill-or-be-killed survival reaction) into an intense, out-of-control, emotional eruption.

I know of *only one* way to break compulsive cycles like this, and in the process expand consciousness toward greater freedom. It is to become aware of the *premovement before it graduates into a full-blown movement sequence*. It is to extinguish the spark before it ignites the tinder, as emphasized by Buddhist teachings.

Many times in the past, I walked with my dog in the Colorado Mountains.

Pouncer, a dingo mix, was imbued with a strong instinctual urge to chase deer and other swift creatures of the upland forests. Try as I might, it was not possible to neutralize this "habit" by reprimanding him. If I tried to call him back or foolishly admonished his behavior when he returned, breathless and panting from the chase, it was of no avail. However, if when we encountered deer up ahead, at the *very moment* his posture changed (just hinting at his readiness to leap forward), I would firmly but gently say, "No, Pouncer. Heel." He would then calmly continue on our walk, striding enthusiastically by my side. Then there is the following story of a brash young samurai sword fighter and a venerated Zen master.

Two Horns of the Dilemma

The vital balancing act between expression and restraint requires that when we experience a strong emotional feeling, we need *not* necessarily act upon it, as this teaching story demonstrates.

A young, brash samurai swordsman confronted a venerated Zen master with the following demand: "I want you to tell me the truth about the existence of heaven and hell."

The master replied gently and with delicate curiosity, "How is it that such an ugly and untalented man as you can become a samurai?"

Immediately, the wrathful young samurai pulled out his sword and raised it above his head, ready to strike the old man and cut him in half. Without fear, and in complete calm, the Zen master gazed upward and spoke softly: "This is hell." The samurai paused, sword held above his head. His arms fell like leaves to his side, while his face softened from its angry glare. He quietly reflected. Placing his sword back into its sheath, he bowed to the teacher in reverence. "And this," the master replied again with equal calm, "is heaven."

Here the samurai, his sword held high at the peak of feeling full of rage (and at the moment *before* executing the prepared-for action), learned to hold back and *restrain* his rage instead of mindlessly expressing it. In refraining (with the master's quick guidance) from making his habitual emotional expression of attack, he transformed his "hell" of rage to a "heaven" of peace.

One could also speculate on what unconscious thoughts (and images) were stirred when the master provoked the swordsman's ire. Perhaps the samurai was startled and at first even agreed with the characterization that he was ugly and untalented. This strong reaction to this insult (we might hypothesize) derived from his parents, teachers and others who humiliated him as a child. Perhaps he had a mental picture of being shamed in front of his school classmates. And then the other micro-fleeting "counter thought"—that no one would dare to call him that again and make him feel small and worthless. This thought and associated (internal) picture, coupled with a momentary *physical sensation of startle*, triggered the rage that led him down the compulsive, driven road to perdition. That was, at least, until his "Zen therapist," precisely at the peak of rage, kept him from habitually expressing this "protective" emotion (really a defense against his feelings of smallness and helplessness) and forced him to the ownership of his *real* power and peaceful surrender.

In the examples of Pouncer and the Zen master, choice occurred at the critical moment *before* executing attack. With the Zen master's critical intervention, the samurai held back and *felt* the *preparation* to strike with his sword. In this highly charged state he paused and was able to restrain and transmute his violent rage into intense energy and a state of clarity, gratefulness, presence and grace. It is the ability to hold back, restrain and *contain* a powerful emotion that allows a person to creatively channel that energy. Containment (a somatic rooting of Freud's "sublimation") buys us time and, with self-awareness, enables us to separate out what we are imagining and thinking from our physical sensations. And this fraction of a second of restraint, as we just saw, is the difference between heaven and hell. When we can maintain this "creative neutrality," we begin to dissolve the emotional compulsion to react as though our life depends on responses that are largely inappropriate. *The uncoupling of sensation from image and thought is what diffuses the highly charged emotions and allows them to transform fluidly into sensation-based gradations of feelings.* This is not at all the same as suppressing or repressing them. For all of us, and particularly for the traumatized individual, the capacity to transform the "negative" emotions of fear and rage *is* the difference between heaven and hell.

The power and tenacity of emotional compulsions (the *acting out* of rage, fear, shame and sorrow) are not to be underestimated. Fortunately, there are practical antidotes to this cascade of misery. With body awareness, it is possible to "deconstruct" these emotional fixations. As an aside, let's take a peak at the inner working of our brains and minds as we free ourselves from the tyranny of driven emotions such as fear and rage. The thin sliver of brain tissue that makes us conscious is found in the prefrontal cortex, the forward part of our frontal lobes. In particular there are two loci. The one toward the side is called the dorsolateral prefrontal cortex. This part makes conscious our relationship to the outside world. The second part, located toward the middle, is called the medial prefrontal cortex. This is the only part of the cerebral cortex that apparently can modify the response of the limbic or emotional brain—particularly the amygdala, which is responsible for intense survival emotions. The medial prefrontal cortex (particularly the insular cingulate cortex) *receives direct input from muscles, joints and visceral organs and registers them into consciousness.*[153] Through awareness of these interoceptive sensations (i.e., through the process of tracking bodily sensations), we are able to access and modify our emotional responses and attain our core sense of self.

A first step in this ongoing process is refusing to be seduced into (the content of) our negative thoughts or swept away by the potent or galvanized drive of an emotion, and instead *returning to the underlying physical sensations.* At first this can seem unsettling, even frightening. This is mostly because it is unfamiliar—we have become accustomed to the (secondary) habitual emotions of distress and to our (negative) repetitive thoughts. We have also become used to searching for the source of our discomfort outside of ourselves. We simply are unfamiliar with experiencing something *as it is*, without the encumbrance of analysis and judgment. As the sensation-thought-emotion complex is uncoupled, experiencing moves forward toward subtler, freer contours of feeling. Eugene Gendlin, the originator of the term *felt sense*,[154] conveys this with simplicity when he says, "Nothing that feels bad is ever the last step." This experiential process involves the capacity to hold the emotion in abeyance, without allowing it to execute in its habitual way. This holding back is not an act of suppression but is rather one of forming a bigger container, a larger experiential vessel, to hold and differentiate the sensations and feelings. "Going into" the emotional expression is frequently a way of trying to "release" the tension we are feeling, while avoiding deeper feelings. It is akin to a whistling teakettle letting off steam but really making no lasting change in its capacity to hold charge (as steam). If, on the other hand, one imagines a strong rubber balloon or bladder being filled with steam, you would see the size of the bladder expanding to contain this increasing "charge." With containment, emotion shifts into a different sensation-based "contour" with softer feelings that morph into deepening, sensate awareness of "OK-ness." This is the essence of emotional self-regulation, self-acceptance, goodness and change.

Let's take the example of anger. *The feeling of anger is derived from the (postural) attitude of wanting to strike out and hit.* However, if one begins to attack—hitting, kicking, tearing, biting—the feeling of anger then shifts rapidly to that of hitting, kicking, and so on. In other words, and contrary to common belief, as you *execute* the preparation for action, the underlying feelings are diminished if not lost.[155] When we cry, for example, our sadness often "magically disappears." However, this may be more like the teakettle just letting off steam, without changing the underlying sadness. Some of the fundamental "expressive" therapies may fall into the trap of trying to drain the emotional swamp through undue emphasis on habitual venting. Yet, what may be visible when the very deepest wells of sadness are touched is a single, trickling tear. As for anger, recall a time when you shook your fist in anger at another person or were the recipient of such behavior. Was this a time when you *really* needed to defend yourself, or was it rather a way to let off steam and to bully the other person? This kind of intimidation is commonly seen in domestic violence. What was the effect of your action on their behaviors and theirs on yours? In any case, when we allow ourselves to be swept away into uncontained emotional expression, we may actually *split off* from what we are feeling. We are held hostage by these habitual emotions, unaware that they can only be transformed if we consciously restrain and resist being triggered into the expressive phase. The samurai lost his false self and found salvation by such a momentary interruption.

Containment promotes choice between a number of possible responses where previously there were only those of fear, rage, defensiveness and helplessness. In primitive life we needed to rapidly assess whether an individual we met in the forest was friend or foe, safe or dangerous. Would he attack? Should we attack first to protect ourselves, or would it be better to move quietly away? However, in modern times we are more apt to need our social skills to differentiate: do we like this person or dislike them, and what do they mean to us? Rather than coming to fisticuffs, we might first try to socially engage by conversing with the person; we might try to "disarm" him with an authentic smile. We are not acting out of emotion but rather are guided by sensate feelings—like or dislike? And most importantly we need to do this *before* we actually act—before we strike out with angry words. This way we enhance the capacity to prioritize possible motoric (and moment-to-moment) actions; we are able to choose which would be the most appropriate action.[156]

What Feelings Do for Us

Biologically, the expression of emotion serves primarily as a vital *signaling* function. For example, when we are frightened, both our face and our entire posture let everyone around us know directly that we sense danger lurking out there in the forest or bushes. When the bomb went off at the 1996 Atlanta Olympics, the "deer in the headlights," "get me out of here" look on swimmer Janet Evans's face signaled to everyone (there and on TV) that we're all in danger. Had she run from the scene, it is likely that many would have followed her nonverbal command. The look of fear is unmistakable. The eyes are wide open with raised eyebrows. The mouth is partially opened with the corners strongly retracted, and the ears drawn back.[157]

A herd of grazing elk being surveyed by an encroaching wolf pack employs their own method. Even knowing of their presence, the elk continue grazing—that is until one of its members first senses that the wolf has penetrated the "strike-ready" perimeter. Then in grunting and stiffening, all the others are signaled to follow its lead, dashing together toward safety.

However, fear can also stimulate panic. People are frequently hurt or die because of "deer in the headlights" freezing. Emotion here could certainly not be said to be adaptive. If we freeze walking across the street or while driving our car, catastrophe is surely at hand. Similarly, nausea and the accompanying disgust appropriately signal, both to oneself and to others, that an ingested substance should not be eaten. However, this response is counterproductive (even detrimental) when it is someone's persistent pattern of engaging with food that is *not* tainted. This maladaptive response can be triggered by people also. Disgust, as a habitual reaction to an appropriate sexual touch or warm embrace, can destroy a relationship and ruin a person's life.

A further example of emotional signaling is that of a baby crying in distress. This call for a mother's attention is a life-or-death wail because if the baby cannot compel her ministrations, he will surely die. The baby is clearly signaling a life-preserving need, and the sound is such that the mother cannot readily ignore it. Yet, when as adults, we cry at our abandonment, this plaintive wail does little to bring back the lover who has fallen in love with someone else. In fact, habitual grief can rob us of our energy and prevent us from moving on with our lives and creating connections with someone new. In all three of these cases, life is supported by the signal function of emotion but is negated by its unabated, malapropos continuance.

We seem to be caught in an intractable contradiction here. In the case of loss, it may be that only by moving through (by feeling) grief can we transition toward a tolerance and courage that allow us to love again, while holding the haunting awareness that, inevitably, time may yet again claim our newly beloved for its own. Similarly, a certain amount of anger can help us remove obstacles in our lives, while *habitual and explosive* anger is almost always corrosive to relationships and the pursuit of what we truly want and need in life. It even frequently puts the pugilist or soldier in a compromised position. To help resolve this apparent paradox, we must first of all understand that emotions (which are reactive) and feelings (which are rooted in fluid internal sensations) are quite different. They are different in their respective functions and in the way they color our lives.

From a functional point of view, bodily/sensate feelings are the compass that we use to navigate through life. They permit us to estimate the *value* of the things to which we must incorporate or adapt. Our attraction to that which sustains us and our avoidance of that which is harmful are the essence of the feeling function. All feelings derive from the ancient precursors of approach and avoidance; they are in differing degrees positive or negative.

Sensation-based feelings guide the adaptive response to (e)*valuations*. Emotions, on the other hand, occur precisely when behavioral adaptations (based on these valuations) have failed! Contrary to what both Darwin and James thought, fear is not what directs escape; nor do we feel fear because we are running from a source of threat. The person who can freely run away from threat does not feel fear. He only feels danger (avoidance) and then experiences the action of running. It is solely when escape is prevented that we experience fear. Likewise, we experience anger when we are unable to strike our enemy or otherwise successfully resolve a conflict. I don't expect you to accept this proposition as true but only ask you to keep an open inquiring mind. What has happened, you might ask, to our instinctual emotions, as described by Darwin? The answer is simply that they are still there. However, the critical intermediary steps that Darwin failed to recognize were later discovered by the carriers of his legacy, the ethologists.

A scene from an upland meadow helps to illustrate the differentiation of feelings and emotions. While you are strolling leisurely in an open meadow, a shadow suddenly moves in the periphery of your vision. Instinctively, all of your movement is arrested (with the feeling of a startle); reflexively you crouch in a somewhat flexed posture. After this momentary "arrest response," your head automatically turns in the direction of the shadow or sound. You attempt to localize and identify the source. Your neck, back, legs and feet muscles all coordinate so that your whole body turns and then extends. Your eyes narrow, while your pelvis and head shift horizontally, giving you an optimal view of the surroundings and an ability to focus panoramically. This initial two-phase action pattern is an instinctive orientation preparing you to respond flexibly to many possible contingencies; it generates the feeling tone of "expectant curiosity." The initial arrest-crouch flexion response minimizes detection by possible predators and possibly offers some protection from falling objects. Primarily, though, it provides a convulsive jerk that interrupts any motor patterns already in motion. Then, through scanning, it flexibly prepares you for the fine-tuned behaviors of exploration (for sources of food, shelter and mating) or for defense against predation (experienced as danger and not fear).

If it had been an eagle taking flight that cast the shadow, a further orientation of tracking-pursuit would likely occur. Adjustments of postural and facial muscles coordinate unconsciously. The new "attitude of interest," when integrated with the contour of the rising eagle image, is perceived as the *feeling of excitement*. This aesthetically pleasing sense, recognized as the feeling of enjoyment, is affected by past experience. It may also, however, be one of the many powerful archetypal predispositions or undercurrents that each species has developed over millennia of evolutionary time. Most Native Americans, for example, have a very special, spiritual, mythic relationship with the eagle. Is this a coincidence, or is there something imprinted deeply within the structures of the brain, body and soul of the human species that responds intrinsically to the image of eagle with a correlative excitement and awe? Most organisms possess dispositions, if not specific approach/avoidance responses, to large moving contours.*

If the initial shadow had been from a raging grizzly bear (rather than from a rising eagle), a very different reaction would have been evoked: *the preparation to flee*. This is not, as James discovered, because we think "bear," evaluate it as dangerous and *then* run. It is because the contours and features of the large, looming, approaching animal cast a particular light pattern upon the retina of the eye. This stimulates a configuration of neural firing that is registered in the phylogenetically primitive brain regions. This "pattern recognition" triggers, in turn, the *preparation for defensive responding before* it is registered in consciousness.[†] These unconscious responses derive from genetic predispositions (as well as from the outcomes of previous personal experiences with similar

---

* A chick or small mammal would respond by scurrying to hide or escape.
† This is analogous to the blind sight phenomenon.

large animals). Primitive, nonconscious circuits are activated, triggering preset constellations or tendencies of defensive posturing. Muscles, viscera and autonomic nervous system activity cooperate in preparing for escape. This preparation is sensed kinesthetically and is internally joined, as a gestalt, to the image of the bear. *Preparation for defensive movement and image are fused* and registered together as the *feeling of danger.* Motivated by this feeling and *not* by fear, we continue to scan for more information (a grove of trees, some rocks) while at the same time drawing on our ancestral and personal memory banks. Probabilities are nonconsciously computed, based on such encounters over millions of years of species evolution, as well as on what we have learned individually does or does not work. We prepare for the next phase in this unfolding drama. Without thinking, we orient toward a large tree with low branches. An *urge* is experienced to flee and climb. If we run, freely oriented toward the tree, we have the *feeling of directed running.* The urge to run (experienced as the feeling of danger) is followed by successful running (experienced as escape rather than fear or anxiety).

On the other hand, let us consider a situation where escape is impossible—where you are trapped. This time you chance upon a starved or wounded bear standing in the path and blocking your escape (as in walking out of a steep box canyon). In this case, the defensive preparedness for flight, concomitant with the *feeling of danger,* is *thwarted.* The feeling of danger will then abruptly change into the *emotional state of fear.* Response is now restricted to non-directed, desperate flight, to rage-counterattack or to freeze-collapse. The latter affords the possibility of diminishing the bear's urge to attack. If it is not cornered or hurt, and is able to clearly identify the human being as helpless and of no threat, the bear usually will not attack the intruder, going on its own way.

The Greek root for *angst* is descriptive, meaning to "press tight" or to strangle. As conveyed in Edward Munch's iconic painting, *The Scream,* our entire physiology and psyche become precipitously constricted in anxious terror. While it may afford a last-ditch survival function, fear is the killer of life. Pi (in the book *The Life of Pi*) tells us about this Achilles heal:

It is life's only true opponent. Only fear can defeat life. It
is a clever, treacherous adversary, how well I know. It has
no decency, respects no law or convention, shows no
mercy. It goes for your weakest spot, which it finds with
unerring ease ... Reason comes to do battle for you. You
are reassured. Reason is fully equipped with the latest
weapons of technology. But, to your amazement, despite
superior tactics and a number of undeniable victories, reason is laid low. You feel yourself weakening, wavering.
Your anxiety becomes dread. Fear turns fully to your body,
which is already aware that something terribly wrong is
going on. Already your lungs have flown away like a bird
and your guts have slithered away like a snake. Now your
tongue drops dead like an opossum, while your jaw begins
to gallop on the spot. Your ears go deaf. Your muscles
begin to shiver as if they had malaria and your knees to
shake as though they were dancing. Your heart strains too
hard, while your sphincter relaxes too much. And so with
the rest of your body. Every part of you, in the manner
most suited to it, falls apart. Only your eyes work well.
They always pay proper attention to fear. [They are constantly on the prowl for more objects of fear.]

Recall the case story of Sharon (in Chapter 8). She was the woman
who had the horrific experience of working on the eightieth floor of
the World Trade Center on September 11, 2001. During her session I
guided her to the experience of being led down the staircase by a Port
Authority employee and encountering a locked door on the seventieth
floor. Suddenly trapped and unable to complete the escape, her body
became paralyzed with fear. In working through this experience, which
reestablished her running reflexes, she opened her eyes (toward the end
of our session), looked at me and said, "I thought it was fear that gets
you through ... but it's not ... It's something more powerful, something much bigger than fear ... It's something that transcends fear."
And what a deep biological truth she reveals here.

Finally, the feeling of danger is the awareness of a *defensive attitude*. It prepares us to defend ourselves through escape or camouflage. Similarly, when our aggression is not thwarted, but is clearly directed, we don't feel anger but instead experience the *offensive attitude of* protection, combativeness and assertiveness. Anger is thwarted aggression, while (uninhibited) aggression embodies self-protection. *Healthy aggression is about getting what you need and protecting what you have.* One sees this in the behaviors of neighborhood dogs. Dog 1 is at home in his yard, and then dog 2 comes along. Both dogs lift their legs and inscribe with their pee a territorial border. If they each stay on their own side, there will be no further problems. However, if the interloper (dog 2) breaches this boundary, the dog 1 will probably kick up dirt with its hind legs as a warning salvo. If dog 2 heeds this display, then again the situation calms. However, if dog 2 does not comply, then dog 1 will likely begin to growl and snarl. Finally, if dog 2 does not move on, there will be a vicious biting attack.

To summarize: it is only when the normal orientation and defensive resources have failed to resolve a situation that non-directed flight, paralysis or collapse come into play. Rage and terror-panic are the *secondary* emotional anxiety states that are evoked when the orientation processes, and the preparedness to flee or attack (felt originally as danger), are not successful. This only occurs when primary aggression does not resolve the situation, is blocked or is inhibited.

Changing How We Feel

One dreary rainy January afternoon, in the warm, musty stacks of the Berkeley graduate library, I was sorting through the innumerable books on theories of emotion. This was well before the advent of computers and Google, and my search strategy was to find a relevant area in stacks, the literary catacombs, and spend the day browsing for related material. It seemed to me that there were nearly as many theories of emotion as there were authors. With my heuristic "search engine," I came across a treasure trove—the visionary work of a woman named Nina Bull. This book, called *The Attitude Theory of Emotion*,[158] clarified what

I was observing with my early clients. It gave me a clear conceptual understanding for the process of emotional change.

Working at Columbia University in the 1940s and 1950s, Bull conducted remarkable research in the experiential tradition of William James. In her studies subjects were induced into a light hypnotic trance, and various emotions were suggested in this state. These included disgust, fear, anger, depression, joy and triumph. Self-reports from the subjects were noted. In addition, a standardized procedure was devised whereby the subjects were observed by other experimenters. These observers were trained to accurately view and record changes in the subject's postures. The postural patterns, both self-reported and observed by experimenters, were remarkably consistent across multiple subjects. The pattern of disgust, for example, involved the internal sensations of nausea—as if in preparation to vomit along with the observed behavior of turning away. The pattern as a whole was labeled "revulsion" and could vary in intensity from the milder form of dislike to an almost violent urge to turn away and vomit. This latter response could be recognized as an effort to eject something toxic, or as a means of preventing being fed something that one doesn't like. This type of reaction is seen when children are abused or forced to do something against their will—something that they cannot "stomach." This could be anything from forced bottle feeding to forced fellatio or, often, something they cannot stomach metaphorically.*

Bull analyzed the *fear* response and found it consisted of a similar compulsion to avoid or escape and was associated with a generalized *tensing up or freezing of the whole body*. It was also noted that subjects frequently reported the desire to get away, which was opposed by an inability to move. This opposition led to paralysis of the entire body (though somewhat less in the head and neck). However, the turning

---

* See episode 74 of A&E's *Intervention* (season 6, episode 2), in which a girl named Nicole had been forced to perform fellatio by her next-door neighbor (and father's best friend) for several years. Once her family found out, they tried to cover it up, and Nicole was forced to live next door to the man for years after. Later, Nicole developed an overactive gag reflex, leaving her unable to swallow anything, including her own saliva. She was placed on a feeding tube.

away in fear was different from that of disgust. Associated with fear was the additional component of turning toward potential resources of security and safety.

Bull discovered that the emotion of *anger* involves a fundamental split. There was, on the one hand, a primary compulsion to attack, as observed in a tensing of the back, arms and fists (as if preparing to hit). However, there was also a strong secondary component of tensing the jaw, forearm and hand. This was self-reported by the subjects, and observed by the experimenters, as a way of controlling and inhibiting the primary impulse to strike.

In addition, these experiments explored the bodily aspects of sadness and depression. Depression was characterized, in the subject's consciousness, as a chronically *interrupted* drive. It was as though there was something they wanted but were unable to attain. These states of depression were frequently associated with a sense of "tired heaviness," dizziness, headache and an inability to think clearly. The researchers observed a weakened impulse to cry (as though it were stifled), along with a collapsed posture, conveying defeat and apparent lethargy.

We all recognize that there is a fundamental difference between negative and positive emotions. When Bull studied the patterns of elation, triumph and joy, she observed that these positive affects (in contrast to the negative ones of depression, anger and disgust) did *not* have an inhibitory component; they were experienced as *pure action*. Subjects feeling joy reported an expanded sensation in their chests, which they experienced as buoyant, and which was associated with free deep breathing. The observation of postural changes included a lifting of the head and an extension of the spine. These closely meshed behaviors and sensations facilitated the freer breathing. Most subjects feeling joy reported feeling "ready for action." This readiness was accompanied with energy and the abundant sense of purpose and optimism that they would be able to achieve their goals.

Understanding the contradictory basis of the negative emotions, and their structural contrast to the positive ones, is revealing in the quest for wholeness. All of the negative emotions studied were comprised of two *conflicting impulses*, one propelling action and the other inhibiting (i.e., thwarting) that action. In addition, when a subject was "locked" into joy by hypnotic suggestion, a contrasting mood (e.g., depression, anger or sadness) *could not be produced unless the (joy) posture was first released.* The opposite was also true; when sadness or depression was suggested, it was not possible to feel joy unless that postural set was first changed.

The facial, respiratory and postural responses that supported positive affects are opposite to those seen in depression. There is a poignancy to this truth that was revealed years ago in a simple exchange between Charlie Brown and Lucy (from Charles M. Schulz's comic strip *Peanuts*). While walking together, Charlie, slumped and shuffling, is bemoaning his depression. Lucy suggests that he might try standing up straight, to which Charlie replies, "But then I wouldn't have a depression to complain about" as he continues on his way resigned, slouched and downtrodden. And what are we to do if we don't have an ever-vigilant Lucy to elucidate the ever-perplexing obvious? However, as correct as Lucy was in a metaphoric sense, mood changing is not a matter of simply willing postural change (like a proud military stance). Indeed, altering one's psychological disposition is a much more complex and subtle process that fundamentally involves, instead, the spontaneous and subconscious changing of postural states through body awareness.

The extensive work of psychologist Paul Ekman[159] supports the role of facial posture in the generation of emotional states. Ekman trained numbers of subjects to contract only the specific muscles that were observed during the expression of a particular emotion. Remarkably, when subjects were able to accomplish this task (without being told what emotion they were simulating), they often experienced those feelings, including appropriate autonomic arousal states.

In a quirky experiment, Fritz Strack of the University of Würzburg, Germany, had two groups of people judge how funny they found some cartoons. In the first group, the subjects were instructed to hold a pencil between their teeth *without it touching their lips.* This procedure forced them to smile (try it yourself). The second group was asked to hold the pencil with their lips, but this time not using their teeth. This forced a frown.

The results reinforced Ekman's work, revealing that people experience the emotion associated with their expressions. In Strack's work those with even a forced smile felt happier and found the cartoons funnier than did those who were forced to frown.

To get even weirder, Richard Wiseman[160] posted a series of jokes on a humor website. The basic template of the joke was that there are two cows in a field. One cow says, "Moo," and the other cow responds, "I was going to say that." When this joke was modified with different animals, by far the funniest was two ducks sitting in a pond. One of the ducks says, "Quack," and the other duck responds, "I was going to say that." It was indeed the "k" sound heard in "quack" and "duck" that was experienced as especially funny. Once again it may have been the facial feedback (as the pencil experiment) that made the people feel particular mirth.

Nikolaas Tinbergen, in his Nobel acceptance speech titled "Ethology and Stress Disease,"[161] described and extolled the beneficial effects of a method of postural reeducation called the *Alexander method*. Both he and his family, in undergoing Alexander's treatment process, had experienced dramatic improvement in sleep, blood pressure, cheerfulness, alertness and resilience to general stress. Other prominent scientists and educators had also written of the benefit of this treatment. These included John Dewey, Aldous Huxley and scientists like G. E. Coghill, Raymond Dart, and even the great doyen of physiology and earlier Nobel Prize recipient, Sir Charles Sherrington. While admiration from such prominent individuals is provocative, it hardly constitutes rigorous scientific proof. On the other hand, it is unlikely that men of such intellectual rigor had all been duped.

F. M. Alexander and Nina Bull had each recognized the intimate role of bodily tension patterns in behavior. Alexander, an Australian-born Shakespearean actor, had made his discovery quite accidentally. One day, while performing Hamlet, he lost his voice. He sought help from the finest doctors in Australia. Getting no relief, and desperate, he pursued assistance from the most influential physicians in England. Without a cure, and given that acting was his only profession, Alexander returned home in great despair.

As the story goes, his voice returned spontaneously, only to elusively vanish again. Alexander took to observing himself in the mirror, hoping that he might notice something that correlated with his erratic vocal capacity. He did. He observed that the return of his voice was related to his posture. After numerous observations, he made the startling discovery that there were distinctly different postures—one associated with voice and another with no voice. To his surprise, he discovered that the posture associated with the strong and audible voice felt wrong, while the posture of the weak or absent voice felt right. Alexander pursued this observational approach for the good part of nine years. He came to the realization that the mute posture felt good merely because it was familiar, while the postural stance supporting voice felt bad only because it was unfamiliar. Alexander discovered that certain muscular tensions could cause a compression of the head-neck-spine axis, resulting in respiratory problems and consequently the loss of voice. Decreasing these tensions would relieve the pressure and allow the spine to return to its full, natural extension. Attending to this disparity allowed Alexander to cure himself of his affliction. Thus, through better mind-body communication, he was able to recover much of his natural ease of movement, leading to an economy of effort as well as improved performance. Realizing that he had the makings of a new career, Alexander gave up acting and began working with fellow actors and vocalists with similar performance problems. He also began working with musicians whose bodies were twisted and in pain from the strained postures they believed were required for playing their instruments. The great violinist Yehudi Menuhin was one of his students. A number of famous pop stars and actors, including Paul McCartney, Sting and Paul Newman, had received treatments from Alexander method teachers and loudly sung their praises. However, even today, this method remains rather obscure, in part because it requires a demanding and refined focus.*

---

* Many of Alexander's principles inspired the work of Moshe Feldenkrais and Ida Rolf.

Alexander's therapeutic work (described in his book *The Use of the Self* [162]) consists of very gentle manipulations, first exploratory and then corrective. It is essentially a reeducation of one's entire muscular system. Treatment begins with the head and neck and subsequently includes other body areas. *There is no such thing as a right position*, he discovered, *but there is such a thing as a right direction.*

Let us now combine Alexander's observations (of posture's effect on function) with Lucy's wise insight into the cause of Charlie Brown's unnecessary, but self-perpetuating, suffering. What we come to is the profound implication of body-self-awareness in the change process. A direct and effective way of changing one's functional competency and mood is through altering one's postural set and thence changing proprioceptive and kinesthetic feedback to the brain. [163] Recall that the medial prefrontal cortex (which receives much of its input from the body) is the only area of the neocortex that can alter the limbic system and, in turn, emotionality. Hence, *the awareness of bodily sensations is critical in changing functional and emotional states.* We are once again reminded that it is primarily through the motivated awareness of internal sensations that the corrosive dragons of negative emotional states can be tamed. Remember how, instead of expressing his habitual rage, the samurai's personal hell was arrested, exposed and brought into awareness by the impeccable timing of the Zen master. It was only when the brash samurai learned to momentarily hold back, contain and "feel into" himself that he was able to transform his rage into bliss. Such is the alchemy of emotional transformation.

Attitude: Reconciling Emotions and Feelings

Just how does posture alter one's mood and effect a lasting change? Recall how Nina Bull demonstrated that intense emotions occur only when emotional action is restrained. Or said in another way, it is the restraint that allows *the postural attitude to become conscious for the attitude to become a feeling-awareness.* This is in partial agreement with the well-known neurologist Antonio Damasio's argument that emotion "is the consciousness of the body." This perspective is also in alignment with William James's peripheral theory of emotion, in which "we are afraid because we are running away from the bear." However, what I believe they both have missed, and what Nina Bull has deeply grasped, is the *reciprocal relationship between the expression of emotion and the sensate feeling of emotion.* When we are "mindlessly" expressing emotion, that is precisely what we are, in fact, doing. Emotional reactivity almost always precludes conscious awareness. On the other hand, restraint and containment of the expressive *impulse* allows us to become aware of our underlying postural attitude. Therefore, it is the restraint that brings a feeling into conscious awareness. Change only occurs where there is mindfulness, and mindfulness only occurs where there is bodily feeling (i.e., the awareness of the postural attitude).

A person who is deeply feeling is not a person who is habitually venting anger, fear or sorrow. Wise and fortunate individuals feel their emotions in the quiet of their interiors, learn from their feelings and are guided by them. They act intuitively and intelligently on those feelings. In addition, they share their feelings when appropriate and are responsive to the feelings and needs of others. And, of course, because they are human, they blow up from time to time; but also they look for the root of these eruptions, not primarily as being caused by another, but as an imbalance or disquiet within themselves.

While physical feelings are both quantitatively and qualitatively distinguishable from emotions, both derive ultimately from the instincts. The five categorical emotional instincts described by Darwin are fear, anger, sorrow, disgust and joy. However, feelings, as the consciousness of a bodily attitude, come in a virtually infinite range and blend. These include the bittersweet longing for an absent friend or tender mirth at a child's spontaneity. The Darwinian emotions correspond to distinct instincts, while feelings express a blending of (sensate-based) nuances and permutations. In addition, bodily feelings embody a relationship between an object or situation and our welfare. They are, in that sense, an elaboration of the basic affective valances of approach and avoidance. Feelings are the basic path by which we make our way in the world. In contrast, (fixated) emotional states derive from frustrated drives or engagement of the last-ditch mobilization of emergency (fight/flight/freeze). With the paucity of saber-toothed tigers, this critical reaction of last resort rarely makes sense in modern life. However, we are compelled to deal with a myriad of very different threats, such as speeding cars and overly eager surgeons, for which we lack much in the way of evolutionarily prepared protocols.

Emotions are our constant companions, enhancing our lives and detracting from them. How we navigate the maze of emotions is a central factor in the conduct of our lives, for better or for worse. The question is: under what conditions are emotions adaptive—and conversely, when are they maladaptive? In general, the more that an emotion takes on the quality of shock or eruption, or the more that it is suppressed or repressed, the more prominent is the maladaptation. Indeed, often an emotion begins in a useful form and then, because we suppress it, turns against us in the form of physical symptoms or in a delayed and exaggerated explosion. Anger and resentment, when denied, can build to an explosive level. There is a popular expression that is apt here: "That which we resist, persists." As damaging as emotions can be, repressing them only compounds the problem. However, let it be duly noted that the difference between repression/suppression and restraint/containment is significant though elusive. Remember once more how the samurai warrior delicately, but definitively, arrested his compulsion to strike, allowing him to feel his (former) murderous rage simply as pure energy—and ultimately as the bliss of feeling alive.

As the successful parent knows, this strategy works well with children. Rather than suppress the child, encouraging a habit of repression, these parents help the child by providing a timely interruption, while guiding the child to feel his anger and source his needs and desires. This is what healthy aggression is about. On the other hand, we have the permissive parent who lets the child go out-of-control with temper tantrums, as the samurai was about to do but with lethal consequences. The effective parent, however, provides and channels the child's aggression in a useful way. They do this by both allowing the child to feel her anger and then helping the child to understand what she is mad about.

If emotions are not too extreme and are approached with a certain stance, they can serve the function of guiding our behaviors—even moving them toward positive goals. Here's an example with which most of us can identify. Bob comes home from work and finds his house in chaos. He is furious and wants to yell at Jane and the kids, but he "stuffs" his rage. By bedtime he cannot unwind and has an acute attack of gastric reflux. His wife, after a trying day herself, wishes to make some contact with her husband. She wants him to share something about his day or how he is feeling and asks if anything is wrong. He utters, "Nothing, I'm just tired," and turns his attention to the raw, sour, burning taste of gastric juices in his throat. Jane smolders, accusing him of being distant and remote. She laments that she cannot get a feel for where he is at; she complains that she "cannot feel him." He withdraws further.

Alternatively, they might have an attacking/counterattacking fight that culminates in her remembering something he did to upset her two years ago … To this perceived blaming he replies that he doesn't even remember what she is talking about; and so far as he is concerned it never even happened. "What is wrong with you?" he murmurs under his breath. He is unaware that (1) when a woman becomes (emotionally) activated, she remains stressed for a much longer time than a man. The woman's pounding heart and racing thoughts remain stuck. And (2) in her racing thoughts, Jane tries to locate an explanation for her runaway heart, *believing* that if she can find the cause (identifying it as a real external threat—as is biologically intended), then she could settle down. In scanning her memory banks in this activated state, she stumbles across the time when (she perceived) Bob hurt her. Seizing on this "explanation" for her distress, she feels compelled to act upon it, "throwing it in Bob's face." In this way, Jane is doing what her physiology compels while he perceives that "she is blaming him for nothing." This dance of daggers intensifies his defensiveness and seething anger. Locked in mortal combat, they both reach for a Valium. As the Valium (which relaxes their muscles) kicks in, they both feel better—it seems to both of them that the blowup was over nothing. Bob hopes that tomorrow will be a clean slate, and Jane wonders why in the world she dragged up that two-year-old event, no less beating Bob over the head with it. However, when they awake the next morning, they are disconnected physically, emotionally, psychologically and spiritually.

Furthermore, research shows that this type of unresolved conflict impairs the couple's immune system, depressing it and reducing the capacity for wound healing over the next several days.*

Rewind and replay: Bob comes into the house. Faced with the chaos, he feels angry, but neither suppresses nor explodes. This time, supported by his wife's centered, calm presence, he attends tentatively to his body. He notices his heart racing, while the muscles of his arms, shoulders, back, neck and jaw are tightening. After sharing his awareness with his wife, Bob has the fleeting glimpse of a bomb ready to explode. He feels the impulse to punch with his fists; his anger intensifies momentarily but then subsides. The vise grip in his tensed muscles begins to loosen. (These muscles had been engaged, as Nina Bull demonstrated, to inhibit the original urge to punch.) Bob sighs in relief as his legs begin, gently, to tremble. He "lets in" his wife's supportive presence and then suddenly recalls, "Oh yeah, that's what it was. Before I left the office, Alex, the supervisor, and I were discussing a marketing plan for the new widget. Alex and I had strongly differing opinions; we just couldn't seem to agree. I felt competitive. We were combative, but in a good way. I felt forceful and clear. I suppose we could have hammered it out. Instead we stopped short of a solution when I remembered that Alex was dating the boss's daughter. I stifled my power and ingenuity, and then, yes, that's when I felt myself go into a rage. I wanted to throttle Alex but then retreated. I just wanted to leave and go home.

---

* In a study of 150 couples, mostly in their sixties, researchers found that women who behaved in a hostile manner during marital disputes were more likely to have atherosclerosis, especially if their husbands were also hostile. In men, hostility—their own or their wives—was not related to atherosclerosis. However, men who behaved in a dominating or controlling manner—or whose wives behaved in that way—were more likely to have clogged coronary arteries. "The only group of men that had very little atherosclerosis were those where both they and their wives were able to talk about a disagreement without being controlling at all," Smith said. "So the absence of a power play in the conversation seemed to be heart protective for men," he concluded (Dr. Timothy Smith, University of Utah, Reuters, March 3, 2006).

The rest of the day I silently fumed. And then, when things were, well, the way they usually are at home, I wanted to explode. I felt the same seething rage I had felt at work. I guess I was triggered to blow when I set foot into the familiar mess at home; I just wanted to blow off steam. I was … well, really afraid that I could hurt you or the kids. So instead, I just went off to read the paper and simmered silently behind my paper fortress. I didn't want to blow up at you and the kids. Really, what I wanted was the calm contact I am getting from you now." This state of calm, unlike the temporary relief provided by the Valium in the first scenario, is a real shift in his perception of safety, an enduring one. It is achieved by a process of self-regulation and social engagement, rather than the temporary masking offered by a tranquilizer—though both act to relax the tight muscles. This collaborative experience is what brings Bob and Jane closer together.

The *feeling of combativeness* that Bob experienced at the office was powerful, focused and motivating. Had he not stopped himself, he might have entered into a productive negotiation with Alex. However, when he thwarted this process (out of a perceived threat that may or may not have even really existed), his directed feeling of healthy aggression (for getting what he needed and protecting what he had), erupted into (impotent) rage. This abrupt transition—from a fluid, organizing *feeling process* into a disorganizing, nonproductive, reactive *emotional state*—is what was so brilliantly studied by Nina Bull.

So why do we get stuck with our negative emotional states, habitually wearing them like our only set of shirt and trousers? Many people (like the young samurai) use their rage to intimidate. Others indulge habitual sadness and remain helpless victims. For Bob and Jane (in the initial scenario), their emotions served to separate them.

In 1978, after completing my doctoral work, I took a paid vacation as a teacher in residence at the Esalen Institute, nestled above the roiling sea of the breathtakingly serrated Big Sur coast. As part of my duties, I conducted what was called the open-seat forum. In this group setting, members of the Esalen community could come in and receive free therapy. My duties were executed on Monday and Thursday afternoons. After several weeks I became perplexed by an intriguing phenomenon.

Thursdays were quite calm, and the impromptu clients were generally working productively. However, Mondays were quite a different story. It was as if there were firecrackers going off on the Fourth of July. One person after another would come to see me and, without prompting, would either break down in jagged sobs or pummel pillows with undirected (and impotent) rage.

A possible explanation for this weekly divergence came to me unexpectedly. One day as I walked past the bulletin board outside the office, I noticed a note announcing that a particular group, which encouraged hyperventilation and strong emotional catharsis, had been canceled for that Wednesday evening. It was set to resume the following week. Hmm, I wondered, would this ordinarily calm Thursday be like the chaotic Mondays? And it was.

Earlier that same year, my brother Jon had published a landmark study in the medical journal *Lancet.*[164] In this research, he had given a group of patients recovering from jaw surgery either an IV drip of morphine or a placebo that consisted of physiological saline. Both groups were told that they were being given a powerful painkiller. Fully two-thirds of the patients who received the saline placebo had as profound an effect of pain relief as did the group of patients who received a solid dose of morphine, pain abatement's gold standard.*

Jon's findings, amazing in their own right, were surpassed by the next phase of the research. When patients were given the placebo plus Naloxone, the placebo response was completely negated. Naloxone is a drug that has absolutely no effect whatsoever when administered to a sober individual (not unlike the effect of Viagra on an individual whose dosage is followed by a leisurely walk with the dog). However, when administered in the emergency room to addicts who have overdosed on heroin, it makes them stone sober in seconds. The mode of action of Naloxone is as an opiate antagonist. This means that Naloxone attaches to opioid receptors throughout the brain, thereby blocking the attachment and action of both the exogenous opiate drugs, including

---

* In the cases where the placebo did not work, the patients were quickly given the real morphine so that their unnecessary suffering was short-lived.

morphine and heroin, as well as the body's own endogenous (internally self-generated) opiates, called endorphins. What Jon and his colleagues had demonstrated with these experiments was that the brain possesses its own pain mediating system. The analgesic effect of these endogenous endorphins can be just as powerful as the strongest known opioid drugs like morphine!

What occurred to me at Esalen was the possibility that I had witnessed the effects of opiate withdrawal during our Monday sessions. This was in stark contrast to Thursdays, when the previous night's opiate orgy, stimulated by the hyperventilating catharsis, produced a "stoned," spaced-out group of participants. These Thursday groups were populated by community members who had recently gotten their drug fix on Wednesday and did not crave another one. In particular, I wondered if the intense emotional abreactions I observed on Mondays were a method by which participants released their own internal opiates (endorphins), essentially giving themselves a fix, not unlike a shot of morphine.

Excited about my hypothesis, I telephoned my brother. Since it was not yet known that the brain regions and neural pathways responsible for physical and emotional pain were nearly identical, Jon's response was not encouraging. "Peter," he said, pitying my naïveté, "don't be silly," while managing to get in a well-deserved jab at his older sibling—a rivalry reasserted. However, a few years later, Bessel van der Kolk replicated Jon's experiment.[165] This time the focus was on Naloxone's blocking the endorphins released by *emotional, rather than physical, pain*. He studied a common treatment for posttraumatic stress disorder (PTSD) administered, at that time, to Vietnam vets in the nation's VA hospitals. These unfortunate soldiers were repeatedly provoked into "reliving" their horrific battlefield experiences. In this "therapy," they were forced, for example, to watch gory war movies like *Platoon* with their arms tied to a chair. These exposures frequently catapulted the veterans into intense emotional abreactions. However, when Naloxone was administered before these cathartic sessions (depriving them of their self-induced endorphin rush) they soon lost interest in taking part in further "therapeutic" sessions.

As I observed many workshop attendees over the years (returning time and time again), I couldn't help but wonder if they were also inducing their own chemical highs. Their repeated and cathartic dramatizations, screaming at their parents or pounding pillows in endless anger, seemed to be rewarding, bringing them back for further fixes. In my own life, I also wondered whether there was an addictive quality to some of my earlier painful and turbulent relationships that I appeared to be creating and re-creating.

While cathartic expressions of emotion in therapy sessions can be of value, reliance on emotional release stems from a fundamental misunderstanding about the very nature of feelings and emotions. The work of Nina Bull provides us with insight, both into the nature of habitual emotions and into why *feelings accessed through body awareness, rather than emotional release, bring us the kind of lasting change that we so desire.*

CHAPTER 14

Trauma and Spirituality

If you bring forth that which is within you,
Then that which is within you
Will be your salvation.
If you do not bring forth that which is
   within you,
Then that which is within you
Will destroy you.
   —The Gnostic Gospels

In a lifetime of working with traumatized individuals, I have been struck by the intrinsic and wedded relationship between trauma and spirituality. From my earliest experiences with clients suffering from a daunting array of crippling symptoms, I have been privileged to witness profound and authentic transformations. Seemingly out of nowhere, as with Nancy from Chapter 2, who was "held in warm tingling waves," such unexpected "side effects" appeared as these individuals mastered the monstrous trauma symptoms that had haunted them—emotionally, physically and psychologically. These surprises included ecstatic joy, exquisite clarity, effortless focus and an all-embracing sense of oneness. In addition, many of my clients described deep and abiding experiences of compassion, peace and wholeness. In fact, it was not unusual after that profound internal shift of feeling the "goodness of self," perhaps for the first time, to refer to their therapeutic work as "a holy experience." While these individuals realized the classic goals of enduring personality and behavioral changes, these transcendent side effects were simply too potent and robust to overlook. I have been compelled to follow these exciting and elusive enigmas with wonder and curiosity for many decades.

Because the formal diagnosis of trauma, as Posttraumatic Stress Disorder (PTSD) in the *Diagnostic and Statistical Manual of Mental Disorders III*, was still over a decade away when my newfound odyssey was in its infancy, I didn't have a formulated set of *pathological* criteria to unduly distract me. I was freer to observe in the tradition of the ethologists. From this vantage point, and without a premeditated list of symptoms, I was able to monitor my clients' bodily reactions and self-reports as I participated in their transformative process of healing. The highly charged physiological reactions described in the earlier chapters, including shaking and trembling (when experienced as a safe discharge) together with dramatic spontaneous changes in temperature, heart rate and respiration, helped to restore their equilibrium. These reactions also promoted a relaxed readiness, an aptitude similar to that cultivated in Zen and in the martial arts such as aikido.

In sorting through these types of involuntary, energetic and deeply moving experiences, I realized that my clients' reactions manifested what was right and normal—rather than what was wrong and pathological. In other words, they exhibited *innate* self-regulating and self-healing processes. And as the animals went on about their daily business after such discharge reactions, so too did my clients reengage into life with renewed passion, appreciation and acceptance.

At the same time, they frequently touched into a variety of experiences that I learned to appreciate as spiritual encounters such as Nancy's feelings of aliveness, warmth, joy and wholeness. In moving toward an understanding of this intrinsic relationship between trauma ("raw, latent survival energy") and spirituality, I was excited to come across a formative article by Roland Fischer published in the prestigious journal *Science*. A surprising and unexpected tenet emerged: that spiritual experience is welded with our most primitive animal instincts.

Transcendental States

Roland Fischer's article, titled "A Cartography of the Ecstatic and Meditative States,"[166] described a schema for showing the association of various parasympathetic and sympathetic (autonomic-instinctual) activities with mystical and meditative experiences. While the details of his work are well beyond the scope of this short chapter, suffice it to say, I suspected that his view of the psychophysiological underpinning of various mystical states paralleled the range of "transpersonal" experiences that my clients were encountering as they unwound and released their traumas.

Trauma represents a profound compression of "survival" energy, energy that has not been able to complete its meaningful course of action. When in the therapeutic session, this energy is *gradually* released or titrated (Step 4 in Chapter 5) and then redirected from its symptomatic detour onto its natural course, one observes (in a softer and less frightening form) the kinds of reactions I observed with Nancy. At the same time, the numinous qualities of these experiences gracefully, automatically and consistently became integrated into the personality structure. The ability to access the rhythmic release of this bound energy makes all the difference as to whether it will destroy or vitalize us.

Primitive survival responses engage extraordinary feats of focused attention and effective action. The mother who lifts the car off of her trapped child mobilizes vast (almost superhuman) survival energy. These same energies, when experienced through *titrated body sensing*, can also open to feelings of heightened focus, ecstasy and bliss. The ownership of these primordial "oceanic" energy sensations promotes embodied transformation and (as suggested in Fischer's cartography) the experience of "timelessness" and "presence" known in meditation as "the eternal now." In addition, it appears that the very brain structures that are central to the resolution of trauma are also pivotal in various "mystical" and "spiritual" states.[167]

In the East, the awakening of *Kundalini* at the first (or survival) chakra center has long been known to be a vehicle for initiating ecstatic transformation. In trauma, a similar activation is provoked, but with such intensity and rapidity that it overwhelms the organism. If we can gradually access and reintegrate this energy into our nervous system and psychic structures, then the survival response embedded within trauma can also catalyze authentic spiritual transformation.

As I began to explore the relationship between trauma transformation and the Kundalini experience, I searched for confirmation of this connection. Around that time (the mid-1970s) I met a physician named Lee Sannella in Berkeley, California. He shared with me a large compilation of notes he had taken about individuals who were experiencing spontaneous Kundalini awakenings. I was intrigued by how similar many of these reactions were to those of my early clients. Sannella's notes formed the basis for his valuable book, *The Kundalini Experience, Psychosis or Transcendence?*[168] This phenomenon has been described by great contemporary adepts such as Gopi Krishna.[169] In addition, C. G. Jung's book *The Psychology of Kundalini Yoga*[170] (based on a 1932 seminar) gives an erudite exposition but concludes, ironically, that Kundalini is unlikely to ever be experienced in the West. However, Jung goes on to say, "The life of feeling is that primordial region of the psyche that is most sensitive to the religious encounter. Belief or reason alone does nothing to move the soul: without feeling, religious meaning becomes a vacant intellectual exercise. This is why the most exuberant spiritual moments are emotively laden." The essence of religious experience is an act of feeling the animating force—the *spiritus* within the lived encounter. When my clients experienced this élan vital surging forth from within them, it was not surprising that they also encountered aspects of religious awe.

Over the years I had the opportunity to show some videos of my clients' sessions to Kundalini teachers from India. These were wonderful exchanges. The yoga masters, with genuine and disarming humility, seemed as interested in my observations as I was in their vast knowledge and intrinsic knowing.

"Symptoms" frequently described in Kundalini awakenings may involve any of the following: involuntary and spasmodic body movements, pain, tickling, itching, vibrations, trembling, alternations of hot and cold, changed breathing patterns, temporary paralysis, crushing pressure, insomnia, hypersensitivity to light and sound, synesthesia, unusual or extremes of emotions, intensified sex drive, sensations of physical expansion, dissociation and out-of-body experiences, as well as hearing "inner sounds," such as roaring, whistling and chirping. These sensations associated with Kundalini awakenings are often more forceful and explosive than those I observed with my clients. As I developed my methodology, I learned to help clients gradually touch into their bodily-energy sensations so that they were rarely overwhelmed. In general, focusing inward and becoming curious about one's inner sensations allows people to experience a subtle inner shift, a slight contraction, vibration, tingling, relaxation and sense of openness. I have named this shift from the feelings of dread, rage or whatever one likes to avoid toward "befriending" one's internal sensations *pendulation*, the *intrinsic rhythm* pulsing between the experienced polarities of contraction and expansion/openness (Step 3 in Chapter 5). Once people learn to access this rhythmic flow within, "infinite" emotional pain begins to feel manageable and finite. This allows their attitude to shift from dread and helplessness to curiosity and exploration.

The mystical text *Hermetic Kybalion* says, "Everything flows, out and in; everything has its tides; all things rise and fall; the pendulum-swing manifests in everything; the measure of the swing to the right is the measure of the swing to the left; rhythm compensates." The application of this perennial philosophy to trauma is the very principle that allows sensations and feelings that had previously been overwhelming to be processed and transformed in present time. In this way, trauma, when transformed, parallels Kabalistic philosophy.

Trauma, Death and Suffering

Yea, though I walk through the valley of
the shadow of death,
I will fear no evil.
—Psalm 23

It would be an error to equate trauma with suffering and suffering, in turn, with transformation. At the same time, however, in virtually every spiritual tradition suffering is understood as a doorway to awakening. In the West, this connection can be seen in the biblical story of Job and, powerfully, in Psalm 23. It is found as the dark night of the soul in medieval mysticism—and, of course, in the passion of Christ. In Buddhism an important distinction is made between suffering and unnecessary suffering. According to the Buddha, "When touched with a feeling of pain, the ordinary person laments ... becomes distraught ... contracts ... so he feels two pains ... just as if they were to shoot a man with an arrow and, right afterward, were to shoot him with another ... so that he would feel the pains of two arrows ..." Trauma sufferers are so frightened of their bodily sensations that they recoil from feeling them. It is as though they believe that by feeling them they will be destroyed or, at the very least, make things worse. Hence they remain stuck. In this way, they shoot themselves with the second arrow—FDR's "fear of fear itself." With support and guidance, however, they are able to gradually learn to befriend and transform their trauma-based sensations.

In both the Buddhist and Taoist traditions, four pathways are said to lead to spiritual awakening.[171] The first is death. A second route to freedom from unnecessary human suffering can come from many years of austere meditative contemplation. The third gateway to liberation is through special forms of (tantric) sexual ecstasy. And the fourth portal is said, by these traditions, to be trauma. Death, meditation, sex and trauma, in serving as great portals, share a common element. They are all potential catalysts for profound surrender.

The ability to feel the *physical sensations* of paralysis (without becoming overwhelmed) and surrender to them is the key in transforming trauma. When we are able to touch into that deathlike void even briefly, rather than recoil from it, the immobilization releases. In this way the second arrow of unnecessary suffering is eliminated. The "standing back" from fear allows the individual to emerge from the strangulation of trauma. As people "experience into" the time-limited paralysis sensations (in the absence of fear), they contact the "mini-deaths" that lie at the eye of the hurricane, at the very heart of trauma. This visitation is an opportunity to enter the rich portal of death. It is well known that many people who have had near death experiences (NDEs) undergo positive personality transformations. At the right time, traumatized individuals are encouraged and supported to feel and surrender into the immobility/NDE states, liberating these primordial archetypal energies while integrating them into consciousness.

In addition, the "awe-full" states of horror and terror appear to be connected to the transformative states such as awe, presence, timelessness and ecstasy. They share essential psychophysiological and phenomenological roots. For example, stimulation of the amygdala (the brain's smoke detector for danger and rage) can also evoke the experience of ecstasy and bliss.[172] This seems to support an approach that guides individuals *through* their *awe-full* feelings of fear and horror toward those of joy, goodness and *awe*.

Andrew Newberg and his colleagues have, in their seminal book *Why God Won't Go Away*,[173] brought together a vast amount of research on the brain substrates underlying a variety of different spiritual experiences. The application of this type of brain research to trauma transformation is a rich area worthy of further research and exploration.

Regulation and the Self

As below, so above.

—*Kybalion*

In review: The autonomic nervous system (ANS) gets its name from being a relatively autonomous branch of the nervous system. Its basic, yet highly *integrated* function has to do with the regulation of energy states and the maintenance of homeostasis. The ANS is composed of two distinctly different branches.* Its sympathetic branch supports

---

* Recall from Chapter 6 that the parasympathetic branch is divided into a primitive (nonmyelinated) and an evolutionarily recent (myelinated) branch.

overall energy mobilization. If you are physically cold, perceive threat, or are sexually aroused, the sympathetic nervous system increases the metabolic rate and prepares you for action. The parasympathetic branch, on the other hand, promotes rest, relaxation, gestation, nurturance and restitution of tissue and cellular function.

When the level of activation of the sympathetic branch of the autonomic nervous system is very low, we are apt to be feeling somewhat lethargic. At moderate levels of sympathetic activity, we are generally doing or preparing to do something active.[174] This level of arousal is usually experienced as being alert, as well as pleasurably excited. In this realm there is typically a smooth back-and-forth shifting between moderate levels of sympathetic and parasympathetic activity serving a *balanced* physiological state called homeostasis. I call this flexible, seesawing, shifting range of arousal *dynamic equilibrium* and *relaxed alertness* along with energy, passion and focus.

In mammals, this capacity for self-regulation is essential. It endows the animal with the capability to make fluid shifts in internal bodily states to meet changes in the external environment. Animals with developed orbitofrontal systems have evolved the capacity to switch between different emotional states. This ability (known as affect regulation) allows animals to vary their emotions to appropriately match environmental demands. In humans, this highly evolved adaptive function, according to Schore and others, is the basis for the core sense of self.[175] These same circuits in the orbitofrontal cortex receive inputs from the muscles, joints and viscera. The sensations that form the inner landscape of the body are mapped in the orbitofrontal portions of the brain.[176] Hence, as we are able to change our body sensations, we change the highest function of our brains. Emotional regulation, our rudder through life, comes about through *embodiment*.

Embodiment and Refinement

For in my flesh I shall see God.
—Book of Job

Curse the mind that mounts the clouds in
　　search of
mythical kings and only mystical things,
mystical things cry for the soul
that will not face the body as an equal place
and I never learned to touch for real
down, down, down where the iguanas feel.
　　—Dory Previn song

Traumatized people are fragmented and disembodied. The constriction of feeling obliterates shade and texture, turning everything into good or bad, black or white, for us or against us. It is the unspoken hell of traumatization. In order to know who and where we are in space and to feel that we are vital, alive beings, subtleties are essential. Furthermore, it is not just acutely traumatized individuals who are disembodied; most Westerners share a less dramatic but still impairing disconnection from their inner sensate compasses. Given the magnitude of the primordial and raw power of our instincts, the historical role of the church and other cultural institutions in subjugating the body is hardly surprising.

In contrast, various (embodied) spiritual traditions have acknowledged the "baser instincts" not as something to be eliminated, but rather as a force in need of, and available for, transformation. In Vipassana meditation and various traditions of tantric Buddhism (such as Kum Nye), the goal is "to manifest the truly human spiritual qualities of universal goodwill, kindness, humility, love, equanimity and so on."[177] These traditions, rather than renouncing the body, utilize it as a way to "refine" the instincts. The essence of embodiment is not in repudiation, but in living the instincts fully as they dance in the "body electric," while at the same time harnessing their primordial raw energies to promote increasingly subtle qualities of experience.[178]

As the song by Dory Previn suggests, mystical experiences that are not experienced in the body just don't "stick"; they are not grounded. Trauma sufferers live in a world of chronic dissociation. This perpetual state of disembodiment keeps them disoriented and unable to engage in the here and now. As mentioned earlier, trauma survivors, however, are not alone in being disembodied; a lower level of separation between body/mind is widespread in modern culture, affecting all of us to a greater or lesser degree.

Recall the distinction made in the German language between the word *Körper*, meaning a physical body, and *Leib*, which translates to English as the "lived (or living) body." The term *Leib* reveals a much deeper generative meaning than does the purely physical *Körper*, which is not unlike "corpse." A gift of trauma recovery is the rediscovery of the living, sensing, knowing body. The poet and writer D. H. Lawrence inspires us all with this reflection on the living, knowing body:

> My belief is in the blood and flesh as being wiser than the intellect. The body-unconscious is where life bubbles up in us. It is how we know that we are alive, alive to the depths of our souls and in touch somewhere with the vivid reaches of the cosmos.

Trauma sufferers, in their healing journeys, learn to dissolve their rigid defenses. In this surrender they move from frozen fixity to gently thawing and, finally, free flow. In healing the divided self from its habitual mode of dissociation, they move from fragmentation to wholeness. In becoming embodied they return from their long exile. They come home to their bodies and know embodied life, as though for the first time. While trauma is hell on earth, its resolution may be a gift from the gods.

Finally, Jack London describes the enlightenment afforded by meeting and transforming trauma. He writes, in *The Call of the Wild*, "There is an ecstasy that marks the summit of life, and beyond which life cannot rise. And such is the paradox of living, this ecstasy comes when one is most alive, and it comes as a complete forgetfulness that one is alive." This awakening of our life force, transmuted from survival to ecstatic aliveness, is truly the intrinsic gift laid at our feet and waiting to be opened through this journey of sweet surrender to the sensate world within, whether we are survivors of trauma or simply casualties of Western culture.

Epilogue

Too much or too little? This question has quietly dogged me in the writing of *In an Unspoken Voice*. As one chapter was completed, two more suggested themselves; and so on. Finally, *basta!* At least for now. My solution to this hydra-like dilemma takes the form of gestating two more books. I am, perhaps, a little like the mother who, after experiencing the agonizing labor pains of birth, some months later, blithely thinks that it might be a good idea to have another child. I fear that I have fallen into that tender trap. After I have adequately recovered from the postpartum letdown of publishing this book, I have two subsequent projects in mind.

Two areas that I felt were not sufficiently addressed in this book concern traumatic memory and the intimate relationship between trauma and spirituality. The first book planned is tentatively titled *Memory, Trauma and the Body;* the second will be called *Trauma and Spirituality.*

Of the many misconceptions and misunderstandings about trauma, confusion about so-called traumatic memory ranks among the greatest and potentially most problematic. Fundamentally, traumatic memories differ from other memories in crucial ways. This first book will methodically explore both the various types of memory as well as the role of these distinct memory systems in the formation and treatment of trauma. Unfortunately, however, rather than exploring these differences in an open and informed scientific forum, two opposing camps of extremists in the "trauma wars" have developed: one that believes that all trauma memories are false (i.e., are confabulated) and another that contends that they are all true, accurate recordings of events exactly as they occurred. In this book we will open this discourse toward balancing the truth about "false memories" and the inherent falsity of "true memories." It is only by understanding the role of the body in registering traumatic experience that we come to a coherent understanding of "traumatic memory," as well as its clinical role in the therapeutic process.

This exploration takes us beyond the two unbalanced polarities (of memories being either false or true) to a deeper understanding of the nature and healing of trauma.

The second book (written with Marianne Bentzen) will explore, in depth, the intrinsic relationship between spirituality and trauma. In the course of working with trauma for over forty years, it has become clear to me that there exists a welded, parallel and interwoven relationship between the transformation of trauma and various aspects of spiritual experiences. In this book we will show how both effective trauma healing and authentic spirituality are part of an embodied developmental process and discipline that draw humans toward greater presence and put us in touch with the numinous experiences that are often attributed to a god, soul or spirit.

In the meantime, for more information on trauma healing, including our training programs, please visit the following websites:

> www.traumahealing.com
> www.somaticexperiencing.com

A companion DVD session of Dr. Levine's poignant work with a Marine serving in Iraq and Afghanistan and suffering from severe PTSD and Traumatic Brain Injury (TBI) can be purchased from www.psychotherapy.net.

Notes

CHAPTER 1

1. Starr, A., et al. (2004). Symptoms of Posttraumatic Stress Disorder after Orthopaedic Trauma. *Journal of Bone and Joint Surgery, 86,* 1115–1121. Ponsford, J., Hill, B., Karamitsios, M., & Bahar-Fuchs, A. P. (2008). Factors Influencing Outcome after Orthopedic Trauma. *Journal of Trauma: Injury, Infection, and Critical Care, 64* (4), 1001–1009. Sanders, M. B., Starr, A. J., Frawley, W. H., McNulty, M. J., & Niacaris, T. R. Posttraumatic Stress Symptoms in Children Recovering From Minor Orthopaedic Injury and Treatment. (2005). *Journal of Orthopaedic Trauma, 19* (9), 623–628.

2. Shalev, A. Y., et al. (1998). A Prospective Study of Heart Rate Response Following Trauma and the Subsequent Development of Posttraumatic Stress Disorder. *Archives of General Psychiatry, 55,* 553–559.

3. von Franz, M.-L. (1970, 1992). *The Golden Ass of Apuleius: The Liberation of the Feminine in Man.* Boston & London: Shambhala Publications.

4. *I Ching,* Hexagram #51, The Arousing (Shock, Thunder) Six in the third place. Wilhelm, R., & Baynes, C. (1967). *The I Ching or Book of Changes,* with foreword by Carl Jung, Bollingen Series XIX. Princeton, NJ: Princeton University Press (1st ed. 1950).

5. Ibid., 10.

CHAPTER 2

6. Ratner, S. C. (1967). Comparative Aspects of Hypnosis. In J. E. Gordon (Ed.), *Handbook of Clinical and Experimental Hypnosis* (pp. 550–587). New York: Macmillan.

7. Gallup, G. and Maser, J. (1977). Tonic Immobility: Evolutionary Underpinnings of Human Catalepsy and Catatonia. In J. D. Maser and M. F. P. Seligman (Eds.), *Psychopathology: Experimental Models.* San Francisco: Freeman.

8. Maser, J. and Bracha, S. (2008). Anxiety and Posttraumatic Stress Disorder in the Context of Human Brain Evolution: A Role for Theory in *DSM-V? Clinical Psychology: Science and Practice 15 (1),* 91–97.

9. Levine, P. A. (1997). *Waking the Tiger: Healing Trauma.* Berkeley: North Atlantic Press.

CHAPTER 3

10. Rubel, A., O'Nell, C., & Collado-Ardon, R. (1984). *Susto: A Folk Illness.* Berkeley: University of California Press.

11. Kraepelin, E. (2009). *Lectures on Clinical Psychiatry.* General Books LLC (Original work published 1904).

CHAPTER 4

12. E. Marais (1922). *The Soul of the Ape.* London: Penguin Press.

13. James, W. (1884), What is an Emotion? *Mind, 9,* 188–205. Bull, N. (1946). Attitudes: Conscious and Unconscious. *The Journal of Nervous and Mental Disease, 103* (4), 337–345. Bull, N. (1962). *The Body and Its Mind: An Introduction to Attitude Psychology.* New York: Las Americas. 1962. Ekman, P. (1980). Biological and Cultural Contributions to Body and Facial Movement in the Expression of Emotions. In A. O. Rorty (Ed.), *Explaining Emotions* (pp. 73–101). Berkeley and Los Angeles, University of California Press.

14. Havens, L. (1979). Explorations in the Uses of Language in Psychotherapy: Complex Empathic Statements. *Psychiatry, 42,* 40–48.

15. The Proceedings of the National Academy of Sciences, Nov, 2004 (Reported in the *New York Times,* Science section, November 16, 2004).

16. Rizzolatti, R., & Sinigaglia, C. (2008). *Mirrors in the Brain: How Our Minds Share Actions and Emotions.* New York: Oxford University Press.

17. Steven Burnett quoted in Carey, B. (July 28, 2009). In Battle, Hunches Prove to Be Valuable, *New York Times,* Science section.

18. Gallup, G., and Maser, J. (1977). Tonic Immobility: Evolutionary Underpinnings of Human Catalepsy and Catatonia. In J. Maser & M. F. P. Seligman (Eds.), *Psychopathology: Experimental Models.* San Francisco: Freeman.

19. Cannon, W. B. (1929). *Bodily Changes in Pain, Hunger, Fear and Rage: An Account of Recent Research Into the Function of Emotional Excitement.* New York: Appleton-Century-Crofts. Bracha, H. et al. (2004). Does "Fight or Flight" Need Updating? *Psychosomatics 45,* 448–449.

20. Levine, P. A. (1991). Revisioning Anxiety and Trauma. In M. Sheets (Ed.), *Giving the Body Its Due.* Albany: SUNY Press. Levine, P. A. (1978). Stress and Vegetotherapy. *Journal of Energy and Character* (Fall 1978). Levine, P. A. (1996). *Waking the Tiger: Healing Trauma.* Berkeley: North Atlantic Books. Moskowitz, A. K. (2004). "Scared Stiff": Catatonia as an Evolutionary-Based Fear Response. *Psychological Review, 111* (4), 984–1002. Marx, B. P., Forsyth, J. P., Gallup, G. G., Fuse, T., Lexington, J. (2008). Tonic Immobility as an Evolved Predator Defense: Implications for Sexual Assault Survivors. *Clinical Psychology: Science and Practice* 15, 74–94. Zohler, L. A. (2008). Translational Challenges with Tonic Immobility. *Clinical Psychology: Science and Practice* 15, 98–101.

21. Levine, J. D., Gordon, N. C., Bornstein, J. C., & Fields, H. L. (1979). Role of pain in placebo analgesia. *Proceedings of the National Academy of Science, 76* (7), 3528–3531. Also see van der Kolk, B., Greenberg, M., Boyd, H., & Krystal, J. (1985). Inescapable Shock, Neurotransmitters, and Addiction to Trauma. *Biological Psychiatry, 20* (3), 314–25.

22. Suarez, S. D., & Gallup, G. G. (1979). Tonic Immobility as a Response to Rape in Humans: a Theoretical Note. *The Psychological Record, 2* 315–320. Finn, R. (2003, January 1). Paralysis Common Among Victims of Sexual Assault. *Clinical Psychiatry News.*

23. Livingstone, D. (1857). *Missionary Travels and Researches in South Africa.* London: John Murray Press.

24. Murchie, G. (1978). *The Seven Mysteries of Life.* Boston: Houghton Mifflin.

25. Scaer, R. (2001). *The Body Bears the Burden: Trauma, Dissociation, and Disease.* Binghamton: Haworth Medical Press.

26. Gallup, G. G. (1977). Tonic Immobility: The Role of Fear and Predation. *Psychological Record, 27,* 41–61.

27. Ibid. Gallup, G., & Maser, J. (1977). Tonic Immobility: Evolutionary Underpinnings of Human Catalepsy and Catatonia. In J. D. Maser & M. F. P. Seligman (Eds.), *Psychopathology: Experimental Models.* San Francisco: Freeman.

28. Ratner S. C. (1967). *Comparative Aspects of Hypnosis.* In J. E. Gordon (Ed.), *Handbook of Clinical and Experimental Hypnosis* (pp. 550–587). New York: Macmillan.

29. de Oliveira L., Hoffman, A., Menescal-de-Oliveira, L. (1997). The Lateral Hypothalamus in the Modulation of Tonic Immobility in Guinea Pigs. *Neuroreport 8* (16), 3489–3493. Leite-Panissi, C. R. A., Coimbra, N. C., & Menescal-de-Oliveira, L. (2003). The Cholinergic Stimulation of the Central Amygdala Modifying the Tonic Immobility Response and Antinociception in Guinea Pigs Depends on the Ventrolateral Periaqueductal Gray. *Brain Research Bulletin, 60,* 167–178.

30. Marx, B. P., Forsyth, J. P., Gallup, G. G., Fuse, T., Lexington, J. (2008). Tonic Immobility as an Evolved Predator Defense: Implications for Sexual Assault Survivors. *Clinical Psychology: Science and Practice 15,* 74–94.

31. Kahlbaum, K. L. (1973). *Catatonia* (T. Pridan, Trans.). Baltimore: Johns Hopkins University Press. (Original work published 1874)

32. Conan Doyle, A. Services and Accounts; Personal Commercial Service Providers. In M. Ashley (Ed.), *The Mammoth Book of New Sherlock Holmes Adventures.* New York: Carroll & Graf.

33. Marx, B. P., Forsyth, J. P., Gallup, G. G., Fuse, T., Lexington, J. (2008). Tonic Immobility as an Evolved Predator Defense: Implications for Sexual Assault Survivors. *Clinical Psychology: Science and Practice 15,* 74–94.

34. Ibid.

35. Finn, R. (2003, January 1). Paralysis Common Among Victims of Sexual Assault. *Clinical Psychiatry News.* and Marx, B. P., Forsyth, J. P., Gallup, G. G., Fuse, T., Lexington, J. (2008). Tonic Immobility as an Evolved Predator Defense: Implications for Sexual Assault Survivors. *Clinical Psychology: Science and Practice 15,* 74–94.

36. See: Morgan, C. A., Wang, S., Southwick, S. M., Rasmusson, A., Hazlett, G., Hauger, R. L., Charney, D. S. (2000). Plasma Neuropeptide-Y Concentrations in Humans Exposed to Military Survival Training. *Biological Psychiatry, 47* (10), 902–909.

37. Solomon, M., & Siegel, D. (Eds.). (2003). *Healing Trauma: Attachment, Mind, Body, and Brain.* New York: W. W. Norton & Company. Kessler, R., Sonnega, A., Bromet, E., Hughes, M., Nelson, C. (1995). Posttraumatic Stress Disorder in the National Comorbidity Survey. *Archives of General Psychiatry, 52* (12),1048–60.

38. Schore, A. N. (1999). *Affect Regulation and the Origin of the Self: The Neurobiology of Emotional Development.* London: Psychology Press.

39. Herman, J. (1997). *Trauma and Recovery: The Aftermath of Violence: From Domestic Abuse to Political Terror.* New York: Basic Books. Eckberg, M. (2000). *Victims of Cruelty: Somatic Psychotherapy in the Healing of Posttraumatic Stress Disorder* (illustrated ed.). Berkeley: North Atlantic Books.

40. Gallup, G., & Maser, J. (1977) Tonic Immobility: Evolutionary Underpinnings of Human Catalepsy and Catatonia. In J. D. Maser & M. F. P. Seligman (Eds.), *Psychopathology: Experimental Models* San Francisco: Freeman.

41. Terr, L. (1992). *Too Scared to Cry: Psychic Trauma in Childhood.* New York: Basic Books. Levine, P. A., & Kline, M. (2007). *Trauma through a Child's Eyes: Awakening the Ordinary Miracle of Healing.* Berkeley: North Atlantic Press.

42. Levy, D. (1945). Psychic Trauma of Operations in Children. *American Journal of Diseases of Childhood, 69* (1), 7–25.

43. Everything Is Not Okay. (July 1993). *Reader's Digest.*

44. Starr, A., et al. (2004). Symptoms of Posttraumatic Stress Disorder after Orthopaedic Trauma. *Journal of Bone and Joint* Surgery, *86,* 1115–1121. Sanders, M. B., Starr, A. J., Frawley, W. H., McNulty, M. J., & Niacaris, T. R. (2005). Posttraumatic Stress Symptoms in Children Recovering from Minor Orthopaedic Injury and Treatment. *Journal of Orthopaedic Trauma, 19* (9), 623–628.

45. Ibid., ii.

46. Geisz-Everson, M., & Wren, K. R. (2007). Awareness under Anesthesia. *Journal of PeriAnesthesia Nursing, 22,* 85–90.

47. Liska, J. (2002). *Silenced Screams.* Park Ridge, IL: AANA Publishing, Inc.

48. Kahlbaum, K. L. (1973). *Catatonia* (T. Pridan, Trans.). Baltimore: Johns Hopkins University Press. (Original work published 1874)

49. Hess, W. R. (1949). *Das Zwuchenhim.* Basel: Schwabe.

50. van der Kolk, B. A., McFarlane, A., & Weisaeth, L. (Eds.). (2006). *Traumatic Stress: The Effects of Overwhelming Experience on Mind, Body, and Society.* New York: Guilford Press.

51. Murray, H. (1967). Dead to the World: The Passions of Herman Melville. In E. S. Schneidman (Ed.), *Essays in Self-Destruction, 3-29.* New York: Science House.

52. Damasio, A. (2000).*The Feeling of What Happens: Body and Emotion in the Making of Consciousness.* Boston: Mariner Books.

CHAPTER 5

53. Schore, J., & Schore, A. (2008). Modern Attachment Theory: The Central Role of Affect Regulation in Development and Treatment. *Clinical Social Work Journal, 36* (1), 9–20.

54. Salzen, E. A. (1991). On the Nature of Emotion. *International Journal of Comparative Psychology, 5,* 47–110. Bull, N. (1951). *The Attitude Theory of Emotion.*

New York: Nervous and Mental Diseases Monographs. Morris, D. (1956). The Feather Postures of Birds and the Problem of the Origin of Social Signals. *Behavior 9*, 75–113.

55. Levine, P. A. (1978). Stress and Vegetotherapy. *Journal of Energy and Character* . Levine, P. A. (1991). Revisioning Anxiety and Trauma. In M. Sheets-Johnstone (Ed.), *Giving the Body Its Due*. New York: SUNY Press. Levine, P. A. (1996). *Waking the Tiger: Healing Trauma*. Berkeley: North Atlantic Books.

56. Kahlbaum, K. L. (1973). *Catatonia* (T. Pridan, Trans.). Baltimore: Johns Hopkins University Press. (Original work published 1874)

57. Bernard, C. (1957). *An Introduction to the Study of Experimental Medicine*. Mineola, NY: Dover Publications. (Original work published 1865)

CHAPTER 6

58. Porges, S. W. (2001). The Polyvagal Theory: Phylogenetic Substrates of a Social Nervous System. *International Journal of Psychophysiology 42*, 123–146.

59. Ekman, P. (1980). Biological and Cultural Contributions to Body and Facial Movement in the Expression of Emotions. In A. O. Rorty, *Explaining Emotions*. Berkeley: University of California Press.

60. Jackson, J. H. (1958). Evolution and Dissolution in the Nervous System. In *Selected Writings of John Hughlings Jackson* (pp. 45–84). London: Staples.

61. Lanius, R. A., Williamson, P. C., Densmore, M., et al. (2001). Neural Correlates of Traumatic Memories in Posttraumatic Stress Disorder: A Functional MRI Investigation. *American Journal of Psychiatry, 158*, 1920–1922.

62. Ibid. Lanius, R. A., Williamson, P. C., Densmore, M., et al. (2004). The Nature of Traumatic Memories: A 4-T fMRI Functional Connectivity Analysis. *American Journal of Psychiatry, 161*, 36–44.

63. Blakeslee, S. (2008). *The Body Has a Mind of Its Own: How Body Maps in Your Brain Help You Do (Almost) Everything Better.* New York: Random House.

64. Levine, P. (1977). *Accumulated Stress Reserve Capacity and Disease*. Doctoral thesis, University of California–Berkeley, Department of Medical Biophysics, Microfilm 77-15-760. Levine, P. (1986). Stress. In M. Coles, E. Donchin, and S. Porges (Eds.), *Psychophysiology: Systems, Processes, and Application; A Handbook*. New York: Guilford Press.

65. Souther, A. F., & Banks, M. S. (1979). *The Human Face: A View from the Infant's Eye*. Paper presented at the biennial meeting of the Society for Research in Child Development, San Francisco, March 15–18.

66. Lorenz, K. (1949). *King Solomon's Ring*. London: Methuen.

67. Markoff, J. (2009). Scientists Worry Machines May Outsmart Man. *New York Times*, Science section, July 26.

68. Carey, B. (2009). After Injury, Fighting to Regain a Sense of Self. *New York Times*, Science section, August 9.

69. Buber, M. (1971). *I and Thou*. New York: Free Press.

70. Porges, S. W. (1998). Love: An Emergent Property of the Mammalian Autonomic Nervous System. *Psychoneuroendocrinology, 23* (8), 837–861.

71. Lanius, R. A., & Hopper, J. W. (2008). Reexperiencing/Hyperaroused and Dissociative States in Posttraumatic Stress Disorder. *Psychiatric Times, 25* (13).

72. Damasio, A. R. (2000). *The Feeling of What Happens.* New York: Harvest Books.

73. Van der Kolk, B. A., & McFarlane, A. (2006). *Traumatic Stress: The Effects of Overwhelming Experience on Mind, Body, and Society.* New York: Guilford Press.

74. Van der Hart, O., Nijenhuis, E. R. S., & Steele, K. (2006) *The Haunted Self: Structural Dissociation and the Treatment of Chronic Traumatization.* New York: W. W. Norton. Courtois, C. A., & Ford, J. D. (Eds.). (2009). *Treating Complex Traumatic Stress Disorders: An Evidence-Based Guide.* New York: Guilford Press. Fosha, D. (2000). *The Transforming Power of Affect: A Model for Accelerated Change.* New York: Basic Books. Paivio, S. C., & Pascual-Leone, A. (2010). *Emotion-Focused Therapy for Complex Trauma: An Integrative Approach.* Washington, DC: American Psychological Association.

75. Darwin, C. (1872). *The Expression of Emotions, Man, and Animals.* New York: Appleton.

76. Hadhazy, A. (2010). Think Twice: How the Gut's "Second Brain" Influences Mood and Well-Being. *Scientific American,* February 12.

77. Lowry, T. (1967). *Hyperventilation and Hysteria.* Springfield, IL: Charles C. Thomas. Robert Whitehouse, PhD, personal communication, 2008.

78. Porges, S. W. (2009). The Polyvagal Theory: New Insights into Adaptive Reactions of the Autonomic Nervous System. *Cleveland Clinic Journal of Medicine, 76* (suppl. 2).

79. Levine, P. A. (2008). *Healing Trauma: A Pioneering Program for Restoring the Wisdom of Your Body.* Boulder, CO: Sounds True. Figure used with permission from Sounds True, www.soundstrue.com.

80. Richter, C. D. (1957). On the Phenomenon of Sudden Death in Animals AND Man. *Psychosomatic Medicine, 19* (3), 191–198.

CHAPTER 7

81. Sperry, R. W. (1952). Neurology and the Mind-brain Problem. *American Scientist, 40,* 291–312.

82. Held, R., & Hein, A. (1963). Movement-Produced Stimulation in the Development of Visually Guided Behaviours. *Journal of Comparative and Physiological Psychology, 56,* 872–876.

83. Held, R. (1965). Plasticity in Sensory-Motor Systems. *Scientific American, 213,* 84–94.

84. Edelman, G. (1987). *Neural Darwinism: The Theory of Neural Group Selection.* New York: Basic Books.

85. Rizzolatti, G., & Craighero, L. (2004). The Mirror-Neuron System. *Annual Review of Neuroscience, 27,* 169–192.

86. Preston, S. D., & de Waal, F. B. M. (2002). Empathy: Its Ultimate and Proximate Bases. *Behavioral and Brain Sciences, 25*, 1–72.

87. Havens, L. (1979). Explorations in the Uses of Language in Psychotherapy: Complex Empathic Statements. *Psychiatry, 42*, 40–48.

88. Ekman, P. (1980). Biological and Cultural Contributions to Body and Facial Movement in the Expression of Emotions. In A. O. Rorty (Ed.), *Explaining Emotions.* Berkeley: University of California Press.

89. Sherrington, C. (2010). *The Integrative Action of the Nervous System.* Republished by Nabu Press (2010).

90. Gisell, A. (1945). *Embryology of Behavior.* New York: Harper.

91. Levine, P., & Macnaughton, I. (2004). Breath and Consciousness. In I. Macnaughton (Ed.), *Body, Breath, and Consciousness: A Somatics Anthology.* Berkeley: North Atlantic Books. Robert Whitehouse, PhD, personal communication, 2008. Lowry, T. (1967). *Hyperventilation and Hysteria.* Springfield, IL: Charles C. Thomas.

92. Levine, J. D., & Fields, H. L. (1984). Placebo Analgesia—A Role for Endorphins? *Trends in Neurosciences, 7* (8), 271–273.

93. Leite-Panissi, C. R. A., Coimbra, N. C., & Menescal-de-Oliveira, L. (2003). The Cholinergic Stimulation of the Central Amygdala Modifying the Tonic Immobility Response and Antinociception in Guinea Pigs Depends on the Ventrolateral Periaqueductal Gray. *Brain Research Bulletin, 60*, 167–178.

94. Boyesen, G. (1994). *Über den Körper die Seele heilen: Biodynamische Psychologie und Psychotherapie* (7th ed.). Munich: Kösel, 1994.

95. Gendlin, E. (1982). *Focusing* (2nd ed.). New York: Bantam Books.

CHAPTER 8

96. Cooper, J. (1994). *Speak of Me as I Am: The Life and Work of Masud Khan.* London: Karnac Books.

97. Myron Sharaf (author of *Fury on Earth: A Biography of Wilhelm Reich*), personal communication.

98. Phelps, E. A., et al. (2009). Methods and Timing to Treat Fears. *New York Times*, December 10, 2009.

99. LeDoux, J., & Gorman, J. (2001). A Call to Action: Overcoming Anxiety through Active Coping. *American Journal of Psychiatry, 158*, 1953–1955.

100. Damasio, A. (1999). *The Feeling of What Happens.* San Diego: Harcourt.

101. Tulku, T. (1975). *Reflections of Mind: Western Psychology Meets Tibetan Buddhism* (4th ed.). Berkeley: Dharma Publishing.

102. Van der Kolk, B., et al. (1996). Dissociation, Somatization, and Affect Dysregulation: The Complexity of Adaptation of Trauma. *American Journal of Psychiatry, 153* (7), 83–93.

103. Danieli, Y. (1998). *International Handbook of Multigenerational Legacies of Trauma* (Springer Series on Stress and Coping). New York: Plenum.

104. Lifton, R. J. (1996). *The Broken Connection: On Death and the Continuity of Life*. Arlington, VA: American Psychiatric Publishing.

105. Levine, P. A., & Kline, M. (2006). *Trauma through a Child's Eyes: Awakening the Ordinary Miracle of Healing*. Berkeley: North Atlantic Books.

106. Levine, P. A., & Kline, M. (2008). *Trauma-Proofing Your Kids: A Parents' Guide for Instilling Confidence, Joy and Resilience*. Berkeley: North Atlantic Books.

107. Terr, L. (1992). *Too Scared to Cry: Psychic Trauma In Childhood*. New York: Basic Books.

CHAPTER 10

108. Goodall, J. (1999). *Reason for Hope: A Spiritual Journey* (p. 188). New York: Warner Books.

109. Eibl-Eibesfeldt, I. (1971). *Love and Hate: The Natural History of Behavior Patterns*. New York: Holt, Reinhart and Winston.

110. de Waal, F. (2005). *Our Inner Ape*. New York: Penguin.

111. Sapolsky, R. M. (2005). *Monkeyluv*. New York: Scribner.

112. Hauser, M. (2006). *Moral Minds: How Nature Designed Our Universal Sense of Right and Wrong*. New York: Ecco. Hauser, M. (2000). *Wild Minds: What Animals Really Think*. New York: Henry Holt. Bekoff, M. (2007). *Minding Animals: Awareness, Emotions, and Heart* (reprint ed.). New York: Oxford University Press.

113. Darwin, C. (2004). *The Descent of Man* (p. 100). New York: Penguin.

114. Sapolsky, R. M. (2004). *Why Zebras Don't Get Ulcers* (3rd ed.). New York: Holt Paperbacks.

115. Darwin, C. (2009). *The Expression of the Emotions in Man and Animals*. London: Cambridge University Press. Regrettably, this edition omits Darwin's magnificent drawings.

116. Ibid., p. 239.

117. Lorenz, K. (1966). *On Aggression* (p. 240). London: Methuen.

118. Meerloo, J. A. (1971). *Intuition and the Evil Eye: The Natural History of a Superstition*. Wassenaar, Netherlands: Servire.

119. Llinás, R. R. (2002). *I of the Vortex: From Neurons to Self*. Cambridge, MA: MIT Press.

120. Blakeslee, S. (2006). Cells That Read Minds. *New York Times*, Science section, January 10.

121. Richter, C. P. (1957). On the Phenomenon of Sudden Death in Animals and Man. *Psychosomatic Medicine, 19*, 191–198.

122. Lacey, J. I. (1967). Somatic Response Patterning and Stress: Some Revisions of Activation Theory. In M. H. Appley & R. Trumbell (Eds.), *Psychological Stress: Issues in Research*. New York: AppletonCenturyCrofts.

CHAPTER 11

123. Papez, J. (1937). A Proposed Mechanism of Emotion. *Archives of Neurology and Pathology, 38*, 725–743.

124. Maclean, P. (1990). *The Triune Brain in Evolution: Role in Paleocerebral Functions*. New York: Springer.

125. Jung, C. G. (1969). *The Structure and Dynamics of the Psyche* (p. 152). Princeton, NJ: Princeton University Press.

126. Hess, W. R. (1981). *Biological Order and Brain Organization: Selected Works of W. R. Hess*. New York: Springer.

127. Gellhorn, E. (1967). *Principles of Autonomic-Somatic Integrations*. St. Paul: University of Minnesota Press.

128. Damasio, A. (2005). *Descartes' Error: Emotion, Reason, and the Human Brain*. New York: Penguin.

129. Damasio, A. (1999). *The Feeling of What Happens: Body and Emotion in the Making of Consciousness*. San Diego: Harcourt.

130. Ferrier, D. (1886). *The Functions of the Brain* (p. 401). London: Smith, Elder.

131. Leitch, M. L. (2005). Just Like Bodies, Psyches Can Drown in Disasters. *New York Times*, May 31.

CHAPTER 12

132. Budbill, D. (2005). *While We've Still Got Feet*. Port Townsend, WA: Copper Canyon Press.

133. Ray, R. A. (2008). *Touching Enlightenment: Finding Realization in the Body*. Boulder, CO: Sounds True.

134. Dhar, P. L. (2005). Holistic Education and Vipassana. Available at http://www.buddhismtoday.com/index/meditation.htm.

135. Hume, D. (1980). *A Treatise of Human Nature: Being an Attempt to Introduce the Experimental Method of Reasoning into Moral Subjects*. New York: Oxford University Press.

136. Krishnamurti, J. (2007). *As One Is: To Free the Mind from All Conditioning*. Prescott, AZ: Hohm Press.

137. *Parabola* magazine, 2002.

CHAPTER 13

138. Damasio, A. (2000). *The Feeling of What Happens: Body and Emotion in the Making of Consciousness*. San Diego: Harcourt.

139. Goleman, D. (1997). *Emotional Intelligence: Why It Can Matter More Than IQ*. New York: Bantam.

140. Van der Kolk, B. A., & van der Hart, O. (1989). Pierre Janet and the Breakdown of Adaptation in Psychological Trauma. *American Journal of Psychiatry, 146* (12), 1530–1540.

141. Myron Sharaf, personal communication.

142. Fosha, D. (2000). *The Transforming Power of Affect: A Model for Accelerated Change*. New York: Basic Books.

143. Binet, A. (1908). "Qu'est ce qu'une émotion? Qu'est ce qu'un acte intellectuel?" *L' Année Psychologique, 17*, 1–47.

144. Panksepp, J. (2004). *Affective Neuroscience: The Foundations of Human and Animal Emotions* (Series in Affective Science). New York: Oxford University Press.

145. Wozniak, R. H. (1999). William James's *Principles of Psychology* (1890). In *Classics in Psychology, 1855–1914: Historical Essays*. Bristol, UK: Thoemmes Press.

146. Libet, B. (1985). Unconscious Cerebral Initiative and the Role of Conscious Will in Voluntary Action. *Behavioral and Brain Sciences, 8*, 529–539. See also the many commentaries in the same issue, pp. 539–566, and in *Behavioral and Brain Sciences, 10*, 318–321. Libet, B., Freeman, A., & Sutherland, K. (1999). *The Volitional Brain: Towards a Neuroscience of Free Will*. Thorverton, UK: Imprint Academic.

147. Libet, B. (1981) The Experimental Evidence of Subjective Referral of a Sensory Experience Backwards in Time. *Philosophy of Science, 48*, 182–197.

148. Wegner, D. M., & Wheatley, T. P. (1999). Apparent Mental Causation: Sources of the Experience of Will. *American Psychologist, 54*, 480–492.

149. Wegner, D. M. (2003). *The Illusion of Conscious Will*. Cambridge, MA: MIT Press.

150. Damasio, A. (1995). *Descartes' Error: Emotion, Reason, and the Human Brain*. New York: Harper Perennial.

151. Weiskrantz, L. (1986). *Blindsight: A Case Study and Implications*. Oxford: Oxford University Press.

152. Sacks, O. (1996). *The Man Who Mistook His Wife for a Hat* (p. 146). New York: Vintage Books.

153. See note 1.

154. Gendlin, E. (1982). *Focusing* (2nd ed.). New York: Bantam Books.

155. Bull, N. (1951). *Attitude Theory of Emotion*. New York: Nervous and Mental Disease Monographs.

156. Llinas, R. R. (2001). *i of the Vortex: From Neurons to Self*. Cambridge, MA: MIT Press.

157. Ekman, P. (2008). *Emotional Awareness: Overcoming the Obstacles to Psychological Balance and Compassion*. New York: Holt.

158. See note 18.

159. See note 20.

160. NewScientist.com, May 09, 2007.

161. Tinbergen, N. (1974). Ethology and Stress Disease. *Science, 185*, 2027.

162. Alexander, F. M. (1932). *The Use of the Self*. London: Orion Publishing.

163. Blakeslee, S. (2007). *The Body Has a Mind of Its Own: How Body Maps in Your Brain Help You Do (Almost) Everything Better*. New York: Random House.

164. Levine, J., Gordon, N. C., & Fields, H. L. (1978). The Mechanism of Placebo Analgesia. *Lancet, 2* (8091), 654–657.

165. Van der Kolk, B. A., & Saporta, J. (1992). The Biological Response to Psychic Trauma: Mechanisms and Treatment of Intrusion and Numbing. *Anxiety Research (UK), 4,* 199–212.

CHAPTER 14

166. Fischer, R. (1971). A Cartography of the Ecstatic and Meditative States. *Science, 174* (4012).

167. Newberg, A., D'Aquili, E., & Rause, V. (2002). *Why God Won't Go Away: Brain Science and the Biology of Belief.* New York: Ballantine Books.

168. Sannella, L. (1987). *The Kundalini Experience: Psychosis or Transcendence.* Lower Lake, CA: Integral Publishing.

169. Krishna, G. (1997). *Kundalini: The Evolutionary Energy in Man.* Boston: Shambhala.

170. Jung, C. G. (1996). *The Psychology of Kundalini Yoga.* Princeton, NJ: Princeton University Press.

171. Chödrön, P. (2002). *The Places That Scare You: A Guide to Fearlessness in Difficult Times.* Boston: Shambhala.

172. Robert Heath, personal communication, conference on the Biology of the Affectionate Bond, Esalen Institute, Big Sur, California, 1978.

173. See note 2.

174. Levine, P. A. (1986). Stress. In M. Coles, E. Donchin, and S. Porges (eds.), *Psychophysiology: Systems, Processes, and Application; A Handbook.* New York: Guilford Press.

175. Schore, A. N. (1994). *Affect Regulation and the Origin of the Self: The Neurobiology of Emotional Development.* Hillsdale, NJ: Lawrence Erlbaum.

176. Damasio, A. (2000). *The Feeling of What Happens: Body and Emotion in the Making of Consciousness.* San Diego: Harvest Books.

177. Dhar, P. L. (2005). Holistic Education and Vipassana. Available at http://www.buddhismtoday.com/index/meditation.htm.

178. Levine, P. A. (2005). *Healing Trauma: A Pioneering Program for Restoring the Wisdom of Your Body.* Boulder, CO: Sounds True.

About the Author

Peter A. Levine, PhD, holds
medical biophysics and psy
of Somatic Experiencing®
to healing trauma, a
Human Enrichme
work throughout the
cultures. Dr. Levine was
ment of the space shuttle p.
World Affairs Task Force of H
developing responses to large-sca
fare. Levine's international best seller,
has been translated into twenty-two la
include the prevention of trauma in childrer
books, with Maggie Kline, in this area: *Traum*
and *Trauma-Proofing Your Kids*. Levine's origina
field of Body-Psychotherapy was honored in 2010 wi.
Life Time Achievement award from the United States
Body Psychotherapy (USABP). For further information on
trainings, projects and literature, visit www.traumahealing.
www.somaticexperiencing.com.